ICT Horizons:
Building Digital Skills for Schools and Colleges

By Patrick Justus, Ph.D.

Copyright © 2024 Patrick Justus

Contact the author:

pcjustus@gmail.com

This author also published:

- Mastering Cybersecurity Excellence
- ICT Functional Skills
- Footprints of Resilience: Story of the Boy from Ibusa

Self-published and printed by Amazon KDP.

Printed in the United Kingdom.

Table of Contents

Dedication 17
Preface 18
Introduction 19
Foreword 20
About the Author 21
Acknowledgement 22
Chapter 1: Basic Computer System 23
    Learning Objectives: 23
    1.1 INTRODUCTION TO THE COMPUTER SYSTEM 23
        1.1.1 Basic Components of a Computer System 24
        1.1.2 Hardware Components of Computer System 25
        1.1.3 Peripheral Connectivity 28
        1.1.4 Nature, Capabilities, and Limitations of Hardware 30
    1.2 SYSTEM UNIT: The Heart of the Computer 31
        1.2.1 Key Internal Components 31
        1.2.2 Categories of System Units by Shape and Size: 32
    1.3 EXTERNAL COMPONENTS: Connecting the System to the Outside World 33
        1.3.1 Common External Components: 33
        1.3.2 Key Storage and Communication Devices 33
    1.4 COMPONENTS AT THE REAR OF A SYSTEM UNIT 34
        1.4.1 Internal Components: The Backbone of the System Unit 34
        1.4.1 Essential Internal Components 34
        1.4.2 Connecting Peripherals and Data Transfer Methods 35
        1.4.3 The Four Components of a Computer System ("The 4wares") 36
        1.4.4 The Interrelationship of the 4wares 36
    1.5 INPUT DEVICES OVERVIEW 37
        1.5.1 Manual Entry Devices 37
        1.5.2 Automatic Entry Devices 38
        1.5.3 Specialised Input Devices 42
    1.6 OPTICAL AND MAGNETIC READERS 44
    1.7 IMAGE AND SOUND INPUT DEVICES 46
    1.8 OUTPUT DEVICES OVERVIEW 46
        1.8.1 Types of Output Devices 46
        1.8.2 Printers 47
        1.8.3 Additional Output Methods 48

- 1.8.4 Sound Production 48
- 1.9 MOTHERBOARD AND PROCESSOR OVERVIEW 49
  - 1.9.1 Components of the CPU 50
  - 1.9.2 Registers in Detail 51
- 1.10 DATA REPRESENTATION 51
  - 1.10.1 Binary Language 52
  - 1.10.2 Bits and Bytes 52
  - 1.10.3 Words 52
  - 1.10.4 Importance of Data Representation 52
  - 1.10.5 Applications of Data Representation 53
- 11.1 MACHINE CYCLE 53
  - 1.11.1 Definition 53
  - 1.11.2 Phases of the Machine Cycle 53
  - 1.11.3 The Complete Cycle: Fetch-Decode-Execute-Store 55
  - 1.11.4 Illustration of a Machine Cycle 55
  - 1.11.5 Importance of the Machine Cycle 55
  - 1.11.6 Modern Enhancements to the Machine Cycle 56
- 1.12 SPEED AND PERFORMANCE 56
  - 1.12.1 Measurement 56
  - 1.12.2 Factors Affecting Performance 57
  - 1.12.3 Evolution 57
  - 1.12.4 Applications of High-Performance CPUs 58
- 1.13 DATA STORAGE SYSTEMS 60
  - 1.13.1 Data Storage 60
  - 1.13.2 Categories of Data Storage Systems 60
  - 1.13.3 Secondary Storage (Mass Storage) 62
- Tutorial Activity 1 - Basic Computer System 64
  - Quizzes and Questions 64

Chapter 2: Software & Its Applications 67
- Learning Outcomes 67
- 2. Introduction 67
- 2.1 SOFTWARE 67
- 2.2 CATEGORIES OF SOFTWARE 68
  - 2.1.1 System Software 68
  - 2.1.2 Application Software 72
  - 2.1.3 Key Features and Characteristics of Software 74

2.2 OPERATING SYSTEMS (OS) 75
    2.2.1 Definition of an Operating System 75
    2.2.2 Functions of the Operating System 75
    2.2.3 Components of an Operating System 77
2.3 INTERRUPTS & CPU 78
    2.3.1 Interrupts 78
    2.3.2 Types of Interrupts 79
    2.3.3 Handling Multiple Interrupts 79
    2.3.4 Example of Interrupt Handling in Action: 81
    2.3.5 Summary of Interrupts & CPU Operations: 81
Tutorial Activity 2 - Software & Its Applications 82
    Quizzes and Questions 82

Chapter 3: Computer Logic and Data Representation 84
Learning Objectives 84
3.1 COMPUTER ARCHITECTURE AND LOGIC GATES: The Foundation of Computing Systems
.... 84
    3.1.1 Structure and Elements of Computing through Logic Gates 84
    3.1.2 Applications of Logic Gates in Key Computing Processes 85
    3.1.3 Key Characteristics of Computing with Logic Gates 85
3.2 DEFINITION OF LOGIC GATES 86
    3.2.1 Basic Types of Logic Gates 86
    3.2.2 Combined Logic Operations 87
    3.2.3 Complex Truth tables 88
3.3 DATA REPRESENTATION AND NUMBER SYSTEMS 90
    3.3.1 The Binary System 90
    3.3.2 Binary Addition and Subtraction 90
3.4 Converting Between Number Systems 92
    3.4.1 The Denary (Decimal) System 92
    3.4.2 The Octal System 92
    3.4.3 Activities for Reinforcement 93
3.5 Hexadecimal Number System 94
    3.5.1 Hexadecimal to Denary Conversion 94
    3.5.2 Hexadecimal to Binary and then to Denary Conversion 94
    3.5.3 Denary to Hexadecimal Conversion (Long Division Method) 95
Tutorial Activity 3 - Computer Logic and Data 95
    Quizzes and Questions 95

References 99

Chapter 4: ICT Laws and Ethics 100

Learning Outcomes: 100

4.1 DATA, INFORMATION, AND KNOWLEDGE 100

4.1.1 Definition of Data 101

4.1.2 Definition of Information 101

4.1.3 Transforming Data into Information 102

4.1.4 Definition of Knowledge 103

4.1.5 Knowledge Expert Systems 104

4.2 DATA SOURCES 105

Learning Outcomes 105

4.2.1 Introduction 105

4.2.2 Range of Data Sources 105

4.2.3 Advantages and Disadvantages 106

4.2.4 Issues in Data Sources 108

4.2.5 Importance of Accuracy 109

4.2.6 Value of Information 109

4.2.7 Information as a Commodity 109

4.2.8 Ensuring Information Quality 111

4.3. ICT AND THE LAW 112

Learning Outcomes 112

4.3.1 Introduction 112

4.3.2 Control of Information 112

4.3.3 Copyright, Designs and Patents Act (1986/1998) 113

4.3.4 Computer Misuse Act (1990) 115

4.3.5 Data Protection Act (1984/1998/2000/2018) 118

4.3.6 Health and Safety at Work Act (1986) 124

4.3.7 Common Health Risks Associated with IT Work 125

4.3.8 Poor Ergonomic Setup 126

4.3.9 Good Ergonomic Setup 127

4.3.10 Visual Examples 128

Tutorial Activity 4 - ICT Laws and Ethics 130

Quizzes and Questions 130

References 132

CHAPTER 5: INFORMATION AGE 133

Learning Outcomes 133

5. TECHNOLOGY OF DIFFERENT INFORMATION AGES 133
5.1 THE EVOLUTION OF INFORMATION AGES 133
5.2.1 The Stone Age 133
5.2.1 Tool Types and Innovations 134
5.2.2 Cultural and Practical Legacy 134
5.2.3 Impact on Human Advancement 134
5.2.4 Prehistoric Stone Age Tools 135
5.3 THE IRON AGE 135
5.3.1 Applications of Iron and Steel 135
5.3.2 Ironworking in Nigeria 135
5.3.3 Societal Impacts of Iron Age Materials 136
5.4 THE MIDDLE AGES 137
5.4.1 Advancements in Toolmaking 137
5.4.2 Projectile Weapons and Hunting Innovations 137
5.4.3 Artistic and Written Expression 137
5.4.4 Middle Age Tools 138
5.5 THE INDUSTRIAL AGE 139
5.5.1 Origins and Global Spread 139
5.5.2 Key Characteristics of the Industrial Age 139
5.5.3 Societal Impact 140
5.5.4 The Industrial Age vs. the Information Age 140
5.5.5 Key Points of Comparison and Debate 140
5.6 ELECTRONIC AGE (CURRENT AGE) 141
5.6.1 Key Features of the Electronic Age 141
5.6.2 Impact on Human Life and Society 142
5.6.3 Socioeconomic Changes 143
5.6.4 Defining Characteristics of the Electronic Age 143
5.7 CLASSIFICATIONS OF COMPUTERS 144
5.7.1 History of Computers by Generation 144
5.8 CLASSIFICATIONS BY FUNCTIONALITY 146
5.8.1 Analog Computers 146
5.8.2 Digital Computers 147
5.8.3 Hybrid Computers 147
5.9 CLASSIFICATIONS BY SIZE 148
5.9.1 Mainframe Computers 148
5.9.2 Minicomputers 148

- 5.9.3 Microcomputers 148
- 5.9.4 Supercomputers 149
- 5.9.5 Ubiquitous Computers 149
- 5.10 CLASSIFICATION BY DEGREE OF VERSATILITY 149
  - 5.10.1 General-Purpose Computers 149
  - 5.10 2 Dedicated or Special-Purpose Computers 151
  - 5.11 Illustrative Examples Across Eras 152
- Tutorial Activity 5 - Information Age 153
  - Quizzes and Questions 153

Chapter 6: Bridging the Digital Divide and Evolving Economies 156

- Learning Outcomes: 156
- 6.1 OVERVIEW 156
  - 6.1.2 What is the Digital Divide? 156
  - 6.1.3 Digital Divide and Education 157
  - 6.1.4 The Old Economy vs. The New Economy 158
  - 6.1.5 Impact of the Digital Divide 160
  - 6.1.6 Strategies to Bridge the Digital Divide: 160
  - 6.1.7 Illustration & Quantification: 160
- Tutorial Activity 6 - Bridging the Digital Divide and Evolving Economies 162
  - Quiz and Questions 162

Chapter 7: The ICT Professional: A Comprehensive Guide to Roles, Skills, Ethics, and Careers 164

- Learning Outcomes 164
- 7.1 THE ICT PROFESSIONAL 164
  - 7.1.1 Legal Context of ICT: Social, Moral, and Ethical Issues 165
- 7.2.2 Social Issues in the Introduction and Use of ICT 165
  - 7.2.3 Job Loss and Workforce Displacement 165
  - 7.2.4 Access to Information and the Digital Divide 165
  - 7.2.5 Control Over Information and Access 165
- 7.3 MORAL ISSUES IN ICT USAGE 166
  - 7.3.1 Privacy Concerns in ICT 166
  - 7.3.2 Content Regulation and Harmful Material 166
  - 7.3.3 Ethical Issues in ICT Practice 166
  - 7.3.4 Employer and Worker Ethics in ICT 168
  - 7.3.5 Professional Codes of Conduct 168
- 7.4 ESSENTIAL SKILLS AND QUALITIES NEEDED BY ICT PROFESSIONALS 168

- 7.4.1 Technical Skills with Illustrative Examples 168
- 7.4.2 Core Abilities Needed by ICT Staff 169
- 7.4.3 Personal Qualities of ICT Staff 169
- 7.4.4 Responsibilities of ICT Professionals 169
- 7.5. SKILLS BEYOND TECHNICAL EXPERTISE 169
  - 7.5.1 Strategic Planning 170
  - 7.5.2 Management Information Systems (MIS) Skills 170
  - 7.5.3 Illustrative Scenario: Integrating Skills and Qualities 170
  - 7.5.4 Codes of Practice vs. Legal Requirements 170
  - 7.5.5 Professional Body Example: 171
- 7.6 ROLE OF PROFESSIONAL BODIES IN ICT 171
- 7.7 CAREER OPPORTUNITIES FOR ICT PROFESSIONALS 172
- 7.8 FUTURE DIRECTIONS AND EMERGING TRENDS IN ICT CAREERS 173
- 7.9 EMBRACING GREEN COMPUTING 174
  - 7.9.1 Key Aspects of Green Computing: 174
  - 7.9.2 Benefits of Green Computing: 175
- Activity 7 Answers - The ICT Professional: A Comprehensive Guide to Roles, Skills, Ethics, and Careers 176
  - Quizzes and Questions 176

Chapter 8: Capabilities & Limitations of Computers & ICT 178
- Learning Outcome 178
- 8. INTRODUCTION 178
- 8.1 HISTORICAL CONTEXT OF COMPUTERS AND ICT 179
- 8.2 COMPUTING POWER AND STORAGE CAPACITY IN THE 21ST CENTURY 179
- 8.3 DEPENDENCE ON ICT 181
- 8.4 THE FUTURE OF ICT 182
- 8.5 LIMITATIONS OF ICT 182
- 8.6 THE EMERGENCE OF NEW TECHNOLOGY 183
- Tutorial Activity 8 - Capabilities & Limitations of Computers & ICT 185
  - Quizzes and Questions 185
- References 187

Chapter 9: Social Impact of Computers & ICT 188
- Learning Outcomes 188
- 9. SOCIAL IMPACT OF COMPUTERS & ICT 188
- 9.1 INFORMATION TECHNOLOGY, PEOPLE, AND SOCIETY 189
- 9.2 THE NEED FOR INFORMATION 190

9.3 THE ELECTRONIC OFFICE ... 191
9.4 HOME COMPUTING ... 192
9.5 COMPUTERS IN SMALL BUSINESSES, SHOPS, AND CHURCHES ... 193
9.6 COMPUTERS IN EDUCATION ... 194
9.7 SOCIAL TRENDS STEMMING FROM THE USE OF COMPUTERS AND ICT ... 195
9.8 ARGUMENTS FOR AND AGAINST COMPUTERS ... 197
9.9 PERSONAL PRIVACY ... 198
9.10 THE EFFECT OF ICT ON EMPLOYMENT AND SKILL DEVELOPMENT ... 199
9.11 ESSENTIAL ICT SKILLS IN THE MODERN WORKPLACE ... 200
9.12 SOURCES OF ICT TRAINING ... 201
9.13 ROLE AND APPLICATIONS OF COMPUTERS AND ICT ... 201
9.14 COMPUTERS & ICT IN FINANCIAL INSTITUTIONS ... 202
9.15 COMPUTERS IN HOSPITALS AND MEDICINE ... 203
9.16 COMPUTERS IN THE HOME ... 203
19.17 COMPUTERS IN RETAIL ... 204
9.18 ROLE OF ICT IN EDUCATION ... 204
9.19 ICT IN MANUFACTURING FIRMS ... 207
9.20 ICT IN HEALTH AND SAFETY ... 208
9.21 COMPUTER-BASED TRAINING (CBT) ... 208
9.22 ARTIFICIAL INTELLIGENCE (AI) ... 208
9.23 ROLE AND APPLICATIONS OF ICT IN FILMS & MOVIES ... 209
9.24 ROLE AND APPLICATIONS OF ICT IN TRANSPORTATION ... 210
9.25 ROLE AND APPLICATIONS OF ICT IN GOVERNMENT ... 210
9.26 THE GLOBAL CONNECTIVITY ... 211
Tutorial Activity 9 - Social Impact of Computers & ICT ... 212
Quizzes and Questions ... 212
Chapter 10: Network Systems Concepts ... 214
Learning Outcome ... 214
10.1 NETWORK SYSTEMS CONCEPTS ... 214
10.1.1 What is a Network System? ... 214
10.1.2 Components of a Network ... 215
10.1.3 Why Have Network Systems? ... 218
10.1.4 Types of Networks ... 218
10.1.5 Classifications of Network Systems ... 220
10.2 NETWORK TOPOLOGY ... 223
10.2.1 Bus Topology ... 223

10.2.2 Star Topology 224

10.2.3 Ring Topology 225

10.2.4 Mesh Topology 225

10.2.5 Hybrid Topology 226

10.2.6 Overview of Internetworking Devices 227

10.3 FROM NETWORK CONCEPTS TO STANDARDS 229

10.3.1 Standards in Network Systems 229

10.3.2 The OSI Model: An Overview 230

10.3.3 Connection-Oriented Communication 230

10.3.4 Connectionless Communication 231

10.3.5 The Seven Layers of the OSI Model 232

10.3.6 Basic Functions of the Layers of the OSI Model 233

10.3.7 Significance of the OSI Model 235

10.3.8 Communication Process: Data Encapsulation and Decapsulation 236

10.4 TCP/IP REFERENCE MODEL (INTERNET SUITE) 236

10.4.1 Layers of the TCP/IP Reference Model 236

10.4.2 Comparison with the OSI Model 237

10.4.3 Significance of the TCP/IP Model 239

10.5 CASE STUDY 1 239

10.6 TRENDS IN NETWORK SYSTEM DESIGN 240

10.6.1 Modern Network System Design 240

10.6.2 Designing Local Area Networks (LANs) 242

10.6.3 Overview of Available Internetworking Technologies 243

10.7 OUTPUT ANALYSIS 247

10.7.1 Challenges in Internetwork Design: 248

10.7.2 CASE STUDY 2 249

10.7.3 Example of a Typical Enterprise Internetwork 250

10.7.4 Design Considerations for EIA Training Centre 251

10.7.5 Summary of LAN Technologies 252

10.8 NETWORK PERFORMANCE MEASUREMENT 252

10.8.1 Key Parameters for Measuring Network Performance 252

10.8.2 Example Calculation of Maximum Data Rate 254

10.8.3 Practical Considerations 254

Tutorial Activity 10 - Network Systems Concepts 255

Quizzes and Questions 255

Reference: 256

Chapter 11: Basic Data Transmission Systems 257

Learning Outcome 257

11.1 Data Transmission & Communication Systems Concepts 257

11.2 Transmission Media 258

11.2.1 Cables 258

11.2.2 Radio Signal Transmission 261

11.2.3 Microwave Transmission 262

11.2.4 Communication Satellite 263

11.3 TRANSMISSION METHODS 264

11.3.1 Baseband Transmission 264

11.3.2 Broadband Transmission 265

11.4 TRANSMISSION MODES 266

11.4.1 Asynchronous Transmission 266

11.4.2 Synchronous Transmission 267

11.5 TRANSMISSION DIRECTIONS 267

11.5.1 Simplex 267

11.5.2 Half-Duplex 268

11.5.3 Full-Duplex 268

11.5.4 Asymmetric Duplex 269

11.6 TRANSMISSION RATE 269

Tutorial Activity 11 - Basic Data Transmission Systems 271

Quizzes and Questions 271

Chapter 12: The Internet and Security Challenges in ICT 273

Learning Outcomes 273

12. THE INTERNET 273

12.1 WHAT IS THE INTERNET? 274

12.1.1 Core Terminology of the Internet 274

12.1.2 Internet vs. World Wide Web 274

12.1.3 Internet Services 275

12.1.4 Evolution of the Internet 275

12.1.5 The Future of the Internet: First World vs. Third World Perspectives 276

12.2 IDENTIFYING CYBERSECURITY THREATS 276

12.2.1 Computer Viruses 276

12.2.2 What is a Computer Virus? 276

12.2.3 Why are Viruses Created? 277

12.2.4 Warning Signs of a Virus Infection 277

12.2.5 Types of Computer Viruses 277

12.2.6 Examples of Notorious Computer Viruses 279

12.2.7 How to Protect Against Viruses 279

12.2.8 Sources of Virus Infection 280

12.2.9 Actions a Company Should Take Against Viruses 280

12.2.10 List of Popular Antivirus Software 280

12.2.11 Issues with Viruses in Academic Environments 281

Tutorial Activity 12 - The Internet and Security Challenges in ICT 282

Quizzes and Questions 282

Chapter 13: Web Technology and Emerging Web Trends 284

Learning Outcomes 284

13 INTRODUCTION TO WEB TECHNOLOGY 285

13.1 FUNDAMENTALS OF WEB ARCHITECTURE AND NETWORKING 285

13.1.1 Web Architecture and Components 286

13.1.2 N-Tier System Architecture 286

13.1.3 Client/Server (Request/Response) Model 287

13.1.4 Internet Service Provider (ISP) 289

13.2 WEB STANDARDS, TOOLS, AND SECURITY 289

13.2.1 Web Standards 289

13.2.2 Web Browsers 290

13.2.3 Web Servers 291

13.2.4 Proxy Server & Firewall 292

13.2.5 OpenRSM Server 293

13.2.6 Internetworking Technology 294

13.2.7 Scope of Networks 295

13.2.8 How Does a Computer Send a Request to a Web Server on the Other Side of the World? 296

13.3 WEB PROTOCOLS AND COMMUNICATION 299

13.3.1 Importance of TCP/IP: 299

13.3.2 Key Components of TCP/IP: 299

13.3.3 TCP/IP Protocol Architecture 299

13.3.4 HTTP and HTTPS: Web Communication Protocols 302

13.3.5 Email Protocols 302

13.4 WEB APPLICATIONS AND THEIR IMPACT 305

13.4.1 Other Applications in the Web Ecosystem 305

13.5 EVOLUTION AND FUTURE OF THE WEB 308

13.5.1 Web 1.0: Static Web 308

13.5.2 Web 2.0: The Dynamic and Interactive Web 309

13.5.3 Web 3.0: The Semantic and Intelligent Web 309

13.6 CHARACTERISTICS OF WEB 4.0: THE INTELLIGENT WEB 311

13.6.1 Key Features of Web 4.0 311

13.6.2 Applications of Web 4.0 311

13.7 CHARACTERISTICS OF WEB 5.0: THE EMOTIONAL WEB 312

13.7.1 Key Features of Web 5.0 312

13.7.2 Applications of Web 5.0 312

13.8 FUTURE OF WEB TECHNOLOGIES 312

Tutorial Activity 13 - Web Technology and Emerging Web Trends 313

Quizzes and Questions 313

Chapter 14: Cloud Computing 316

Learning Outcome 316

14. CLOUD COMPUTING 316

14.1 TYPES OF CLOUD COMPUTING 317

14.1.1 Public Cloud 317

14.1.2 Private Cloud 318

14.1.3 Hybrid Cloud 319

14.2 CLOUD SERVICES AND SECURITY: IaaS, PaaS, SaaS, and Compliance 320

14.2.1. Cloud Services Technology Model 320

14.2.2 Infrastructure as a Service (IaaS) 321

14.2.3 Platform as a Service (PaaS) 322

14.2.4 Software as a Service (SaaS) 323

14.2.5 Everything as a Service (XaaS) As organisations grow and globalise, the 323

14.3 CLOUD SERVICES COMPLIANCE AND DATA PRIVACY 324

14.3.1 Cloud Services Compliance and Policy 324

14.3.2 Security Considerations and Challenges in Cloud Computing 324

14.3.3 Data Protection and Privacy 324

14.3.4 Compliance Issues 324

14.3.5 Security Challenges 325

14.3.6 Gartner's 7 Advisory Considerations for Cloud Adoption 325

Tutorial Activity 14 - Cloud Computing 326

Quizzes and questions 326

Reference 327

Chapter 15: The Role of Communication Systems and Telematics 328

Learning Outcomes 328

15.1 INTRODUCTION TO COMMUNICATION SYSTEMS AND TELEMATICS 328

15.2 THE DEVELOPMENT OF TELEMATICS 329

15.3 APPLICATIONS AND IMPACT OF TELEMATICS 329

15.4 THE ROLE OF COMMUNICATION SYSTEMS IN BUSINESS 330

Tutorial Activity 15 - The Role of Communication Systems and Telematics 332

Quizzes and Questions 332

Chapter 16: E-Commerce 335

Learning Outcomes 335

16. UNDERSTANDING E-COMMERCE 335

16.1.1 E-Commerce Today 335

16.1.2 E-Commerce Models and Applications 335

16.1.3 E-Commerce Transaction Models 336

16.1.4 Inter-Organisational Information Systems (IOS) 337

16.1.5 Benefits of IOS 338

16.1.6 Globalisation and E-Commerce 339

16.1.7 Globalisation and Trade 341

16.1.8 The Impact of E-Commerce 341

Tutorial Activity 16 - E-Commerce 344

Quizzes and Questions 344

Chapter 17: Web Design and Development 347

Learning Outcomes 347

17.1 WEBSITE DESIGN 347

17.1.1 Types of Websites 347

17.1.2 Common Web Elements 348

17.1.3 Purpose of Text & Graphics 348

17.1.4 Hyperlinks 349

17.2 WEBSITE DEVELOPMENT PROCESS 349

17.2.1 Key Stages of the Website Development Process 350

17.2.2 Importance of the SDLC in Website Development 351

17.2.3 Considerations for Designing Website 352

17.2.4 Implementation 353

17.2.5 Example HTML Structure 354

17.2.6 Evaluation and Testing 357

17.2.7 Publishing the Website 358

17.2.8 Web Server 359

17.2.9 Maintenance 360

17.3 CAREERS IN WEBSITE DEVELOPMENT 361

Tutorial Activity 17 - Web Design & Development. 362

    Quiz and Questions 362

Reference 365

Chapter 18: Cybersecurity Strategies for ICT Systems 366

Learning Outcomes 366

18. Modern Cybersecurity Practices and Risk Mitigation 366

18.1 CYBERSECURITY RISKS AND RISK MANAGEMENT 366

    18.1.1 Cybersecurity Risk 366

    18.1.2 Cybersecurity Risk Assessment 368

    18.1.3 Cybersecurity Risk Management 369

18.2 MITIGATION, CONTROL, AND PROTECTION MECHANISMS 370

18.3 DATA BACKUP AND CONTINGENCY PLANNING 373

18.4 Emerging Technologies in Cybersecurity 375

Tutorial Activity 18 - Cybersecurity Strategies for ICT Systems 377

    Quizzes and Questions 377

Chapter 19: Foundations of Software Design and Development. 379

Learning Outcomes 379

19.1 Introduction 380

    19.1.1 Overview of Software Design & Development 381

    19.1.2 Elements of Software Development 381

    19.1.3 Roles in Software Development 382

19.2 Programming Paradigms 382

    19.2.1 Procedural Programming 383

    19.2.2 Object-Oriented Programming 384

    19.2.3 Event-Driven Programming 385

19.3 Programming Features and Data Types 385

    19.3.1 Features of Programming Languages 386

    19.3.2 Programming Constructs 386

    19.3.2 Methods of Translation 387

    19.3.3 Understanding Syntax and Keywords 387

    19.3.4 Variables and Data Types 388

    19.3.5 Common Types of Data Types 388

    19.3.6 Benefits of Data Types 389

19.4 Computer Programming Languages 389

19.4.1 Definition of Computer Programming Languages 389

19.4.2 Generations of Computer Programming Languages.. 389

19.4.3 Characteristics of Programming Languages 390

19.4.4 Examples of Common Programming Languages... 391

19.4.5 Fourth Generation Languages (4GLs) 391

19.4.6 Advantages of 4GLs: 392

19.4.7 Activities for Reinforcement 392

19.4.8 Tasks to do.. 392

Tutorial Activity 19 - Foundations of Software Design and Development......................... 394

Quiz Questions, Exercises 394

Conclusion 396

References 397

Dedication

To God first, my Redeemer, whose grace and guidance have been my unwavering source of strength.

To my family, whose unconditional love and support have been the cornerstone of every achievement and aspiration in my life.

To my students, past and present, whose curiosity, determination, and resilience remind me of the profound impact education can have in shaping futures.

And to all the visionaries, educators, and learners striving to bridge the digital divide and foster a more inclusive, equitable, and connected world - this book is dedicated to you.

Preface

The world we live in today is inseparably intertwined with technology. From how we communicate, work, and learn to the innovations that shape industries and improve lives, Information and Communication Technology (ICT) sits at the core of modern society. It is both a tool and a driving force, reshaping our world at an unprecedented pace. This book, *ICT Horizons: Building Digital Skills for Schools and Colleges,* stems from my passion for technology and a steadfast commitment to empowering learners with the knowledge and skills they need to excel in a digital society.

Over the years, as an educator and ICT professional, I have had the privilege of witnessing the transformative power of technology in action. I have seen students develop newfound confidence as they master complex concepts and practical skills. I have observed how innovative ICT solutions can propel businesses to new heights. At the same time, I have been acutely aware of the challenges we face, from navigating the digital divide to addressing the growing need for accessible and comprehensive educational resources in technology.

This book is my contribution to bridging those gaps. Designed with students, educators, and aspiring professionals in mind, *ICT Horizons* blends foundational knowledge with practical application. Each chapter not only delves into critical ICT concepts but also emphasizes real-world relevance, encouraging critical thinking and problem-solving. The inclusion of tutorial activities at the end of each chapter further reinforces understanding, offering readers opportunities to engage with the material through self-assessment and practical exploration.

Whether you are stepping into the field of ICT for the first time or seeking to enhance your existing expertise, this book is crafted to serve as your companion on this learning journey. It is my hope that it not only enriches your understanding of ICT but also inspires you to explore its vast possibilities.

I encourage you to approach this book with curiosity and enthusiasm. Ask questions, challenge assumptions, and actively engage with the material, for ICT is more than a field of study - it is a transformative force with the potential to empower individuals and uplift communities.

Welcome to *ICT Horizons.* Your journey into the ever-evolving world of technology begins here.

Dr Patrick Justus

Introduction

In today's rapidly evolving digital landscape, the role of Information and Communication Technology (ICT) has become increasingly pivotal in shaping the future of education. "ICT Horizons: Building Digital Skills for Schools and Colleges" is a comprehensive guide designed to equip students, educators, and institutions with the essential digital skills necessary to navigate this transformative era.

The title, "ICT Horizons," captures the essence of what this book aims to achieve: to expand the digital horizons of learners by exploring the ever-changing frontiers of technology. Just as horizons represent the broadening limits of our world, this book pushes those limits in terms of knowledge, skills, and potential applications in ICT. It reflects the idea that the digital realm is vast and ever-expanding, offering boundless opportunities for those who are prepared to engage with it.

The subtitle, "Building Digital Skills for Schools and Colleges," emphasizes the core mission of this book: to equip learners with the necessary tools and understanding to thrive in a digital society. In schools and colleges, students are at a crucial stage in their academic and professional lives. This book provides them with the foundational digital competencies required for success, while also delving into more advanced topics that will empower them to make meaningful contributions in the world of technology.

As technology continues to shape every aspect of our lives - from communication and education to business and healthcare - this book serves as a roadmap for developing the critical digital literacy and skills needed to succeed. Whether you are a student looking to enhance your ICT proficiency or an educator seeking to foster a digital-first mindset, "ICT Horizons" offers valuable insights, practical applications, and a deep understanding of the role technology plays in modern learning environments.

Foreword

Welcome to the captivating realm of Information and Communication Technology (ICT). As we enter an age characterised by swift technological advancements, this book serves as your guiding compass, navigating you through the vibrant landscape where innovation intersects with everyday life. Envision a world where communication knows no borders, knowledge is readily accessible, and technology empowers you to create, connect, and collaborate in unprecedented ways. This is the reality we inhabit today and is merely the beginning.

Titled, ICT Horizons: Building Digital Skills for Schools and Colleges, this book is an invaluable resource for learners, educators, and professionals alike, offering a thorough exploration of both fundamental and advanced ICT concepts. Spanning 19 meticulously organised chapters, it invites readers on an insightful journey through essential themes of computing, from the evolution of the Information Age to the latest advancements in e-commerce, cybersecurity, software design, and programming fundamentals. Each chapter promotes theoretical understanding, practical activities, and skills application, equipping learners to confidently tackle real-world scenarios.

As an experienced educator and ICT professional, the author has expertly blended clarity, depth, and practicality to create a resource that aligns seamlessly with academic curricula and industry demands. This book exemplifies the transformative power of education in bridging the digital divide and empowering individuals to thrive in the digital landscape.

Whether you are a student embarking on your ICT journey or an educator seeking to inspire future generations, this book will surely enhance your understanding and appreciation of the dynamic world of ICT. I warmly invite you to embark on this enlightening journey through information and communication technology. May it empower you to harness technological potential and positively contribute to our interconnected global community.

Dr Imad Guenane
Principal Lecturer
Head of Curriculum Development and Employability
University of Sunderland in London, UK.

About the Author

Dr Patrick Justus is a seasoned educator, accomplished ICT expert, and curriculum developer with over 34 years of experience in teaching, learning, assessing, mentoring, and leadership. Holding a B.Sc. (Hon.) in Software Engineering, an M.Sc. in Distributed Computer Systems, and a Ph.D. in Information Systems, he has dedicated his career to demystifying complex technological concepts and equipping learners with the skills needed to excel in the digital age.

Currently, Dr Justus is a Senior Lecturer at the London College of Business Studies and a mentor at the University of Greenwich, where he shares his wealth of knowledge guiding aspiring professionals and students toward achieving their academic and career goals. His teaching journey has spanned diploma, higher education, and professional development programs, making him a versatile educator who effectively tailors his materials to diverse audiences.

Dr Justus's professional expertise encompasses a broad spectrum of ICT fields, including computer architecture, software engineering, and cybersecurity. His teaching journey has taken him across some of the most prestigious academic institutions in the UK, where he served as a Lecturer and Senior Lecturer at Harlow College, Barking & Dagenham College, College of North West London, South Essex College, Newham College, and Twin Employment & Training. Each role reinforced his passion for education and his ability to inspire students in diverse learning environments.

Beyond his UK-based roles, Dr Justus has also made significant contributions on the global stage. As an expatriate, he served as the Pioneer Head of ICT and Network Manager at the British Nigeria Academy, Abuja, where he played a pivotal role in shaping the institution's technological framework and advancing its digital transformation. As a passionate advocate for digital literacy, he has led efforts to promote equitable access to technology in underserved communities, reflecting his commitment to education's transformative power.

Driven by a mission to inspire curiosity and innovation in ICT, Dr Justus continues to explore emerging technologies and create content that bridges the gap between theoretical concepts and practical applications. His commitment to excellence is reflected in this book, which synthesizes decades of experience into an accessible, comprehensive guide for learners at all levels.

Outside the classroom, Dr Justus enjoys delving into the latest advancements in technology and sharing insights that empower others to thrive in the ever-evolving world of technology and business.

Acknowledgement

The completion of this book would not have been possible without the unwavering support and encouragement of numerous individuals and organisations.

First and foremost, I extend my heartfelt gratitude to my family and friends for their patience and understanding throughout this journey. Your support has been my greatest source of strength.

I would also like to acknowledge my colleagues and students, whose insights, questions, and feedback have profoundly shaped the content of this book. Your curiosity and enthusiasm for learning have been a constant source of inspiration.

A special thank you to my apprenticeship students, James, Oliver, Dylan, Alex, Leo, and Philip, among others, for their respective dialogues, curiosity, and workplace insights. Their diverse perspectives have been instrumental in refining the material presented here.

Lastly, I am deeply grateful for the advancements in technology and education that have made it possible to share knowledge across boundaries and generations. It is my hope that this book will empower readers to embrace the transformative potential of ICT and contribute meaningfully to the digital future.

With appreciation,

Patrick Justus, Ph.D.

Chapter 1: Basic Computer System

Learning Objectives:

By the end of this topic, students will be able to:

- Describe the term "computer system."
- Identify the internal and external components of a computer system.
- Explain the term "4wares":
    - Hardware
    - Software
    - Firmware
    - People-ware
- Analyse the relationship between hardware, software, firmware, and people-ware.
- Understand the Nature, Capabilities, and Limitations of Hardware
- Differentiate between parallel and serial communication.
- Understand various methods of connecting peripherals to a computer system.
- Understand input and output devices overview
- Understand motherboard and processor overview
- Understand data representation, machine cycle, measurements
- Understand CPU speed and performance
- Understand Data Storage System, their types, and characteristics.

1.1 INTRODUCTION TO THE COMPUTER SYSTEM

A computer system is a versatile and indispensable tool in modern society, designed to process, store, and communicate information efficiently. It is an electronic system composed of interdependent hardware and software components, working together to perform a wide array of tasks. These tasks range from basic data entry and retrieval to complex computations, multimedia processing, and networking.

Computer systems play a critical role in nearly every aspect of daily life, including education, business, healthcare, entertainment, and personal productivity. They provide users with the ability to analyse large datasets, automate repetitive tasks, connect with others globally, and access vast repositories of knowledge.

At the heart of every computer system is its ability to execute instructions. This capability is facilitated by:

1. **Hardware Components:** The tangible, physical elements such as processors, memory, input/output devices, and storage.

2. **Software Components:** Intangible programs and operating systems that provide instructions for the hardware to perform specific tasks.

Modern computer systems are designed to meet diverse user needs, whether it is a personal computer (PC) for individual use, a server for hosting applications, or a supercomputer for advanced scientific research.

Understanding the fundamentals of computer systems is essential for anyone navigating today's digital world. It empowers users to make informed decisions about technology, optimise its use, and appreciate its impact on society.

This section will explore the structure, components, and functionality of computer systems, laying the foundation for a deeper understanding of how they operate and contribute to the digital age.

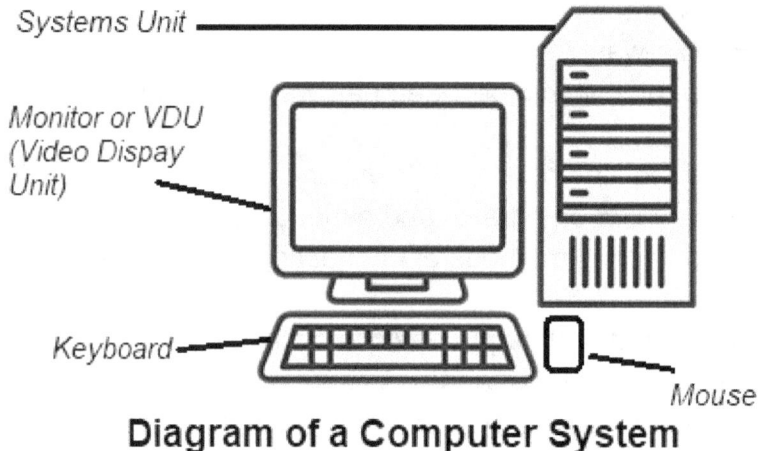

Diagram of a Computer System

1.1.1 Basic Components of a Computer System

A computer system operates as a cohesive unit, bringing together various essential components to process data and deliver meaningful outputs. Each component plays a specific role, ensuring the system functions efficiently to meet user requirements.

Below are the fundamental components of a computer system:

- **Input Devices:** Tools like keyboards, mice, scanners, and microphones allow users to input data into the system.

- **Processing Unit:** The Central Processing Unit (CPU), often called the brain of the computer, processes data by executing instructions.

- **Output Devices:** Monitors, printers, and speakers present processed data in a human-readable or usable form.

- **Storage Devices:** Hard drives, SSDs, and optical drives store data permanently or temporarily for use in processing tasks.

- **Software:** Programs and operating systems that define how the hardware operates and execute specific tasks.

- **Human Operator:** A critical part of the system, the user provides instructions, interacts with the software, and interprets the output.

Peripheral devices like printers, external drives, and networking equipment further extend the capabilities of a computer system.

Basic Components of a Computer Systems

1.1.2 Hardware Components of Computer System

Hardware represents the physical, tangible elements of a computer system. These components form the core infrastructure that facilitates data entry, processing, storage, and output. Without hardware, software instructions cannot be executed, making it an essential part of computing.

Key Categories of Hardware Components

1. **Input Devices:** Devices like keyboards, mice, joysticks, and scanners are the starting points for data entry into the system.
2. **Processing Unit:** The CPU is the central hub for data manipulation, logic execution, and control of system operations. It includes:
    - **Arithmetic Logic Unit (ALU):** Handles mathematical calculations and logic operations.

- **Control Unit (CU):** Directs data flow between components.
- **Cache Memory:** Provides high-speed storage for frequently accessed data.

3. **Memory:** Includes:
   - **RAM (Random Access Memory):** Temporary storage for active tasks and processes.
   - **ROM (Read-Only Memory):** Permanent storage for system firmware and essential instructions.
4. **Storage Devices:** Long-term data storage solutions such as:
   - **Hard Drives (HDD):** Magnetic storage for bulk data.
   - **Solid State Drives (SSD):** Faster, more durable storage solutions without moving parts.
   - **Optical Drives:** For reading/writing CDs, DVDs, or Blu-rays.
5. **Output Devices:** Convert processed data into a usable format, such as visual displays (monitors), printed documents (printers), or sound (speakers).
6. **Motherboard:** The primary circuit board that connects and enables communication between all hardware components.
7. **Power Supply Unit (PSU):** Converts electrical energy to a usable form for the computer.

Block Diagram of a Computer System

A block diagram provides a simplified representation of a computer system, illustrating the primary hardware components and their interactions. This visual framework helps to understand how data and control signals flow through the system.

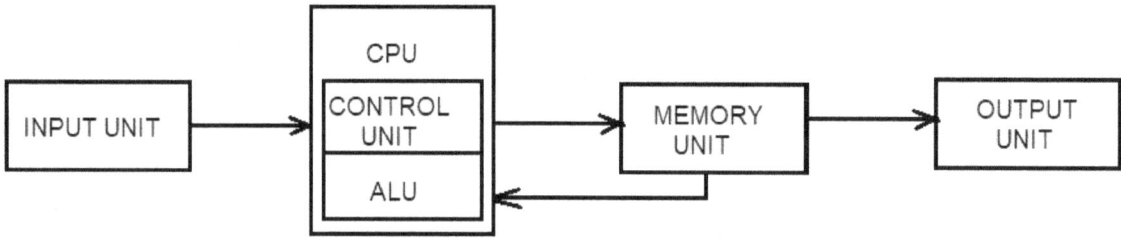

A BLOCK DIAGRAM OF COMPUTER SYSTEM

Key Components of the Block Diagram

1. **Input Unit**
    - **Purpose:** Facilitates data entry into the computer system. It converts human-readable data (analogue) into machine-readable form (digital) for further processing.
    - **Examples:** Keyboard, mouse, scanner, microphone.
    - **Process:** Inputs data and sends it to the Central Processing Unit (CPU) for processing.

2. **Central Processing Unit (CPU)**
   The CPU is the brain of the computer and processes all instructions received from input devices or software. It consists of three major subcomponents:

   a. **Arithmetic Logic Unit (ALU):**
    - Performs arithmetic calculations (e.g., addition, subtraction) and logical operations (e.g., comparisons).

   b. **Control Unit (CU):**
    - Directs the flow of data between the CPU, memory, and peripherals.
    - Interprets instructions and controls execution.

   c. **Accumulator (Scratch Pad Memory):**
    - Temporarily holds intermediate results of calculations and data during processing.

   d. **Registers:**
    - Temporary storage locations within the CPU that hold data or instructions being processed.

3. **Memory Unit**
    - More on this topic later. Memory unit stores data and instructions required during processing. It is divided into two main types:

      a. **Primary Memory (RAM and ROM):**
        - RAM (Random Access Memory): Stores data temporarily while the computer is running.
        - ROM (Read-Only Memory): Contains permanent data and instructions required for booting.

      b. **Secondary Memory (Storage Devices):**
        - HDDs, SSDs, and external storage devices for permanent storage of data and software.

4. **Output Unit**

- o Converts processed data into human-readable format.
- o **Examples:** Monitor (displays visual output), printer (produces hardcopy output), speakers (output audio signals).

5. **Communication Buses**
   - o **Data Bus:** Transfers actual data between the CPU, memory, and peripherals.
   - o **Address Bus:** Transfers information about where data should be stored or retrieved.
   - o **Control Bus:** Transfers control signals to coordinate the activities of hardware components.

6. **Storage Unit**
   - o This includes both **primary storage** for temporary data and **secondary storage** for permanent data retention. Examples include RAM, SSDs, and hard drives.

3. Flow of Data in the Block Diagram

1. **Input Phase:**
   Data is input through devices like a keyboard or mouse.

2. **Processing Phase:**
   The CPU processes the input data using instructions stored in memory.

3. **Storage Phase:**
   Data and instructions are stored temporarily (RAM) or permanently (HDD/SSD).

4. **Output Phase:**
   Processed data is sent to output devices like monitors, printers, or speakers for presentation to the user.

1.1.3 Peripheral Connectivity

Peripheral devices are hardware components connected to the CPU, either internally or externally, to expand the computer's functionality. While they operate under the CPU's control, they perform specific tasks related to input, output, storage, or communication. By understanding hardware components and their interconnectivity, students can better appreciate how computers operate as integrated systems, from data input to output and everything in between.

Peripheral devices are grouped into the following categories based on their functionality:

- **Input Devices:**
  Input devices capture raw data and send it to the CPU for processing. Examples include:

    o **Keyboard:** Allows users to input text and commands.

    o **Mouse:** Enables point-and-click navigation.

    o **Scanner:** Converts physical documents into digital format.

- **Processing Devices:**
  These devices are integral to data transformation, with the CPU playing a central role:

    o **Graphics Processing Unit (GPU):** Handles rendering of images, video, and 3D applications.

    o **Motherboard:** Houses the CPU and connects all hardware components for seamless communication.

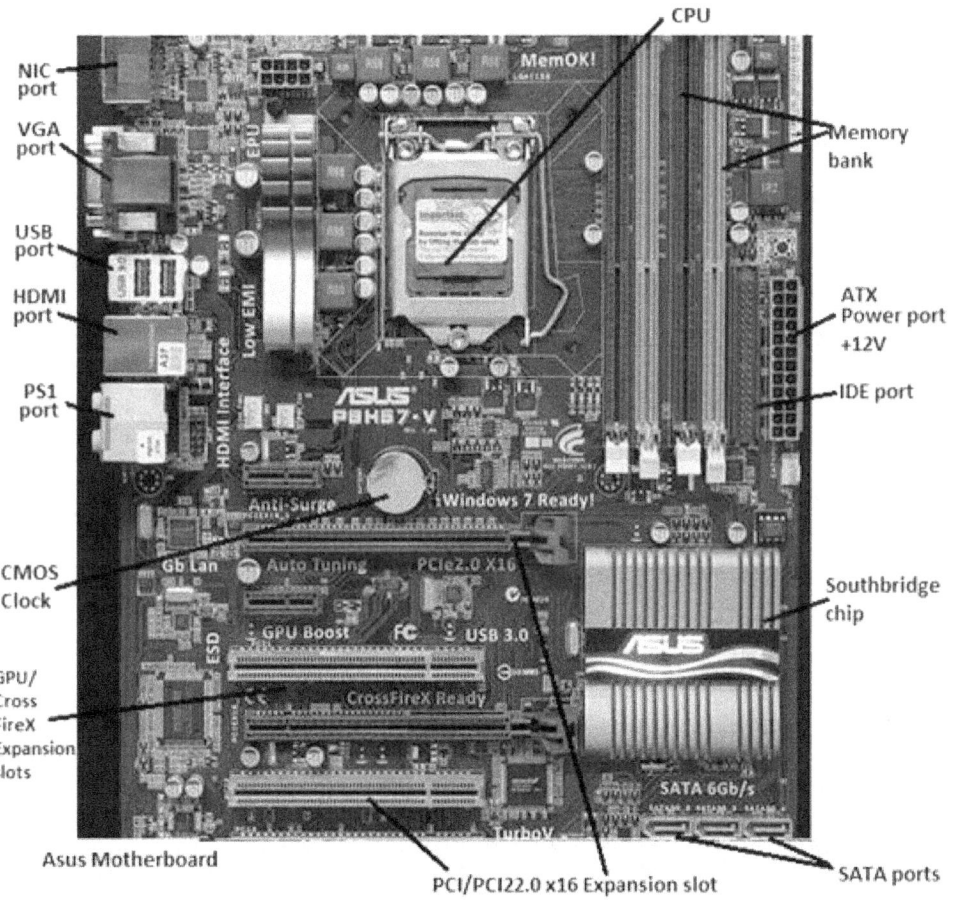

Asus Motherboard

- **Output Devices:**
  Output devices display or present the processed data as information, either in digital or physical form:
    - **Monitor:** Displays softcopy (digital) output on the screen.
    - **Printer:** Produces hardcopy (physical) output on paper.
    - **Speakers:** Output audio signals from the computer.

- **Storage Devices:**
  Storage devices are essential for saving data for future use, ranging from volatile to non-volatile memory:
    - **Primary Storage (RAM):** Temporarily holds data and instructions currently in use.
    - **Secondary Storage (HDD, SSD):** Stores data persistently even when the computer is off.
    - **Removable Storage (USB Drives, DVDs):** Portable options for storing and transferring data.

- **Communication Devices:**
  These facilitate data exchange between the computer and external systems or networks:
    - **Network Interface Cards (NIC):** Enable wired or wireless network connectivity.
    - **Modems:** Convert digital signals into analogue for internet access and vice versa.

1.1.4 Nature, Capabilities, and Limitations of Hardware

- **Nature:**
    - Hardware operates under the direction of software, executing tasks as instructed.
    - It includes both internal (e.g., CPU, GPU) and external (e.g., printers, external drives) components.

- **Capabilities:**
    - High-speed processing enables quick data manipulation.
    - Vast storage capacities accommodate large datasets.
    - Advanced peripherals enhance user interaction and task efficiency.

- **Limitations:**
    - Hardware components are susceptible to wear and tear over time.

- Performance depends on compatibility with software and other hardware.
- Limited by physical constraints, such as size and energy consumption.

1.2 SYSTEM UNIT: The Heart of the Computer

The **system unit** is the central component of a computer system, serving as the housing and framework for the essential hardware that enables the computer to function. Typically enclosed in a metal or plastic case, the system unit houses various internal components and provides the infrastructure for connections to external devices. These vital components work in tandem to provide the computing power needed for modern applications. From storage devices to power supply and cooling mechanisms, each part plays a crucial role in ensuring the efficient operation of the computer.

1.2.1 Key Internal Components

The primary components found within the system unit include:

- **Motherboard**
  The motherboard is the foundational circuit board (or printed circuit board) of the computer. It hosts the Central Processing Unit (CPU), Random Access Memory (RAM), and connectors for other components like storage drives, expansion cards, and external interfaces. Essentially, it acts as the nervous system of the computer, facilitating communication between t+he different parts. The motherboard also features slots for peripheral cards such as graphics and sound cards. See picture of a motherboard above.

- **Central Processing Unit (CPU)**

  The CPU, often referred to as the "brain" of the computer, is responsible for executing instructions from programs. It processes all the computational tasks that enable the system to run applications and perform complex calculations. Modern CPUs are designed with multiple cores, allowing them to handle several tasks simultaneously (multithreading), significantly enhancing performance.

- **Random Access Memory (RAM)**
  RAM provides temporary storage for data that is actively being used or processed by the CPU. This volatile memory allows fast access to data, ensuring that running applications can operate smoothly. Once the system is powered off, all data in RAM is lost, which is why it is primarily used for short-term data storage while the system is running.

- **Storage Drives**
  Storage drives are where the computer's data is permanently stored. These can be **Hard Disk Drives (HDD)** or **Solid-State Drives (SSD)**.
    - **HDDs** use spinning magnetic disks to store data, offering large storage capacities at a lower cost, but with slower data access speeds.
    - **SSDs**, on the other hand, store data on flash memory chips, making them faster, more reliable, and energy-efficient, though typically at a higher cost per gigabyte.

- **Power Supply Unit (PSU):**
  The **PSU** converts **alternating current (AC)** from a wall outlet into **direct current (DC)**, which is required by the internal components of the computer. The PSU is crucial for ensuring that the system receives a steady and safe power supply for smooth operation.

- **Input/Output Ports:**
  These are connectors that allow the computer to interface with external devices like keyboards, mice, printers, and monitors. Common types of I/O ports include **USB ports**, **HDMI**, and **audio jacks**.

1.2.2 Categories of System Units by Shape and Size:

- **Desktop Case**
  A **desktop case** is typically placed flat on a desk or table, with the monitor positioned above or adjacent to it. This design is often compact, making it ideal for home offices or environments with limited space.

- **Tower Case**
  A **tower case** stands upright, offering a more spacious design that allows for better airflow and expansion opportunities. These cases come in different sizes:

- **Mini Tower** is ideal for smaller, budget-conscious setups.
- **Mid Tower** is the most common size for personal and professional use, offering ample space for additional components.
- **Full Tower** cases provide the largest capacity for high-performance systems and are often used by gamers or professionals who require substantial processing power and storage.

1.3 EXTERNAL COMPONENTS: Connecting the System to the Outside World

The front panel of the system unit typically includes various external components that allow users to interact with the computer and expand its functionality. These components are essential for connecting external peripherals, providing storage options, and ensuring efficient communication between the user and the computer.

1.3.1 Common External Components:

- **CD/DVD Drive**
  CD/DVD drives enable users to read and write data on compact discs (CDs) and digital versatile discs (DVDs). Though largely replaced by digital downloads and streaming services, optical drives are still useful for playing media and installing software from physical discs.

- **Floppy Drive**
  Once a staple for data storage and file transfer, floppy drives have become obsolete in most modern systems. These drives were used to read and write data to floppy disks, typically with capacities ranging from 720 KB to 1.44 MB.

- **USB Ports**
  USB ports are one of the most versatile and commonly used connectors on modern computers. They enable the connection of peripherals such as external hard drives, printers, mice, and keyboards. USB ports are available in various versions (USB 2.0, 3.0, 3.1) that support different data transfer rates and compatibility with older and newer devices.

- **LED Indicators**
  LED indicators on the front of the system unit provide users with visual feedback on the status of the computer, such as power status, hard drive activity, or error conditions. These lights are essential for troubleshooting and monitoring the health of the system.

1.3.2 Key Storage and Communication Devices

- **Floppy Disk Drive**
  Although outdated, the floppy disk drive is a relic from the early days of personal computing. It was used to read and write data on floppy disks, which were commonly used for file storage and software distribution during the 1980s and early 1990s.

- **CD-ROM Drives**
  CD-ROM drives are used to read data from compact discs. The drive's speed is often indicated by a multiplier (e.g., 16x, 52x) representing the rate at which data can be read compared to the original speed of the CD. While still found in some systems, these drives are becoming less common as digital distribution takes over.

- **CD-R & CD-RW**
  CD-R (Recordable) and CD-RW (Rewritable) drives allow users to burn data onto CDs. CD-RWs can be rewritten multiple times, making them a reusable storage option, while CD-Rs can only be written once.

- **DVD Drive**
  DVD drives offer higher data storage capacities compared to CD drives, allowing users to read and write DVDs with larger files, such as movies or software packages.

- **Blu-Ray & DVD-9**
  Blu-ray drives support high-definition content and offer large storage capacities for data, ideal for high-definition video and large software installations. DVD-9 is a dual-layer format, offering more space than standard DVDs.

1.4 COMPONENTS AT THE REAR OF A SYSTEM UNIT

The back of a system unit contains interfaces to various devices. The interfaces are located at the back, probably because access to them is not needed for everyday use. The common interface ports to be found at the rear of a system unit are pictured here – *identify them if you can:*

1.4.1 Internal Components: The Backbone of the System Unit

Inside the system unit lies an intricate network of components that work together to ensure the computer runs efficiently. These components are critical to the functionality of the system and include power distribution, storage connection, and cooling mechanisms.

1.4.1 Essential Internal Components

- **Power Supply Unit (PSU)**
  The **PSU** remains an essential component of the internal system unit. It ensures that the system receives the correct power levels needed to

function, converting AC power into the DC power that various components require. Without a stable and efficient PSU, the system could experience power surges or failures.

- **Expansion Slots**
  Expansion slots allow for the addition of peripheral cards, such as graphics cards, sound cards, or network cards, expanding the capabilities of the computer. These slots are designed to be compatible with specific types of cards (e.g., PCI Express).

- **SATA and IDE Connectors**
  SATA (Serial ATA) and IDE (Integrated Drive Electronics) connectors are used to link storage devices like hard drives and solid-state drives to the motherboard. SATA connectors have become the standard in modern computers, offering faster data transfer rates compared to IDE.

- **Cooling Fans**
  As computers become more powerful, **cooling fans** play a crucial role in regulating temperatures within the system unit. Excess heat can lead to component failure, so fans are strategically placed to circulate air and prevent overheating, ensuring the longevity of the system's components.

1.4.2 Connecting Peripherals and Data Transfer Methods

To optimise the functionality of a computer, peripherals and storage devices must be properly connected, and the data transfer methods used must support the necessary speeds for efficient operation.

- **LPT (Parallel) vs. COM (Serial) Ports**

    - **LPT (Parallel) Ports:** Used primarily for connecting printers, parallel ports transfer multiple bits of data simultaneously, which increases transfer speeds.

    - **COM (Serial) Ports: Serial ports** transmit data one bit at a time, making them suitable for long-distance communication, as seen in modems.

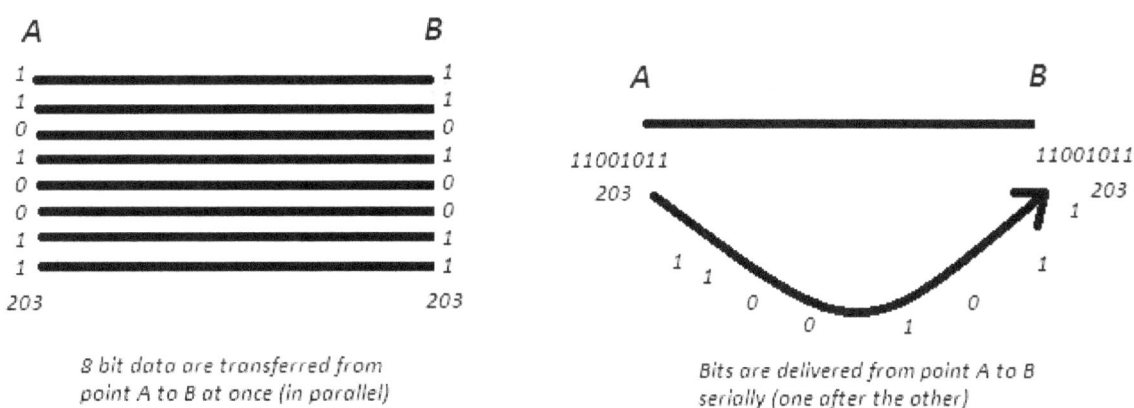

Parallel Transmission Vs. Serial Transmission of Data

- **USB (Universal Serial Bus)**
  USB ports are the most common interface for connecting peripherals. Over the years, the USB standard has evolved:
    - **USB 2.0:** Supports transfer rates of up to 480 Mbps.
    - **USB 3.0:** Offers a much higher transfer rate of up to 5 Gbps, making it ideal for high-speed devices like external hard drives.
- **SATA (Serial ATA)**
  SATA is the standard for connecting storage devices in modern systems:
    - **SATA I:** Offers transfer speeds of up to 150 Mbps.
    - **SATA II:** Provides faster speeds and improved performance.
    - **SATA III:** Supports speeds of up to 6 Gbps, allowing for faster data access and retrieval from hard drives and SSDs.

SATA III Cable, Socket

1.4.3 The Four Components of a Computer System ("The 4wares")

1. **Hardware**
   Refers to the physical components of the computer system, such as the system unit, monitor, keyboard, and mouse. Example: A **graphics card** is hardware that enhances visual output for gaming or graphic design.

2. **Software**
   Comprises the programs and instructions executed by the computer. Software can be system software (like operating systems) or application software (like word processors). Example: **Microsoft Word** is application software used for word processing.

3. **Firmware**
   Permanent software embedded in the hardware, providing low-level control for the device. An example is the **Basic Input/Output System (BIOS)**, which initialises hardware during the boot process.

4. **People-ware**
   Encompasses the users and professionals who interact with and manage the system. This includes both technical personnel (like IT support) and end-users (like office workers).

1.4.4 The Interrelationship of the 4wares

In a computer system, the relationship between hardware, software, firmware, and people-ware is crucial for functionality:

- **Hardware** requires **firmware** to operate correctly.

- **Software** interacts with **hardware** through the operating system, which relies on **firmware** for low-level control.

- **People-ware** is essential for managing and troubleshooting the system, ensuring effective utilisation of its capabilities.

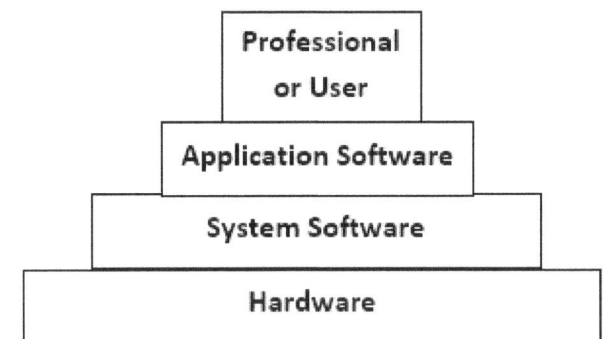

Relationship between Computer/ICT Systems

1.5 INPUT DEVICES OVERVIEW

Input devices are essential for entering data into a computer system. They can be classified into two main categories: manual entry and automatic entry devices.

1.5.1 Manual Entry Devices

These devices require user interaction to input data:

- **Keyboard**
  The primary input device for computers. Most keyboards use the **QWERTY** layout, where each key functions as a switch sending a code to the keyboard driver, which then translates it into a character. For example, when the 'A' key is pressed, the keyboard sends a signal indicating the character 'A' to the computer.

Keyboard

- **Mouse**

Mouse

A pointing device that allows users to select items within a Graphical User Interface (GUI). Modern optical mice have replaced traditional ball-based mice, offering improved precision and reduced maintenance. For example, optical mice use a laser or LED light to detect movement, allowing for smoother navigation.

- **Keypad**
  Similar to a keyboard but typically has a smaller number of keys, often used in specific applications like calculators or security systems.

Keypad

- **Microphone**

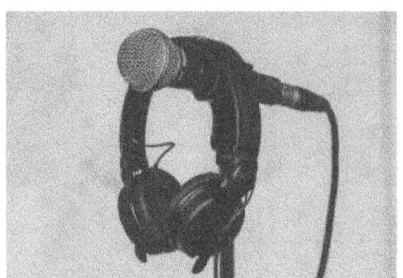

Microphone, Headphone

  Captures audio input, allowing for voice commands or voice recordings. Increasingly used in applications for voice recognition and automated services.

- **Joystick**
  Primarily used in gaming and simulation, allowing users to control movement in a 3D environment by tilting and moving the stick.

Joystick

1.5.2 Automatic Entry Devices

Automatic entry devices are specialised tools designed to input data into a computer system without requiring manual intervention, often streamlining processes and increasing efficiency in various industries. These devices capture and transmit information automatically, reducing human error and saving time. Here are some of the most common types of automatic entry devices:

• **Barcode Reader**

A barcode reader is a device that scans and decodes barcodes - patterns of lines and spaces that represent data encoded in a visual format. These readers capture the visual representation of data and translate it into numerical or alphanumeric codes that a computer can interpret.

Barcodes are widely used in various industries, including retail, libraries, and warehouse management, for efficient tracking of products, inventory, and items. By eliminating the need for manual data entry, barcode readers significantly enhance accuracy and speed in data processing.

When a barcode is scanned, the reader decodes the embedded information and inputs it into a computer system. This technology has become fundamental in modern business operations, streamlining processes such as inventory management, point-of-sale transactions, and asset tracking. The use of barcode readers ensures fast, reliable, and precise data capture, making them an indispensable tool in automation and logistics.

- **Swipe Cards**

Swipe cards are commonly used for access control in secured areas or systems. These cards contain magnetic strips or embedded chips that store data such as the user's identity or access privileges. When a user swipes the card through a reader, the system verifies the information and grants or denies access accordingly. This system is prevalent in corporate environments, educational institutions, and various forms of electronic payment systems.

- **Sensors**

Sensors are devices that automatically input data based on changes in the environment. Examples include temperature sensors that detect changes in temperature, light sensors that adjust screen brightness, or motion detectors that trigger actions in smart homes. Sensors are critical for applications that require constant monitoring, such as in industrial systems, weather stations, or healthcare devices. By converting environmental stimuli into data, sensors enhance automation and responsiveness in various systems.

- **Scanners**

Scanners are devices designed to convert physical documents, photographs, or images into digital formats such as JPEG, PDF, or TIFF. This process facilitates easy storage, retrieval, sharing, and manipulation of data, making scanners indispensable in modern document management systems.

Scanners operate using light sensors to capture the image of a document and translate it into a digital representation. Many models employ Charge-Coupled Device (CCD) technology, which ensures high-quality image capture by detecting variations in light and colour with exceptional precision. Advanced scanners can achieve resolutions of up to 3000 dots per inch (dpi), allowing for detailed and accurate reproductions of the original material.

These devices are particularly valuable in environments where efficient handling of paper documents is essential, such as offices, libraries, and healthcare institutions. Scanners streamline workflows by digitising records, reducing the dependency on physical storage, and enabling efficient data integration into digital systems. With features like optical character recognition (OCR), scanners can also convert printed text into editable digital formats, further enhancing their utility in tasks like archiving, editing, and data analysis.

QR Code Scanners

Quick Response (QR) codes are a type of matrix barcode that can store a variety of data, such as URLs, product information, contact details, or other encoded messages. QR code scanners are devices or applications that quickly decode this information when the QR code is scanned. These scanners can be hardware devices, such as handheld scanners, or software-based, often integrated into smartphones or mobile devices. QR code scanners have become integral to numerous modern-day applications, including:

- **Payment Systems:** QR codes are widely used in mobile payment services, such as mobile banking apps, Apple Pay, Google Pay, and others. Users can scan QR codes to make payments quickly and securely at retail outlets or during online transactions.

- **Mobile Applications:** Many mobile applications use QR codes as a way to initiate actions, download apps, authenticate users, or link accounts. For instance, users can scan a QR code to download a new app directly without typing in a URL or visiting an app store.

- **Product Tracking and Inventory Management:** Businesses rely on QR codes to track product information and supply chain logistics. Scanners can instantly access inventory records or product information stored in the QR code.

- **Event and Ticketing:** QR codes are commonly used for event entry, where attendees can scan the QR code on their ticket to gain entry, ensuring faster processing and reducing the risk of counterfeit tickets.

The speed, versatility, and convenience of QR code scanners make them indispensable in modern technological and commercial workflows.

ANPR (Automatic Number Plate Recognition)

Automatic Number Plate Recognition (ANPR) is an advanced technology system designed to identify vehicles by scanning and interpreting the characters on their number plates. ANPR technology uses optical character recognition (OCR) and high-resolution cameras to capture the alphanumeric characters on vehicle registration plates and process them into digital data. ANPR is deployed in a variety of industries and applications, including:

- **Toll Collection:** ANPR is used on highways and toll roads to automate vehicle registration and toll payments without requiring physical tickets or manual payment.

- **Parking Management:** Many parking facilities employ ANPR systems to identify vehicles entering and exiting parking areas. This allows for automated billing and the prevention of unauthorised parking.

- **Traffic Monitoring and Law Enforcement:** ANPR enables law enforcement agencies to monitor vehicle movement, detect stolen cars, identify unregistered vehicles, and investigate criminal activities. It is often used in road policing operations and traffic surveillance cameras.

- **Border Control and Security:** ANPR is deployed at borders to scan vehicles crossing international entry points, improving the accuracy and speed of vehicle inspections and security checks.

The use of ANPR enhances traffic flow, reduces administrative bottlenecks, and improves security by providing law enforcement and transportation management with real-time vehicle recognition capabilities.

RFID (Radio Frequency Identification)

Radio Frequency Identification (RFID) is a wireless communication technology that uses radio waves to identify, track, and monitor objects, assets, or individuals carrying RFID tags. These tags store encoded data that can be transmitted to RFID readers via radio waves without requiring direct contact or line-of-sight scanning. RFID technology has a broad range of applications across industries due to its speed, ease of use, and accuracy.

Common uses of RFID include:

- **Inventory and Supply Chain Management:** RFID tags are embedded into products, containers, or pallets to enable automated inventory tracking, reducing the need for manual checks. They streamline supply chain logistics by providing real-time visibility of inventory movement.

- **Access Control:** RFID is widely used for secure entry into restricted areas, offices, buildings, and facilities. Employees or visitors use RFID-enabled badges to gain access to secure entry points, replacing traditional keys or swipe cards.

- **Asset Tracking:** Organisations employ RFID to track high-value assets, such as equipment, vehicles, or electronics. The tags make it easier to locate and monitor assets, preventing theft and loss.

- **Retail and Point of Sale:** RFID allows retailers to streamline the checkout process by enabling "self-checkout" options. Customers can pay for items by simply passing them over an RFID reader without manual scanning of barcodes.

- **Transportation and Logistics:** RFID tags are used to track vehicles, shipments, or cargo containers in transit. This improves tracking accuracy, enhances visibility, and optimises delivery routes.

- **E-Passport Chip:** An e-passport contains a small, embedded RFID chip that securely stores the holder's personal information, including name, nationality, date of birth, passport number, and biometric data such as a digital photograph or fingerprints. At border control points, specialised RFID readers or e-passport readers scan this chip wirelessly to verify identity and streamline the immigration process. This enhances security, expedites processing times, and ensures accurate identification at international border crossings.

Functionality of E-Passport Chip

- **Biometric Identification:** The stored biometric data allows border control officials to match physical features (e.g., facial recognition or fingerprints) with the data in the chip.
- **Fast Processing:** RFID readers enable quick, contactless scanning, reducing wait times at border points.
- **Enhanced Security:** The data stored in the chip is encrypted, making it difficult to counterfeit or tamper with the passport.

RFID's ability to transmit data wirelessly without direct contact has revolutionised industries by enabling faster, more efficient, and secure data capture. Its versatility ensures its continued use across diverse applications worldwide.

1.5.3 Specialised Input Devices

Specialised input devices are tailored to meet specific user needs, offering more precise or unique forms of interaction with computers. These devices are often used in professional, creative, or specialised applications where standard input devices like keyboards and mice are not as effective.

- **Graphics Tablet and Light Pen**

    - **Graphics Tablet**
      A graphics tablet allows for precise drawing or sketching on a computer screen using a stylus or pen-like device. This tool is popular among graphic designers, digital artists, and illustrators, providing a more natural way to create digital artwork compared to using a mouse. The tablet captures the movement of the stylus and translates it into digital input, offering high accuracy for detailed drawings.

Graphics Pen Tablet
H420
Konga.com

    - **Light Pen**
      A light pen is a pointing device that allows users to interact directly with a display screen by detecting light from the screen itself. Unlike a mouse, the light pen enables users to draw, write, or select items directly on the screen. This device is less common today but was historically used for graphic design, education, and early forms of computer-aided design (CAD).

• **Touch Screen**

A touch screen detects the position of a user's finger on the display surface, enabling interaction with applications and menus by directly touching the screen. This technology is widely used in devices like smartphones, tablets, and kiosks due to its intuitive interface. Touchscreens eliminate the need for external input devices like a mouse or keyboard, allowing for more portable and interactive user experiences.

Amazon.com: 17" Touch Screen ...
amazon.com

• **Concept Keyboard**

Concept Keyboard
ict4u.net

A concept keyboard uses pictures, symbols, or images instead of traditional alphanumeric keys. This type of keyboard is often employed in specialised environments like point-of-sale systems, where users need to quickly select predefined options without requiring literacy in a specific language. Concept keyboards are particularly useful for children, elderly users, or in settings like cafeterias or self-service machines, where ease of use is critical.

• **Biometric Data Entry**

Biometric data entry refers to the use of unique human characteristics for identification and access control. These can be classified as physiological or behavioural modalities. Common forms of biometric entry include fingerprint recognition, retina scans, voice recognition, and palm prints. These systems are increasingly used in secure environments, offering a higher level of security than traditional passwords. Biometric data is difficult to replicate, making it ideal for applications in personal security, banking, and law enforcement.

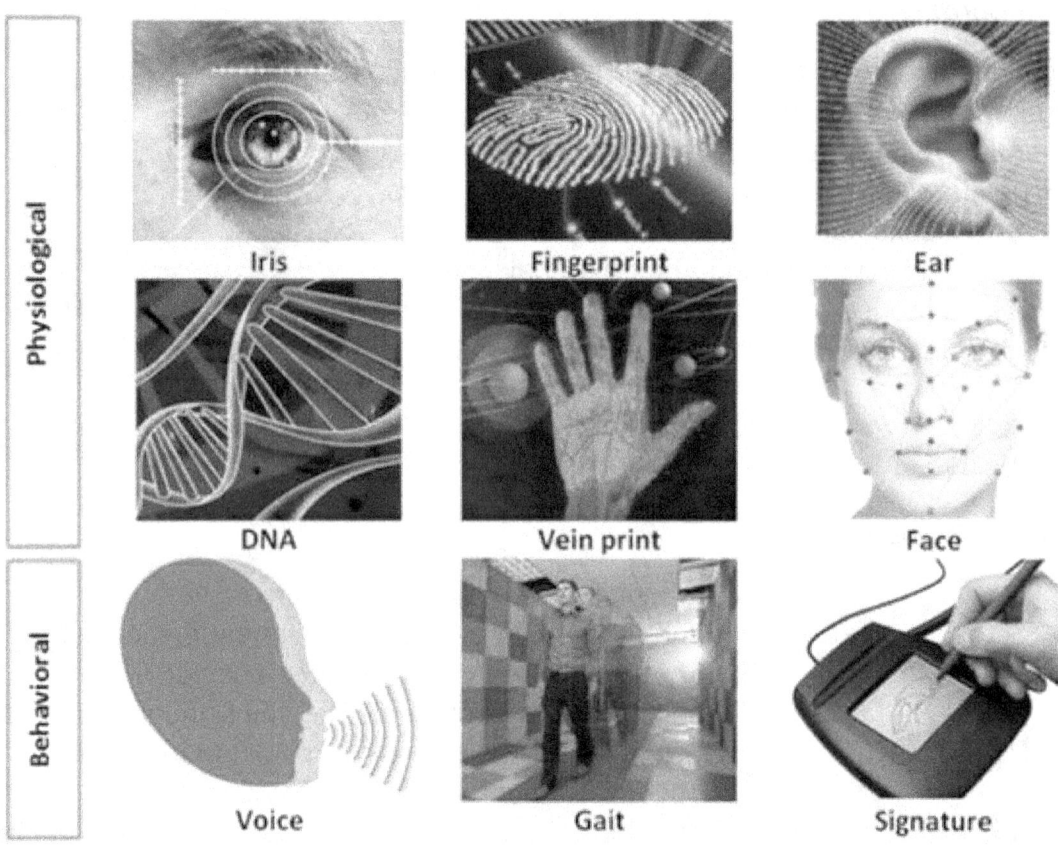

Various types of biometric modalities - by Imed Bouchrika (A Survey of using Biometrics for Smart Visual Surveillance)

- **Voice Data Entry (VDE)**

Voice Data Entry (VDE) allows users to input information into a system through spoken commands. This technology has evolved significantly, with modern systems capable of understanding and processing complex speech patterns. Popular applications of VDE include virtual assistants like Siri and Google Assistant, which enable users to control devices, search the web, and manage schedules hands-free. Voice recognition is increasingly being used in environments like healthcare, automobile, customer service, and smart home systems.

1.6 OPTICAL AND MAGNETIC READERS

Optical and magnetic readers are specialised input devices designed to capture and interpret data from physical media, enabling automated data entry. These devices play a crucial role in industries where fast and accurate data processing is required, such as banking, retail, and document management.

Digitiser

A digitiser converts analogue data (such as temperature readings, pressure data, or graphic drawings) into digital format, enabling more precise processing and analysis. This device is particularly useful in graphic design, engineering, and scientific applications where analogue data needs to be transformed into a digital representation for further analysis or editing.

Barcode Scanner

As already discussed above, a barcode scanner, also known as a barcode reader, is a device used to capture and interpret the data encoded in barcodes. It works by scanning the barcode with a laser or image sensor, then translating the black and white pattern into numerical or alphanumeric data. This data is sent to a computer or software system for automated processing. Barcode readers are widely used in retail, logistics, inventory management, and healthcare for tasks like product identification, tracking, and billing.

Optical Character Recognition (OCR):

Optical Character Recognition (OCR) is a technology that enables a system to read stylised characters (printed or handwritten) from paper documents and convert them into editable text. OCR is widely used in Point of Sale (POS) systems and document scanning applications, reducing the need for manual data entry and improving efficiency in document management and processing.

Optical Mark Reader (OMR)

An Optical Mark Reader (OMR) detects marks made on forms, such as those on multiple-choice exams, surveys, or lottery tickets. The system reads the positions of marks on a paper form, processing them quickly and accurately.

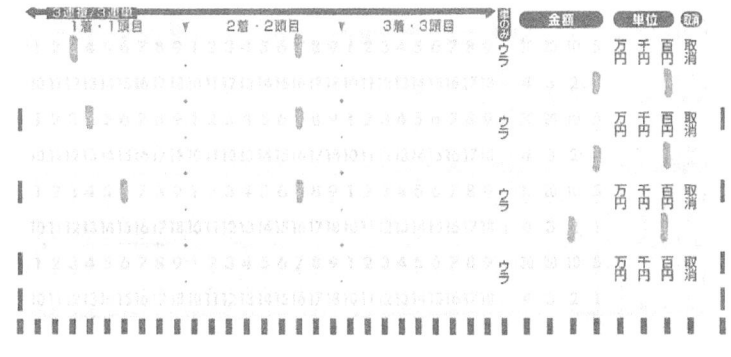

OMR is commonly used for scoring exams, processing questionnaires, and tallying votes in elections.

Magnetic Ink Character Recognition (MICR)

Magnetic Ink Character Recognition (MICR) is a specialised system for reading magnetised characters printed on documents, most commonly used in **banking** for cheque processing. The magnetic ink allows for fast and secure recognition of characters, ensuring that documents are processed accurately and efficiently.

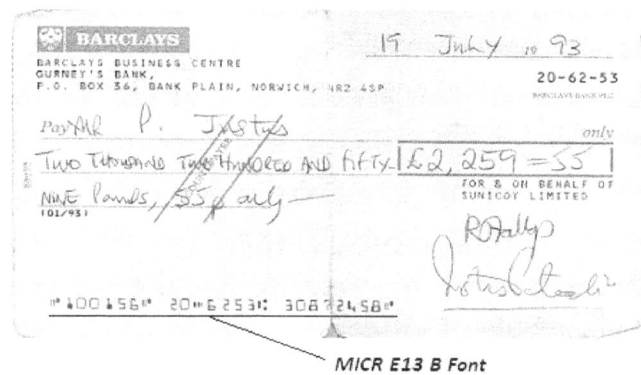

MICR E13 B Font

1.7 IMAGE AND SOUND INPUT DEVICES

Image and sound input devices are designed to capture visual and auditory data, converting them into digital formats that can be processed, analysed, and stored on a computer. These devices are essential for multimedia applications, including photography, video production, and sound recording.

1Scanners and Cameras

- See section on Manual Entry Devices above.

- **Cameras**
  Digital **cameras** capture still images or videos and convert the analogue signals into a digital format. Cameras come in various forms, from handheld devices to webcams and professional-grade video equipment. The captured data can then be processed, edited, and shared or stored digitally.

Pixels and Colour Depth

The quality of digital images is largely determined by **pixels** and **colour depth**. **Pixels** are the smallest unit of a digital image, with more pixels generally resulting in higher image resolution. **Colour depth** refers to the number of bits used to represent the colour of a single pixel. A higher bit depth allows for a greater range of colours, leading to more accurate and vibrant images.

Speech Recognition

Speech recognition systems convert spoken language into text or commands, allowing users to interact with computers using their voice. From simple command-based systems to advanced applications like **Siri**, **Google Assistant**, and **Amazon Alexa**, speech recognition technology has become a core part of modern computing. These systems are designed to understand and process natural language, enabling more intuitive interaction with technology.

1.8 OUTPUT DEVICES OVERVIEW

Output devices are hardware components that take processed data from the computer and present it to users in a human-readable or perceivable form. These devices are essential for converting computational results into formats that can be understood and interacted with, whether through visual displays, sound, or other forms of output.

1.8.1 Types of Output Devices

Monitors (Visual Display Unit - VDU):
Monitors are the most common output devices used to display visual content from the computer. They come in various types, each offering different advantages in terms of resolution, power consumption, and design. Some of the key monitor types include:

- **CRT (Cathode Ray Tube)**
  The CRT is an older display technology used in early computer monitors and television sets. It works by firing electron beams onto a phosphor-coated screen, creating images by varying the intensity of these beams. While CRTs can produce high-resolution images, they have largely been replaced by more modern technologies due to their bulky size, high energy consumption, and lower resolution compared to newer display types.

- **LCD (Liquid Crystal Display)**
  LCDs use liquid crystals that modulate light to create images. These displays are more energy-efficient and thinner than CRTs, offering clearer images and lower power consumption. They are now the standard for everything from laptops and smartphones to television screens. LCDs provide sharp, detailed images, and they use much less electricity, making them more environmentally friendly.

- **LED (Light Emitting Diode)**
  LED displays are an advanced form of LCD technology, using semiconductor diodes that emit light. LEDs offer brighter, more vibrant colours, higher contrast ratios, and energy efficiency compared to traditional LCDs. They are commonly used in modern televisions, computer monitors, and mobile devices. Additionally, LED displays have a longer lifespan, which enhances their overall value.

- **Plasma Displays**
  Plasma displays use ionised gases to create images, providing superior colour accuracy and the ability to produce larger screen sizes. Plasma screens are often used in high-end home entertainment systems due to their excellent visual quality and rich colour representation. However, they are generally more expensive and consume more power compared to other display technologies, which has led to their gradual replacement with LED-based displays.

1.8.2 Printers

Printers are output devices that produce hard copies of documents, images, or designs. They vary in terms of printing quality, speed, and functionality. Common types of printers include:

- **Dot Matrix Printer**
  Dot matrix printers are impact printers that create characters by striking an ink-soaked ribbon against paper. While their print quality is lower compared to modern printers, they are still used for printing multi-part stationery or carbon copies.

- **Ink-Jet Printer**
  Ink-jet printers use a non-impact method, spraying small droplets of ink onto paper to form images or text. These printers offer higher print quality, especially for colour images, making them suitable for printing photos and

high-quality documents.

- **Laser Printer**
  Laser printers use a laser beam to produce high-resolution text and images. Known for their speed, precision, and efficiency, laser printers are commonly used in office environments where high-volume printing is required. They produce clear, sharp prints and are generally more cost-effective in the long run.

- **Line Printer**
  Line printers are high-speed impact printers used for printing large volumes of text at once. They are designed for industrial applications or bulk printing, such as generating reports, and tend to be faster but less refined than inkjet or laser printers.

- **Plotters**
  Plotters are specialised printers used to create high-precision line drawings and technical illustrations, often used in engineering, architecture, and design applications. Unlike regular printers, plotters can draw continuous lines and curves, making them ideal for producing blueprints, maps, and other technical documents.

1.8.3 Additional Output Methods

In addition to monitors and printers, there are other forms of output devices that convey information in different ways:

- **LED Indicators**
  LED indicators are small light-emitting diodes that signal various statuses such as "power on," "battery charging," or "error" conditions. These are often used in devices to provide simple, visual feedback.

- **Buzzers**
  Buzzers are used to produce sound alerts or notifications, often in situations where the user needs immediate attention or when an event occurs (e.g., an alarm or error message).

- **Microform Outputs (COM)**
  Microform outputs, such as microfilm or microfiche, are used to store documents at a reduced size for archival purposes. These outputs are mainly used for long-term storage of documents in libraries, governmental agencies, and archives.

1.8.4 Sound Production

Sound production devices are used to convert digital data into audible sound. This could include anything from music and spoken words to system alerts and notifications. Common technologies used in sound production include:

- **Digital Audio Formats**
  Formats like WAV and MP3 store audio data either in a compressed or uncompressed format. These formats allow for efficient storage of sound, making them suitable for music, speech, or other audio playback applications.

- **MIDI (Musical Instrument Digital Interface):**
  MIDI is a protocol that allows electronic instruments and computers to communicate with each other. It is used in digital music production and synthesisers, allowing musicians to compose, record, and play music electronically. Unlike audio formats, MIDI files contain data that represent musical notes and instrument sounds, rather than actual audio recordings.

1.9 MOTHERBOARD AND PROCESSOR OVERVIEW

The motherboard is the central hub of a computer system, serving as the foundational circuit board that houses and connects various components. It holds the Central Processing Unit (CPU), Random Access Memory (RAM), and provides connectors for storage drives, expansion cards, and external interfaces. The motherboard plays a crucial role in facilitating communication between all the different parts of the computer, similar to how the nervous system coordinates activities in the human body. It also includes expansion slots for additional components such as graphics cards, sound cards, and network cards, allowing users to enhance the computer's functionality.

The **Central Processing Unit (CPU),** often referred to as the "brain" of the computer, is responsible for executing instructions and processing data. The efficiency and speed of the CPU directly influence the computer's overall performance. Modern CPUs often feature multiple cores, enabling them to handle multiple tasks simultaneously, a process known as multithreading, which significantly boosts computational power.

Computer System vs. Von Neumann Architecture

The diagram below illustrates the **Von Neumann Architecture**, which depicts the components and the flow of information within a computer system.

Computer Systems - Von Neumann Architecture

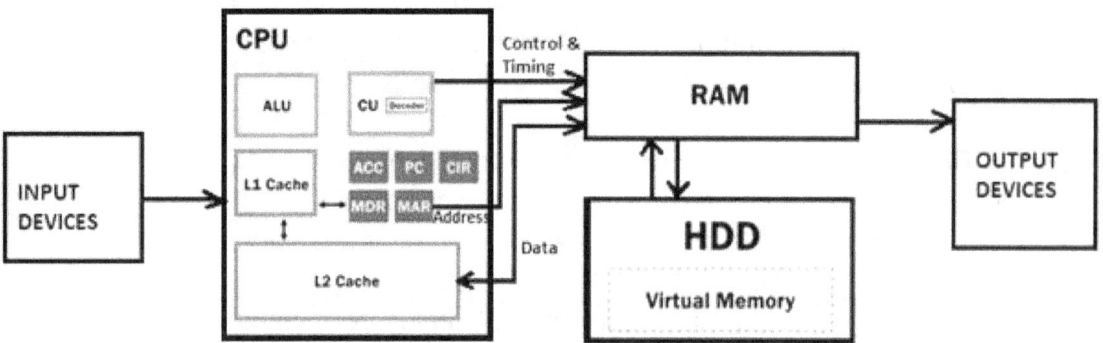

This foundational design shows the relationship between various hardware components, including input devices, the CPU, RAM, the Arithmetic/Logic Unit (ALU), the Control Unit (CU), the hard disk drive (HDD), and output devices.

1.9.1 Components of the CPU

The CPU (Central Processing Unit) serves as the central hub for organising and executing instructions from either the user or the software. It consists of several key components, with the following being noteworthy:

- **Arithmetic and Logic Unit (ALU):**
  The ALU performs mathematical calculations (addition, subtraction, multiplication, division) and logical operations (AND, OR, NOT). For example, when a user performs a calculation in a spreadsheet, the ALU processes the numbers to produce the result.

- **Control Unit (CU):**
  The CU orchestrates the operations of the CPU by directing the flow of data within the system. It retrieves instructions from memory, decodes them, and sends commands to the ALU and other components to execute the instructions.

- **Registers:**
  Registers are small, high-speed storage locations within the CPU that temporarily hold data and instructions. They facilitate rapid access during processing, which is essential for performance.

The Von Neumann Architecture emphasizes the sequential processing of data and instructions, forming the basis of modern computing systems.

1.9.2 Registers in Detail

Registers are integral to the CPU's function, particularly during the **fetch-execute cycle**, which consists of retrieving, decoding, and executing instructions. The main types of registers include:

- **Program Counter (PC):**
  The Program Counter keeps track of the address of the next instruction to be executed.

- **Memory Address Register (MAR):**
  The MAR holds the address of the memory location from which data is to be read or written.

- **Memory Buffer Register (MBR):**
  The MBR stores data being transferred to or from memory, acting as a buffer during data transfer.

- **Current Instruction Register (CIR):**
  The CIR holds the instruction currently being executed by the CPU.

Together, these registers facilitate the smooth operation of the CPU, ensuring efficient data processing and execution of tasks.

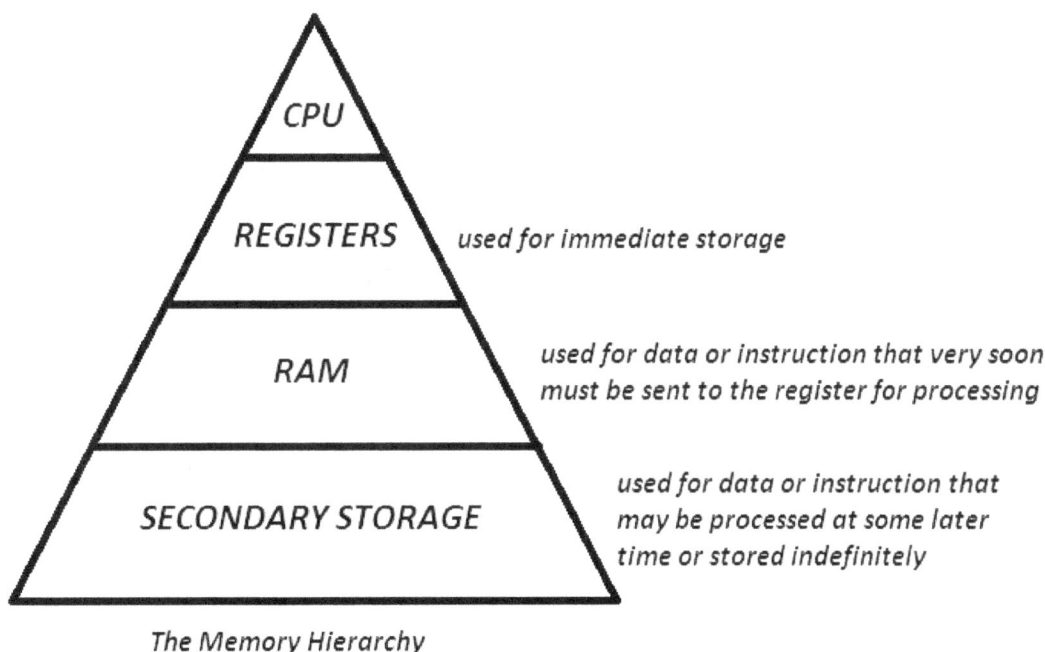

The Memory Hierarchy

1.10 DATA REPRESENTATION

Data representation is fundamental to computing, as computers rely on digital systems to interpret, store, and manipulate information. At the heart of this process is the binary language, which forms the basis of all computations. Data representation forms the foundation of digital computing, ensuring that complex operations can be broken down into simple binary instructions. From individual bits to words and bytes, these fundamental units of data allow modern systems to perform a wide range of tasks with speed and precision.

1.10.1 Binary Language

Computers operate using the binary numeral system, which employs only two symbols: **1** and **0**. Each digit in a binary number represents an **on** (1) or **off** (0) state in a circuit, enabling computers to process complex instructions through simple operations.

1.10.2 Bits and Bytes

- **Bit (Binary Digit)**
  The smallest unit of data in computing, a bit represents a binary value of **1** or **0**. Bits form the building blocks of all digital information.

- **Byte**
  A byte consists of 8 bits and is widely regarded as the basic unit of data in computer systems. Each byte can represent up to 256 unique values (2^8), making it suitable for encoding characters in systems like ASCII (American Standard Code for Information Interchange).

- **Nibble**
  A lesser-known unit, a nibble consists of 4 bits (half a byte), commonly used in representing hexadecimal values.

1.10.3 Words

In computing, a word is a fixed-sized unit of data that a CPU processes as a single entity.

- Word sizes vary depending on system architecture:
  - **16-bit systems**: Can process 2^2 = 65,536 unique values.
  - **32-bit systems**: Process larger data sets more efficiently, enabling modern software and applications.
  - **64-bit systems**: Handle vast amounts of data, supporting advanced computing and multitasking.
- The word size determines the CPU's capacity to address memory, impacting overall system performance.

1.10.4 Importance of Data Representation

- **Efficiency in Processing**:
  Binary systems allow computers to process data at incredible speeds, optimising memory usage and minimising errors.

- **Universal Standard**:
  Binary encoding forms the foundation for all modern computing devices, ensuring consistency across platforms.

- **Data Encoding**:
  Various data types - text, images, audio, and video - are represented in binary, enabling seamless communication between devices.

1.10.5 Applications of Data Representation

- **Text Representation**:
  Characters and symbols are encoded using systems like **ASCII** (American Standard Code for Information Interchange) or **Unicode**, allowing computers to store and display text in different languages.

- **Graphics**:
  Pixels in images are represented by binary codes indicating their colour and intensity, forming the basis of digital imaging.

- **Multimedia**:
  Audio and video data are encoded as binary streams, enabling storage, playback, and streaming.

11.1 MACHINE CYCLE

The machine cycle is the core process through which a Central Processing Unit (CPU) executes instructions, enabling a computer to perform tasks. It represents the sequence of steps the CPU follows to process a single instruction, divided into distinct phases that ensure accurate and efficient operation. This cycle occurs billions of times per second in modern processors, forming the basis of all computing processes.

The machine cycle remains a cornerstone of computer architecture, providing the foundation for all computational tasks. By breaking down complex operations into manageable phases, it ensures that computers function with speed, accuracy, and reliability.

1.11.1 Definition

The machine cycle encompasses the actions taken by the CPU to fetch, decode, execute, and sometimes store the results of an instruction. The cycle is traditionally broken down into two main phases:

a) Instruction Cycle

b) Execution Cycle

1.11.2 Phases of the Machine Cycle

a) Instruction Cycle

This phase involves retrieving and interpreting the instruction, which consists of the following steps:

- **Fetch**:
    - The Control Unit (CU) reads the next instruction from the memory address specified by the Program Counter (PC).
    - This instruction is then transferred to the Current Instruction Register (CIR).
- **Decode**:
    - The Control Unit decodes the fetched instruction to determine the specific operation to perform.
    - If necessary, the memory locations or registers involved are identified.

The instruction cycle ensures that the CPU is prepared to perform the desired task.

b) Execution Cycle

In this phase, the actual operation specified by the instruction is carried out. It involves:

- **Execution**:
    - The Arithmetic Logic Unit (ALU) or other functional units perform the required operation, such as arithmetic calculations (e.g., addition, subtraction) or logical comparisons (e.g., AND, OR).
    - For example, if the instruction is to add two numbers, the ALU retrieves the operands from registers or memory, performs the addition, and stores the result.
- **Write Back (Store)**:
    - The result of the operation is written back to the memory, or a CPU register for future use.

The execution cycle is where the actual task is completed, converting the decoded instruction into tangible outcomes.

The Machine Cycle

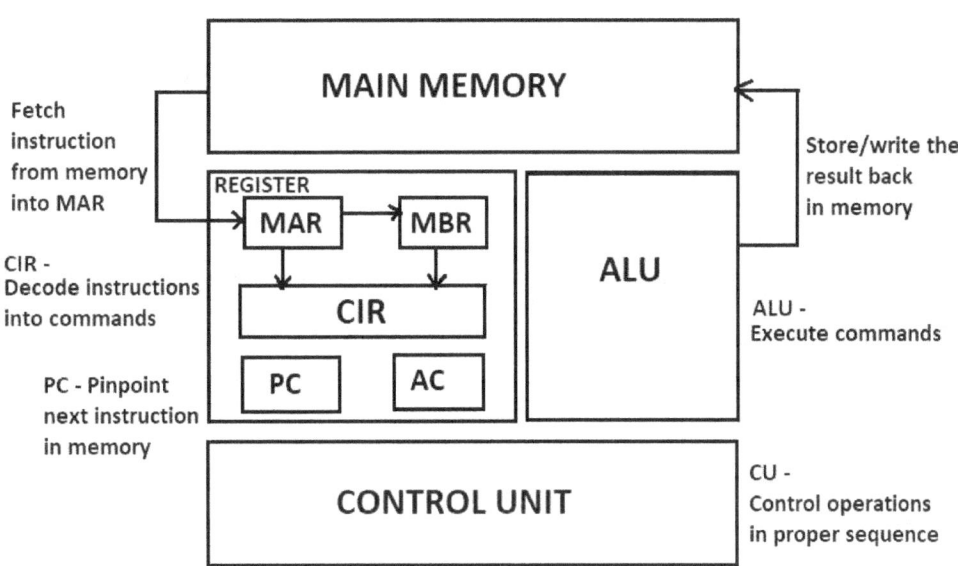

1.11.3 The Complete Cycle: Fetch-Decode-Execute-Store

The machine cycle can also be viewed as a **four-step process**, often referred to as the **Fetch-Decode-Execute-Store cycle**:

1. **Fetch**: Retrieve the instruction from memory.
2. **Decode**: Interpret the instruction.
3. **Execute**: Perform the instruction using the CPU's functional units.
4. **Store**: Save the result in memory or a register.

This cycle repeats continuously for every instruction, enabling seamless processing.

1.11.4 Illustration of a Machine Cycle

Consider an instruction to **add two numbers** stored in memory locations:

1. The Control Unit fetches the instruction and operands from memory.
2. The instruction is decoded to identify the operation (addition).
3. The ALU executes the addition, using the operands.
4. The result is stored back in a designated memory location or register.

1.11.5 Importance of the Machine Cycle

- **Efficiency**:
  The machine cycle ensures that instructions are processed systematically, optimising CPU performance.

- **Automation**:
  It automates task execution, requiring no manual intervention once the program is loaded.

- **Precision**:
  Each phase of the cycle is meticulously controlled, reducing errors and ensuring accurate results.

1.11.6 Modern Enhancements to the Machine Cycle

In modern CPUs, technologies like **pipelining** and **parallel processing** enhance the machine cycle:

- **Pipelining** allows multiple instructions to overlap in execution, with different stages of the cycle occurring simultaneously.

- **Parallel Processing** enables multiple cores to process separate instructions, significantly improving performance.

1.12 SPEED AND PERFORMANCE

The speed and performance of a Central Processing Unit (CPU) are critical factors that determine how efficiently a computer can execute tasks and process data. These metrics are influenced by several factors, including clock speed, architecture, and the presence of advanced features like multi-core processing and hyper-threading. With ongoing advancements, CPUs continue to play a pivotal role in driving innovation and meeting the increasing demands of modern computing.

1.12.1 Measurement

The performance of a CPU is typically measured using the following metrics:

- **MIPS (Million Instructions Per Second):**
  MIPS is a unit that quantifies the number of instructions a CPU can execute in one second, expressed in millions. This metric provides a basic indication of the processor's speed. For instance, a CPU with a rating of 100 MIPS can execute 100 million instructions every second. While useful, MIPS does not account for variations in instruction complexity, making it a less precise measure for comparing processors with different architectures.

- **FLOPS (Floating-Point Operations Per Second):**
  FLOPS is a more specialised metric used to measure a CPU's ability to perform floating-point calculations. Floating-point operations are essential for scientific computations, simulations, and graphics rendering. FLOPS is particularly relevant in high-performance computing (HPC) and supercomputers. For example, modern supercomputers are capable of achieving speeds in the range of exaFLOPS (quintillions of FLOPS), enabling breakthroughs in fields like climate modelling and molecular simulations.

1.12.2 Factors Affecting Performance

- **Clock Speed:**
  Measured in gigahertz (GHz), the clock speed of a CPU indicates how many cycles it can complete per second. Higher clock speeds generally mean faster performance, but efficiency also depends on the CPU's architecture and ability to process instructions within each cycle.

- **Number of Cores:**
  Modern CPUs often feature multiple cores, allowing them to execute multiple tasks simultaneously. Multi-core processors are particularly beneficial for multitasking and running applications optimised for parallel processing, such as video editing and 3D rendering.

- **Cache Memory:**
  Cache memory is a small amount of high-speed storage located within the CPU. It stores frequently accessed data and instructions, reducing the time required to fetch information from main memory (RAM). Larger and more advanced caches can significantly enhance performance.

- **Instruction Set Architecture (ISA):**
  The ISA defines the set of instructions a CPU can execute. Advanced ISAs, such as those supporting vector operations or specialised machine learning instructions, enable processors to handle complex tasks more efficiently.

1.12.3 Evolution

The architecture of CPUs has undergone remarkable advancements over the years, resulting in substantial improvements in speed and performance. Key milestones in CPU evolution include:

- **Pipeline Architecture:**
  Introduced in processors like Intel's 80486, pipeline architecture allows multiple instructions to be processed simultaneously at different stages of execution. This innovation enables more efficient use of the CPU's resources, significantly increasing processing speed.

- **Superscalar Architecture:**
  Modern CPUs often use superscalar designs, which allow multiple instructions to be issued and executed per clock cycle. This approach maximises parallelism and improves overall throughput.

- **Hyper-Threading Technology:**
  Technologies like Intel's Hyper-Threading enable a single physical core to appear as two logical cores to the operating system. This allows the processor to handle multiple threads more efficiently, improving multitasking and performance in applications optimised for multi-threading.

- **Advances in Lithography:**
  Over time, CPUs have become smaller and more power-efficient thanks to

advancements in semiconductor fabrication techniques. Modern processors are built on processes as small as 3 nanometres, enabling billions of transistors to fit on a single chip, which improves both performance and energy efficiency.

1.12.4 Applications of High-Performance CPUs

High-performance CPUs play a crucial role in enabling seamless functionality, speed, and efficiency across various domains of modern computing. These processors are engineered to handle intensive computational tasks, ensuring optimal performance in scenarios requiring rapid data processing, multitasking, and responsiveness. Below are some key areas where high-performance CPUs are central:

1. Gaming

- Modern video games demand exceptional processing power to deliver immersive experiences.
- **Graphics Rendering**: High-performance CPUs work alongside GPUs to process intricate 3D environments, lighting effects, and textures in real time.
- **Physics Simulation**: Realistic interactions, such as object collisions, explosions, and character movements, require CPUs capable of performing complex calculations rapidly.
- **Artificial Intelligence (AI)**: Games increasingly incorporate advanced AI for non-playable characters (NPCs), requiring CPUs that can process and adapt AI algorithms in real time.
- **Virtual Reality (VR) and Augmented Reality (AR)**: These applications push processing requirements even further, demanding ultra-low latency and high-speed performance for smooth user experiences.

2. Data Science and Machine Learning

- The rise of big data and AI has amplified the need for high-performance CPUs in analytical and predictive applications.
- **Training Machine Learning Models**: CPUs with high Floating-Point Operations Per Second (FLOPS) are essential for running iterative processes on large datasets, optimising models efficiently.
- **Real-Time Analytics**: Tasks like fraud detection, recommendation systems, and dynamic pricing rely on the ability to process vast amounts of data almost instantaneously.
- **Scientific Computing**: Fields such as genomics, climate modelling, and particle simulations demand CPUs capable of performing precise, large-scale calculations.

3. Content Creation

- The creative industries, encompassing video production, graphic design, animation, and sound editing, rely heavily on high-performance CPUs to manage resource-intensive workflows.

- **Video Editing and Post-Production**:
    - CPUs with multiple cores and threads enable smooth editing, rendering, and colour grading of high-resolution videos, including 4K and 8K formats.
    - Tasks like transcoding and applying visual effects require extensive processing power to maintain efficiency.

- **3D Modelling and Rendering**:
    - Applications in architecture, game development, and filmmaking depend on CPUs to handle intricate calculations for object rendering, lighting, and texture mapping.

- **Audio Production**:
    - High-performance CPUs process complex audio effects, real-time sound synthesis, and multi-track mixing without latency issues.

4. Engineering and Scientific Research

- Engineering simulations, such as finite element analysis (FEA), fluid dynamics, and circuit design, demand CPUs capable of solving complex mathematical problems efficiently.

- **Astronomy and Physics**: Research institutions use high-performance CPUs for tasks like simulating the cosmos, modelling black hole dynamics, and processing data from telescopes.

- **Pharmaceutical Research**: CPUs play a role in drug discovery by performing simulations of molecular interactions and analysing vast datasets from experiments.

5. Financial and Business Applications

- The financial industry relies on high-performance CPUs for tasks requiring speed and precision:
    - **Algorithmic Trading**: Rapid processing of market data and executing trades within milliseconds.
    - **Risk Analysis and Forecasting**: CPUs handle complex statistical models to assess financial risks and predict market trends.

6. Everyday Computing and Consumer Technology

- While high-performance CPUs are often associated with specialised applications, they also enhance everyday technologies:

- **Smartphones and Tablets**: Advanced CPUs power features like real-time language translation, facial recognition, and augmented reality.
- **Smart Home Devices**: Devices such as smart speakers, smart TVs and home automation systems rely on efficient processing to understand commands and control devices seamlessly.

7. The Importance of High-Performance CPUs

High-performance CPUs are foundational to the modern digital landscape. By enabling rapid and efficient data processing across diverse applications, they empower innovation, enhance productivity, and elevate user experiences in both professional and personal contexts.

1.13 DATA STORAGE SYSTEMS

1.13.1 Data Storage

Data storage is a fundamental component of any computer system, responsible for holding information that the system can retrieve and use to execute tasks. Data storage is divided into different types based on characteristics such as data retention duration, speed, and purpose. Understanding these storage types helps users manage and access data efficiently across different scenarios.

1.13.2 Categories of Data Storage Systems

Data storage systems are typically divided into two main categories: Primary Storage and Secondary Storage.

1. Primary Storage (Main Memory)

Primary storage, also known as main memory, refers to the computer's internal memory that provides fast, direct access to the processor. It is where the operating system, applications, and currently processed data reside temporarily while a computer is running. Primary storage is usually volatile, meaning data is lost when power is switched off.

2. Characteristics of Primary Storage:

- **Size**: Typically measured in megabytes (MB) or gigabytes (GB), depending on the memory's capacity.
- **Volatility**: Primary storage is generally volatile, meaning that it only retains data while the computer is powered on.
- **Speed**: It offers fast access speeds compared to secondary storage.

3. Types of Primary Storage:

1. **RAM (Random Access Memory):**

    - RAM is a type of volatile memory that temporarily stores data and program instructions that the CPU needs to access quickly.
    - It allows data to be read and written quickly, facilitating fast performance.
    - **Example**: When you open a browser or a document, the data is temporarily stored in RAM, enabling quick access while the application is in use.

2. **ROM (Read-Only Memory):**
    - ROM is a non-volatile memory that retains data even when the computer is turned off. It typically contains firmware - permanent software instructions for initial hardware functions.
    - Since ROM is read-only, its contents cannot be modified or erased under normal circumstances.
    - **Example**: The BIOS (Basic Input/Output System) in a computer is stored in ROM, allowing the system to boot up when powered on.

3. **Cache Memory:**
    - Cache is a high-speed memory located close to the CPU that stores frequently accessed data, reducing the need for the CPU to access slower main memory.
    - This type of memory is particularly useful for storing repeated tasks or commands, enhancing processing speed and performance.
    - **Example**: Web browsers often use cache memory to store website data, allowing frequently visited pages to load faster.

1.13.3 Secondary Storage (Mass Storage)

Secondary storage, also referred to as mass storage, is used for long-term data retention. Unlike primary storage, secondary storage is non-volatile, meaning data is preserved even when the computer is powered off. Secondary storage devices store files, applications, and the operating system permanently or until the data is deleted by the user.

1. Characteristics of Secondary Storage:

- **Non-Volatile**: Data remains intact without power, ensuring long-term data retention.

- **Higher Capacity**: Typically, secondary storage has a higher storage capacity than primary storage.

- **Slower Access Speed**: Data retrieval is slower than primary storage due to physical read/write mechanisms.

2. Types of Secondary Storage:

a. **Magnetic Disks**:

- Magnetic disks are widely used as storage media in computers, primarily in the form of hard drives (HDDs).
- Data is stored magnetically in tracks and sectors on spinning disks and read/write heads access data.
- **Example**: Traditional hard drives in desktop computers and laptops use magnetic disks to store operating systems, applications, and personal files.

b. **Optical Discs**:

- Optical storage devices, including CDs (Compact Discs), DVDs (Digital Versatile Discs), and Blu-ray discs, use laser technology to read and write data.
- Data is written as a series of pits and lands on the disc's surface and is read by a laser beam.
- **Examples**:
    - **CDs**: Used for music, software, and small data storage (up to 700 MB).

- **DVDs**: Commonly used for movies and data storage, offering greater capacity than CDs (up to 4.7 GB for a single-layer disc).
- **Blu-ray Discs**: Provide even higher storage capacity, making them suitable for high-definition videos (up to 25 GB per layer).

3. Comparison of Primary and Secondary Storage

To understand the role each storage type plays in data management, let's consider some comparisons:

Feature	Primary Storage	Secondary Storage
Volatility	Typically, volatile	Non-volatile
Access Speed	Faster	Slower
Usage	Temporary storage for active data	Long-term data retention
Capacity	Smaller	Larger
Examples	RAM, ROM, Cache Memory	HDDs, SSDs, CDs, DVDs, Blu-rays

Example Exercise:

Identify a device you use daily (e.g., smartphone, laptop) and list one type of primary storage and one type of secondary storage it contains. Explain how each storage type contributes to your device's performance.

Example Answer:

- **Device**: Smartphone.
- **Primary Storage**: RAM, which allows me to switch between apps quickly.
- **Secondary Storage**: Internal SSD (Solid State Drive), where all my photos, videos, and app data are stored permanently. RAM enables faster app performance, while the SSD provides ample storage capacity for long-term data retention.

Tutorial Activity 1 - Basic Computer System

Quizzes and Questions

Multiple Choice Questions (MCQs)

1. What does the term "computer system" primarily refer to?
   a) A single hardware component
   b) A combination of hardware, software, and other components working together
   c) Only the software applications installed on a machine
   d) The physical keyboard and monitor setup

2. Which of the following is an example of firmware?
   a) Microsoft Word
   b) BIOS
   c) Hard disk drive
   d) RAM

3. The 4wares of a computer system include:
   a) Software, middleware, hardware, networks
   b) Hardware, software, firmware, people-ware
   c) People-ware, network-ware, hardware, firmware
   d) Firmware, hardware, middleware, people-ware

4. Which type of communication transfers data one bit at a time?
   a) Parallel communication
   b) Serial communication
   c) Asynchronous communication
   d) Bus communication

5. Which method is commonly used to connect modern peripherals to a computer?
   a) Ethernet ports
   b) USB (Universal Serial Bus)
   c) Parallel ports
   d) PS/2 connectors

6. What is the primary role of hardware in a computer system?
   a) To design software
   b) To execute tasks under software instructions
   c) To prevent wear and tear of components
   d) To enhance data storage permanently

7. Which of the following is NOT a capability of modern hardware?
   a) High-speed data processing
   b) Vast storage capacity
   c) Immunity to physical wear and tear
   d) Enhanced user interaction through peripherals

8. What type of hardware is considered an external component?
   a) CPU
   b) Motherboard
   c) Printer
   d) GPU

9. Which of these is a limitation of hardware?
   a) It is immune to software bugs.
   b) It can process data at infinite speeds.
   c) Its performance depends on software compatibility.
   d) It doesn't consume energy.

Short Answer Questions

1. Define the term "computer system" and explain its importance.

2. Identify three input devices and three output devices.

3. Explain the difference between hardware and software.
   run on the hardware to perform specific tasks, like operating systems or applications.

4. Describe the role of the motherboard in a computer system.

5. What is the significance of CPU speed and how is it measured?

6. Explain the role of software in directing hardware operations.

7. List two capabilities of modern hardware.

8. What are two common limitations of hardware?

True/False Questions

1. Firmware is a combination of hardware and software that provides permanent instructions for the hardware to function.

2. Parallel communication transfers data one bit at a time.

3. People-ware refers to the human users and administrators involved in operating and managing a computer system.

4. The BIOS is an example of software that can be uninstalled.

5. Data representation in a computer is always in binary form.

6. Hardware can operate independently without any software instructions.

7. External components like printers and external drives are considered part of the hardware.

8. The size and energy consumption of hardware are not limitations.

Fill-in-the-Blank Questions

8. The CPU and GPU are examples of _____ hardware components.
9. Hardware performance is limited by _____ constraints such as size and energy consumption.
10. _____ peripherals enhance user interaction and improve task efficiency.

Essay Questions

1. Analyse the relationship between hardware, software, firmware, and people-ware, providing examples of how they work together in a computer system.
2. Discuss the methods of connecting peripherals to a computer system and their evolution from parallel ports to modern wireless technologies.

Activity: Matching

Match the following components to their category:

1. Keyboard
2. BIOS
3. RAM
4. Monitor
5. Operating System

Options:
a) Hardware
b) Firmware
c) Software
d) Input Device
e) Output Device

Scenario-Based Question

Scenario: A user has a high-performance computer but experiences frequent crashes while running a graphics-intensive program. Based on the nature and limitations of hardware, what could be the possible reasons?

Chapter 2: Software & Its Applications

Learning Outcomes

By the end of Chapter 3, students will be able to:

- Define software and understand its importance in computing.
- Differentiate software categories, including system software and application software.
- Provide examples of software types, such as operating systems, utility programs, and application software.
- Explain the core features and characteristics of software categories.
- Define the Operating System (OS) and describe its role in managing computer hardware and software.
- Recognise examples of various operating systems used in modern computing.
- Describe the functions of an OS, such as file management, memory management, and input/output (I/O) control.
- Distinguish between primary and secondary data storage systems, noting their characteristics and uses.
- Understand Interrupts, their types, and significance in multitasking.

2. Introduction

In computing, software and operating systems (OS) are fundamental to a computer's functioning. They act as a bridge between users and hardware, enabling seamless execution of tasks and the management of system resources. This chapter introduces these essential components, helping students gain foundational knowledge of software and operating systems.

We begin by defining software and exploring its types: system software and application software. This includes examining how they interact with hardware to perform specific functions. Next, we'll discuss operating systems, detailing their purpose, structure, and main components. Finally, we'll explore data storage systems and interrupts, both of which are crucial for multitasking and efficient system processing.

This chapter provides an engaging mix of explanations, examples, and interactive activities, equipping students to understand and apply these concepts in everyday computing experiences.

2.1 SOFTWARE

Software is a crucial component of any computer system, consisting of a collection of instructions or programs that direct the computer on how to execute specific tasks. Unlike hardware, which is the physical component that can be touched (like the keyboard, monitor, and internal components), software is intangible. It cannot be physically seen or held but is observed through the actions and tasks it performs.

When you open a document, play a game, or browse the internet, you're interacting with software that tells the computer how to accomplish these tasks. Software, therefore, acts as an intermediary between the user and the hardware, allowing the computer to execute a wide variety of functions.

Example: Word processing software, such as Microsoft Word, enables users to create, edit, and format documents. Though users cannot physically interact with Microsoft Word itself, they can perceive its presence and utility through the document editing tools it provides.

2.2 CATEGORIES OF SOFTWARE

Software can be broadly categorised into two main types, each playing a distinct role in computer functionality:

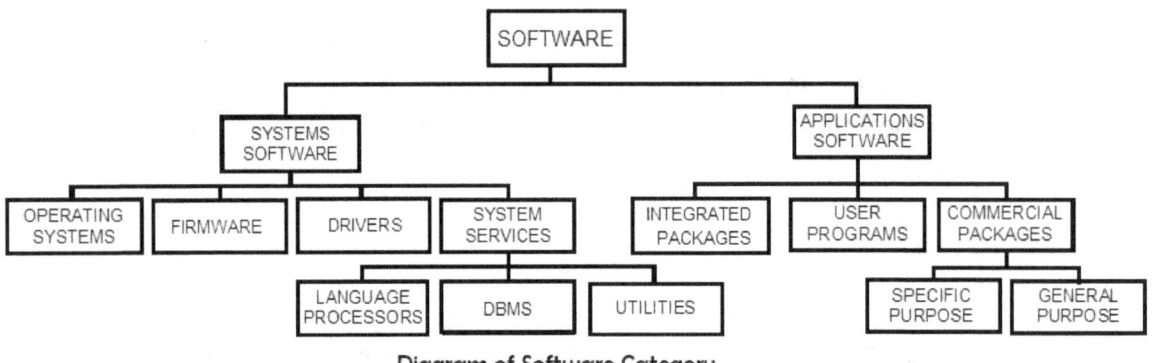

Diagram of Software Category

2.1.1 System Software

System software is essential for the operation and management of computer hardware. It serves as the foundational layer on which application software operates, ensuring efficient communication between hardware and software while maintaining the stability and functionality of the computing environment. Without system software, the computer would be unable to execute even the most basic tasks.

Key Components of System Software

1. **Operating Systems (OS)**
   The operating system is the most critical component of system software. It acts as an intermediary between the user, application software, and hardware, managing system resources such as memory, processing power, and storage. The OS ensures that all programs can run without conflicts and provides essential services for application software to function effectively.

- **Functions of an Operating System:**
  - **Resource Management:** Manages CPU time, memory allocation, and input/output (I/O) devices.
  - **File Management:** Organises data in storage devices, allowing easy access and manipulation.
  - **User Interface (UI):** Provides interfaces like command-line interfaces (CLI) or graphical user interfaces (GUI) for user interaction.
  - **Multitasking and Multithreading:** Allows multiple processes to run simultaneously and efficiently.
  - **Security:** Protects system data and user information from unauthorised access.

- **Examples of Popular Operating Systems**
  - **DOS (Disk Operating System):** An early command-line OS designed for file management and application execution.
  - **Windows:** A widely used graphical OS with a user-friendly interface, suitable for personal and business environments.
  - **Linux:** An open-source OS valued for its stability, security, and customisation, commonly used in servers and programming.
  - **macOS:** Developed by Apple, known for its intuitive design and seamless integration with Apple hardware.
  - **Android and iOS:** Operating systems designed specifically for mobile devices, enabling smartphone functionality.

2. **System Services**
System services are additional software components that enhance the OS by providing specialised functions essential for system and application performance.

- **Language Processors**
These are software tools that convert code written in programming languages into machine-readable instructions that the CPU can execute.
  - **Compilers:** Translate entire high-level programs into machine code before execution, producing standalone executable files.
  - **Interpreters:** Translate and execute high-level programs line-by-line, enabling immediate error detection and debugging.
  - **Assemblers:** Convert assembly language, a low-level human-readable code, into machine code.

- **Database Management Systems (DBMS)**
The DBMS is a specialised software used under system services to manage

the storage, organisation, retrieval, and updating of data within a computer system. It acts as an interface between the user and the database, streamlining the handling of large volumes of structured information. By integrating with the operating system, DBMS enhances file system management, enabling efficient data processing, storage, and retrieval crucial for modern computing applications.

- Role in File System Management
    - DBMS is a key component of file system management, ensuring efficient and organised data handling for storage and retrieval. Unlike basic file storage systems, which store data in unstructured formats, a DBMS provides structured frameworks that enable:
    - **Data Organisation:** DBMS uses tables, rows, and columns to arrange data logically, making it easy to locate and access specific information.
    - **Storage Management:** It optimises the use of storage resources, ensuring data is stored compactly and efficiently.
    - **Data Retrieval:** Queries, written in languages like SQL (Structured Query Language), allow users to fetch specific data quickly.
    - **Data Integrity and Security:** DBMS ensures data accuracy, enforces constraints, and protects information from unauthorised access.
- Features of a DBMS in System Services
    - **Centralised Data Management:** Facilitates a single repository for data, reducing redundancy and ensuring consistency.
    - **Indexing and Searching:** Speeds up data retrieval through advanced indexing techniques.
    - **Transaction Management:** Maintains data integrity during operations by ensuring transactions are processed entirely or not at all.
    - **Backup and Recovery:** Provides tools to safeguard data against loss and restore it during failures.
- Examples of DBMS Software
    - **MySQL:** A widely used open-source DBMS for web applications.
    - **Oracle DB:** Known for its scalability and reliability in enterprise environments.
    - **Microsoft SQL Server:** A robust solution for database management in business applications.

- **Utility Programs**
These are specialised software tools designed to optimise, maintain, and secure the computer system.

- **Antivirus Software:** Scans for and removes malicious software, protecting the system from cyber threats.
- **Disk Defragmenter:** Reorganises fragmented data on a storage drive, improving data retrieval speed.
- **Backup Software:** Creates copies of data to prevent loss in the event of hardware failure or accidental deletion.
- **Compression Tools:** Reduce file sizes for storage efficiency (e.g., WinRAR, 7-Zip, Zip).
- **Disk Cleanup Tools:** Remove unnecessary files to free up storage and improve system performance.

3. **Firmware**

Firmware is a specialised form of system software embedded into hardware devices. It provides the essential instructions for how the device communicates with other hardware and software components. Unlike application software, firmware operates at a lower level, directly controlling hardware functions.

- **Examples of Firmware**
    - BIOS/UEFI: Firmware that initiates hardware components during startup and loads the OS.
    - Embedded System Software: Found in devices like routers, washing machines, and smart TVs, enabling them to perform their specific tasks.

4. **Drivers**

Device drivers are system software components that enable the operating system and applications to communicate with hardware devices such as printers, graphics cards, and storage devices.

- **Functions of Drivers**
    - Facilitate hardware-software interaction.
    - Provide instructions for operating hardware-specific features.
    - Ensure compatibility between the OS and connected devices.

Role of System Software in Computing

System software forms the backbone of a computer system, managing hardware resources and providing an environment for application software to perform effectively. Its various components work together to ensure that the system remains functional, secure, and efficient, catering to both basic and advanced computing needs.

2.1.2 Application Software

Application software is designed to enable users to perform specific tasks ranging from document creation to complex data analysis. Unlike system software, which manages hardware and system resources, application software directly addresses user needs by providing tools and features tailored to specific or general purposes. These programs are fundamental for productivity, creativity, and problem-solving across various domains.

Categories of Application Software

1. **Commercial Application Packages**
   These are software products developed for broad usage, generally available for purchase or subscription. They are classified into:
   - **General-purpose Applications:**
     These versatile tools are designed for everyday tasks applicable across various fields. Examples include:
     - **Word Processors (e.g., Microsoft Word):** For creating, editing, formatting, and printing documents, widely used in offices, schools, and at home.
     - **Spreadsheets (e.g., Microsoft Excel):** Used for organising data, performing calculations, generating graphs, and analysing trends.
     - **Presentation Software (e.g., PowerPoint):** Helps in creating slideshows, incorporating text, images, videos, and animations for effective communication.
     - **Database Management Systems (e.g., Microsoft Access):** Used for storing, retrieving, and managing structured data efficiently.
   - **Specific-purpose Applications:**
     These are specialised tools tailored to meet the requirements of specific industries or tasks. Examples include:
     - **Payroll Software (e.g., QuickBooks):** Automates payroll processes by calculating wages, deductions, and taxes.
     - **Computer-Aided Design (CAD) Software (e.g., AutoCAD):** Utilised by architects and engineers to create precise 2D or 3D models of structures and products.
     - **Graphic Design Software (e.g., Adobe Photoshop):** Allows artists and designers to create and manipulate digital images and illustrations.

2. **Integrated Software Packages**
   Integrated software combines multiple applications within a single suite,

streamlining workflows and ensuring compatibility across tools. These suites are ideal for users requiring a variety of tools in one environment. Examples include:

- **Microsoft Office Suite:** Combines Word, Excel, PowerPoint, and Outlook, offering tools for document creation, data analysis, presentations, and communication.
- **Google Workspace:** A cloud-based suite including Docs, Sheets, Slides, and Gmail, enabling online collaboration and real-time editing.
- **Zoho One:** Provides a unified solution with applications for customer relationship management (CRM), project management, and finance.

3. **User Programs**
User programs, also referred to as **custom software** or **end-user programs**, are created by individuals or organisations to meet specific, unique requirements not addressed by commercial or integrated software packages.
    - **Features of User Programs:**
        - **Tailored Functionality:** Designed to solve a specific problem or automate a particular process for a user or business.
        - **Customisation:** Flexible and adjustable based on user preferences.
        - **Examples of User Programs:**
            - A company-developed **inventory management tool** tailored to its supply chain.
            - A user-written Python script for automating data entry tasks.
            - Custom programs for educational purposes, such as quizzes, attendance tracking systems or students' performance tracking and report card system.
    - **Advantages of User Programs:**
        - **Exact Fit:** Addresses specific needs more effectively than general-purpose software.
        - **Control:** Users or organisations maintain full control over the program's features and updates.
    - **Disadvantages of User Programs:**
        - **Development Cost and Time:** Requires significant resources to design, develop, and maintain.

- **Limited Support:** Unlike commercial software, user programs may lack extensive support or regular updates.

Importance of Application Software

Application software is essential for productivity in personal and professional environments. It simplifies complex tasks, enhances efficiency, and supports collaboration. Whether using general-purpose tools for day-to-day work or custom user programs for specialised needs, application software forms a critical link between users and computing systems.

By categorising and understanding different types of application software, users can make informed decisions about which tools best suit their requirements, ensuring maximum utility and effectiveness.

2.1.3 Key Features and Characteristics of Software

Software has certain defining features and characteristics that set it apart from hardware. Understanding these characteristics helps in distinguishing between different types of software and recognising their respective roles.

- **Intangibility**: Unlike hardware, which is physical and tangible, software is intangible. It exists as a set of instructions or code that can only be experienced through the tasks it enables. You can see the results of using software (such as a document or a game interface), but the software itself cannot be physically touched.

- **Updatability**: Software can be frequently updated to improve performance, add new features, or fix bugs. These updates help software stay relevant and compatible with new technology, which can extend its usability over time. For example, operating systems often release periodic updates to enhance security and functionality.

- **Complexity**: Software can range from simple programs with a single function to complex systems with multiple components working together. For instance, a basic calculator app is simple software, while an operating system is complex software, coordinating numerous applications and hardware resources simultaneously.

- **Compatibility**: Software must often be compatible with specific hardware, operating systems, or other applications. For example, software written for Windows OS may not be directly compatible with Mac OS, requiring either a different version or adaptation.

- **User Interface (UI)**: The user interface determines how users interact with the software, whether through command-line input, graphical buttons, or touch-based navigation. Software with a well-designed UI is generally easier to use and more accessible.

Example Exercise: Identify two software applications you use regularly, categorise them as system or application software, and describe their main functions and features. Explain how they help you perform specific tasks or enhance your computer's performance.

Example Answers:

- **Microsoft Word**: Application software, allows for document creation and editing, helping users format and save written content.
- **Windows Defender**: System software, utility program, protects against malware and viruses, ensuring secure computer operation.

2.2 OPERATING SYSTEMS (OS)

2.2.1 Definition of an Operating System

An Operating System (OS) is essential system software that allows a computer to function by managing both the hardware and software resources. It provides a foundational environment where application software can run, allocating resources to programs and serving as an interface between the user and the computer hardware. The OS ensures that the computer system operates efficiently by coordinating tasks and managing hardware components like the CPU, memory, and storage.

The OS essentially bridges the gap between the user and the hardware, translating user commands into actions that the computer hardware can execute. Without an OS, users would need to communicate directly with hardware, which would be complex and inefficient.

Example: The Windows Operating System (OS) enables users to manage files, connect to the internet, and run applications such as word processors, games, and browsers. It allocates system resources (like CPU time and memory) to applications as needed, facilitating multitasking and user-friendly operation.

2.2.2 Functions of the Operating System

An operating system performs several critical functions that support computer operation and make it easier for users to interact with the machine. Some of the main functions include:

1. **File Management**:
    - The OS organises, stores, retrieves, and manages data in a structured way. It provides users with a way to create, delete, read, and write files, and to organise them within directories or folders.
    - The OS maintains a hierarchical file structure and enables users to search for and access files efficiently.

- **Example**: Windows OS allows users to create folders, move files, and search for specific files using File Explorer.

2. **Memory Management**:
   - The OS allocates and deallocates memory to different applications, ensuring that multiple programs can run simultaneously without conflicts. It manages primary memory (RAM) by assigning space to processes and freeing up memory when processes complete.
   - Memory management prevents application crashes due to insufficient memory and enhances system performance.
   - **Example**: When running multiple applications, Windows OS manages memory so that each program receives the necessary resources, allowing users to switch between applications smoothly.

3. **Input/Output (I/O) Control**:
   - The OS manages communication between the computer and connected peripheral devices like keyboards, mice, printers, and storage devices. It coordinates the flow of data to and from these devices to ensure accurate and timely processing.
   - **Example**: When a user types on a keyboard, the OS translates the input into readable data on the screen.

4. **Interrupt Management**:
   - The OS handles interruptions from devices and applications that require immediate CPU attention. This allows the OS to prioritise tasks, balancing system demands by assigning higher priority to critical tasks and deferring less urgent ones.
   - **Example**: When printing a document, the printer sends an interrupt request. The OS temporarily pauses other tasks, allowing the CPU to process the printing command, ensuring smooth operation.

5. **Security Management**:
   - The OS provides security features to protect data and system resources from unauthorised access. This includes managing user permissions, enforcing password protection, and using encryption to safeguard sensitive information.
   - **Example**: Windows OS enables users to set permissions, restricting certain files or applications to specific users, and employs firewalls to monitor and control network traffic for security.

2.2.3 Components of an Operating System

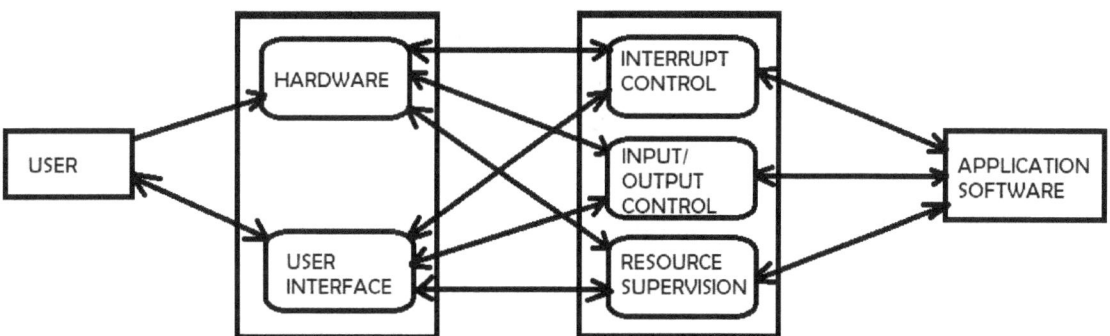

DIAGRAM OF THE ELEMENTS OF THE OPERATING SYSTEM

An operating system is made up of several key components, each playing a specific role in managing the computer system's resources and facilitating user interaction:

- **User Interface (UI)**:
    - The user interface is the component through which users interact with the computer. There are two primary types of user interfaces:
        - **Command-Line Interface (CLI)**: Allows users to type commands for execution (e.g., DOS, Linux CLI).
        - **Graphical User Interface (GUI)**: Provides a visual interface with icons, windows, and menus, making it more intuitive for users to interact with the OS (e.g., Windows, macOS).

- **Input/Output (I/O) Control**:
    - Managed by the BIOS (Basic Input/Output System), I/O control handles communication with peripheral devices, facilitating the input and output processes. This includes initial tasks like booting up the computer, as well as managing ongoing communication between the OS and devices such as keyboards, monitors, and printers.
    - The BIOS enables basic functions, such as reading data from storage devices or displaying text on the screen.

- **Interrupt Control**:
    - Interrupt control enables the OS to manage priorities among tasks by pausing low-priority tasks and allowing high-priority requests to be processed immediately. This feature is crucial for efficient resource allocation, as it ensures that urgent tasks, such as responding to user commands or handling hardware requests, are addressed without delay.

- **Resource Supervision**:
    - The OS supervises system resources, including the CPU, memory, and storage. This ensures that each application receives the necessary resources without interfering with other processes. Resource supervision helps maintain stability, prevents crashes, and optimises the system's performance.
    - The OS also manages resources based on user permissions, helping protect sensitive data from unauthorised access.

Example Exercise:

Identify an operating system you use frequently, describe one key function, and explain how it enhances your interaction with the computer.

Example Answer:

- **Operating System**: macOS.
- **Function**: Memory Management.
- **Explanation**: macOS manages memory effectively, allowing me to run multiple applications like Safari, Photoshop, and Mail without lag. It allocates memory to each application, optimising performance and preventing crashes.

2.3 INTERRUPTS & CPU

2.3.1 Interrupts

Interrupts are essential signals used by the computer's hardware to communicate with the CPU (Central Processing Unit) and manage multiple tasks efficiently. They allow the CPU to pause its current operations temporarily, address specific events or needs, and then resume its primary task. This process is crucial for multitasking and efficient processing within a computer system.

Definition and Purpose of Interrupts:

An interrupt is a signal sent from a hardware or software source that requires immediate CPU attention. The CPU receives this signal, temporarily halts its current task, and directs its resources to handle the interrupt. Once the interrupt task is addressed, the CPU returns to its original task, maintaining system efficiency and allowing seamless task switching.

Example:

When you're typing on a word processor and receive a notification, the CPU pauses word processing to handle the notification's display, then returns to your document. This is an example of an interrupt that prioritises real-time user interaction.

2.3.2 Types of Interrupts

Interrupts are broadly categorised based on the role and handling level they play in the interrupt processing system. Each type of interrupt serves a distinct purpose and helps the CPU identify and manage interrupts more effectively.

1. **First-Level Interrupt Handler (FLIH):**

    - The first-level interrupt handler, or "interrupt service routine (ISR)," is responsible for immediately recognising the interrupt source. It identifies the device or software source requesting attention.
    - **Example**: When a mouse click occurs, the FLIH identifies this as an input device interrupt and signals the CPU to process the action.

2. **Second-Level Interrupt Handler (SLIH):**

    - The second-level interrupt handler is tasked with executing specific code to resolve the interrupt. After the FLIH identifies the source, the SLIH processes the necessary response to complete the interrupt task.
    - **Example**: For a keyboard press, the SLIH might translate the keystroke into character data and display it on the screen.

2.3.3 Handling Multiple Interrupts

When multiple interrupts occur, the CPU uses specific strategies to prioritise and manage them effectively.

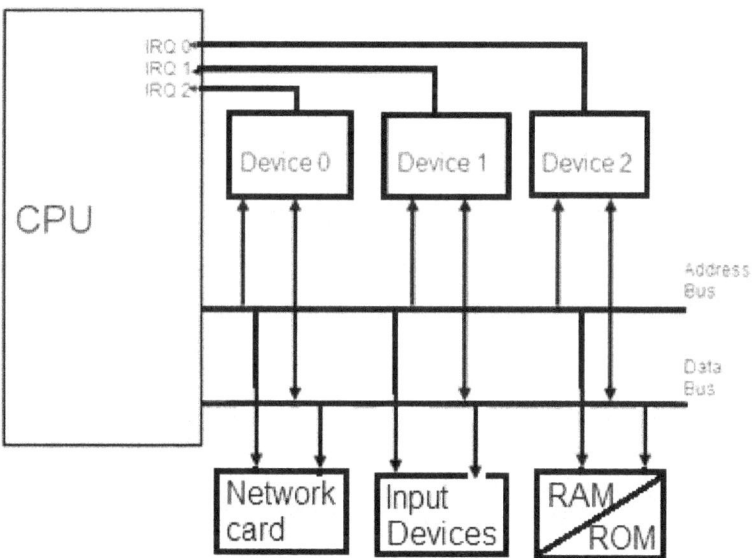

Diagram of Multiple Interrupt Lines

Two common methods for handling simultaneous interrupts are **Polling** and **Vectored Interrupts**. Both commonly specify a bus-interrupt priority level; and while vectored devices exhibit an interrupt vector, polled devices do not.

1. Polling:

- Polling involves the CPU periodically checking each device in a sequence to see if any require attention. While effective, this method can slow down performance, as it involves continuous checking.

- **Example**: Polling may be used in systems where regular checks for updates are necessary, such as in basic embedded systems where CPU demands are low.

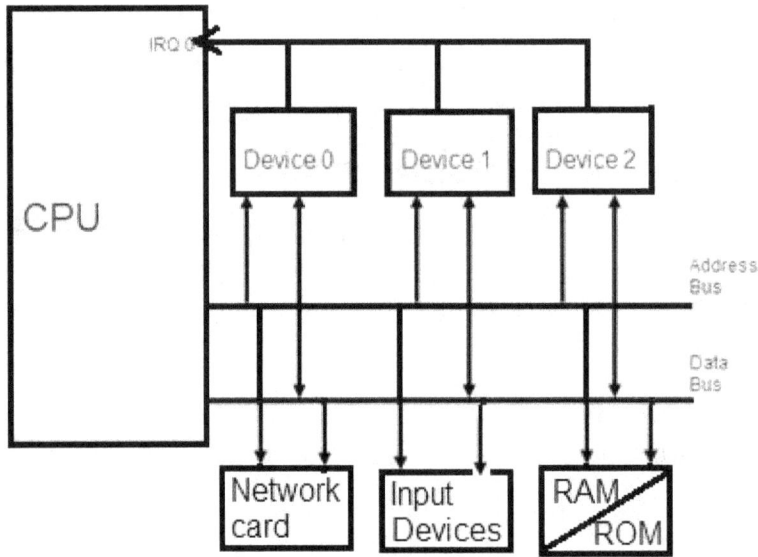

Diagram of Polled Interrupt Structure

2. Vectored Interrupts:

- Vectored interrupts assign a unique identifier to each interrupt type. This method allows the CPU to recognise and address specific interrupts quickly, based on priority levels, resulting in a faster response than polling.

- **Example**: In a high-performance system like a smartphone, vectored interrupts prioritise essential tasks, such as touch inputs or incoming calls, enabling quicker responses.

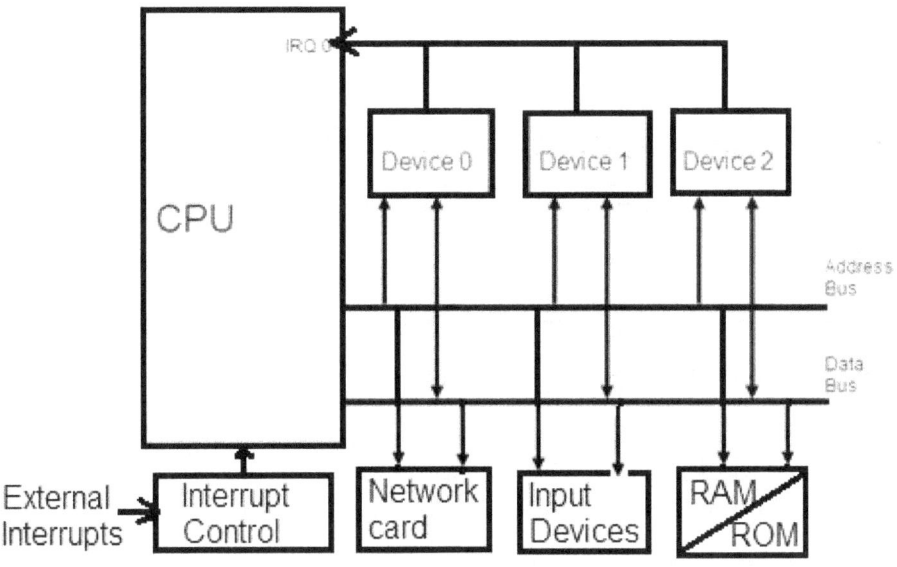

Diagram of Vector Interrupt Structure

2.3.4 Example of Interrupt Handling in Action:

Imagine using a music player on your computer while also typing a document. When a new message notification appears, an interrupt is triggered. With vectored interrupts, the CPU can immediately identify and prioritise this notification (a high-priority interrupt) over the background tasks (e.g., music playback). It then displays the notification to the user and returns to music playback and typing tasks without delay.

2.3.5 Summary of Interrupts & CPU Operations:

Component	Description
Interrupt	Signal prompting the CPU to pause a task to address an event.
First-Level Interrupt Handler	Identifies the source of the interrupt.
Second-Level Interrupt Handler	Executes the code needed to address the interrupt.
Polling	The CPU checks devices in a sequence to see if they need attention.
Vectored Interrupts	Unique identifiers for each interrupt, enabling prioritised and faster responses.

Tutorial Activity 2 - Software & Its Applications

Quizzes and Questions

Multiple Choice Questions (MCQs)

1. Which of the following best defines software?
   a) The physical parts of a computer
   b) Programs and instructions that enable hardware to perform tasks
   c) A collection of transistors and chips
   d) Network connections between devices

2. What type of software is responsible for managing hardware resources and providing a platform for other software to run?
   a) Application software
   b) Utility programs
   c) System software
   d) Multimedia software

3. Which of the following is an example of application software?
   a) Microsoft Excel
   b) Windows 11
   c) Antivirus software
   d) BIOS

4. What is the primary role of an Operating System (OS)?
   a) Design user interfaces
   b) Connect to the internet
   c) Manage hardware and software resources
   d) Store user data permanently

5. Which of the following is NOT a function of an OS?
   a) File management
   b) Memory management
   c) I/O control
   d) Creating software applications

Short Answer Questions

1. Define interrupts and their importance.

2. Describe two types of interrupts.

3. Explain methods for handling multiple interrupts.

4. Define system software and provide two examples.

5. What is the difference between primary and secondary storage?

6. List and explain three core functions of an operating system.

7. Provide examples of three operating systems commonly used in computing.

8. Explain the concept of an interrupt and its importance in multitasking.
9. Explain the difference between primary and secondary storage.
10. Name two types of primary storage and describe their characteristics.
11. Magnetic disks store data on spinning platters; optical discs use lasers for storage.

True/False Questions

1. System software includes utility programs and application software.
2. The Operating System is an example of system software.
3. RAM is an example of secondary storage.
4. File management is one of the core functions of an operating system.
5. Interrupts help the CPU to focus on one task at a time without any external disturbances.

Essay Questions

1. Differentiate between system software and application software, providing examples of each.
2. Discuss the functions of an Operating System, focusing on how it manages files, memory, and I/O operations.

Matching Activity

Match the following examples to their software category:

1. Microsoft Word
2. Linux
3. Disk Cleanup Tool
4. macOS
5. Google Chrome

Options:
a) Application Software
b) System Software
c) Utility Software

Chapter 3: Computer Logic and Data Representation

Learning Objectives

By the end of this chapter, learners will be able to:

- Define and explain computer architecture and its structure and elements through logic gates.
- Define and explain the function of basic logic gates.
- Construct truth tables for different logic operations.
- Design logic circuits based on given specifications and truth tables.
- Perform binary arithmetic, including addition and subtraction.
- Understand data representation across different number systems: binary, denary (decimal), octal, and hexadecimal.
- Convert between binary, denary, octal and hexadecimal number systems.

3.1 COMPUTER ARCHITECTURE AND LOGIC GATES: The Foundation of Computing Systems

While computer architecture focuses on the high-level design of computing systems, its functionality at the most fundamental level depends on logic gates - the building blocks of digital circuits. These gates underpin the operation of all computing hardware, enabling the execution of complex instructions through basic binary logic.

Logic gates are the invisible architects of computer systems, enabling the execution of every instruction and data processing task. By understanding the principles and applications of gates, we can appreciate how fundamental operations cascade into the higher-level functionality described in computer architecture. This alignment highlights how simple binary logic forms the backbone of modern computing.

Logic Gates and Their Role in Computer Architecture

Logic gates are electronic components that perform basic Boolean logic operations (AND, OR, NOT, etc.) on binary inputs (0s and 1s) to produce a single binary output. They form the foundation of circuits that process data in computer systems.

3.1.1 Structure and Elements of Computing through Logic Gates

1. **Central Processing Unit (CPU)**
   The CPU operates based on the principles of logic gates, where millions of gates work together to execute instructions.

   - **Arithmetic Logic Unit (ALU):** Built with logic gates to perform operations such as addition, subtraction, AND, OR, and XOR.

- **Control Unit (CU):** Utilises logic circuits to interpret and execute instructions by orchestrating the movement of data.

2. **Memory Systems**
    - **Data Storage:** Memory cells are constructed using combinations of logic gates (e.g., flip-flops) to store binary data.
    - **Address Decoding:** Logic gates are used to manage memory access by selecting specific memory locations.

3. **Input/Output (I/O) Operations**
   Logic gates are critical in managing data transfer between input/output devices and the CPU. For example:
    - **Encoders and Decoders:** Convert data formats or signals using logic gates.
    - **Multiplexers:** Use logic gates to route data efficiently.

4. **Control and Interconnect Systems**
   Logic gates ensure synchronization and communication between different subsystems:
    - **Timing Circuits:** Use flip-flops and oscillators.
    - **Bus Controllers:** Enable smooth data transfer using combinational and sequential logic.

3.1.2 Applications of Logic Gates in Key Computing Processes

1. **Arithmetic and Data Processing:**
    - Addition and subtraction are implemented using **half adders** and **full adders**, which are combinations of AND, OR, and XOR gates.
    - Multiplication and division involve more complex circuits made from basic gates.

2. **Data Flow Control:**
    - Logic gates enable decision-making in data routing, as seen in **multiplexers** and **demultiplexers**.

3. **Error Detection and Correction:**
    - **Parity generators** and **checkers**, built from XOR gates, ensure data integrity during transmission.

3.1.3 Key Characteristics of Computing with Logic Gates

- **Speed:** Operations are performed at the speed of light, determined by the physical properties of gates.
- **Scalability:** Millions of gates are integrated into microprocessors to perform more complex tasks.

- **Simplicity:** Complex functions are broken down into smaller tasks handled by basic gate operations.
- **Reliability:** Digital circuits built with gates are robust and precise, critical for error-free processing.

3.2 DEFINITION OF LOGIC GATES

Logic gates are the fundamental building blocks of digital circuits, used to perform basic logical operations on binary data. These gates process binary inputs (0s and 1s) and yield a single binary output, which is essential in controlling computer functions and decision-making in digital devices.

3.2.1 Basic Types of Logic Gates

Understanding individual logic gates provides insight into how complex computer operations are achieved. This section introduces the three primary types of gates: NOT, AND, and OR.

1. **NOT Gate (Inverter)**
    - **Function**: The NOT gate, also known as an inverter, outputs the opposite (or inverse) of its input. If the input is 1, the output is 0, and if the input is 0, the output is 1.
    - **Symbol**: The NOT gate is represented by a triangle followed by a small circle.
    - **Truth Table**:

NOTE GATE

A	NOT A
0	1
1	0

2. **AND Gate**
    - **Function**: The AND gate produces an output of 1 only when both inputs are 1; otherwise, it outputs 0. This gate is used in situations where both conditions need to be true.
    - **Symbol**: The AND gate is represented by a D-shaped symbol with two input lines and one output line.
    - **Truth Table**:

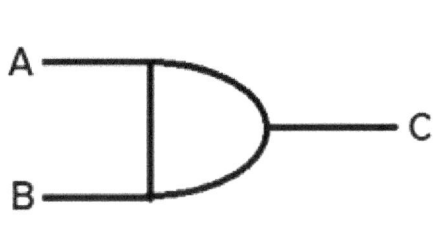

A	B	A AND B
0	0	0
0	1	0
1	0	0
1	1	1

3. **OR Gate**
   - **Function**: The OR gate outputs 1 if at least one of its inputs is 1. This gate is commonly used when any condition can be true to trigger an output.
   - **Symbol**: The OR gate is represented by a curved shape with two input lines and one output line.
   - **Truth Table**:

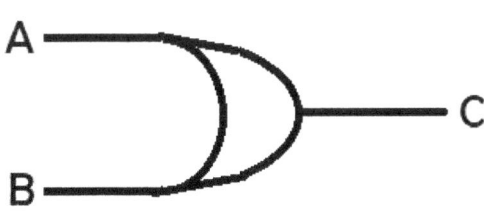

A	B	A OR B
0	0	0
0	1	1
1	0	1
1	1	1

3.2.2 Combined Logic Operations

Combining these logic gates can create more complex operations. For example, combining NOT, AND, and OR gates can help control outputs based on multiple conditions. The following truth table demonstrates these combinations:

A	B	NOT A	A AND B	A OR B
0	0	1	0	0
0	1	1	0	1
1	0	0	0	1
1	1	0	1	1

Using Symbols

+ means OR

· means AND

A bar above a letter $\overline{A}$ means NOT; therefore, $\overline{A}$ is **NOT A**. **NOT** may also be shown by a single inverted comma A':

$A + B = A \text{ OR } B$
$A \cdot B = A \text{ AND } B$

$\overline{A} + \overline{B} = \text{NOT A OR NOT B'}$
$A' \cdot B' = \text{NOT A AND NOT B}$

3.2.3 Complex Truth tables

In the above examples we have our results as a table. These tables are known as TRUTH TABLES or OPERATION TABLES. They are constructed by passing all possible binary input values for a given number of input bits through the LOGIC CIRCUIT.

If we have 2 input bits (variables) A and B, we have 4 possible combinations (0 – 3).

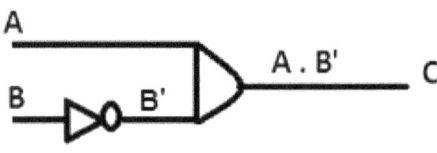

A	B	B'	A . B'
0	0	1	0
0	1	0	0
1	0	1	1
1	1	0	0

With 3 input bits (variables) A, B, C we have 8 possible combinations (0 – 7)

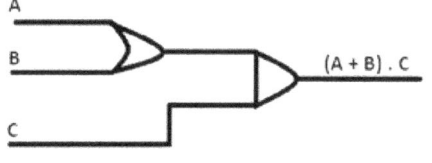

A	B	C	A + B	(A + B).C
0	0	0	0	0
0	0	1	0	0
0	1	0	1	0
0	1	1	1	1
1	0	0	1	0
1	0	1	1	1
1	1	0	1	0
1	1	1	1	1

Activity 1

Create a Logic Circuit

Objective: Design a circuit that outputs 1 if inputs X and Y match (i.e., X = Y).

Instructions: Students will use an AND gate and a NOT gate to achieve the required logic. If both inputs are either 1 or 0, the circuit should output 1; otherwise, the output should be 0.

Example: If X and Y are both 1 and both 0, the output should be 1. Otherwise, the output should be 0.

Activity 2

1. What is the relationship between the number of inputs bits and the range of the counter?
2. Draw some of your own logic circuits. Trace them through and produce truth tables.
3. Suppose that it is required to produce a suitable logic circuit from the following specification:

    A circuit has two binary inputs, X and Y. The output from the circuit is 1 when the two inputs are the same; otherwise, the output is 0.

    i) Produce a simple truth table to define the circuit.

    ii) In fully defining the circuit, the truth table below emerged.

    iii) *Classwork:* Draw a circuit diagram to illustrate the truth table below:

X	Y	$\overline{X}$	$\overline{Y}$	$\overline{X}.\overline{Y}$	X.Y	$\overline{X}.\overline{Y}+X.Y$
0	0	1	1	1	0	1
0	1	1	0	0	0	0
1	0	0	1	0	0	0
1	1	0	0	0	1	1

3.3 DATA REPRESENTATION AND NUMBER SYSTEMS

Computers rely on various number systems to process and represent data. Binary, denary (decimal), and octal systems are essential for understanding computer logic operations. This section introduces each system and covers how to convert between them.

3.3.1 The Binary System

The binary system is the base-2 number system, using only two digits: 0 and 1. Each binary digit (or "bit") represents an increasing power of 2, starting from the rightmost digit. Binary is fundamental in computers because it aligns with digital logic, where a 0 represents "off" and a 1 represents "on."

3.3.2 Binary Addition and Subtraction

Binary Addition: Binary addition follows the same basic principles as decimal addition but carries over once the sum reaches 2 (i.e., 1 + 1). Here's how binary addition works:

Binary Operation	Result
0 + 0	0
0 + 1	1
1 + 0	1
1 + 1	0 (carry 1)

Example: To add 101 and 011 in binary:

1. Align the numbers:

    101

    + 011

    1000

2. Compute from right to left:
    - Rightmost bit: 1 + 1 = 0 (carry 1)
    - Middle bit: 0 + 1 + 1 (carry) = 0 (carry 1)
    - Leftmost bit: 1 + 1 (carry) = 1.

Binary Subtraction: Binary subtraction uses the same approach as decimal subtraction but borrows when subtracting 1 from 0. The borrowing rules are:

Binary Operation	Result
0 - 0	0
1 - 0	1
1 - 1	0
0 - 1	1 (borrow 1)

Example: To subtract 011 from 101:

1. Align the numbers:

    101

    - 011

    010

2. Perform each subtraction from right to left:
    - Rightmost bit: 1 - 1 = 0
    - Middle bit: 0 - 1 = 1 (borrow 1)
    - Leftmost bit: 1 - 0 = 1.

3.4 Converting Between Number Systems

Converting between binary, decimal (denary), and octal systems is essential for understanding data representation in computers.

1. **Binary to Decimal**: Multiply each binary digit by 2 raised to the position's power (starting from 0 on the right).

2. **Decimal to Binary**: Divide the decimal number by 2, recording the remainders, until reaching 0.

3. **Binary to Octal**: Group binary digits in sets of three (from right to left) and convert each group to its octal equivalent.

Activity:

- Convert the binary number 10110110 to decimal.

Solution:

$$1 \times 2^7 + 0 \times 2^6 + 1 \times 2^5 + 1 \times 2^4 + 0 \times 2^3 + 1 \times 2^2 + 1 \times 2^1 + 0 \times 2^0 = 128 + 32 + 16 + 4 + 2 = 182.$$

3.4.1 The Denary (Decimal) System

The denary system is the standard counting system using ten digits (0-9). Each digit's position represents a power of 10.

- **Positional Notation**: For example, the number 753 can be broken down as follows:

753 = (7×100) + (5×10) + (3×1)

3.4.2 The Octal System

The octal system uses eight digits (0-7) and is often used in computing as a shorthand for binary.

- **Conversions**:
  - Convert octal 347 to binary:
    - 3(011),4(100),7(111) → 011100111
  - Convert octal 347 to decimal: 3×64+4×8+7×1=231

Activity:

Convert Decimal Numbers: Convert the following decimal numbers to octal:

- 63
- 100

- 155

3.4.3 Activities for Reinforcement

To reinforce the concepts covered in this chapter, students can engage in the following activities:

Practice Conversions

- Use worksheets to practice converting between binary, decimal, and octal number systems.

Logic Circuits

- Draw logic circuits for various truth tables involving three variables.
- For example, create a circuit for the output of A AND (B OR C).

Binary Complements

- Calculate the binary complement of given binary numbers.
- Represent integers in sign-and-magnitude and two's complement notation.

Quiz

1. **What is the output of an AND gate when both inputs are 0?**
    - a) 0
    - b) 1
    - c) Undefined

2. **Which gate inverts the input signal?**
    - a) AND Gate
    - b) OR Gate
    - c) NOT Gate

3. **Convert the binary number 1101 to decimal.**
    - a) 13
    - b) 14
    - c) 12

Answers

1. a) 0
2. c) NOT Gate
3. a) 13

3.5 Hexadecimal Number System

The hexadecimal (or Hex) number system is a base-16 system, using digits **0–9** and letters **A–F** to represent values 10–15, respectively. In Hex, each digit is a **nibble** (four binary digits), and its place values increase by powers of 16.

e.g.,

base 16	16^3	16^2	16^1	16^0
positional value	4096	256	16	1

thus $296_{10} = 128_{16}$

3.5.1 Hexadecimal to Denary Conversion

To convert a Hex number to its denary (decimal) equivalent:

1. Separate each Hex digit and assign its positional power of 16.
2. Multiply each digit by its power of 16.
3. Sum all the results.

Example: Convert 128 H to decimal:

- 128 H = (1×256) + (2×16) + (8×1) = 256 + 32 + 8 = 296 10

3.5.2 Hexadecimal to Binary and then to Denary Conversion

1. Convert each Hex digit to a 4-bit binary equivalent.
2. Concatenate the binary groups.
3. Convert the resulting binary to decimal by applying binary place values.

Example: Convert 554 H to decimal:

- Separate each digit: 5,5,4
- Convert to binary: 5 = 0101, 5 = 0101, 4 = 0100
- Concatenate: 0101 0101 0100
- Convert binary 0101 0101 0100 to decimal:
  - Calculate each place: (2048×0) + (1024×1) + (512×0) + (256×1) + (128×0) + (64×1) + (32×0) + (16×1) + (8×0) + (4×1) + (2×0) + (1×0) = 1364
- Therefore, 554 H =1364

3.5.3 Denary to Hexadecimal Conversion (Long Division Method)

To convert a decimal number to Hex:

1. Divide the number by 16.
2. Write down the remainder.
3. Use the quotient for the next division.
4. Repeat until the quotient is zero.
5. The Hex number is the remainders read from bottom to top.

Example: Given a larger number; 52653(H), convert it to denary number:

Using the powers of 16, starting from right to left:

16^4	16^3	16^2	16^1	16^0
(65536)	(4096)	(256)	(16)	(1)
5	2	6	5	3

(65536*5) + (4096*2) + (256*6) + (16*5) + (1*3)

327680 + 8192 + 1536 + 80 + 3 = 337,491

Also, to prove that 337491 to 52653 H:

$337491_{10} = 52653_{16}$

Use the long division method as follows:

337,491 divides by 16 = 21093 remainder 3

21093 divides by 16 = 1318 remainder 5

1318 divides by 16 = 82 remainder 6

82 divides by 16 = 5 remainder 2

5 divides by 16 = 0 remainder 5

- Reading the remainder from bottom up, we get 52653 H.

Thus, 337491 = 52653 H.

Tutorial Activity 3 - Computer Logic and Data

Quizzes and Questions

Representation

Multiple-Choice Questions (MCQs)

1. **Which of the following is NOT a basic logic gate?**
   A. AND
   B. OR
   C. ADD
   D. NOT

2. **What is the output of an OR gate if both inputs are 0?**
   A. 1
   B. 0
   C. Depends on the circuit
   D. Undefined

3. **Which number system is used internally by computers for data representation?**
   A. Binary
   B. Decimal
   C. Octal
   D. Hexadecimal

4. **What is the binary addition of 1011 and 1101?**
   A. 10010
   B. 10100
   C. 11100
   D. 100000

5. **Which component of computer architecture performs arithmetic and logical operations?**
   A. Control Unit
   B. Arithmetic Logic Unit (ALU)
   C. Memory Unit
   D. Input/Output Unit

Short-Answer Questions

1. **Define the function of a NOT gate.**

2. Construct a truth table for an AND gate with two inputs.

Input A	Input B	Output (A AND B)
0	0	0
0	1	0
1	0	0
1	1	1

3. Convert the decimal number 45 into binary and octal.

4. What is the importance of truth tables in designing logic circuits?

5. Explain how data is represented in the binary number system.

Problem-Solving Questions

1. Design a circuit that outputs 1 only when both inputs are 1 or both inputs are 0.

2. Perform the binary subtraction 1101−1011101 - 1011101−101.

3. Convert the octal number 72 into binary and decimal.

4. Given the truth table, identify the logic gate:

Input A	Input B	Output
0	0	0
0	1	1
1	0	1
1	1	1

Open-Ended Discussion Questions

1. Why is binary arithmetic crucial for computer systems?

2. Discuss the role of logic gates in modern computing devices.

3. Explain how truth tables are used to verify the functionality of a logic circuit.

Additional Activity 3.1

Convert the following:

1. Convert 574 to Hexadecimal
2. Convert 160 H to decimal
3. Convert 444 H to decimal
4. **Convert the following decimal numbers to Hexadecimal:**
    - a. 635
    - b. 100
    - c. 155
    - d. 200
    - e. 254
5. **Convert the following Hexadecimal numbers to decimal:**
    - a. 5A00 H
    - b. 66E0 H
    - c. 1741 H
    - d. 4F76 H

Activity 3.2

Complete the conversions in the following table:

Decimal	Binary	Octal	Hexadecimal
52			
		1204	
			CC
	1001001		

References

Tanenbaum, A. S., & Austin, T. (2012). Operating Systems: Design and Implementation. Pearson.

Stallings, W. (2018). Operating Systems: Internals and Design Principles. Pearson.

Tanenbaum, A. S., & **Austin, T.** (2013). *Structured Computer Organisation* (6th ed.). Pearson.

- This textbook provides a comprehensive look at computer architecture, covering key topics such as logic gates, circuits, and processor design.

Hennessy, J. L., & **Patterson, D. A.** (2019). *Computer Architecture: A Quantitative Approach* (6th ed.). Morgan Kaufmann.

- This book focuses on the principles of computer architecture and their application, with a strong emphasis on logic gates and data representation.

Sharma, A. (2011). *Digital Logic and Computer Design*. McGraw-Hill Education.

- A detailed introduction to digital circuits and logic gates, offering foundational knowledge needed to understand computer architecture.

Chapter 4: ICT Laws and Ethics

Learning Outcomes:

By the end of this chapter, learners will be able to:

- Differentiate between data, information, and knowledge, understanding their interrelationships and roles in decision-making.
- Understand data sources, their key types, their roles, and the methods used to extract and process them, including data value judgement.
- Identify and explain key laws and regulations related to data handling, information management, and knowledge sharing, particularly in the context of ICT.
- Understand ICT and the Law, focusing on the frameworks, regulations, and guidelines that govern ICT use, their significance and challenges they present.
- Assess the ethical, social, and legal implications of ICT in managing data and information in various sectors (e.g., healthcare, education, business).
- Evaluate the impact of ICT on data privacy, security, and governance, highlighting potential risks and challenges faced by organisations and individuals.
- Discuss the global and local regulatory frameworks governing ICT, focusing on data protection acts, copyright laws, and digital rights.
- Apply knowledge of ICT-related laws to real-world scenarios, proposing strategies for compliance and risk mitigation in data management and information systems.
- Analyse the role of ICT in knowledge creation and dissemination, and its broader impact on society and the economy.

4.1 DATA, INFORMATION, AND KNOWLEDGE

Understanding the relationship between data, information, and knowledge is fundamental across various disciplines, including computing, business, and data management. These concepts form a hierarchy that transforms raw facts into actionable insights, enabling effective decision-making and problem-solving.

Data refers to raw, unprocessed facts or figures that lack context or meaning on their own. For example, numbers, text, or symbols collected during an observation or transaction are considered data.

Information is the next step, where data is processed, organised, and structured to provide context and relevance. Information answers specific questions, such as "who," "what," "where," and "when." For instance, sales data organised into a report showing daily revenue trends becomes meaningful information.

Knowledge arises when information is analysed, interpreted, and applied within a specific context. It involves understanding the "how" and "why" behind the information, leading to insights that guide strategic actions. For example, analysing revenue trends to identify patterns and predict future sales is an application of knowledge.

This section delves deeper into their definitions, interconnections, and how each contributes to building effective decision-making frameworks. By comprehending the transformation from data to knowledge, individuals and organisations can harness their resources more efficiently and gain a competitive edge.

4.1.1 Definition of Data

Data refers to raw, unprocessed facts and figures that lack inherent meaning when presented in isolation. It includes individual items such as numbers, words, dates, images, sounds, or measurements. These raw elements serve as the foundational building blocks for computer systems and other analytical processes. For example:

- "42"
- "rabbits"
- "4:00 PM"
- "2010"
- "apples"
- "08031122244"
- "800 Naira"
- "Kaduna"
- "90"

These examples are standalone pieces of data that require additional context or processing to become meaningful. In computing, data is typically stored in databases, with each item described by an attribute or field name. Data exists in various formats, such as:

- **Text**: Words or alphanumeric characters
- **Numbers**: Counts, measurements, or statistical values
- **Dates**: Temporal data for referencing events
- **Graphics and Images**: Visual data for analysis or presentation
- **Sounds**: Audio files or sound waves

Without further organisation or context, these items remain raw and disconnected.

4.1.2 Definition of Information

Information is the result of processing, organising, or structuring data in a way that adds context and meaning. When data is manipulated through sorting, calculation, or categorisation, it transforms into information that can inform decisions or convey understanding.

Example of Transformation:

- **Data**: "42", "apples" (or "42 apples")

- **Information**: "There are 42 apples in that box, which were eaten by rabbits over the past week."

Here, the raw data ("42 apples") becomes meaningful when additional context is provided. The BBC Education defines information as a "collection of words, numbers, or pictures that possess meaning."

Information is vital for decision-making and problem-solving across various sectors, from business to healthcare and education.

4.1.3 Transforming Data into Information

The process of converting data into information involves organisation, analysis, and contextualisation. This transformation often requires the use of structured headings or categorisation to add meaning.

Example of Unstructured Data:

Larry	Yes	
Jamila	Yes	
Maya	Yes	
Kieran	Yes	
Amina	Yes	
Shola	No	Yes
Musa	No	No

This table is merely a collection of data. Without appropriate headings, its purpose and meaning are unclear. However, when organised with headings such as "Student Name," "Attendance," and "Absence Authorised," it becomes information that can be analysed for patterns or trends in attendance.

Example of Structured Data:

Student Name	Attendance	Absence Authorised?
Larry	Yes	
Jamila	Yes	
Maya	Yes	
Kieran	Yes	
Amina	Yes	

Student Name	Attendance	Absence Authorised?
Shola	No	Yes
Musa	No	No

Data Collection Methods:

Data is collected through various means, both manual and automatic, such as:

- **Manual Input**: Teachers entering student grades or attendance records.
- **Automatic Input**: Sensors measuring temperature or barcode scanners capturing product details at a Point of Sale (POS).

Efficient organisation and input methods ensure that data can be transformed into actionable information.

4.1.4 Definition of Knowledge

Knowledge is the understanding derived from processed information. When information is newly acquired and previously unknown, it becomes knowledge. Knowledge emerges from the application and interpretation of information. It represents an individual's or system's understanding of information in context, enabling decision-making, predictions, judgment and problem-solving.

Relationship Between Data, Information, and Knowledge:

- **Data**: Raw facts (e.g., "42 apples").
- **Information**: Processed data (e.g., "42 apples were consumed in a week by rabbits").
- **Knowledge**: Application of information to a scenario (e.g., "To prevent shortages, supply 50 apples per week").

Examples of Knowledge Application:

- **Agriculture**:
  - **Example 1**: "In the last five years, the tomato yield in Kaduna has grown by 10% annually. This year, it is expected to increase by an additional 10%. Thus, we need to secure markets for 10% more tomatoes." Here, the application of historical data informs future decisions, representing knowledge.
    - Historical data: "Tomato yields in Kaduna increased by 10% annually over the last five years."
    - Knowledge: "Expect a 10% increase this year and secure markets for the surplus."

- **Safety Assessment**:
    - **Example 2**: "The car appeared to have flat tires, with a pool of petrol underneath and smoke emerging from the bonnet. I decided to evacuate the area." The assessment of the situation leads to informed decision-making, again demonstrating knowledge gained from information.
        - Information: "The car has flat tires, petrol leaking, and smoke emerging."
        - Knowledge: "Evacuate the area to avoid potential hazards."

Knowledge enables individuals and organisations to draw actionable insights from information, improving outcomes and decisions.

4.1.5 Knowledge Expert Systems

Knowledge expert systems are advanced computer programs designed to simulate human decision-making by applying predefined rules to vast amounts of information. They process structured data to generate conclusions or recommendations.

Applications of Knowledge Expert Systems:

- **Education**:
    - A spreadsheet program automatically calculates student grades based on inputted test scores, transforming data into reports.
- **Healthcare**:
    - Diagnostic programs analyse symptoms and medical histories to suggest potential treatments.
- **Aviation**:
    - Autopilot systems control aircraft using data from sensors, adhering to programmed flight rules.

While knowledge expert systems improve efficiency and decision-making, they are not infallible. Their effectiveness depends on the accuracy of the rules and data provided by humans. They are best used to supplement human expertise rather than replace it entirely.

In summary, the progression from data to knowledge forms the backbone of effective decision-making in computing and beyond. While data serves as the raw material, information provides structure and meaning, and knowledge enables actionable insights. Advanced technologies, like knowledge expert systems, further enhance our ability to process and apply information, underscoring the critical role of data management in modern society.

4.2 DATA SOURCES

Learning Outcomes

By the end of this section, students should be able to:

- Describe a range of data sources.
- Identify specific types of data sources with examples.
- State the advantages and disadvantages of different data sources.
- Explain the effects of data quality on information and its value judgment.

4.2.1 Introduction

Data sources are the origins or locations from which data is collected, gathered, or generated for analysis, processing, and decision-making. They form the foundation of information systems, ensuring organisations have the raw material required to create meaningful insights and knowledge. Data can be collected manually or automatically, structured or unstructured, and derived from a variety of mediums depending on the context and purpose.

In the digital age, data sources are vast and diverse, ranging from traditional records to sophisticated real-time streams, and their reliability and accuracy are critical for effective outcomes. Understanding the types, characteristics, and significance of these sources is essential for ensuring that the information derived is accurate, relevant, and actionable.

This section delves into the key types of data sources, their roles in information management, and the methods used to extract and process data from them. It also examines challenges related to data integrity and provides strategies for selecting and utilising appropriate sources effectively.

4.2.2 Range of Data Sources

Data sources can be categorised into several types: traditional, modern, automated, electronic, and sensor-based sources.

- **Traditional Data Sources**: These originate from paper documents such as price tags, tickets, invoices, and questionnaires. Data from these sources is manually entered into computers using input devices like keyboards and mice.

- **Automated Data Sources**: With technological advancements, automated data sources have emerged, including systems like barcode scanners commonly found in supermarkets and libraries.

- **Optical Character Recognition (OCR)** is utilised for transcribing printed documents. Magnetic Ink Character Recognition (MICR) is specifically used with bank cheques, while Optical Mark Recognition (OMR) is employed for processing multiple-choice questionnaires and lottery systems.

- **Electronic Data Sources**: These include handheld electronic devices used in parcel clearance, price tracking in goods ordering, and meter reading systems.
- **Sensor-Based Data Sources**: Sensors are frequently integrated with embedded systems for real-time data collection. Examples include:
    - Traffic light control systems
    - Climate control systems in homes and offices
    - Satellite monitoring systems
    - Weather monitoring systems
    - Car engine management systems
    - Healthcare monitoring systems
    - Household appliances like microwaves and washing machines

4.2.3 Advantages and Disadvantages

Automated data entry systems have become increasingly integral to business operations across various industries. While they offer numerous advantages, there are also significant drawbacks that organisations must consider before implementing such systems.

Advantages of Automated Data Entry Systems

- **Increased Speed of Transaction Processing**:
  Automated data entry systems can process transactions at a much faster rate compared to manual entry. This speed is particularly beneficial in environments where quick processing is essential, such as retail or hospitality. For instance, a supermarket using an automated Point of Sale (POS) system can significantly reduce customer wait times during checkout, leading to improved customer satisfaction and retention.

- **Higher Accuracy**:
  Automated systems reduce the likelihood of human error associated with manual data entry. This increased accuracy is vital in maintaining the integrity of data, especially in industries that require precise information, such as finance, healthcare, and logistics. Errors in data entry can lead to significant issues, including financial discrepancies, mismanagement of inventory, or even legal consequences.

- **Reduced Human Error**:
  By minimising the involvement of human operators, automated systems decrease the chances of mistakes that can occur due to fatigue, distraction, or lack of training. For example, an automated system can consistently capture data correctly from scanned barcodes or RFID tags, reducing the risk of mis-keyed data in inventory management.

- **Cost Efficiency Over Time**:
  Although initial setup costs can be high, automated data entry systems can lead to long-term savings by increasing efficiency and productivity. They can

decrease labour costs associated with manual data entry and reduce the expenses related to errors, such as correction costs or losses due to inaccurate data.

- **Enhanced Data Management**:
Automated systems often come with advanced data management features, such as real-time analytics and reporting tools. This capability allows businesses to analyse trends, monitor performance, and make informed decisions quickly. For example, supermarkets can analyse customer purchasing patterns to optimise inventory levels and improve marketing strategies.

- **Scalability**:
As businesses grow, automated data entry systems can be scaled more easily than manual processes. Organisations can handle increased transaction volumes without a proportional increase in labour costs or time. This scalability is crucial for businesses anticipating growth or fluctuating demands, such as during holiday seasons.

Disadvantages of Automated Data Entry Systems

- **High Initial Costs**:
Implementing automated data entry systems can be expensive. The costs associated with purchasing hardware and software, integrating systems, and migrating data from legacy systems can add up quickly. For example, implementing a comprehensive POS system in a supermarket may exceed N4,000,000 (£1,800 approx.), which can be a significant investment for smaller businesses.

- **Personnel Training**:
Training employees to use new automated systems can be time-consuming and costly. Staff may require extensive training to become proficient in operating new technology, which can temporarily disrupt operations and reduce productivity. Additionally, there may be resistance to change from employees accustomed to manual processes.

- **Dependence on Technology**:
Organisations may become overly reliant on automated systems, making them vulnerable to system failures or technical issues. If a POS system crashes or experiences downtime, it can halt transactions and lead to lost sales. This dependence can also create challenges during power outages or network failures, necessitating backup plans.

- **Limited Flexibility**:
Automated systems may not adapt well to changes in business processes or unforeseen circumstances. For example, if a supermarket introduces a new product line that requires modifications in data entry processes, the automated system may need significant reprogramming or updates, incurring additional costs and delays.

- **Security Concerns**:
  The increased use of technology in data entry raises concerns about data security and privacy. Automated systems can be susceptible to cyberattacks, data breaches, and unauthorised access. Businesses must invest in robust cybersecurity measures to protect sensitive information, which can further increase overall costs.

- **Potential Job Displacement**:
  While automation can lead to increased efficiency, it may also result in job displacement for employees whose roles become redundant. For example, if a supermarket automates its entire checkout process, cashiers may find their jobs at risk. This shift can lead to workforce challenges and require careful management of personnel transitions.

In summary, while automated data entry systems offer substantial benefits such as increased speed, accuracy, and efficiency, businesses must also consider the associated disadvantages, including high implementation costs and potential job displacement. A thorough cost-benefit analysis and strategic planning can help organisations effectively leverage automation while mitigating its drawbacks. Understanding these factors is essential for businesses aiming to improve their operational efficiency through automated solutions.

4.2.4 Issues in Data Sources

While various data sources offer numerous benefits for organisations, they also present significant challenges that can affect the quality and reliability of the information produced. Errors in data entry can stem from multiple factors, leading to inaccuracies that can have serious implications for decision-making and operational efficiency. Key issues include:

- **Human Mistakes**:
  Manual data transcription is prone to human errors, including typos, misinterpretation of data, and oversight in recording information. These mistakes can arise during the initial collection of data or when entering it into digital systems. For instance, if an employee incorrectly transcribes survey results, the resulting data analysis could lead to misguided conclusions and poor strategic decisions.

- **Malfunctioning Sensors or Equipment**:
  Technological failures can significantly impact data accuracy. Sensors or devices used for automated data collection may malfunction, yielding incorrect results. For example, a temperature sensor that is out of calibration can provide faulty readings that affect environmental monitoring or manufacturing processes. Ensuring regular maintenance and calibration of equipment is crucial to minimising such errors.

- **Misinformation from Surveys or Questionnaires**:
  Surveys and questionnaires can be influenced by human biases, leading to inaccurate or misleading information. Respondents may misunderstand

questions, provide socially desirable answers, or omit critical details due to memory recall issues. For instance, in a survey about health behaviours, respondents might underreport unhealthy habits, skewing the results and impacting public health initiatives.

- **Data Source Reliability**:
The credibility of data sources is paramount. Using unreliable sources can lead to compromised data integrity. For example, relying on outdated or unverified datasets can result in analysis based on flawed assumptions. Organisations should prioritise sourcing data from reputable and validated sources to enhance overall data quality.

4.2.5 Importance of Accuracy

To mitigate errors and enhance data quality, data entry systems must incorporate robust validation and verification mechanisms. Accuracy is crucial for various applications, especially in fields such as environmental science, finance, and healthcare. For instance, environmentalists rely on accurate data collection to conduct effective Environmental Impact Assessments (EIAs) for new developments. Accurate data helps assess potential impacts on ecosystems, guides regulatory compliance, and informs stakeholders about environmental consequences. Implementing validation checks, such as double-entry systems, cross-referencing data, and real-time error alerts, can significantly improve the reliability of data input.

4.2.6 Value of Information

Data transforms into valuable information when it is analysed, summarised, or processed meaningfully for the user. The value of this information is often assessed based on its utility in decision-making processes. For example, a business might analyse customer purchasing patterns to inform inventory management and marketing strategies. However, the value of information is dependent on several factors:

- **Accuracy**: Inaccurate data can lead to flawed analyses and poor decisions, undermining the overall value of the information.

- **Relevance**: Information must be pertinent to the specific needs of the user. For example, financial forecasts are only valuable if they align with the strategic objectives of an organisation.

- **Context**: The context in which information is used affects its perceived value. For example, real-time sales data is highly valuable during peak shopping seasons but may be less relevant during off-peak times.

4.2.7 Information as a Commodity

Information is often considered a **commodity** because it holds economic value in today's data-driven world. Just like tangible goods such as oil or gold, information can be bought, sold, traded, or utilised to generate profit. This notion has become especially prominent with the rise of the **information economy**, where businesses, governments, and individuals rely heavily on data and information to make decisions, improve efficiency, and gain a competitive edge.

Key Points: Why Information is a Commodity

- **Economic Value of Information**:
    - Organisations invest heavily in collecting, storing, analysing, and distributing information because it directly impacts their ability to make informed decisions, strategise, and innovate.
    - For example, market research data helps businesses tailor their products to meet customer needs, while financial reports guide investments.

- **Quality Determines Value**:
    - The monetary value of information is directly linked to its **quality** - which includes attributes such as accuracy, reliability, timeliness, relevance, and completeness.
    - Low-quality information can lead to poor decisions, wasted resources, and potential financial losses. For instance, incorrect customer data in a marketing campaign can lead to ineffective targeting and lost revenue.

- **Competitive Advantage**:
    - Organisations that possess high-quality information are better equipped to predict market trends, understand consumer behaviour, and adapt to changes. This creates a competitive edge in industries where knowledge drives success.
    - For example, companies like Google and Amazon thrive on their ability to collect and analyse massive amounts of high-quality information about user preferences and market patterns.

- **Information as a Tradable Asset**:
    - Data brokers, for instance, trade consumer information, such as purchasing habits and preferences, with businesses looking to enhance their marketing efforts.
    - Similarly, intellectual property, like patents or proprietary algorithms, is a form of high-value information that can be licensed or sold.

- **Legal and Ethical Implications**:
    - Since information is valuable, organisations must also protect it from theft, misuse, or loss. This has given rise to laws and frameworks like the Data Protection Act and General Data Protection Regulation (GDPR) to ensure ethical handling and prevent exploitation.

4.2.8 Ensuring Information Quality

To maximise the value of information, organisations must prioritise its quality by:

- **Validating Accuracy**: Ensuring data inputs are correct and verified before analysis.
- **Timely Updates**: Keeping information up to date to maintain relevance.
- **Relevance**: Filtering out unnecessary or irrelevant information.
- **Completeness**: Collecting all necessary data points to avoid gaps in understanding.

In summary, information is treated as a commodity because it holds intrinsic monetary value and is essential for decision-making, strategic planning, and innovation. Organisations that ensure the quality of their information stand to gain the maximum benefits, both economically and operationally.

4.2.9 Consolidation: Overheads in Maintaining Relevant Information

To maintain information that is up-to-date and relevant, organisations must consider several overheads related to data management. These factors help streamline operations and ensure data integrity:

- **Data Collection Methods**:
  Organisations should utilise efficient data collection methods tailored to their needs. This may include online surveys, direct input from field staff, or automated data capture from sensors.

- **Data Conversion or Direct Input Processes**:
  Effective processes for converting raw data into usable formats are essential. This includes determining how data will be entered into systems - whether through manual entry, automated uploads, or direct integration from other software.

- **Frequency of Data Collection**:
  Regular and timely data collection ensures that information remains relevant. Organisations should establish protocols for how often data is collected, ensuring it aligns with operational needs and strategic objectives.

- **Control Mechanisms for Data Integrity**:
  Implementing controls such as access restrictions, user authentication, and audit trails helps maintain data integrity and prevent unauthorised changes.

- **Validation Procedures**:
  Consistent validation processes should be in place to verify data accuracy. This includes automated checks for errors during entry and periodic reviews of collected data.

- **Processing Cycles**:
  Organisations need to define clear cycles for data processing, including data

cleaning, analysis, and reporting. Establishing these cycles helps manage workload and ensures timely access to insights.

- **Output Formats and Their Frequency**:
  Data should be presented in formats that meet the needs of users. This may include reports, dashboards, or visualisations. Regular updates to these outputs ensure stakeholders receive the most current and relevant information.

4.3. ICT AND THE LAW

Learning Outcomes

By the end of this section, students should be able to:

- Describe the various information controls, regulations, legislations, and laws covering the following:
    - Copyright, Licensing, and Piracy
    - Computer Misuse Act
    - Data Protection Act
    - Health and Safety at Work Act – Guidelines
    - Hackers and Hacking
    - Malpractice and Crime
    - Internet Ethics, Security, and Censorship
    - Hardware and Software Ergonomics
- Identify the basic concepts, significance, and challenges of ICT laws.
- Explain the importance of ICT law.

4.3.1 Introduction

The integration of Information and Communication Technology (ICT) into all aspects of modern life has necessitated the development of laws and regulations to guide its use, protect users, and address ethical and security challenges. This section focuses on understanding the various laws, regulations, and guidelines that govern ICT use, ensuring that students can recognise their significance and navigate the challenges they present.

ICT laws are established frameworks designed to ensure the responsible and ethical use of technology. They govern the production, distribution, and use of ICT tools and services, addressing issues like intellectual property, privacy, security, and workplace safety.

4.3.2 Control of Information

The rapid evolution of technology has dramatically transformed how information is created, stored, and shared. However, the legal framework surrounding the use and control of information is still in a state of flux, leading to ongoing debates and complexities regarding ownership, access, and protection. The rules governing information technology (IT) have far-reaching implications for its development, usage, and ethical considerations. As we navigate this complex landscape, several critical questions arise:

1. **Is a Computer Program a Form of Property That Can Be Stolen?**
   The classification of computer programs as property raises important legal and ethical questions. Traditionally, property rights are associated with tangible items, but digital assets challenge this notion. The argument is that computer programs, being intellectual creations, should be protected under intellectual property laws. This raises the issue of whether unauthorised copying, distribution, or use of software constitutes theft, similar to stealing a physical object. Cases like the Microsoft vs. Harmony Gold case highlight the importance of legal protections for software creators to prevent piracy and ensure they receive recognition and compensation for their work.

2. **Can Computer Data Be Considered Property?**
   The question of whether computer data can be classified as property is multifaceted. Data, particularly personal data, is increasingly viewed as an asset with significant value. For instance, companies that collect and analyse consumer data leverage this information for targeted marketing and strategic decision-making, highlighting its economic importance. However, the debate continues over ownership rights - do individuals retain ownership of their personal data, or does it become the property of the organisations that collect it? Legislation like the General Data Protection Regulation (GDPR) in the European Union seeks to address these issues by granting individuals rights over their personal data and imposing strict guidelines on data handling.

3. **Who Has the Right to Store and Access Personal Data?**
   As organisations increasingly rely on data for operations and decision-making, the question of who has the right to store and access personal data becomes critical. Legal frameworks such as the GDPR establish that individuals have the right to control their personal information, including how it is collected, stored, and used. Organisations must navigate consent requirements, transparency obligations, and security measures to protect personal data. The rising trend of data breaches emphasizes the need for stringent regulations and accountability mechanisms to safeguard sensitive information. Furthermore, ethical considerations around data usage must be addressed, ensuring that individuals are informed and empowered regarding their data rights.

4.3.3 Copyright, Designs and Patents Act (1986/1998)

The **Copyright, Designs and Patents Act** (CDPA) of 1986, updated in 1998, provides the legal framework for copyright protection in the United Kingdom. This legislation is essential for safeguarding the rights of creators and ensuring that their intellectual property is recognised and protected against unauthorised use.

What is Copyright?

Copyright is a form of legal protection granted to the creators of original works, covering a broad range of creative expressions, including:

- Literature (books, articles, poetry)
- Art (paintings, sculptures, graphic designs)
- Music (songs, compositions)
- Broadcasts (radio and television)
- Photography (images)
- Films (motion pictures)
- Audio recordings (soundtracks, podcasts)

Under UK law, computer programs are classified as literary works, thereby granting them copyright protection as well.

Key Aspects of Copyright:

- **Ownership**: Generally, the individual who creates the work is the first owner of the copyright. However, if the work is created as part of an employment arrangement, the employer typically holds the copyright. This principle is rooted in the idea that employers invest resources and provide the environment for the creation of the work.

- **Duration**: Copyright protection in the UK lasts for **75 years** from the end of the year in which the creator passes away. This duration was extended from 50 years as of January 1, 1996, in alignment with European Union directives. In cases involving multiple creators, the copyright lasts for **75 years** after the death of the last surviving creator.

Example:

If an author pens a novel, copyright is automatically granted to them, allowing them control over how the work is used, reproduced, or distributed. However, if the author is employed by a publishing company, the employment contract may stipulate that the publisher holds the copyright, reflecting the investment and resources they provide for publication.

Tutorial:

To gain a comprehensive understanding of copyright protections in different jurisdictions, consider investigating the extent of copyright protections under your own country's law, e.g., **Nigerian law**. Examine whether these protections align with those in the UK or the EU by reviewing the **Nigerian Copyright Act** (Chapter C28 of the Federal Republic of Nigeria 2004), as administered by the **Nigerian Copyright Commission (NCC)**. Key points to investigate include:

- The definition of copyrightable works under your country law
- Duration of copyright protection in your country
- Ownership rights and how they may differ from those in the UK
- Enforcement mechanisms for copyright infringement

- Differences or similarities in terms of exceptions or limitations to copyright (e.g., fair use or fair dealing provisions)

Understanding these aspects will provide insight into how copyright law is applied across different legal systems, highlighting both commonalities and unique characteristics.

4.3.4 Computer Misuse Act (1990)

The **Computer Misuse Act (CMA)** of 1990 is a pioneering legislation enacted in the UK to address the increasing threats of computer-related crimes. The law provides a comprehensive legal framework to combat unauthorised access and misuse of computer systems and data. It marked a significant step in regulating digital behaviour and ensuring that offenders could be prosecuted effectively.

Key Offences Under the CMA

The CMA identifies several key offences designed to protect computer systems and data integrity. These offences include:

1. Unauthorised Access

- This offence involves accessing computer material without proper authorisation. It encompasses activities such as viewing, copying, or using files without permission.
- **Examples**:
    - An employee accessing confidential company reports without authorisation.
    - A student using someone else's login credentials to view restricted academic resources.

2. Intent to Commit Further Offences

- This occurs when an individual gains unauthorised access with the intent to engage in other criminal activities such as theft, fraud, or espionage.
- **Examples**:
    - A cybercriminal breaking into an e-commerce platform to steal customer payment details for financial fraud.
    - A hacker accessing a hospital's database to manipulate patient records for ransom.

3. Unauthorised Modification

- This involves altering, deleting, or adding data to a computer system without permission, often with malicious intent.

- **Examples**:
    - Injecting malware or ransomware into a system to lock users out until a ransom is paid.
    - Deleting critical business data to disrupt operations or cause financial harm.

Examples of Computer Misuse

The CMA covers a range of misuse scenarios, many of which have significant consequences for individuals and organisations:

Hacking

- Unauthorised individuals infiltrate computer systems to steal sensitive information, disrupt operations, or compromise security.
- **Impact**:
    - Theft of trade secrets or customer data.
    - Reputational damage and financial losses for affected organisations.

Piracy

- The illegal copying, sharing, or distribution of copyrighted digital media, including software, music, films, and games.
- **Impact**:
    - Financial losses for creators and industries.
    - Legal penalties for offenders.

Email Abuse

- Activities such as spamming, phishing, or sending malicious emails to deceive recipients into divulging personal or financial information.
- **Impact**:
    - Victims may face identity theft, financial fraud, or loss of sensitive information.

Challenges in Enforcing the CMA

Despite its significance, the enforcement of the CMA faces numerous challenges, including:

1. Complexity of Cybercrimes

- Many cybercrimes involve sophisticated methods, such as encryption and anonymisation, making it difficult for investigators to trace perpetrators.
- Skilled professionals and advanced technologies are required to identify and counteract such crimes effectively.

2. Limited Resources

- Law enforcement agencies often operate with constraints in funding, technology, and staffing, limiting their ability to pursue and resolve computer misuse cases.
- Specialised training programs and resource allocation are essential to address this gap.

3. Jurisdictional Issues

- Cybercrimes frequently cross-national borders, making it challenging to determine jurisdiction and enforce the law.
- International cooperation between law enforcement agencies is required to combat transnational cybercrimes.

4. Rapid Technological Changes

- As technology evolves, new forms of computer misuse emerge, outpacing existing legal frameworks.
- Continuous updates to legislation and enforcement strategies are necessary to address emerging threats.

Importance of the CMA

The Computer Misuse Act serves as a critical tool in:

- **Protecting Digital Assets**: Safeguarding personal, corporate, and governmental data from unauthorised access and misuse.
- **Promoting Responsible Behaviour**: Deterring potential offenders by outlining clear legal consequences for computer misuse.
- **Strengthening Cybersecurity**: Encouraging organisations to adopt robust security measures to prevent breaches.
- **Fostering Trust**: Building confidence among users in the safety and security of digital systems.

The Computer Misuse Act of 1990 remains a cornerstone of digital legislation, addressing the growing complexities of cybercrimes. By defining key offences and outlining penalties, it aims to protect individuals and organisations while adapting to the evolving technological landscape. Addressing the enforcement challenges and ensuring the law remains relevant in a rapidly changing digital world are vital for maintaining its effectiveness.

4.3.5 Data Protection Act (1984/1998/2000/2018)

The **Data Protection Act (DPA)** is a cornerstone of data privacy legislation in the UK, governing the collection, storage, processing, and use of personal data. Initially enacted in **1984**, the Act underwent significant updates in **1998** and **2000** to address emerging technologies and evolving societal expectations surrounding data privacy.

In **2018**, the DPA was revised to align with the **EU's General Data Protection Regulation (GDPR)**, marking a major shift towards more stringent global data privacy standards. This revision aimed to enhance individual rights, establish clearer guidelines for organisations, and adapt to the challenges posed by the digital economy and increased cross-border data flows.

Key Updates Introduced in 2018

The 2018 revision introduced several critical updates to modernise the DPA by reinforcing the UK's commitment to robust data protection practices while aligning with international standards, ensuring that individuals' privacy rights are safeguarded in the modern era:

1. **Alignment with GDPR:**
   - Incorporated GDPR principles, including data portability, enhanced consent standards, and more substantial penalties for non-compliance.

2. **Children's Data Protection:**
   - Imposed stricter requirements for processing children's data, particularly in online services, and mandated parental consent where appropriate.

3. **Data Breach Notifications:**
   - Organisations are required to report data breaches to the Information Commissioner's Office (ICO) within **72 hours** of discovery if the breach poses a risk to individuals' rights.

4. **Data Protection Officers (DPOs):**
   - Certain organisations, such as public authorities, are now required to appoint a **Data Protection Officer (DPO)** to ensure compliance with data protection regulations.

Data Protection Update 2024

The **Data Protection Update 2024** introduces new provisions regulating the processing of information related to identifiable living individuals. It aims to:

1. Regulate services that use personal data to ascertain and verify facts about individuals.

2. Establish rules on access to customer and business data.

This update reflects a continued effort to balance data privacy with the needs of modern information processing and verification services.

October 2024 European Court of Justice (ECJ) Ruling

On October 4, 2024, the **European Court of Justice (ECJ)** issued a significant preliminary ruling regarding the **General Data Protection Regulation (GDPR)**. The court confirmed that a controller's legitimate interest in processing personal data does not necessarily need to be explicitly set out in EU or national law to qualify as a "legitimate interest" under **Article 6(1)(f)** of the GDPR. This decision provides greater flexibility for organisations to justify certain data processing activities.

Relationship Between the Data Protection Act (DPA) and GDPR

The **Data Protection Act (DPA)** has not been replaced by the GDPR. Both frameworks came into effect on **May 25, 2018**, and have since coexisted:

- The **EU GDPR** applies to organisations operating within the European Union.
- Post-Brexit, the **UK General Data Protection Regulation (UK GDPR)** became law on **January 1, 2021**, ensuring continued data protection compliance tailored to the UK's legal framework.

Together, the UK GDPR and the DPA 2018 form the core of the UK's data protection regime.

Data Retention and Investigatory Powers Act 2014

The **Data Retention and Investigatory Powers Act 2014 (DRIPA)** was introduced to maintain critical capabilities in fighting crime and ensuring public safety. This legislation:

- Clarifies existing legal requirements for retaining and accessing data.
- Does not extend current investigatory powers but ensures clarity and legal consistency in their application.

The act underscores the importance of retaining data for investigative and security purposes while adhering to legal safeguards.

Key Terms in the Data Protection Act

Understanding the core concepts of the **Data Protection Act (DPA)** is essential for comprehending how personal data is managed and protected. Three important terms - **Data Subject**, **Data User**, and **Data Controller** - play distinct roles within the framework of data protection. Below is an explanation and differentiation of these terms:

1. Data Subject

A Data Subject is an individual to whom personal data relates. This is the person whose information is collected, processed, stored, or used by an organisation. The Data Subject holds specific rights under the DPA, such as the right to access their data, request corrections, object to processing, or demand erasure.

- **Example:** A customer providing their name, email address, and payment details when purchasing a product online is a Data Subject.

2. Data User

A Data User refers to an individual or organisation that accesses, processes, or uses personal data for specific purposes. They do so under the authority of the Data Controller, following the data protection principles outlined in the DPA. Data Users must handle personal data responsibly, ensuring it is used lawfully and ethically.

- **Example:** A marketing employee who uses customer email addresses to send promotional newsletters acts as a Data User.

3. Data Controller

A Data Controller is an entity (individual, organisation, or public body) that determines the purposes and means of processing personal data. The Data Controller has overall responsibility for ensuring compliance with the DPA, implementing necessary safeguards, and protecting Data Subjects' rights. They may delegate data processing tasks to others but remain accountable for how data is managed.

- **Example:** A retail company that collects and manages customer data for order processing and marketing purposes is the Data Controller.

4. Data Protection Officer (DPO):

A DPO is an individual designated by certain organisations (e.g., public authorities or large companies handling significant personal data) to oversee compliance with data protection laws. The DPO acts independently to advise the organisation and monitor compliance but does not function as an external regulator.

5. Information Commissioner's Office (ICO):

In the UK, the ICO serves as the **regulatory authority** for data protection. It investigates complaints, enforces compliance, and provides guidance on data protection laws. The ICO would be the equivalent of a "Data Ombudsman" in terms of overseeing adherence to data protection laws.

Differentiating the Terms

This table briefly defines the key terms in DPA, their roles, responsibilities, and examples to ensure clarity and completeness:

Term	Role	Responsibility	Example
Data Subject	The individual whose personal data is collected and processed.	Holds rights such as access, correction, and erasure of their data.	A customer providing personal details during an online purchase.

Term	Role	Responsibility	Example
Data User	The person or organisation authorised to access and use personal data.	Must comply with data protection principles when using personal data for authorised purposes.	A staff member using a CRM system to manage client information.
Data Controller	The person or organisation deciding the purposes and means of processing personal data.	Ensures data is processed lawfully, implements safeguards, and upholds the rights of Data Subjects.	A healthcare provider managing patient records for treatment and billing.
Data Protection Officer (DPO)	An individual responsible for overseeing compliance with data protection laws within an organisation.	Monitors compliance, provides advice, and serves as a liaison between the organisation, employees, and regulatory authorities.	A public authority appoints a DPO to ensure compliance with GDPR and the DPA.
Information Commissioner's Office (ICO)	The UK's independent authority responsible for upholding information rights.	Oversees compliance with data protection laws, investigates breaches, and enforces penalties for non-compliance.	The ICO investigating a data breach at a government agency that failed to notify the breach in time.

Key Principles of the Data Protection Act

The Act outlines key principles that remain the foundation of data protection practices, ensuring organisations handle personal data responsibly and transparently:

1. **Fair and Lawful Processing**
   - Personal data must be processed lawfully, fairly, and transparently.
   - **Example:** Organisations must provide clear information on how they collect and use data, often through a privacy notice or policy.

2. **Purpose Limitation**
    - Data should only be used for the specific purposes stated at the time of collection.
    - **Example:** An e-commerce company collecting data for purchases cannot use the information for unrelated marketing without explicit consent.

3. **Data Minimisation**
    - Only data strictly necessary for the stated purpose should be collected.
    - **Example:** A job application form should only ask for relevant information, such as qualifications and contact details, and not unnecessary personal details.

4. **Accuracy**
    - Organisations must ensure data is accurate and up to date to avoid harm or inconvenience to individuals.
    - **Example:** Regularly updating contact information in employee or customer records.

5. **Storage Limitation**
    - Data should not be retained longer than necessary for its intended purpose.
    - **Example:** A business should delete customer data once it is no longer needed for processing orders or complying with legal requirements.

6. **Individual Rights**
    - Data subjects have enhanced rights under the 2018 update, including the right to access, rectify, erase, and restrict the processing of their data.
    - **Example:** Individuals can request the deletion of their data under the "right to be forgotten" if it is no longer needed.

7. **Security**
    - Organisations must take appropriate technical and organisational measures to protect data against breaches or unauthorised access.
    - **Example:** This may include encryption, firewalls, and robust access controls.

8. **Accountability**
    - Organisations must demonstrate compliance with the DPA principles by maintaining records of data processing activities and conducting impact assessments.
    - **Example:** Documenting how personal data is handled and ensuring staff are trained in data protection.

9. **International Transfers**
    - Personal data should not be transferred outside the UK unless the recipient country has adequate data protection measures.
    - **Example:** Organisations using cloud services must ensure data stored abroad meets UK standards for data protection.

Example Scenario: Compliance with the Data Protection Act

Consider a financial institution that collects customer data, such as names, addresses, and financial transactions. To comply with the DPA:

- **Transparency:** Customers are informed about how their data will be used, such as for account management or fraud detection.
- **Security:** Encryption is applied to sensitive information like credit card numbers, and access controls limit data access to authorised staff.
- **Retention Policy:** Records are kept for the required duration (e.g., for legal or regulatory compliance) and securely deleted afterward.

Data Security Measures

Organisations must implement robust security measures to protect personal data, including:

1. **Access Controls:**
    - Use of secure logins, multi-factor authentication, and role-based permissions to limit data access to authorised personnel.

2. **Encryption:**
    - Data encryption ensures that sensitive information, such as medical records or financial data, is protected during storage and transmission.

3. **Regular Audits and Monitoring:**
    - Conducting regular audits helps organisations identify unauthorised access attempts or weaknesses in data security systems.

4. **Data Protection Training:**
   o Providing staff with training on data protection policies and practices ensures compliance and reduces the risk of breaches.
5. **Data Protection Impact Assessments (DPIAs):**
   o Evaluating potential risks associated with new data processing activities helps organisations proactively address privacy concerns.

4.3.6 Health and Safety at Work Act (1986)

The **Health and Safety at Work Act** (HSWA) of 1986 is a crucial piece of legislation in the UK that places a legal duty on employers to ensure the health, safety, and welfare of their employees while they are at work. This includes the safe use of Information Technology (IT) systems, which have become integral to many workplaces.

Employer Responsibilities

1. **Provide Ergonomically Designed Equipment**:
   o Employers must ensure that all equipment, such as chairs and computer screens, is designed to promote comfort and reduce the risk of injury. Ergonomics is vital for minimising physical strain, especially for employees who spend extended periods working at computers.
2. **Ensure Adequate Workstation Conditions**:
   o Workstations should be adequately lit, spacious, and well-organised. This includes providing enough space for employees to move freely and preventing clutter that could lead to accidents.
3. **Encourage Regular Breaks**:
   o Employers should promote regular breaks during work hours to prevent repetitive strain injuries and to mitigate the effects of prolonged sitting and screen time. Breaks are essential for both mental and physical well-being.

Example of Ergonomics

An adjustable office chair that supports proper posture is a prime example of ergonomic design. Such chairs can help prevent back pain and other musculoskeletal disorders among employees who spend long hours seated at their desks. Adjustable desks that allow employees to alternate between sitting and standing can also contribute to better overall health.

4.3.7 Common Health Risks Associated with IT Work

- **Repetitive Motion Injuries (RMIs)**:
  - RMIs often result from prolonged typing or repetitive tasks, leading to conditions such as carpal tunnel syndrome or tendinitis.

- **Eyestrain**:
  - Prolonged exposure to screens can lead to digital eye strain, causing discomfort, headaches, and blurred vision. This condition can be exacerbated by poor lighting and glare from screens.

- **Ozone Irritation**:
  - Emissions from laser printers and other electronic devices can release ozone, which may cause respiratory issues or exacerbate existing health conditions.

Solutions to Mitigate Health Risks

- **Implement Regular Breaks**:
  - Encouraging employees to take short breaks every hour can help reduce the risk of RMIs and eyestrain. Simple stretching exercises or brief walks can be beneficial.

- **Conduct Ergonomic Assessments**:
  - Regular ergonomic assessments of workstations can help identify potential issues and allow for adjustments to be made, such as repositioning equipment or providing additional support.

- **Provide Training**:
  - Training employees on proper posture, workstation setup, and the importance of breaks can enhance their awareness and promote better health practices in the workplace.

Ergonomics in the Workplace

Ergonomics is the science of designing workspaces, products, and systems to fit the people who use them, promoting comfort, efficiency, and safety.

Key Considerations for Ergonomics

1. **Furniture Design**:
   - Ergonomically designed chairs and desks can significantly reduce discomfort and enhance productivity. For instance, chairs should have lumbar support, adjustable height, and armrests.

2. **Workstation Layout**:
    - The arrangement of equipment should minimise strain and promote good posture. This includes placing monitors at eye level and keeping frequently used items within easy reach.

3. **Environmental Factors**:
    - Adequate lighting, proper ventilation, and noise control are critical for improving overall workplace health. Natural lighting, where possible, can reduce eyestrain, while good ventilation helps maintain air quality.

4.3.8 Poor Ergonomic Setup

An improperly arranged workstation can have significant physical and mental health repercussions, as well as create safety risks. A poor ergonomic setup typically features cluttered spaces, disorganised cables, inadequate furniture, and incorrect monitor placement. These setups not only reduce productivity but can also result in long-term health problems.

Key Features of Poor Ergonomic Setup

- **Cluttered Cables:** Tangled or unsecured wires can become trip hazards and cause accidental damage to equipment.

    - **Uncomfortable Chairs:** Chairs lacking proper lumbar support force users into awkward postures, potentially leading to back pain, muscle strain, and fatigue.

    - **Inappropriate Monitor Placement:** Monitors that are too high, low, or not aligned with eye level can cause neck and shoulder strain, headaches, and eye fatigue.

    - **Improper Keyboard and Mouse Positioning:** Misaligned input devices can lead to repetitive strain injuries (RSI), such as carpal tunnel syndrome.

    - **Insufficient Lighting:** Poor lighting conditions can strain the eyes, cause headaches, and make the workstation visually unappealing.

Consequences of Poor Ergonomic Setup:

- **Health Risks:** Chronic discomfort, musculoskeletal disorders, and posture-related injuries.

- **Reduced Productivity:** Physical discomfort can lead to distractions and lower work efficiency.

- **Safety Hazards:** Cluttered and poorly arranged cables can lead to trips and falls.

- **Workplace Dissatisfaction:** Employees may feel undervalued in poorly designed work environments.

4.3.9 Good Ergonomic Setup

A good ergonomic setup prioritises user comfort, efficiency, and health. It ensures that workstations are designed to accommodate individual needs while adhering to ergonomic principles. This type of arrangement minimises health risks, boosts productivity, and promotes a safe, positive working environment.

Key Features of Good Ergonomic Setup

- **Adjustable Furniture:**
    - Chairs with adjustable height, back support, and armrests to promote good posture.
    - Desks designed to allow natural arm positioning and legroom.

- **Monitor Positioning:**
    - Screens positioned at eye level and about an arm's length away to prevent neck strain.
    - Anti-glare screens or proper lighting to reduce eye fatigue.

- **Cable Management:**
    - Properly organised and secured cables to avoid hazards and maintain a tidy appearance.

- **Input Device Arrangement:**
    - Keyboards and mice placed at elbow level, with wrists in a neutral position.
    - Wrist rests or ergonomic input devices for added comfort.

- **Lighting:**
    - Adequate task lighting to minimise eye strain.
    - Use of natural light where possible for a pleasant work environment.

- **Foot Support:**
    - Footrests for individuals who cannot place their feet flat on the ground comfortably.

- **Clutter-Free Environment:**
    - A clean, organised space to promote focus and reduce stress.

Benefits of a Good Ergonomic Setup

- **Health Improvements:** Reduces the risk of musculoskeletal issues, eye strain, and other health-related concerns.
- **Enhanced Productivity:** A comfortable setup allows for extended periods of focused work.

- **Increased Safety:** Proper cable management and furniture placement minimise physical hazards.
- **Positive Work Environment:** Employees feel valued and motivated in well-designed spaces.

4.3.10 Visual Examples

- **Poor Ergonomics:** A cluttered desk with tangled cables, a fixed-height chair offering no back support, and a monitor placed at an incorrect height, forcing the user into awkward postures.

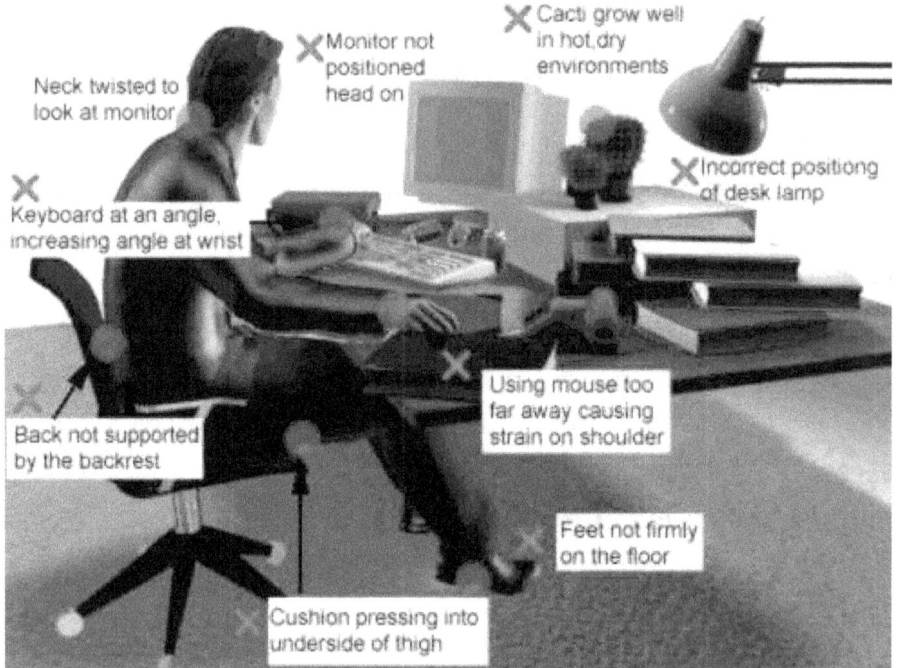

Source unknown: poor seating arrangement of a computer workstation

- **Good Ergonomics:** A clean desk with cables neatly organised, an adjustable chair supporting proper posture, feet firmly on footrest, and a monitor aligned at eye level, creating a comfortable and efficient workspace.

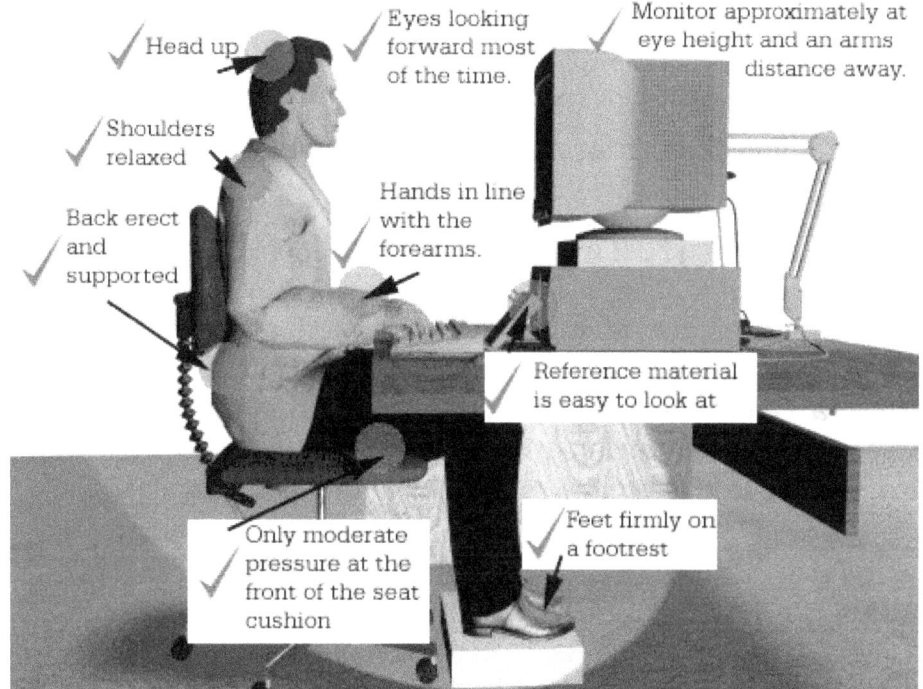

Source unknown: good (ergonomics) seating arrangement of a computer workstation

The Health and Safety at Work Act underscores the critical need to establish a safe and healthy working environment, particularly in the context of IT system usage. By adhering to ergonomic principles and adopting best practices, employers can create a workplace culture that prioritises employee well-being while boosting productivity. Regular training and assessments are essential to address evolving workplace dynamics, ensuring compliance with health and safety regulations. Continuous evaluation and adjustment of workstation setups to meet individual needs further reinforce this commitment, promoting both the physical health and overall efficiency of employees.

Tutorial Activity 4 - ICT Laws and Ethics

Quizzes and Questions

1. Differentiating Data, Information, and Knowledge

Question:
Which of the following best represents the relationship between data, information, and knowledge?
a) Knowledge leads to data, which becomes information.
b) Information is raw and unprocessed, while knowledge is structured data.
c) Data is raw and unprocessed; information is organised and contextualised data; knowledge is derived from information.
d) Data and knowledge are the same, but information is distinct.

2. Understanding Data Sources

Question:
What is the primary role of data sources in information management?
a) To store processed information for decision-making.
b) To provide raw data for processing and analysis.
c) To ensure data is automatically validated.
d) To replace the need for information systems.

Question:
Identify two methods used to extract data from sources.

3. Key Laws and Regulations in ICT

Question:
What is the primary focus of the Data Protection Act?
a) To regulate hardware standards in ICT systems.
b) To safeguard personal data from misuse and unauthorised access.
c) To manage copyright for digital content.
d) To monitor software development practices.

4. Ethical, Social, and Legal Implications of ICT

Question:
Which of the following is an ethical concern related to ICT in healthcare?
a) Ensuring fair use of software licenses.
b) Monitoring employees' use of social media.
c) Protecting patient data from unauthorised access.
d) Reducing energy consumption in server farms.

5. ICT and Data Privacy

Question:
What is a potential risk of poor data governance?
a) Increased efficiency in data processing.
b) Loss of stakeholder trust due to data breaches.

c) Enhanced compliance with regulations.
d) Reduction in legal liabilities for the organisation.

6. Global and Local ICT Regulatory Frameworks

Question:
Which global regulation is known for its comprehensive approach to data protection and privacy?
a) Computer Misuse Act
b) General Data Protection Regulation (GDPR)
c) Health and Safety at Work Act
d) Digital Millennium Copyright Act (DMCA)

7. Real-World Application of ICT Laws

Scenario-Based Question:
A company discovers that an employee has been sharing customer data with a third party without consent. Which law is most likely violated, and what compliance strategy could have prevented this?

8. ICT's Role in Knowledge Creation and Dissemination

Question:
How does ICT contribute to knowledge dissemination?
a) By restricting access to certain information.
b) By automating repetitive tasks to reduce costs.
c) By enabling the sharing of information through digital platforms.
d) By enforcing strict censorship on all online activities.

Bonus Question:

Question:
Discuss one major ethical challenge posed by the increasing use of ICT in education and propose a solution.

References

This Chapter is based on general knowledge and understanding of data privacy, digital rights, and the typical structure of privacy regulations, without referencing any specific sources. However, primary references or official resources on data privacy legislation and practices include:

- Legislation.gov.uk. "Copyright, Designs and Patents Act 1988." Available at legislation.gov.uk.
- Legislation.gov.uk. "Computer Misuse Act 1990." Available at legislation.gov.uk.
- Legislation.gov.uk. "Data Protection Act 1998" and "Data Protection Act 2018." Available at legislation.gov.uk.
- European Commission. "General Data Protection Regulation (GDPR)." Available at ec.europa.eu.
- Health and Safety Executive (HSE). "Health and Safety at Work Act 1974." Available at hse.gov.uk.
- UK Government, Intellectual Property Office. Available at gov.uk/ipo.
- Electronic Frontier Foundation (EFF) – The EFF advocates for digital privacy, free expression, and innovation.
- International Association of Privacy Professionals (IAPP) – The IAPP offers various research papers, best practices, and certification courses on data privacy, useful for understanding global data protection laws.
- Nigerian Data Protection Regulation (NDPR) – Issued by Nigeria's National Information Technology Development Agency (NITDA), the NDPR is a framework similar to GDPR, governing data protection in Nigeria.
- Information Commissioner's Office (ICO) – The ICO is the UK's independent authority set up to uphold information rights. It offers guidance on data protection, privacy rights, and cybersecurity.

CHAPTER 5: INFORMATION AGE

Learning Outcomes

By the end of this chapter, learners will be able to:

- Identify and list the key information ages in human history.
- Describe the defining characteristics of each information age.
- Analyse the impact of each information age on society, technology, and communication.
- Explain how innovations in different ages influenced the development of modern technology.
- Evaluate the progression of information handling from prehistory to the present digital era.
- Classify computers based on their generations, size, purpose, and functionality as influenced by developments across various information ages.

5. TECHNOLOGY OF DIFFERENT INFORMATION AGES

The evolution of technology has been a defining factor in shaping human societies across various information ages. Each era - marked by distinct technological advancements - has revolutionised the way information is created, stored, and shared. From the early use of primitive tools in the Stone Age to the intricate systems of the Information Age, these technological milestones have driven progress and innovation. This section explores the defining technologies of different information ages, examining their impact on communication, industry, and daily life, and highlighting how they laid the foundation for modern digital advancements.

5.1 THE EVOLUTION OF INFORMATION AGES

This premise explores the progression of information ages, offering a concise overview of each era rather than an exhaustive analysis. For a deeper understanding, learners are encouraged to consult specialised literature on the subject. Key highlights of the different information ages are outlined to enable comparisons with the present age of information. By identifying the tools associated with each era, students can appreciate the evolution of human innovation.

5.2.1 The Stone Age

The Stone Age represents a prehistoric era characterised by the use of stone as the primary material for toolmaking. This period is considered the foundation of human technological development, as early humans crafted tools and implements that addressed fundamental survival needs such as hunting, food preparation, and shelter construction. Stone tools were typically shaped or chipped to create a variety of implements, including carving molds, cutting tools, grinding stones, and weapons.

5.2.1 Tool Types and Innovations

Early tools like the **Oldowan tools**, dating back over 2 million years, are believed to be the oldest stone tools, used by early humans for cutting meat, processing plant materials, and breaking bones to access marrow. Later advancements led to more refined tools, such as **Acheulean hand axes**, which showcased improved craftsmanship and functionality. These innovations were pivotal in enabling early humans to adapt to their environment, improve hunting techniques, and develop communal living practices.

Diagram: Stone Age Firelighting Stones

5.2.2 Cultural and Practical Legacy

The ingenuity of Stone Age humans is reflected in tools that continue to be relevant today, particularly in traditional or resource-limited settings. Examples of their enduring influence include:

- **Outdoor Cooking**: Large stones are still used as makeshift cooking tripods or hearths, especially during traditional ceremonies or in rural households.
- **Grinding Stones**: These remain vital in many communities for processing food items. For instance, in some rural Nigerian households, grinding stones are commonly used to prepare ingredients such as tomatoes, peppers, onions, and indigenous delicacies like **egusi** (melon seeds) or **ogbono** (wild mango seeds).

5.2.3 Impact on Human Advancement

Stone Age tools not only provided immediate solutions to everyday challenges but also laid the groundwork for future technological and societal advancements. The use of tools encouraged problem-solving and innovation, fostering the development of complex societies and paving the way for subsequent eras, including the Bronze and Iron Ages.

The Stone Age was not just a period of survival but also a time of experimentation and discovery. It highlights the adaptability and resourcefulness of early humans, whose innovations set the stage for the modern technologies we rely on today. These enduring practices and tools underscore humanity's ability to find practical solutions and adapt materials to meet evolving needs.

5.2.4 Prehistoric Stone Age Tools

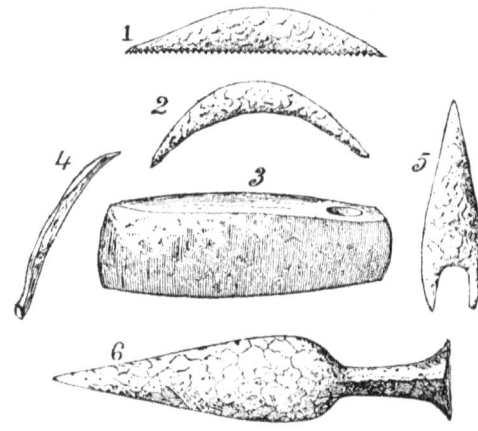

1. Saw-edged flint knife
2. Crescent-shaped flint knife
3. Stone axe
4. Flint flake knife
5. Flint harpoon head
6. Flint knife

Figure 1 depicts a variety of tools characteristic of the Stone Age.

Source: William Dwight Whitney, *The Century Dictionary, an Encyclopaedic Lexicon of the English Language* (New York: The Century Co., 1902) I-109
Copyright: Florida Centre for Instructional Technology, 2009

5.3 THE IRON AGE

The Iron Age succeeded the Bronze Age, marking a significant period in prehistoric times when humans advanced to the widespread use of iron and steel for crafting tools, household items, jewellery, and weapons. This era was characterised by innovations that transformed everyday life, agriculture, and warfare.

5.3.1 Applications of Iron and Steel

During the Iron Age, humans developed tools and utensils that are still relevant in various communities today. Common items included:

- **Household utensils:** Spoons, knives, and cooking pots.
- **Agricultural tools:** Cutlasses, hoes, and tools for clearing vegetation (*e.g., langa langa* for cutting grass).
- **Weapons:** Iron blades and other localised weaponry for hunting or defence.

These advancements reflected the practicality and versatility of iron as a material, revolutionising daily life.

5.3.2 Ironworking in Nigeria

In Nigeria, the early use of ironworks can be traced back to the Nok culture, dating as far back as the 6th century B.C., between 1400 and 1600. The Nok civilisation is renowned for its early adoption of ironworking and its iconic terracotta artifacts.

Subsequently, other prominent kingdoms in Nigeria embraced ironworking for both utilitarian and ceremonial purposes. Examples include:

- **The Benin Kingdom:** Renowned for its artistic and functional ironworks.
- **The Yoruba Kingdom:** Revered Ogun, the god of iron, as a deity central to their belief systems and craftsmanship.

Ironworking also played a spiritual role, particularly among the Ibo people of eastern Nigeria. They crafted iron objects such as Ikenga, a symbolic figure believed to possess supernatural powers. Ikenga was often used for rituals, taking oaths, and as a focal point for sacrifices, reflecting the deep interconnection between ironworking and religious practices.

5.3.3 Societal Impacts of Iron Age Materials

The widespread use of iron had transformative effects on society, influencing:

1. **Agriculture:** The development of durable tools improved farming techniques and food production.
2. **Religious practices:** Iron artifacts held spiritual significance and were integrated into rituals and beliefs.
3. **Socio-cultural evolution:** As iron tools and weapons became widespread, communities adapted to new ways of life, including enhanced craftsmanship, trade, and warfare.

The Iron Age signifies a pivotal step in human innovation, where the mastery of metalworking not only met practical needs but also influenced cultural identity and spiritual expression. It remains a foundational period in the historical and technological development of societies around the world.

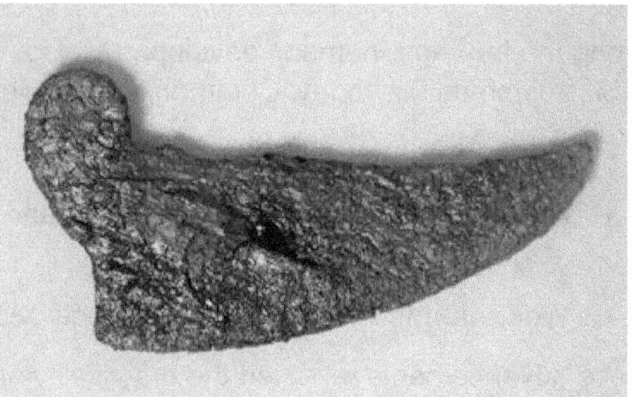

Above: An Iron Age Crucible used for casting bronze. Although iron was used for tools and weapons, bronze was still popular for jewellery and other decorations (width 25mm).

Above: Curved iron knife with spiral handle - perhaps a razor (length 90 mm).

Fig 2 shows some prehistoric Iron Age tools
Source: *National Museum Scotland website.*

5.4 THE MIDDLE AGES

The Middle Age, dating back approximately 200,000 to 400,000 years ago, marks a pivotal period in prehistoric times when human ingenuity and craftsmanship advanced significantly. This era was defined by the development of smaller, more sophisticated toolkits, enabling the creation of tools with greater precision and versatility. The Middle Age stands as a testament to human innovation, characterised by the refinement of tool-making techniques and the emergence of early artistic and written expression. These advancements laid the groundwork for subsequent technological and cultural developments.

5.4.1 Advancements in Toolmaking

During this period, innovations in technology revolutionised tool production:

- **Precision crafting:** Tools were often made using a technique known as the "prepared core technique," allowing a tool to be formed with a single, precise blow.

- **Smaller, portable tools:** Unlike earlier bulky implements, Middle Age tools were lightweight and easy to handle, making them more effective for various tasks.

- **Diverse toolkits:** Items such as hand-held axes, cutting tools, blades, and spearheads became common. These tools were designed for a range of purposes, from hunting to crafting and domestic use.

5.4.2 Projectile Weapons and Hunting Innovations

The Middle Age also saw advancements in hunting technology:

- **Spearheads:** These were hafted onto shafts to create effective hunting weapons.

- **Darts and arrows:** Smaller, smoother spearheads were mounted on slim shafts, giving rise to the use of darts and arrows as projectile weapons. This development marked a leap in hunting techniques, enabling humans to target prey from greater distances.

5.4.3 Artistic and Written Expression

Another hallmark of this era was the creation and use of tools for artistic and written expression. For example, the use of quills made from bird feathers allowed scribes to produce detailed manuscripts and illuminate texts, leading to an increase in literacy and the preservation of knowledge. Feather pens and natural inks were developed for writing, drawing, and calligraphy. These tools not only served functional purposes but also facilitated the growth of early artistic and symbolic communication.

The **printing press**, invented by Johannes Gutenberg in the 15th century, later transformed the dissemination of information, paving the way for the Renaissance.

5.4.4 Middle Age Tools

During the Middle Ages, tools played a crucial role in agriculture, construction, trade, and daily life. The tools used during this period were often simple but highly functional, reflecting the technological limitations and ingenuity of the time.

Agricultural Tools: Farming was the backbone of the economy, and tools like plows, hoes, sickles, scythes, and flails were essential. Wooden plows with iron tips were used to till the soil, while sickles and scythes were employed for harvesting crops.

Construction Tools: Building techniques advanced with the use of hammers, chisels, axes, and saws for shaping wood and stone. These tools were instrumental in constructing cathedrals, castles, and other iconic medieval structures.

Blacksmithing Tools: Blacksmiths used anvils, hammers, tongs, and bellows to forge weapons, armour, and everyday items like nails and horseshoes. The blacksmith's craft was vital for both war and peace.

Trade and Commerce Tools: Merchants and artisans relied on weighing scales, measures, and tools for weaving, leatherworking, and carpentry to produce goods for trade and local use.

Household Tools: Everyday life saw the use of simple tools like knives, hangers, mortars and pestles, and spinning wheels for cooking, grinding, and textile production.

The development and use of these tools not only facilitated daily life but also laid the foundation for technological advancements in later periods.

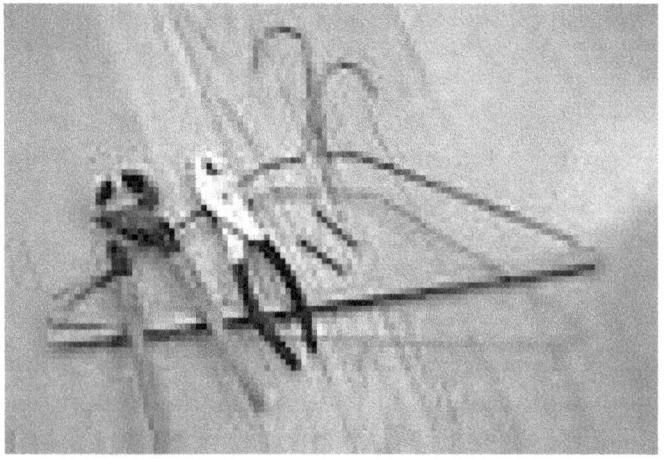

Figure 3 displays a range of tools typical of the Middle Age in great use today, including hand cutters, wire hangers, pliers, hand axes, shovel, spearheads, and blades. These items reflect the period's focus on precision and portability in toolmaking.

Source: National Museum Scotland website (*terriermandotcom.blogspot.com/2007_05_01_arch...*)

5.5 THE INDUSTRIAL AGE

The Industrial Age, also known as the Industrial Revolution, was a transformative period spanning the 18th and 19th centuries. During this time, advancements in agriculture, manufacturing, mining, transportation, and technology triggered profound social, economic, and cultural changes. These developments significantly impacted human conditions and reshaped society.

5.5.1 Origins and Global Spread

The Industrial Age began in the United Kingdom and gradually extended across Europe, North America, Russia, and eventually the rest of the world. Its influence was monumental, altering nearly every aspect of daily life.

5.5.2 Key Characteristics of the Industrial Age

1. **Mechanisation of Labour:**
   - Manual labour on farms transitioned to machine-assisted processes.
   - The use of animals for work was supplemented or replaced by machines powered by steam and coal.

2. **Advancements in Transportation:**
   - The development of improved roads, canal waterways, and railways revolutionised the movement of goods and people.

3. **Technological Innovations:**
   - Mechanisation first took hold in the textile industry, significantly boosting production. For instance, the **cotton gin**, invented by Eli Whitney in 1793, significantly increased cotton production efficiency, transforming the textile industry and driving economic growth. This era not only changed production methods but also led to substantial socioeconomic changes, including urbanisation and the rise of the working class.
   - Advances in iron-making techniques and the use of steam power (derived from coal) increased efficiency.
   - Water wheels and all-metal machine tools further accelerated industrial production.

Jacquard loom, engraving, 1874

At the top of the machine is a stack of punched cards that would be fed into the loom to control the weaving pattern. This method of automatically issuing machine instructions was employed by computers well into the 20th century.

Fig. 4: The Bettmann Archive

4. **Impact on Manufacturing:**
   - Factories became central to production, leading to urbanisation and the rise of industrial cities.
   - Mass production techniques enabled the creation of goods on a previously unimaginable scale.

5.5.3 Societal Impact

The Industrial Age marked a shift from agrarian economies to industrialised ones, with widespread implications:

- **Economic changes:** Industrialisation created new wealth and redefined labour, with industries driving the global economy.
- **Cultural shifts:** Urbanisation led to new social dynamics, while art and literature often reflected the challenges of industrial life.
- **Technological dependency:** Machines and technological advancements became integral to human existence.

5.5.4 The Industrial Age vs. the Information Age

The Industrial Age and the Information Age represent two significant milestones in human history, each defined by its transformative impact on society, economy, and technology. While they are often discussed as distinct eras, their relationship is complex, with overlaps and interconnections that continue to shape the modern world.

5.5.5 Key Points of Comparison and Debate

1. **Continuity:**
   - The Industrial Age introduced mechanisation, mass production, and global trade networks, laying the foundation for much of today's economic infrastructure.
   - Many industrial practices, such as assembly-line manufacturing, remain integral to modern industries, highlighting the enduring relevance of the Industrial Age.

2. **Transition:**
   - The Information Age, emerging in the mid-20th century, is marked by advancements in computing, telecommunications, and data processing.
   - Scholars often view it as a natural evolution of the Industrial Age, with automation and digitalisation enhancing traditional industrial processes.

3. **Interconnection**:
    - Modern technologies, such as the Internet of Things (IoT), artificial intelligence (AI), and robotics, bridge the two eras. For instance, smart factories leverage information technology to optimise industrial production.
    - This blending of technologies demonstrates that the Industrial and Information Ages are not mutually exclusive but coexist in various forms.

The Legacy of the Industrial Age

- The Industrial Age was a period of extraordinary innovation and change that reshaped human life and society. Key achievements include mechanised transportation, urbanisation, and the rise of global markets.
- Its influence persists in contemporary civilisation, from the design of cities to the operation of global supply chains.

The Role of the Information Age

- The Information Age builds on the legacy of the Industrial Age, focusing on the management, analysis, and dissemination of information.
- Innovations such as the internet, cloud computing, and big data analytics represent a shift from physical production to knowledge-based economies.

Conclusion: A Blend of Distinction and Interconnection

While the Industrial Age is often characterised by physical machinery and tangible goods, and the Information Age by intangible data and digital tools, the two eras are deeply interconnected. The blending of industrial processes with information technologies continues to define progress, shaping a hybrid era where the strengths of both ages combine to drive innovation and efficiency.

5.6 ELECTRONIC AGE (CURRENT AGE)

The Electronic Age, often referred to as the Computer Age, Information Age, or Digital Age, is a transformative period that revolutionised how information is transferred, processed, and accessed. Emerging from the technological advancements of the Space Age, this era marks a shift from the industrial economy to one dominated by information, digital innovation, and global connectivity.

5.6.1 Key Features of the Electronic Age

1. **Advancements in Technology:**
    - **Microminiaturisation**: The miniaturisation of electronic components led to smaller, more powerful, and versatile devices.

- **Large-Scale Integration (LSI)**: Enabled compact devices with enhanced processing power, such as smartphones and wearables.
- **Enhanced Storage**: Devices became capable of storing vast amounts of data in reduced physical space, transitioning from floppy disks to cloud storage.

2. **Innovative Devices and Systems:**
   - Computers became smaller, with the introduction of laptops, notebooks, and handheld devices such as smartphones, personal digital assistants (PDAs), iPods, iPads, and smartwatches.
   - Transition from cathode-ray tube displays to flat-screen, terrestrial and OLED technologies for televisions and monitors.
   - Internet-based communication tools like **Voice over IP (VoIP)** revolutionised voice communication, challenging traditional telephony.

3. **Telecommunication and Networking:**
   - The Electronic Age brought about global communication networks, with the Internet enabling real-time connectivity and collaboration enabling instant connectivity across the globe.
   - Technologies like Wi-Fi, fibre optics, and mobile broadband became integral to both personal and professional life.

5.6.2 Impact on Human Life and Society

The Electronic Age has profoundly reshaped nearly every aspect of daily life, including:

- **Workplace Transformation**
   - Automation and digital tools streamlined operations, leading to cost savings but also job redundancies in traditional industries.
   - Remote work, facilitated by video conferencing tools, redefined office culture.

- **Digital Economy**
   - E-commerce platforms such as Amazon and Alibaba transformed retail practices.
   - Contactless payment technologies like e-wallets, swipe cards, and mobile payment apps replaced traditional cash transactions.

- **Education and Learning**
   - Online learning platforms democratised education, allowing access to quality resources across geographic and economic barriers.

- **Everyday Activities**

- Activities like online shopping, social media communication, and streaming entertainment became integral to daily life.

5.6.3 Socioeconomic Changes

The Electronic Age brought both opportunities and challenges:

- **Opportunities:**
    - Enhanced global connectivity and access to information fostered innovation and creativity spurring the growth of industries such as software development, artificial intelligence, and cybersecurity.
    - Global connectivity enabled collaboration across borders, fostering creativity and innovation.
    - New industries emerged, creating jobs in technology, digital marketing, and data analysis.

- **Challenges:**
    - Widespread worker displacement due to automation led to the need for closure of traditional businesses, reskilling programs and other socioeconomic shifts.
    - New legislation and policies were introduced to address issues like data privacy, cybersecurity, and intellectual property rights.

5.6.4 Defining Characteristics of the Electronic Age

The Electronic Age is marked by:

- Heavy reliance on computing technologies, the Internet, and digital sensors.
- The transformation of virtually all aspects of life, from communication and commerce to education and entertainment.
- The seamless integration of technology into human activities, enabling unparalleled productivity and connectivity.

The legacy of the Electronic Age lies in its ability to:

- Drive unprecedented innovation, fostering new industries and lifestyles.
- Present humanity with challenges requiring adaptation, such as navigating digital ethics and managing socioeconomic disparities.

This era continues to shape the modern world, ensuring that technology remains the cornerstone of how we interact, work, and thrive in an interconnected global society.

Fig. 6: Stacked smartphone, ipad, laptop devices

5.7 CLASSIFICATIONS OF COMPUTERS

Computers have undergone a remarkable evolution since their inception, transforming from basic machines into complex systems integral to modern life. This section explores the history of computers by their generational development, their classifications by functionality and type, and their categorisation by size. Thus provides a comprehensive understanding of how computing systems have evolved and how they continue to shape the future.

Fig. 5: A truncated evolution of Apple products, Laura Dishaw (Photo by edtechie99)

5.7.1 History of Computers by Generation

The history of computers can be divided into distinct generations, each characterised by technological advancements that significantly enhanced their functionality, efficiency, and versatility.

First Generation (1941–1956): The Vacuum Tube Era

- Early computers used vacuum tubes for circuitry, which were large, expensive, and prone to overheating.
- Programming was performed using machine language, requiring detailed and labour-intensive coding.

- **Key Developments:**

  o The **ENIAC (Electronic Numerical Integrator and Computer)** performed complex calculations at unprecedented speeds for its time.

  o The **UNIVAC I (Universal Automatic Computer)** marked the transition from experimental devices to practical commercial use.

- **Limitations:**

  o Bulky size, high energy consumption, and limited flexibility hindered widespread use.

The Zuse Z3, 1941, considered the world's first working programmable, fully automatic computing machine.

Courtesy of Wikimedia Commons

Second Generation (1956–1963): The Advent of Transistors

- The invention of **transistors** replaced vacuum tubes, reducing size and improving reliability and performance.

- Higher-level programming languages like COBOL and FORTRAN enabled more sophisticated software applications.

- **Example:**

  o The **IBM 1401**, a highly successful business computer, demonstrated the practical applications of this generation.

Third Generation (1964–1971): The Rise of Integrated Circuits

- **Integrated Circuits (ICs)** allowed multiple electronic components to be embedded on a single chip, enabling greater miniaturisation and efficiency.

- User-friendly features such as keyboards, monitors, and operating systems facilitated broader accessibility.

- **Example:**

  o The **IBM System/360**, a standardised computing platform, ensured compatibility across diverse applications.

Fourth Generation (1971–Present): The Microprocessor Revolution

- The **microprocessor** integrated a Central Processing Unit (CPU) onto a single chip, paving the way for personal computing.
- The era introduced **Graphical User Interfaces (GUIs)** and the Internet, revolutionising work and communication.
- **Examples:**
  - The **Apple II** was instrumental in popularising home computing.
  - The **IBM PC** became the benchmark for business and home computing systems.

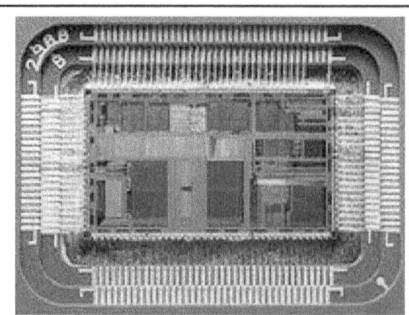

Die of an Intel 80486DX2 microprocessor (actual size: 12×6.75 mm) in its packaging. **Courtesy** of Wikimedia Commons

Fifth Generation (Present–Future): The Age of Artificial Intelligence (AI)

- Advanced technologies such as Artificial Intelligence (AI), quantum computing, and natural language processing define the current era.
- AI systems are revolutionising industries through applications like autonomous vehicles, virtual assistants, and machine learning.
- **Examples:**
  - **IBM Q System One**, a quantum computer, demonstrates the potential for unprecedented computational capabilities.
  - AI-powered tools such as **Alexa** and **Siri** showcase the integration of intelligence in daily life.

5.8 CLASSIFICATIONS BY FUNCTIONALITY

Computers can also be classified based on their functionality and the type of data they process. These classifications reflect the adaptability of computing systems to different tasks and data forms.

5.8.1 Analog Computers

- **Definition and Characteristics:**
  Analog computers are designed to process continuously varying data. These systems excel in handling physical phenomena, such as temperature, speed, and pressure, which change continuously over time. Unlike digital systems, they do not convert data into binary but represent it in physical quantities.

- **Historical Context:**
  Early analogue computers, like the Astrolabe and slide rules, laid the

foundation for modern analogue systems. The Differential Analyser, developed in the 1930s, is a notable example.

- **Applications:**
    - Measuring vehicle speed with speedometers.
    - Monitoring temperature changes using analogue thermometers.
    - Simulating flight conditions in aeronautics.

5.8.2 Digital Computers

- **Definition and Characteristics:**
  Digital computers operate on discrete binary data (0s and 1s). They form the backbone of modern computing systems and are versatile, reliable, and capable of complex data processing.

- **Historical Context:**
  ENIAC (1945) was one of the first digital computers, marking the beginning of the digital revolution.

- **Applications:**
    - Consumer devices like smartphones, laptops, and gaming consoles.
    - Business systems for data analysis and financial modelling.
    - Communication tools like email servers and VoIP systems.

5.8.3 Hybrid Computers

- **Definition and Characteristics:**
  Hybrid computers combine the functionalities of analogue and digital systems, enabling them to process both continuous and discrete data. They are commonly used in specialised fields requiring both types of data processing.

- **Historical Context:**
  Hybrid computers emerged as a response to the limitations of analogue and digital systems, finding applications in fields like medicine and military operations.

- **Applications:**
    - Medical devices, such as ECG machines, which convert analogue patient vitals into digital data for analysis.
    - Weather forecasting systems that integrate continuous environmental data with digital predictive models.

5.9 CLASSIFICATIONS BY SIZE

Computers are also categorised by size and performance capabilities, catering to a variety of needs and scales of operation.

5.9.1 Mainframe Computers

- **Definition and Characteristics:**
  Mainframes are large, powerful systems designed for enterprise-scale data processing and mission-critical applications. They are known for reliability, scalability, and the ability to handle massive amounts of data.

- **Historical Context:**
  The IBM 1401, introduced in the 1960s, revolutionised enterprise computing.

- **Applications:**
  - Banking and financial services, e.g., IBM Z Series.
  - Airline reservation systems and government census data processing.

5.9.2 Minicomputers

- **Definition and Characteristics:**
  Minicomputers, also known as mid-range computers, offer a balance between performance and cost, making them suitable for small to medium-scale tasks.

- **Historical Context:**
  The DEC PDP-11 (1970s) was instrumental in popularising this category.

- **Applications:**
  - Small business servers for inventory management.
  - Educational institutions for research and training.

5.9.3 Microcomputers

- **Definition and Characteristics:**
  Microcomputers are affordable, compact systems designed for personal and office use. They are commonly referred to as personal computers (PCs).

- **Historical Context:**
  The introduction of the IBM PC in 1981 marked the rise of microcomputers in everyday life.

- **Applications:**
  - Desktop systems like HP, Dell Inspiron for office tasks.
  - Portable devices such as Microsoft Surface, Apple MacBook for professional and personal use.

5.9.4 Supercomputers

- **Definition and Characteristics:**
  Supercomputers are built for high-performance tasks, including simulations, scientific research, and complex problem-solving. They boast unparalleled processing speed and power.

- **Historical Context:**
  Cray-1, introduced in 1976, set the benchmark for modern supercomputers.

- **Applications:**
  - Climate modelling, e.g., Fugaku supercomputer.
  - Advanced research in fields like genomics and astrophysics.

5.9.5 Ubiquitous Computers

- **Definition and Characteristics:**
  Also known as embedded systems, these computers are seamlessly integrated into everyday objects, driving the Internet of Things (IoT).

- **Historical Context:**
  Ubiquitous computing gained traction in the 21st century with the advent of smart devices.

- **Applications:**
  - Smart devices like Amazon Echo.
  - Wearable technologies such as Fitbit fitness trackers.

5.10 CLASSIFICATION BY DEGREE OF VERSATILITY

Computers can be classified based on their versatility and purpose, falling into two main categories: general-purpose computers and dedicated or special-purpose computers. This distinction highlights the adaptability of computing systems to various tasks or specific applications.

5.10.1 General-Purpose Computers

Definition and Characteristics
General-purpose computers are flexible machines designed to execute a wide range of instructions and solve diverse problems. They are versatile tools, and their functionality depends on the software applications installed, making them adaptable to numerous environments and industries.

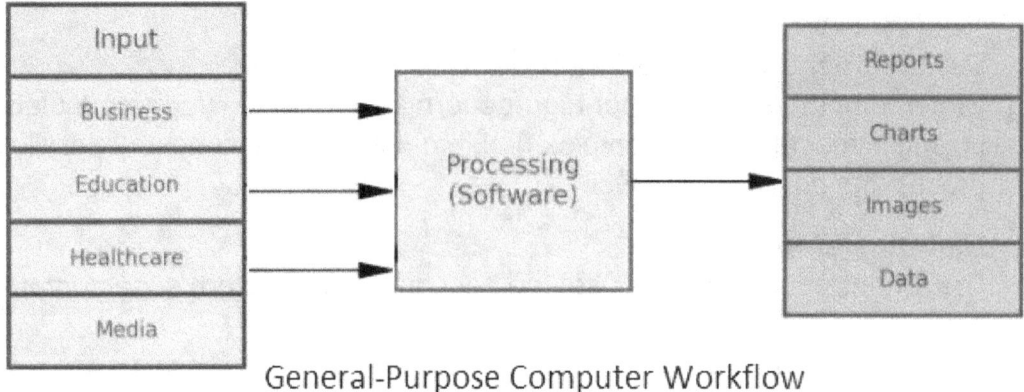
General-Purpose Computer Workflow

Diagram 1 - General-Purpose Computer Workflow: Illustrates the input from various industries, processing through adaptable software, and output in diverse forms like reports and charts.

Applications in Organisations and Use Cases

General-purpose computers are widely used in organisations for various data processing tasks, including:

- **Word Processing:**
  Application software like Microsoft Word, Google Docs enables users to create, edit, and format text documents with professional results. Common features include spell check, templates, and advanced typography tools.

- **Spreadsheets:**
  Programs such as Microsoft Excel, Google Sheets use a grid system to facilitate data entry, arithmetic calculations, and statistical analysis. They allow users to create visual data representations, such as charts and graphs, for decision-making.

- **Database Applications:**
  Examples include MySQL, Oracle Database and Microsoft Access, which allow for the collection, storage, and querying of complex data to produce insights tailored to specific organisational needs.

- **Graphics Packages:**
  Crafting visual content for business, creative projects, or desktop publishing, e.g., Adobe Illustrator, Canva. Graphics software is divided into three categories:

    - **Business Graphics:** For creating charts, graphs, and diagrams used in reports and presentations.

    - **Creative Graphics:** For designing images, illustrations, and multimedia using tools like Adobe Photoshop or CorelDRAW.

    - **Desktop Publishing (DTP):** For combining text and images to produce professional documents like flyers, posters, and newspapers. Advanced DTP software, such as Adobe InDesign, allows for precise layout and text manipulation.

- **Expert Systems:**
  These are AI-driven programs that provide advice or solutions in a specific domain. For instance, medical diagnostic systems assist healthcare professionals in diagnosing illnesses based on symptoms.

5.10 2 Dedicated or Special-Purpose Computers

Definition and Characteristics:

Dedicated or special-purpose computers are tailored to perform a specific task or solve a particular problem. Unlike general-purpose computers, their functionality is limited to the predefined scope of their design.

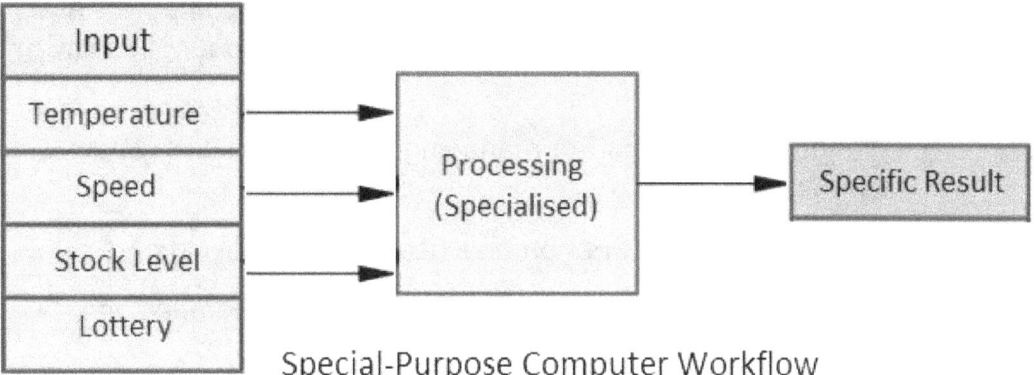

Special-Purpose Computer Workflow

Diagram 2 - Special-Purpose Computer Workflow: Focuses on specific inputs like temperature or speed, processed by dedicated systems, and yielding targeted results such as numerical data or controlled actions.

Applications:

- **Industry-Specific Systems:**

    - **CAD/CAM (Computer-Aided Design/Manufacturing):** Used in engineering and architecture to create precise models and automate production.

    - **Payroll Management Systems:** For automating employee salary calculations and payment processing.

    - **Stock Control Systems:** For tracking and managing inventory levels, orders, and managing supply chains and logistics.

    - **Weather Forecasting Models:** Advanced computations for simulating atmospheric conditions and predicting weather patterns.

    - **FE/HE FEMIS (Further/Higher Education Management Information Systems):** For managing student enrolment and academic records.

    - **Lottery Systems:** For automating lottery draws and ticket validation.

    - **EFTPOS (Electronic Funds Transfer at Point of Sale):** For secure and efficient financial transactions.

- **Industrial Applications:**
  Special-purpose computers are often integrated into automated manufacturing processes, such as:
    - Producing precision-engineered components like cams, gears, and wires.
    - **Robotics** - controlling industrial robots used in manufacturing to automate repetitive tasks like assembly, painting, or welding in factories.

- **Home Appliances:**
  Many modern appliances incorporate special-purpose computers and embedded processors to perform specialised tasks and functionality, including:
    - **Washing Machines:** For managing wash cycles and water temperature.
    - **Microwave Ovens:** For precise heating and cooking.
    - **Vacuum Cleaners:** For automated cleaning schedules and navigation.
    - **Smart refrigerators**: For precise cooling and chilling.

Advantages of Special-Purpose Computers:

- High efficiency in executing the specific tasks they are designed for.
- Optimised performance with minimal resource waste.
- Enhanced reliability due to their simplicity and focus on a singular purpose.

5.11 Illustrative Examples Across Eras

To appreciate the evolution of computing and its influence on society, we can examine key innovations across different eras:

- **Stone Age Tools:** Hand axes and scrapers represent early human ingenuity and problem-solving.
- **Nok Culture Artifacts:** Terracotta sculptures and iron tools from ancient Nigerian civilisations showcase early technological advancements.
- **Middle Age Manuscripts:** Illuminated texts highlight artistic and intellectual achievements.
- **Industrial Revolution Innovations:** Steam engines and mechanised tools demonstrate the transformative power of mechanisation.
- **Modern Digital Devices:** Smartphones, laptops, and IoT gadgets epitomise current technological progress, shaping how we work, communicate, and live.

Tutorial Activity 5 - Information Age

Quizzes and Questions

Multiple Choice Questions (MCQs)

1. Which of the following periods is marked by the development of tools primarily made of stone?
a) Bronze Age
b) Stone Age
c) Industrial Age
d) Information Age

2. The term "Information Age" is often used interchangeably with which of the following?
a) Electronic Age
b) Bronze Age
c) Agricultural Age
d) Space Age

3. What was a significant technological advancement of the Industrial Age?
a) Steam engines
b) Microprocessors
c) Blockchain
d) Cloud computing

4. What is the fundamental unit of data representation in computers?
a) Byte
b) Kilobyte
c) Bit
d) Word

5. Which age saw the first use of iron for tools and weapons?
a) Stone Age
b) Iron Age
c) Bronze Age
d) Information Age

6. Which of the following is a characteristic of first-generation computers?
a) Use of transistors
b) Use of vacuum tubes
c) Use of microprocessors
d) Use of cloud technology

7. Which type of computer is designed for a specific task, such as controlling industrial machines or managing appliances?
a) General-purpose computer

b) Supercomputer
c) Embedded system
d) Mainframe computer

8. Miniaturisation and the use of integrated circuits are defining features of which computer generation?
a) First
b) Second
c) Third
d) Fourth

9. What type of computer is most suitable for running large-scale simulations and complex scientific calculations?
a) Desktop computer
b) Supercomputer
c) Microcomputer
d) Tablet computer

10. Computers classified by size include which of the following categories?
a) Digital and analogue
b) Mainframe, micro, and supercomputers
c) Real-time and hybrid systems
d) Cloud-based and distributed systems

Short Answer Questions

1. Define the term "Information Age" and describe its significance.
2. Explain the difference between the Industrial Age and the Information Age.
3. What were some key tools developed during the Stone Age?
4. How has the transition from the Agricultural Age to the Information Age impacted societies?
5. List two key features of the Bronze Age.
6. Define the term "generation of computers" and explain how they are classified.
7. Differentiate between general-purpose computers and special-purpose computers. Provide an example for each.
8. List and explain the four classifications of computers based on size.
9. How do the developments in various information ages influence the classification of computers?
10. Identify one computer from each generation and describe its purpose.

True/False Questions

1. The Information Age began immediately after the Iron Age.
2. The Industrial Age introduced steam engines and mechanised production.
3. Microminiaturisation is a feature of the Stone Age.
4. In the Information Age, digital technologies became a central part of life.
5. Grinding stones from the Stone Age are still used in some parts of the world today.
6. Mainframe computers are smaller than microcomputers.
7. The fifth generation of computers focuses on artificial intelligence and machine learning.
8. Embedded systems are classified based on their size.
9. The use of vacuum tubes marked the first generation of computers.
10. Laptops are considered a type of microcomputer.

Essay Questions

1. Discuss the impact of the Information Age on education and communication.
2. Compare and contrast the Stone Age and the Information Age in terms of tools, lifestyle, and societal structure.
3. Discuss the classification of computers based on functionality, providing examples for real-time systems, general-purpose systems, and embedded systems.
4. How have technological developments in the Information Age influenced the classification and evolution of computer generations?

Chapter 6: Bridging the Digital Divide and Evolving Economies

Learning Outcomes:

By the end of this Chapter, learners will be able to:

- Explain the Concept of the Digital Divide: Understand the socio-economic and geographic factors contributing to the digital divide.
- Identify key concepts and factors contributing to the digital divide.
- Differentiate Between Old and New Economies: Identify the key differences between traditional and digital-based economies, particularly in terms of production methods, resource use, and value generation.
- Explain the Limitations of the Old Economy: Understand the labour-intensive and resource-heavy nature of the old economy.
- State the Benefits of the New Economy: Recognise the advantages that digital technologies bring to productivity, cost-efficiency, and global economic development.
- Explore strategies to bridge the digital divide.
- Analyse the impact of the digital divide on society.

6.1 OVERVIEW

The concept of the digital divide is fundamental in understanding the disparities that exist between those who have access to technology and those who do not. In today's world, access to digital resources such as the internet, computers, and mobile devices plays a crucial role in education, employment, and communication. The digital divide is not only a matter of physical access to devices but also includes gaps in digital skills, quality of access, and the ability to use technology effectively.

6.1.2 What is the Digital Divide?

The digital divide refers to the gap between individuals, households, or countries that have adequate access to modern information and communication technologies (ICTs) and those who do not. The term first gained prominence in the early 1990s as technological advancements surged, leading to an unequal distribution of internet access, digital skills, and devices such as computers, smartphones, and tablets.

- **Physical Access**: The disparity in owning devices like computers or smartphones.
- **Digital Skills**: The ability to use technology effectively.
- **Quality of Access**: Includes internet speed, device quality, and availability of technological infrastructure.

Origins and Evolution:

- **Early 1990s**: The term gained prominence as computer ownership and internet usage began to spread unevenly across different communities.

- **Political Recognition**: In 1996, U.S. President Bill Clinton and Vice President Al Gore highlighted the digital divide during a political address in Knoxville, Tennessee, emphasizing its impact on education and economic opportunities.

Globally, the digital divide is observed between developed and developing nations, but it also exists within countries, often correlated with income levels, geographic location (urban vs. rural), gender, age, and education.

Example: In the United Kingdom, low-income households are less likely to have broadband access, while in rural areas of Africa or Asia, entire regions may lack stable internet connections, deepening the digital divide.

Key Concepts and Factors

- **Access to Technology:** Availability of computers, internet connectivity, and modern devices.

- **Economic Disparities & Affordability:** The cost associated with acquiring and maintaining ICT tools. Limited financial resources prevent access to devices and internet services.

- **Digital Literacy:** The ability to effectively use digital devices and navigate the internet.

- **Geographical Barriers & Disparities:** Differences in ICT access between urban and rural areas. Rural and remote areas often lack reliable internet infrastructure.

- **Educational Gaps & Opportunities:** Impact on learning and skill development. Lack of digital literacy and education impedes effective technology use.

- **Age Differences**: Older populations may have less familiarity with new technologies.

6.1.3 Digital Divide and Education

One of the most concerning impacts of the digital divide is on education. Schools with more resources can offer students better access to technology, often translating into better educational outcomes. Disadvantaged schools, on the other hand, might lack both devices and internet access, further widening the gap in learning opportunities.

- **Access to Technology in Schools**: In wealthier regions, students might have daily access to computers and the internet, while in underfunded schools, access might be limited to a few hours a week.

- **Home Access**: Students from higher socio-economic backgrounds typically have access to technology at home, whereas lower-income students often rely solely on school or public resources like libraries or internet cafes.
- **Teacher Training**: Providing technology is insufficient without proper training. Teachers must know how to effectively integrate technology into their teaching methods to close the gap in digital literacy.

Example: In a classroom where only 40% of students have computers at home, these students may have a clear advantage over their peers when it comes to completing assignments and accessing online learning resources.

6.1.4 The Old Economy vs. The New Economy

Old Economy Features

The **old economy** is characterised by traditional, labour-intensive industries such as manufacturing, agriculture, and services that rely heavily on physical labour and mechanical processes. Key features include:

- **Time-Consuming**: Processes take longer due to manual work.
- **Labour-Intensive**: Heavy reliance on human workers, which increases operational costs.
- **Mechanical**: Based on physical machinery rather than digital automation.
- **Constrained by Space and Time**: Goods and services are often limited to local markets due to the costs and difficulty of transportation and communication.

New Economy Features:

The **new economy**, driven by digital and information technologies, has redefined how businesses operate. It is characterised by automation, digital communication, and global reach. Key features include:

- **Digital**: Operations and transactions are often automated and based on digital systems.
- **Time and Distance Are Irrelevant**: The internet allows instant global communication and transactions, making geographic limitations insignificant.
- **Knowledge-Based**: The workforce relies more on intellectual capabilities rather than physical labour.
- **Technology-Driven**: The use of computers, software, and internet-based tools defines the new economy.

Comparison Table

Feature	Old Economy	New Economy
Time Consumption	High, due to manual processes	Low, automated processes
Labor Dependency	High	Low, reliant on technology
Operational Basis	Mechanical	Digital
Geographical Limits	Significant constraints	Minimal constraints

Limitations of the Old Economy

The old economy, while foundational, presents significant limitations in the modern world:

1. **Labour Intensiveness**: High dependence on manual labour makes tasks time-consuming and less efficient.

2. **High Costs**: Production and manufacturing costs are higher due to inefficiencies, manual labour, and slower processes.

3. **Low Productivity**: The output is often low in comparison to the resources and time invested.

4. **Logistical Challenges**: High costs of transportation and storage further reduce the profitability of old economy industries.

Benefits of the New Economy

The **new economy** offers numerous advantages over the old economy, particularly in terms of efficiency and innovation:

1. **Low Capital for Business Start-Up**: Digital businesses require less capital to launch, as many tools and platforms are available at low or no cost.

2. **Higher Productivity**: Automation and digital tools significantly boost productivity by reducing manual input.

3. **Lower Production Costs**: Automated processes and digital tools lower costs while increasing output.

4. **Global Reach**: Digital technologies enable businesses to operate globally, overcoming geographic and time-based limitations.

5. **Enhanced Security and Information Systems**: The sophistication of digital systems ensures better protection and data management.

6. **Job Creation and New Opportunities**: The digital economy creates new roles in IT, e-commerce, digital marketing, and more.

Example: The shift from manufacturing physical goods to offering digital services like cloud computing allows companies to operate with lower overhead costs, faster delivery, and higher profitability.

This understanding of the digital divide and the transition from the old economy to the new economy highlights the crucial role technology plays in shaping modern life, business, and education. Closing the digital divide is essential for creating a more inclusive, equitable society where everyone has the opportunity to thrive in the new economy.

6.1.5 Impact of the Digital Divide

- **Economic Inequality:** Limited access can hinder job opportunities and economic advancement.
- **Educational Disparities:** Students without ICT access may fall behind academically.
- **Social Exclusion:** Individuals may miss out on social interactions and community engagement facilitated by ICT.
- **Healthcare Access:** Reduced ability to access online health information and services.

6.1.6 Strategies to Bridge the Digital Divide:

- **Infrastructure Development**: Expanding broadband access to underserved areas.
- **Affordable Technology**: Providing low-cost devices and internet plans.
- **Digital Literacy Programs**: Offering training and education to improve technology skills.
- **Government Initiatives**: Implementing policies that promote equitable access to ICT.

6.1.7 Illustration & Quantification:

- **Global Statistics**: According to the International Telecommunication Union (ITU), as of 2023, approximately 37% of the world's population remains offline, exacerbating global inequalities.
- **Impact of Digital Divide**: Countries with higher internet penetration rates (e.g., South Korea at 96%) versus lower rates (e.g., Afghanistan at 14%).
- In developed countries, the digital divide affects around 15% of the population, while in developing nations, it impacts up to 60%.

Digital Divide: Countries with higher internet penetration rates (e.g., South Korea at 86%) versus lower rates (e.g., Afghanistan at 14%).

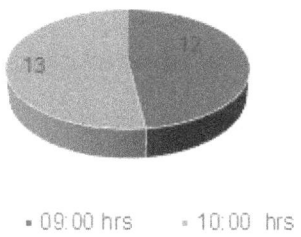

Figure 2a: Global Digital Divide Statistics

Activity 1:

1. **Define the Digital Divide**: What is the digital divide, and how does it affect different regions or groups?

2. **Differentiate Between Old and New Economies**: What are three key differences between the old and new economies in terms of technology and productivity?

3. **State Three Disadvantages of the Old Economy**: What are the limitations of the old economy that hinder growth and innovation?

4. **List Four Benefits of the New Economy**: How has the new economy improved business operations and global communication?

Activity 2:

Analyse the Digital Divide in Your Community

1. **Research:** Investigate the level of ICT access in different socio-economic groups within your community.

2. **Survey:** Conduct surveys to gather data on digital literacy and device availability.

3. **Report:** Present your findings, highlighting the factors contributing to the digital divide and proposing solutions to bridge the gap.

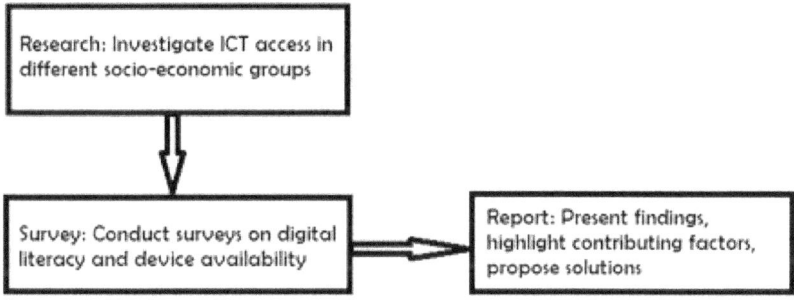

Figure 2b: Analyse the Digital Divide in your Community

Tutorial Activity 6 - Bridging the Digital Divide and Evolving Economies

Quiz and Questions

Multiple Choice Questions

1. **What does the term "digital divide" primarily refer to?**
    - A) The gap between urban and rural areas
    - B) The unequal access to digital technologies and internet services
    - C) Differences in educational systems between countries
    - D) The economic disparity between rich and poor nations

2. **Which of the following is a key characteristic of the old economy?**
    - A) Reliance on digital technologies
    - B) Labour-intensive production methods
    - C) Cost-efficiency and scalability
    - D) Global accessibility of resources

3. **What is one primary benefit of the new economy?**
    - A) Increased dependency on natural resources
    - B) Focus on manual labour for production
    - C) Enhanced global connectivity and collaboration
    - D) Reliance on outdated technologies

4. **Which strategy is most effective for bridging the digital divide?**
    - A) Investing in renewable energy
    - B) Expanding access to high-speed internet in underserved areas
    - C) Promoting traditional agricultural methods
    - D) Reducing global trade partnerships

5. **How does the digital divide impact societies?**
    - A) It reduces technological innovation globally.
    - B) It widens economic inequality and limits access to opportunities.
    - C) It strengthens traditional industries.
    - D) It improves access to healthcare and education.

Short Answer Questions

1. Define the digital divide and list two factors contributing to it.
2. What are three key differences between old and new economies?
3. What are two limitations of the old economy?
4. State three benefits of the new economy.
5. List two strategies to bridge the digital divide.

Analytical Question

1. Discuss how bridging the digital divide can contribute to global economic development. Provide two examples to support your answer.

Chapter 7: The ICT Professional: A Comprehensive Guide to Roles, Skills, Ethics, and Careers

Learning Outcomes

By the end of this chapter, learners will be able to:

1. Understand the roles and contributions of ICT professionals in various domains.
2. Analyse ethical and legal considerations in ICT, including GDPR and professional codes of conduct.
3. Develop key technical and soft skills for effective performance in ICT roles.
4. Explore career paths and opportunities for growth within the ICT industry.
5. Recognise the importance of professional bodies like BCS in promoting standards and ethics.
6. Identify future trends in ICT, such as AI, cloud computing, and green computing.
7. Apply technical expertise and ethical practices to real-world ICT scenarios.

7.1 THE ICT PROFESSIONAL

The rapid evolution of Information and Communication Technology (ICT) has created a demand for skilled professionals capable of navigating complex technological landscapes. The ICT professional is pivotal in driving innovation, managing systems, and ensuring the seamless integration of technology into organisational processes.

An ICT professional encompasses a diverse range of roles, from software developers and network engineers to data analysts and cybersecurity specialists. These individuals possess a blend of technical expertise, problem-solving abilities, and a deep understanding of emerging technologies to address modern challenges in business, education, healthcare, and beyond.

This chapter delves into the key attributes, roles, and responsibilities of ICT professionals, highlighting their critical contributions to the digital economy. It explores their competencies in areas such as system design, project management, and stakeholder collaboration, as well as the ethical and professional standards that guide their practice.

As the digital landscape continues to evolve, ICT professionals play a central role in shaping future innovations and driving sustainable technological growth.

7.1.1 Legal Context of ICT: Social, Moral, and Ethical Issues

The rapid expansion and integration of ICT into all aspects of life have created complex social, moral, and ethical challenges. These challenges influence how ICT is perceived and applied in society, impacting areas such as privacy, employment, equity, and professional responsibility. Addressing these issues requires thoughtful policies, ethical frameworks, and public awareness. Below is a detailed examination of key areas:

7.2.2 Social Issues in the Introduction and Use of ICT

The introduction of ICT brings transformative changes to industries, communities, and individual lives. However, these changes often come with unintended consequences, such as shifts in employment patterns, disparities in access to technology, and challenges in managing information control. New policies and innovative initiatives are essential to mitigate these challenges and promote equitable benefits.

7.2.3 Job Loss and Workforce Displacement

The automation of processes, a hallmark of ICT, often leads to job displacement, particularly in roles traditionally performed by humans.

- **Example**: The adoption of self-checkout systems in retail has reduced the reliance on cashier roles, potentially improving customer convenience but leading to workforce displacement.

- **Solution Illustration**: Companies like Amazon have implemented reskilling programs to help affected employees transition to new roles. For instance, displaced workers can train in managing automated systems or gain expertise in data analytics and system maintenance.

7.2.4 Access to Information and the Digital Divide

ICT has the potential to empower individuals by providing access to critical services, yet disparities in access can exacerbate social and economic inequalities.

- **Issue**: Communities in remote or underserved areas often face limited access to reliable internet, hindering education, healthcare, and economic opportunities. This "digital divide" represents a significant barrier to global equity.

- **Case Study**: India's Digital India initiative seeks to bridge this divide by investing in rural internet infrastructure. This initiative has expanded access to digital services in underserved regions, enabling improvements in education, healthcare delivery, and business opportunities.

7.2.5 Control Over Information and Access

- The centralization of information within ICT platforms raises critical ethical questions about data ownership, privacy, and the influence of technology providers.

- **Power Dynamics Example**: Companies like Meta (Facebook) and X (formerly Twitter) manage vast quantities of user data, giving them significant influence over how information is disseminated and used.
- **Historical Context**: The control of information is not a new concern. During the early 20th century, figures like Joseph Goebbels, Nazi Minister of Propaganda, leveraged media to manipulate public perception. Today, similar challenges persist as ICT firms are scrutinized for ethical management of user data and influence over societal narratives.

7.3 MORAL ISSUES IN ICT USAGE

ICT usage brings up moral considerations that address privacy, content regulation, and responsible use of technology.

7.3.1 Privacy Concerns in ICT

- Surveillance technologies, like CCTV in public places such as the Hong Kong Metro, provide safety monitoring but can also intrude on individual privacy. This footage, if misused, raises ethical concerns about how much personal privacy is sacrificed for security.
- **Example**: The European Union's General Data Protection Regulation (GDPR) enforces strict rules on data privacy, requiring businesses to seek explicit user consent before collecting personal data and setting strict penalties for data misuse.

7.3.2 Content Regulation and Harmful Material

- **Example**: Social media platforms have faced backlash for failing to control harmful or explicit content. For instance, YouTube has implemented AI-based filters to flag and remove inappropriate material, but ethical accountability remains on how effectively these systems moderate content and ensure user safety.

7.3.3 Ethical Issues in ICT Practice

ICT professionals and organisations have significant ethical responsibilities that guide their conduct and decision-making. These responsibilities are essential for fostering trust, ensuring fairness, and minimising harm in the development, deployment, and use of technology. Ethical practices in ICT are not merely aspirational but foundational to sustainable and responsible innovation. Below are some key ethical issues and their implications:

Privacy and Data Protection

ICT professionals must handle user data with care, ensuring it is collected, stored, and used transparently and securely.

- **Issue**: Unethical data practices, such as unauthorised collection or sharing of personal information, can lead to privacy breaches.

- **Example**: High-profile data breaches in companies like Equifax and Facebook have highlighted the risks of poor data governance and the ethical obligation to protect user information.

Equity and Accessibility

Ensuring that ICT solutions are inclusive and accessible to all is a critical ethical responsibility.

- **Issue**: Products and services that ignore the needs of people with disabilities or underserved communities contribute to digital exclusion.
- **Example**: Ethical ICT design includes accessibility features like screen readers and text-to-speech options to accommodate diverse user needs.

Algorithmic Fairness and Bias

ICT professionals must design algorithms that promote fairness and avoid perpetuating biases.

- **Issue**: Biased algorithms can lead to discriminatory practices in areas like hiring, lending, and law enforcement.
- **Example**: Ethical frameworks for AI development, such as those promoted by organisations like IEEE, emphasize the need for fairness, accountability, and transparency in algorithmic decision-making.

Professional Integrity

ICT practitioners have a duty to act with honesty and integrity, avoiding conflicts of interest and unethical behaviours.

- **Issue**: Practices such as plagiarism, misrepresentation of qualifications, or engaging in unauthorised activities undermine professional credibility.
- **Example**: Codes of conduct from organisations like ACM (Association for Computing Machinery) provide guidelines for ethical ICT practices.

Environmental Responsibility

The ICT sector must consider the environmental impacts of its activities, such as electronic waste and energy consumption.

- **Issue**: The production and disposal of ICT equipment contribute to environmental degradation.
- **Example**: Ethical ICT practices include promoting sustainable designs, recycling initiatives, and energy-efficient technologies.

Cybersecurity and Ethical Hacking

Maintaining robust cybersecurity measures is both a technical and ethical responsibility.

- **Issue**: While ethical hacking aims to identify vulnerabilities, misuse of hacking skills for personal gain or harm breaches ethical norms.

- **Example**: ICT professionals must operate within legal and ethical boundaries, adhering to established protocols when testing systems for vulnerabilities.

7.3.4 Employer and Worker Ethics in ICT

- **Employer Obligations**: Employers in ICT have a duty to provide training and development opportunities to keep employees competitive in a rapidly changing field. For instance, if an IT department adopts new software, it's ethically responsible for offering adequate training to reduce the risk of skill gaps.
- **Worker Obligations**: Workers facing job instability may encounter ethical decisions, like whether to share honest assessments of job stability with analysts or managers, especially when such information could affect financial projections or resource allocations.

7.3.5 Professional Codes of Conduct

- **Guideline Example**: Many organisations adopt ethical codes similar to those established by professional bodies like the British Computer Society (BCS). These codes emphasize principles like transparency, fairness, and accountability, which help foster trust in ICT practices by promoting responsible use and management of technology.

7.4 ESSENTIAL SKILLS AND QUALITIES NEEDED BY ICT PROFESSIONALS

ICT professionals require a balanced mix of technical expertise and interpersonal skills to navigate complex technological environments and work effectively within teams. Below is an in-depth look at these essential skills:

7.4.1 Technical Skills with Illustrative Examples

- **Oral and Written Communication Skills**: ICT professionals must often explain technical concepts to colleagues with limited technical knowledge. For instance, an IT consultant explaining a network upgrade's benefits to an HR manager would need to simplify jargon, focusing on productivity improvements and reduced downtime.
- **Problem-Solving Skills**: Effective troubleshooting is critical in ICT roles, where technical issues can arise at any time. For example, a helpdesk support technician may need to remotely diagnose a software issue affecting multiple employees, applying analytical skills to identify and resolve the problem efficiently.
- **Documentation Skills**: Clear, structured documentation underpins consistent, efficient operations. A software developer, for instance, may create user manuals for a new app, ensuring they are accessible to both beginners and advanced users. Well-documented systems also help new team members understand project nuances quickly.

7.4.2 Core Abilities Needed by ICT Staff

- **Team Collaboration**: ICT projects frequently span various departments and require coordinated efforts. For example, developing an e-commerce website involves input from designers (for user interface), backend developers (for functionality), and project managers (for timeline adherence), emphasizing the need for seamless collaboration.

- **Adaptability and Continuous Learning**: In technology, staying updated is essential. A network administrator, for instance, may need to keep pace with evolving cybersecurity protocols to ensure organisational security, demonstrating a commitment to continuous learning.

- **Pressure Management**: Many ICT roles involve high-stakes situations where quick, composed action is necessary. Deploying new software under tight deadlines requires resilience and calm decision-making.

7.4.3 Personal Qualities of ICT Staff

- **Patience and Initiative**: Working with complex systems often demands patience, especially when issues are difficult to troubleshoot. For example, a database administrator updating a system during off-peak hours to prevent operational disruptions shows initiative and foresight in managing responsibilities.

- **Responsibility and Accountability**: Managing sensitive data, like patient records, requires legal and ethical accountability. A data analyst working with client data, for instance, must secure and respect user privacy while abiding by data protection regulations.

7.4.4 Responsibilities of ICT Professionals

- **Ethical Accountability**: ICT professionals must weigh the ethical implications of their actions, particularly concerning data security and privacy. For example, a software developer handling personal user information must follow security protocols to prevent unauthorised access and misuse.

- **Client Care and Professional Image**: The interactions between ICT professionals and clients reflect on the company's reputation. Positive client experiences often hinge on attentive, respectful, and transparent communication, fostering long-term relationships and trust.

7.5. SKILLS BEYOND TECHNICAL EXPERTISE

For career advancement, ICT professionals benefit from developing strategic, business, and leadership skills. These abilities allow them to contribute to organisational growth and innovation beyond daily technical tasks.

7.5.1 Strategic Planning

- **Example**: Senior IT managers use strategic planning to align technology investments with business objectives, like adopting a customer relationship management (CRM) system to streamline customer support and improve response times. This alignment ensures that technology initiatives support long-term business goals.

7.5.2 Management Information Systems (MIS) Skills

- **Application**: Executives and senior ICT professionals use MIS tools, such as Executive Information Systems (EIS), for data-driven decision-making. By analysing market trends, tracking performance metrics, and forecasting organisational needs, they can make informed decisions that guide the company towards growth and efficiency.

7.5.3 Illustrative Scenario: Integrating Skills and Qualities

Imagine an ICT project to implement a secure, cloud-based data management system for a healthcare provider. Below is how these skills and qualities come into play:

- **Communication Skills**: The lead ICT professional must communicate with healthcare staff to understand specific requirements, like data accessibility for remote consultations. The information is then conveyed clearly to the development team.

- **Problem-Solving**: Challenges arise with data transfer and compatibility. The team collaboratively troubleshoots using analytical skills to resolve technical issues swiftly.

- **Strategic Planning**: Project leaders align the new system with business goals, focusing on scalability for future needs, like remote patient care.

- **Ethics and Responsibility**: Due to the sensitivity of patient data, the team ensures the system complies with legal standards like GDPR, protecting data privacy and fostering client trust.

In this scenario, each skill, ability, and quality reinforce the others, creating a cohesive, effective team that successfully implements a secure, scalable solution aligned with business goals and ethical standards.

7.5.4 Codes of Practice vs. Legal Requirements

Understanding the distinction between codes of practice and legal requirements is crucial for ICT professionals, as each framework has different implications for professional conduct and accountability.

- **Code of Practice (Self-Regulation)**: A code of practice is a set of voluntary guidelines established by a professional body, such as the British Computer Society (BCS) or the Institute of Electrical and Electronics Engineers (IEEE). These codes encourage professionals to maintain high standards of ethical behaviour, integrity, and transparency. While these codes outline best practices and ethical standards, they do not carry legal penalties for non-compliance. Instead, they focus on self-regulation, where professionals are expected to hold themselves accountable to industry standards. For instance:

- **BCS Code of Conduct**: This includes requirements to prioritise the public interest, maintain professional competence, and uphold client confidentiality. Violating this code can lead to loss of professional membership but not to legal penalties.

- **IEEE Code of Ethics**: Encourages professionals to work ethically, avoid harm, and be honest about their work's impact on society.

- **Legal Requirements**: These are enforceable laws established by government bodies that ICT professionals must follow. Unlike codes of practice, which rely on self-regulation, legal requirements carry penalties for non-compliance, such as fines or imprisonment. Key examples include:

  - **General Data Protection Regulation (GDPR)**: A European Union law mandating strict data privacy requirements. Organisations must obtain explicit consent from users before collecting personal data. Non-compliance can lead to significant fines.

  - **Computer Misuse Act**: A UK law criminalising unauthorised access to computer systems. Under this act, hacking, data theft, and unauthorised system manipulation are punishable offenses.

7.5.5 Professional Body Example:

Professional organisations like the BCS support both legal compliance and ethical practices by providing ICT professionals with guidelines, self-regulatory practices, and professional development resources. BCS members are encouraged to follow both their code of conduct and legal standards, creating a dual layer of accountability that strengthens professional integrity within the ICT field.

7.6 ROLE OF PROFESSIONAL BODIES IN ICT

Professional bodies, such as the British Computer Society (BCS), play a crucial role in setting industry standards, promoting continuous development, and fostering ethical conduct in ICT.

- **Professional Development**: Through certifications, workshops, and training, professional bodies provide members with opportunities to advance their skills. BCS, for example, offers certifications in areas like project management, cybersecurity, and data analysis, enabling ICT professionals to stay competitive and compliant with evolving industry demands.

- **Ethical Oversight**: Bodies like BCS establish and promote codes of conduct, ensuring that ICT professionals adhere to ethical guidelines. These guidelines encourage members to consider the public interest, maintain client confidentiality, and prioritise cybersecurity measures, helping build trust within the industry and with the public.

- **Networking and Support**: Many professional bodies organise special interest groups (SIGs) where ICT professionals collaborate, share knowledge, and explore emerging trends. For instance, BCS hosts SIGs focused on fields like AI, software engineering, and health informatics, providing platforms for professionals to stay connected and informed on industry developments.

- **Industry Advocacy**: Professional bodies often advocate for policies and standards that protect professionals and consumers. For example, the BCS actively engages with regulatory bodies to address cybersecurity policies, data privacy concerns, and education standards, ensuring the ICT industry remains secure, ethical, and forward-looking.

7.7 CAREER OPPORTUNITIES FOR ICT PROFESSIONALS

ICT professionals have access to a diverse range of career paths that blend technical expertise with problem-solving, customer service, and ethical responsibility. Below are some key roles with insights:

- **Systems Analyst**
    - **Function**: Systems analysts liaise with clients to understand business requirements, then translate these needs into technical specifications for developers. They create detailed plans to improve system efficiency and effectiveness.
    - **Example**: Working in a healthcare setting, a systems analyst might develop a patient data management system that improves data accessibility for medical staff while ensuring compliance with privacy laws.

- **Software Developer**
    - **Function**: Developers design, write, and test code to create software applications, ranging from mobile apps to complex business systems. They work closely with clients to ensure the software meets user needs.
    - **Example Project**: Developing a custom payroll system for a mid-sized company that automates payroll processing, integrates with employee attendance records, and calculates tax deductions in real-time.

- **Database Administrator (DBA)**
  - **Function**: DBAs manage and secure an organisation's databases, ensuring data is stored efficiently, remains accessible, and is protected from unauthorised access.
  - **Example**: A DBA at a bank might oversee a customer database, managing backup procedures, implementing data encryption, and creating access controls to protect sensitive customer information.

- **Cybersecurity Specialist**
  - **Function**: Cybersecurity specialists protect networks and systems from threats like hacking, data breaches, and ransomware attacks. They identify vulnerabilities, create security protocols, and monitor networks for suspicious activity.
  - **Example**: A cybersecurity specialist at a tech company might design a system-wide security policy, monitor potential phishing attempts, and conduct security audits to maintain a robust defence against cyber threats.

- **Web Developer**
  - **Function**: Web developers design and maintain websites, focusing on aesthetics, usability, and functionality. They work to create user-friendly, accessible, and secure websites.
  - **Example**: A web developer at an e-commerce firm might design a website with easy navigation, secure payment options, and fast loading times to improve the customer shopping experience.

These roles involve technical skills as well as collaborative problem-solving, customer orientation, and adherence to ethical standards, making them dynamic and rewarding career choices.

7.8 FUTURE DIRECTIONS AND EMERGING TRENDS IN ICT CAREERS

ICT continues to evolve rapidly, and professionals must stay informed of emerging trends that will shape the future of the field. Below are three key areas to watch:

- **AI and Machine Learning**:

  With AI technology advancing rapidly, ICT professionals specialising in AI are creating predictive models, recommendation algorithms, and automation solutions. AI skills are valuable for developing customer support chatbots, financial forecasting tools, and fraud detection systems. This field offers diverse opportunities for innovation in sectors like healthcare, finance, and retail.

- **Cloud Computing**:

  As businesses increasingly move their operations to cloud platforms, expertise in cloud architecture is essential. Cloud architects design and manage cloud infrastructure, while cloud security specialists focus on securing data in cloud environments. These roles support business scalability, cost-efficiency, and collaboration, making cloud computing expertise highly sought after in the ICT field.

- **Cybersecurity**:

Cyber threats continue to increase, creating a high demand for cybersecurity professionals. These specialists protect sensitive information, maintain regulatory compliance, and secure data from unauthorised access. Emerging trends, like zero-trust security models and AI-driven threat detection, are becoming key tools in cybersecurity, highlighting the need for professionals skilled in these areas to mitigate evolving digital risks.

7.9 EMBRACING GREEN COMPUTING

Green computing, also known as **green IT**, refers to environmentally sustainable practices in the design, production, use, and disposal of computers and other electronic devices. It focuses on reducing the environmental impact of IT operations by conserving energy, minimising waste, and promoting the use of eco-friendly technologies. Green computing is integral to modern IT strategies, as it balances technological advancements with ecological responsibility.

7.9.1 Key Aspects of Green Computing:

- **Energy Efficiency**
    - Developing energy-saving technologies for computers and data centres (e.g., energy-efficient processors, power management features).
    - Using renewable energy sources to power IT infrastructure.

- **Eco-Friendly Manufacturing**
    - Employing sustainable materials in the production of electronic devices.
    - Reducing the use of hazardous substances (e.g., lead, mercury).

- **Optimised Use of Resources**
    - Implementing virtualisation to reduce the number of physical servers.
    - Using thin clients and cloud computing to minimise hardware usage.

- **Recycling and Proper Disposal**
    - Promoting the recycling of electronic waste (e-waste) to recover valuable materials and reduce landfill waste.
    - Ensuring safe disposal of toxic components in compliance with environmental regulations.

- **Green Software Design**
    - Creating software that optimises hardware use to save energy.
    - Ensuring applications are efficient and require minimal computational resources.

- **Extending Equipment Life**
    - Encouraging the reuse or donation of older devices.
    - Repairing and upgrading hardware rather than replacing it.

7.9.2 Benefits of Green Computing:

- **Environmental Protection:** Reduces carbon footprint and e-waste.
- **Cost Savings:** Energy-efficient systems lower electricity bills.
- **Sustainability:** Encourages long-term, responsible use of technology.
- **Regulatory Compliance:** Meets global standards for environmental conservation.

Activity 7 Answers - The ICT Professional: A Comprehensive Guide to Roles, Skills, Ethics, and Careers

Quizzes and Questions

Quiz 1: Roles of ICT Professionals

1. **Question:** Name three key roles of ICT professionals in an organisation.

2. **Question:** What is the primary responsibility of a Network Engineer?
   - **Answer:** To design, implement, and maintain computer networks, ensuring seamless connectivity and security.

3. **Question:** Which ICT role is responsible for securing an organisation's digital assets?

Quiz 2: Skills Required for ICT Professionals

1. **Question:** List two technical skills essential for a Software Developer.

2. **Question:** Why are communication skills important for ICT professionals?

3. **Question:** Identify one emerging skill that ICT professionals should acquire to stay relevant.

Quiz 3: Ethics in ICT

1. **Question:** Why is ethical behaviour important for ICT professionals?

2. **Question:** Provide an example of an unethical action in the ICT field.

3. **Question:** Which professional code of ethics governs ICT professionals in many countries?

Quiz 4: ICT Careers

1. **Question:** Name three career paths available to ICT professionals.

2. **Question:** Which ICT career focuses on designing and managing databases?

3. **Question:** What is the role of an ICT Consultant?

Quiz 5: Future Trends in ICT

1. **Question:** Predict one way that artificial intelligence (AI) may evolve in the future.

2. **Question:** What is the role of quantum computing in future ICT trends?

3. **Question:** Name one challenge associated with future ICT developments.

Classroom Discussion Topics

- Discuss the ethical implications of future ICT trends such as AI and virtual reality.

- Discuss the impact of ethics on the reputation and effectiveness of ICT professionals.
- Debate the relevance of continuous professional development for ICT careers in a fast-evolving industry.
- Explore the role of ICT professionals in advancing sustainability through green computing.

Chapter 8: Capabilities & Limitations of Computers & ICT

Learning Outcome

By the end of this chapter, learners will be able to:

- Trace the historical development of computers and ICT and their evolving applications.
- Evaluate the capabilities of modern computers, including high-speed processing, data storage, and real-time communication.
- Identify limitations and challenges in ICT, such as processing constraints, over-reliance, and ethical considerations.
- Explore emerging technologies like nanotechnology, AI, quantum computing, and high-speed networks and their societal impacts.
- Assess the implications of technological advancements on privacy, security, and societal integration.

8. INTRODUCTION

In today's fast-evolving technological landscape, computers and Information and Communication Technology (ICT) have become indispensable in nearly every facet of modern life. From automating repetitive tasks to revolutionising global communication and enabling groundbreaking scientific research, the capabilities of computers and ICT are vast. They have profoundly impacted industries such as finance, healthcare, education, entertainment, and logistics, reshaping how we work, learn, and interact.

However, despite these remarkable advancements, computers and ICT also have their limitations. Issues such as processing speed constraints, reliance on accurate programming, and vulnerabilities in communication systems highlight the challenges of technological dependence. Moreover, the societal implications of ICT, including the digital divide and concerns over privacy and security, underscore the complexities of integrating technology into every aspect of human activity.

This chapter explores both the powerful capabilities and the inherent limitations of computers and ICT, providing a balanced understanding of their role in shaping the modern world. It delves into the historical development of computing technologies, key functionalities that have driven innovation, and the challenges that remain unresolved as we continue to push the boundaries of what these technologies can achieve.

8.1 HISTORICAL CONTEXT OF COMPUTERS AND ICT

Computers have evolved significantly since their inception in the late 1940s, originally designed to solve complex mathematical problems and conduct physics research. Early computers were renowned for their speed and accuracy compared to human calculations. As storage systems advanced, new applications for computers emerged, influencing various sectors such as stock control, payroll processing, financial management, and machine control.

By the 1970s, the introduction of minicomputers made computing more accessible and affordable. This era saw innovative applications in the insurance industry for generating quotations, laboratory systems for scientific research, and spacecraft control for aeronautical advancements. As the years progressed, computers became integral to graphic design, word processing, and office calculations, further embedding technology into daily operations.

8.2 COMPUTING POWER AND STORAGE CAPACITY IN THE 21ST CENTURY

In the 21st century, computing technology has achieved unprecedented growth in terms of processing power, storage capacity, and accessibility. Modern computers now feature capabilities that were once unimaginable, at costs that make advanced technology available to the masses. The result is a profound transformation in how technology is integrated into our daily lives, industries, and even social structures.

Key Capabilities of Modern Computers

1. **Repetitive Calculations**: Today's computers can perform millions, and even billions, of calculations per second. This speed and accuracy have revolutionised numerous fields:

    - **Banking and Finance**: Computers manage billions of transactions daily, calculating interest, processing loans, and conducting high-frequency trading in stock markets.

    - **Payroll and Billing**: Organisations automate payroll and billing cycles, accurately calculating wages and expenses based on predetermined schedules and inputs.

    - **Scientific Research**: Computers assist scientists in complex simulations, like climate modelling, DNA sequencing, and drug discovery, where accurate calculations are essential.

    - **Satellite Navigation**: Modern GPS systems rely on vast computing power to calculate real-time positions, enabling accurate navigation for millions of users.

    - **Gaming**: Game development leverages high-speed calculations to generate realistic graphics and interactive environments, providing immersive experiences for players.

2. **Vast Storage**: Modern storage devices, from solid-state drives to cloud storage, can store and retrieve enormous amounts of data efficiently.
   - **Customer Billing and Government Databases**: Massive databases hold customer records, billing information, and government data, allowing access and updating at scale.
   - **Stock Control**: Retail and supply chain industries depend on storage solutions to track inventory, reducing shortages and enhancing logistics.
   - **Online Services**: Streaming platforms, social media, and cloud storage services manage and store data for billions of users, offering personalised content and instant access worldwide.
3. **Searching and Sorting**: The ability to retrieve, sort, and organise data quickly has transformed industries:
   - **Banking and Finance**: Banks use advanced searching capabilities to monitor transactions, manage accounts, and detect fraudulent activities.
   - **Law Enforcement**: Databases help law enforcement agencies retrieve suspect information, criminal records, and case files in seconds, improving response times and accuracy.
   - **Retail and E-commerce**: Online retailers rely on efficient data search and sorting to manage customer orders, track deliveries, and offer product recommendations.
   - **Billing Systems**: Automated billing systems search and sort customer data, ensuring accurate and timely invoicing.
4. **Combining Data**: Data analysis tools that combine and process large datasets are pivotal for spotting patterns, trends, and insights:
   - **Medical Research**: Data from clinical trials and patient histories are analysed to identify trends and predict outcomes, aiding in disease prevention and treatment.
   - **Scientific Studies**: Fields like astronomy and environmental science use combined datasets to analyse phenomena, such as star formations or climate change effects.
   - **Law Enforcement and Security**: Combining data across sources helps identify crime patterns, profile suspects, and enhance public safety.
5. **Fast Response**: The capability for real-time processing enables rapid response, which is crucial in several fields:

- **Retail and Banking**: ATMs provide immediate account access, while point-of-sale systems in stores facilitate real-time inventory tracking and payment processing.
- **Engine Management**: Modern vehicles monitor engine health in real-time, alerting drivers to issues and improving safety.
- **Ticket Booking Systems**: From concert tickets to flights, users experience near-instant bookings, with systems updating in real-time to prevent overbooking.
- **Medical Monitoring**: Hospital systems use real-time monitoring to track patients' vital signs, enabling swift intervention in emergencies.

6. **Communication**: ICT advancements have revolutionised communication globally, facilitating near-instantaneous interactions:
   - **Internet and Smartphones**: Internet connectivity and mobile devices have become ubiquitous, allowing people to communicate via email, video calls, and instant messaging regardless of distance.
   - **Satellite Communication**: Satellites support GPS, broadcasting, and international communication, which are essential for navigation, media, and emergency services.
   - **Digital Broadcasting**: Platforms like live streaming allow real-time broadcasts to millions, fostering information-sharing on a global scale.
   - **Social Networks**: Platforms like Facebook, Twitter/X, and WhatsApp connect individuals and businesses, enabling direct communication, marketing, and social interaction.

8.3 DEPENDENCE ON ICT

In highly technological societies, there is a significant reliance on ICT for day-to-day operations. For example:

- **Electricity and Utilities**: Power grids are monitored and controlled by computer systems; a minor malfunction can disrupt electricity supply, affecting millions.
- **Telecommunications**: Networks and internet services depend on reliable ICT infrastructure. Downtime can lead to widespread loss of communication, affecting personal and business activities.
- **Transportation**: Airports, railway systems, and traffic management depend on ICT for efficient operations. Even a brief system failure can cause delays, missed connections, and logistical chaos.
- **Finance and Banking**: Financial institutions rely heavily on ICT for secure transactions, fraud detection, and customer management. A cyberattack or technical failure can lead to data breaches, financial loss, and eroded trust.

The extensive reliance on ICT has led major organisations to invest in disaster recovery plans and backup systems to mitigate the potential impact of technology failures.

8.4 THE FUTURE OF ICT

The future of ICT appears to be characterised by even deeper integration into all aspects of life:

- **Ubiquitous Computing**: Predictions suggest that nearly all manufactured items may incorporate computing hardware. Already, we see examples such as keyless car entry systems and voice-activated home assistants (e.g., Amazon Alexa, Google Assistant).

- **Embedded Technology for Health and Security**: In the U.K., it is anticipated that by 2030, health monitoring devices may be embedded in humans to facilitate constant health tracking. This trend parallels ID chips used in pets, raising potential for similar applications in humans for security, monitoring, and identification purposes.

- **Smart Cities and Infrastructure**: ICT integration in infrastructure could make cities "smart," with sensors managing traffic flow, air quality, and utilities. This could improve urban living but also raises concerns about data privacy and security.

These advancements promise a future where ICT is fully integrated into everyday life, requiring careful consideration of ethical and societal impacts, including issues of privacy, security, and accessibility for all individuals.

8.5 LIMITATIONS OF ICT

While ICT offers numerous advantages, it also presents limitations that must be considered:

- **Processing Speed**: Certain operations require processing speeds beyond current capabilities, such as complex weather forecasting, real-time 3D rendering, audio editing, visual effects production, high-energy simulations, and advanced object recognition tasks.

- **Communication Speed and Capacity**: The internet has its challenges, particularly regarding bandwidth limitations. Large video and audio files necessitate higher processing speeds and reliable broadband connectivity for effective communication.

- **Data Control in Programming**: Developing large-scale systems can be challenging due to programming bugs and potential system overloads from excessive data volumes. Ongoing research aims to create self-repairing programs and intelligent computing solutions.

- **Data Models**: Computers rely on mathematical models to solve problems. However, some complex issues - like nuclear reactions, airflow dynamics in aviation, and intricate traveling systems - remain unsolved, partly due to the complexity of current computer systems.

- **Over-reliance on Technology**: Societal dependence on technology has led to the erosion of traditional skills, diminished social interactions, and privacy concerns. The "digital divide" highlights disparities between those with access to technology and those without.

- **Inappropriate Use of ICT**: Not all challenges are best addressed through ICT solutions. In some cases, manual processes may yield better results. The costs of implementing ICT systems can be high, and they may not always produce consistent or accurate outcomes.

8.6 THE EMERGENCE OF NEW TECHNOLOGY

The rapid pace of technological development continues to drive innovation across diverse fields, impacting daily life, industries, and global society at large. While these advancements open up exciting opportunities for growth and transformation, they also bring about complex challenges related to ethics, privacy, and societal integration. Below is a closer look at some of the key emerging technologies, their applications, and the potential challenges they introduce:

- **Nanotechnology**: This field involves the manipulation of materials at the atomic or molecular level, typically at scales of 1 to 100 nanometres. Nanotechnology holds immense promise in fields like medicine, electronics, and materials science. For example, in healthcare, nanotechnology enables the development of targeted drug delivery systems that can transport medication directly to cancer cells, potentially reducing side effects associated with traditional chemotherapy. In materials science, nanotechnology has led to the creation of stronger, lighter materials, such as carbon nanotubes, which have applications in construction, electronics, and aerospace. However, nanotechnology also presents challenges, including potential health risks associated with nanoparticles and the environmental impact of nanomaterial production.

- **Artificial Intelligence (AI)**: AI encompasses a variety of technologies, including machine learning, natural language processing, and robotics, that enable computers to perform tasks that traditionally required human intelligence. AI is reshaping industries from healthcare to finance by streamlining processes, improving data analysis, and enhancing decision-making. For instance, AI-powered diagnostic tools in healthcare can analyse medical images faster and, in some cases, more accurately than human radiologists, aiding in early disease detection. In finance, AI algorithms are used for fraud detection, real-time trading, and personalised banking. However, the rise of AI raises ethical concerns, particularly regarding job displacement, biases in AI algorithms, and privacy issues. Additionally, the potential for AI to be misused, such as in deepfake creation, presents societal risks that need careful consideration.

- **Ultra-high-Speed Computers**: Advances in computing power, such as quantum computing and new-generation supercomputers, promise to revolutionise data analysis, complex simulations, and large-scale problem-solving. These computers are designed to process information at unprecedented speeds, opening up possibilities for solving problems that were previously unsolvable. For example, quantum computers could potentially solve complex mathematical problems in seconds, where traditional computers would require years. This advancement is particularly significant for fields like climate modelling, drug discovery, and cryptography. However, ultra-high-speed computing also poses security risks; quantum computers could theoretically break traditional encryption methods, making sensitive information vulnerable to cyber-attacks, which could have far-reaching implications for data privacy and national security.

- **High-Speed Wireless Networks (e.g., 5G and beyond)**: As wireless technology continues to advance, the development of ultra-fast networks such as 5G enables quicker and more reliable communication between devices. This is expected to accelerate the adoption of the Internet of Things (IoT), where everything from home appliances to vehicles can connect to the internet, collect data, and communicate seamlessly. High-speed networks enhance real-time applications like telemedicine, autonomous driving, and virtual reality. For example, in healthcare, 5G enables remote surgery by allowing doctors to operate on patients through robotic instruments controlled from miles away. While high-speed networks provide substantial benefits, they also raise concerns over cybersecurity, as increased connectivity creates more entry points for hackers. Additionally, the rollout of 5G infrastructure has sparked debates over privacy and health implications.

- **Enhanced Humans**: This refers to the integration of technology with the human body, either to restore or enhance physical capabilities. Examples include wearable devices, brain-machine interfaces, and biohacking. In healthcare, this has led to innovations such as prosthetics controlled by neural impulses and implants that allow blind individuals to perceive shapes and colours. Wearable devices like smartwatches monitor health metrics such as heart rate, sleep patterns, and blood oxygen levels, helping users maintain better health awareness. However, enhanced human technology presents ethical and societal concerns, especially regarding the potential for creating socio-economic divides based on access to enhancements. Questions about data privacy, consent, and the psychological impacts of human-technology integration also come into play as this field advances.

Tutorial Activity 8 - Capabilities & Limitations of Computers & ICT

Quizzes and Questions

Multiple Choice Questions (MCQs)

1. **Which of the following was an early application of computers in the 1940s?**

    a) Graphic design

    b) Payroll processing

    c) Complex mathematical problem-solving

    d) Online banking

2. **What is a key capability of modern computers in the field of scientific research?**

    a) Real-time 3D rendering

    b) Simulating climate models

    c) Managing billing systems

    d) Enhancing interpersonal communication

3. **Which emerging technology manipulates materials at an atomic or molecular level?**

    a) Artificial Intelligence

    b) Quantum Computing

    c) Nanotechnology

    d) High-Speed Networks

4. **What is one limitation of modern ICT systems?**

a) Over-reliance on traditional labour

b) Data processing speeds beyond current capabilities

c) High costs of implementation

d) Limited ability to perform repetitive calculations

5. Which of the following is a societal concern linked to high-speed networks like 5G?

    a) Increased healthcare costs

    b) Ethical considerations in AI

    c) Privacy and cybersecurity issues

    d) Reduced storage capacity

True or False

1. Computers were initially developed for general-purpose use across industries.
2. Quantum computing could potentially solve complex problems that are unsolvable with traditional computers.
3. The digital divide only affects developing countries.
4. Nanotechnology has no implications for environmental safety.
5. Over-reliance on ICT can lead to a loss of traditional skills and increased privacy concerns.

Short Answer Questions

1. What was the primary focus of early computers, and how did their applications evolve over time?
2. List three key capabilities of modern computers.
3. Identify two ethical considerations associated with Artificial Intelligence.
4. What are the potential risks associated with quantum computing?
5. Explain how ICT has contributed to productivity and cost-efficiency in industries.

Essay/Discussion Questions

1. Discuss the societal implications of emerging technologies like AI, quantum computing, and nanotechnology. How can these advancements be responsibly integrated?
2. Evaluate the limitations of ICT in solving complex real-world problems. Provide examples of areas where traditional methods might still be preferred.
3. How has the evolution of computers and ICT transformed industries like healthcare, finance, and education? Provide specific examples.

References

This Chapter is based on general knowledge and understanding of the capabilities and limitations of computers and ICT in commerce, industry and society at large without referencing any specific sources. However, primary references or official resources that can provide deeper insight into the capabilities and limitations of ICT across various sectors are listed below. They offer factual and in-depth perspectives on how ICT reshapes various sectors and can be valuable for further reading on the broader capabilities and limitations of ICT:

1. **World Bank Reports on Digital Development**: The World Bank offers comprehensive studies and statistics on the role of ICT in driving economic growth, digital transformation, and poverty reduction across both developing and developed nations.

2. **International Telecommunication Union (ITU) Publications**: The ITU provides global standards, data, and research on telecommunications and ICT usage worldwide, covering areas like mobile adoption, internet access, and digital skills development.

3. **OECD Reports on Digital Economy and Innovation**: The Organisation for Economic Co-operation and Development (OECD) publishes research on digital transformation, innovation in business, education, and social sectors, along with trends and policy recommendations.

4. **UNESCO Resources on ICT in Education**: UNESCO has several publications and frameworks on ICT in education, focusing on its implementation, the impact on learning, and its role in improving educational access and quality.

5. **Eurostat and U.S. Bureau of Labour Statistics Data**: Both Eurostat and the U.S. Bureau of Labour Statistics provide data on the use of ICT in industries, the labour market impact, job creation, and productivity metrics within ICT sectors.

6. **McKinsey Global Institute (MGI) Reports**: MGI publishes research on the potential of digital and technological transformations in business, covering topics such as digital economy, AI, automation, and workforce shifts due to ICT.

7. **Research and Reports from Technology Firms**: Companies like Cisco, Microsoft, and IBM frequently publish white papers and reports detailing ICT trends, cybersecurity, the Internet of Things (IoT), and other emerging technologies and their impacts on business and society.

8. **Academic Journals on ICT and Society**: Journals like *Computers in Human Behaviour*, *Information Systems Research*, and *Journal of Information Technology* provide peer-reviewed articles that explore the social and economic impacts of ICT, with studies on e-commerce, digital privacy, cybersecurity, and social media influence.

Chapter 9: Social Impact of Computers & ICT

Learning Outcomes

By the end of this chapter, learners will be able to:

1. Appreciate the social impacts and effects of computers and ICT: Understand how technology influences daily life, workplace dynamics, and broader societal changes.

2. Understand the facts surrounding various situations: Recognise how different aspects of computer technology affect communication, information access, and personal interactions.

3. Formulate arguments for and against computers: Develop critical thinking skills to assess the benefits and drawbacks of technological integration in society.

4. Understand the roles and effective applications of ICT, employment and skill development.

9. SOCIAL IMPACT OF COMPUTERS & ICT

The advent of computers and Information and Communication Technology (ICT) has had a profound and transformative effect on society. These technologies have reshaped not only the way we work and communicate but also how we interact socially, learn, and even perceive the world around us. ICT has brought about unparalleled access to information, enabling individuals from different corners of the globe to connect, collaborate, and share knowledge instantaneously. The rise of social media platforms, online communities, and digital collaboration tools has redefined social dynamics and created new opportunities for self-expression and global engagement.

However, the widespread use of computers and ICT also presents significant challenges and raises important social concerns. Issues such as digital addiction, privacy invasion, and the erosion of face-to-face communication are growing concerns in an increasingly digital society. Additionally, the rapid pace of technological change has contributed to widening social divides, with access to technology and digital literacy often determined by socio-economic status and geographical location.

This chapter examines the various ways in which computers and ICT have influenced social structures, personal relationships, and cultural practices. It explores both the positive and negative social impacts of these technologies, addressing the ethical implications and exploring strategies for ensuring equitable access and responsible use in the digital age.

9.1 INFORMATION TECHNOLOGY, PEOPLE, AND SOCIETY

The evolution of **information technology (IT)** has profoundly reshaped the landscape of human interaction and organisational functionality. From its early days to the present, technology has played a crucial role in transforming how we live, work, and connect with one another.

Historical Context:

- **1980s Mainframe Popularity**: The 1980s marked a significant shift with the introduction of mainframe computers, which were capable of processing vast amounts of data. These systems were predominantly used by large corporations, leading to enhanced data management and operational efficiency in business environments.

- **Rise of Microprocessors**: The subsequent development and affordability of microprocessors allowed computers to become more accessible to the general public. This democratisation of technology led to widespread adoption in homes and small businesses, setting the stage for the digital revolution.

Key Points:

- **Ubiquity of Information Technology**: Today, technology permeates nearly every aspect of life, influencing how individuals work, learn, and communicate. From smartphones to cloud computing, IT is integral to daily routines.

- **Benefits and Challenges**: While IT facilitates increased efficiency, productivity, and access to information, it also presents significant challenges, including privacy issues, social isolation, and job displacement.

Examples of Benefits:

1. **Workplace Efficiency**: Computers enable faster processing of information and communication, leading to increased productivity. Automation tools and software streamline processes, allowing employees to focus on higher-value tasks.

2. **Access to Information**: The internet provides vast resources for learning, research, and personal development. Individuals can access information on nearly any topic, enhancing knowledge and skills.

3. **Improved Communication**: Technology has transformed communication, allowing instant connectivity through emails, social media, and messaging platforms. This connectivity fosters collaboration and strengthens relationships, both personally and professionally.

Challenges:

1. **Digital Divide:** Not everyone has equal access to technology, creating disparities in opportunities. This divide can impact education, employment, and economic advancement, particularly in underserved communities.
2. **Job Displacement:** Automation and AI may lead to the reduction of traditional jobs, impacting employment rates in sectors like manufacturing and retail. While new job opportunities may arise, they often require different skill sets.
3. **Privacy Concerns:** The collection and storage of personal data raise questions about individual privacy and security. Data breaches and unauthorised access can result in identity theft and loss of personal information.

9.2 THE NEED FOR INFORMATION

In our daily lives, information is crucial for effective functioning, particularly in business contexts.

Importance of Information:

1. **Business Operations**: In a retail setting, cashiers rely on accurate pricing information to process sales efficiently. Point-of-sale systems ensure transactions are conducted smoothly, contributing to overall customer satisfaction.

2. **Management Decisions**: Managers utilise data to forecast trends, manage inventory and strategise for future growth. Data-driven decision-making helps organisations remain competitive and responsive to market changes.

Examples of Information Needs:

- **Retail**: A grocery store manager monitors sales data to identify popular products and manage stock levels accordingly. This data-driven approach optimises inventory management and reduces waste.

- **Healthcare**: Medical professionals require up-to-date patient information to provide accurate diagnoses and treatments. Electronic health records (EHRs) facilitate the sharing of critical patient data among healthcare providers.

Efficiency Through Information:

- **Speed and Accuracy**: Quick access to reliable information not only enhances productivity but also reduces costs associated with errors and inefficiencies. Organisations that prioritise data accuracy can significantly improve operational performance.

- **Strategic Planning**: Organisations can utilise data analytics to predict market trends and consumer behaviour, guiding decision-making processes. Businesses that leverage analytics can tailor their strategies to meet evolving customer needs.

Examples of Applications of Computers

Computers serve diverse functions across various industries, enhancing operational efficiency and control.

Industrial Applications:

- **Automation in Manufacturing**: Robots programmed for specific tasks, such as welding in automotive production, increase precision and speed. Automation reduces human error and enhances product quality.
- **Smart Greenhouses**: Automated systems regulate temperature and humidity through sensors, optimising conditions for plant growth. This technology improves agricultural productivity and resource management.
- **Fuel Efficiency Systems**: Technologies that monitor and adjust fuel flow in vehicles reduce emissions and conserve energy. Such systems contribute to sustainability and lower operating costs for transportation companies.

Classroom Discussion

Students are encouraged to brainstorm additional applications of computers across various sectors, such as:

- **Healthcare**: Telemedicine platforms allow for remote consultations, improving access to medical care.
- **Education**: Online learning platforms offer flexible learning opportunities and resources for students worldwide.
- **Transportation**: GPS navigation systems provide real-time traffic updates and route optimisation, enhancing travel efficiency.
- **Finance**: Financial trading algorithms facilitate high-frequency trading, enabling quicker responses to market changes.

9.3 THE ELECTRONIC OFFICE

The concept of the **electronic office** represents the integration of technology into workplace environments to enhance efficiency, streamline operations, and foster collaboration. As businesses embrace digital tools, the electronic office becomes the hub of modern productivity, enabling organisations to function in a more agile and responsive manner.

Components of the Electronic Office:

1. **Standalone Computers**: These individual systems are used for specific tasks like document creation, data entry, and analysis. They are often

equipped with productivity software such as word processors and spreadsheets, making them essential for daily tasks.
2. **Networked Workstations**: Workstations connected to a central server or cloud network facilitate real-time collaboration and information sharing among team members, which is critical for project-based tasks and organisational cohesion.
3. **Peripheral Devices**: Equipment such as printers, scanners, and fax machines support a range of office functions, from document digitisation to communication, increasing versatility in the workplace.

Benefits of the Electronic Office:

- **Enhanced Collaboration**: Teams can seamlessly share documents and communicate in real-time, which improves workflow efficiency, decision-making, and collective problem-solving.
- **Streamlined Processes**: Digital tools reduce time spent on repetitive or administrative tasks, allowing employees to focus on strategic goals and core responsibilities.

Technological Tools in the Electronic Office:

- **Software Applications**: Various applications such as project management tools, accounting systems, and customer relationship management (CRM) platforms help organisations streamline their operations, track progress, and optimise customer relations.
- **Cloud Computing**: Cloud services provide data storage and access over the internet, enabling remote work and collaboration. This facilitates flexibility and ensures that employees can stay connected and productive from virtually any location.

9.4 HOME COMPUTING

The integration of computers into home life has transformed how individuals manage tasks, access entertainment, and communicate. Home computing has brought convenience, accessibility, and versatility into everyday activities, revolutionising the way we interact with information and technology.

Common Home Applications

1. **Smart Appliances**: Modern home devices like washing machines and refrigerators use microprocessors and connectivity to optimise energy consumption, enhance convenience, and provide data on usage patterns.
2. **Entertainment Systems**: Home computers, smart TVs, and gaming consoles provide a diverse range of leisure activities and educational resources, transforming home entertainment and offering interactive learning experiences.
3. **Home Automation**: Automated systems control heating, lighting, and security, which can be managed remotely, promoting energy efficiency and safety. These "smart home" systems also offer customisation options to suit individual lifestyles.

Benefits of Home Computing:

- **Convenience**: With a few clicks, tasks such as online shopping, bill payments, and communication with family and friends can be easily completed. This convenience extends to e-learning platforms, allowing users to develop new skills from home.
- **Access to Information**: The internet offers a wealth of resources for education, health, and personal development. Home computing empowers users to acquire knowledge and stay informed on a wide array of topics.

Challenges of Home Computing:

- **Digital Dependency**: Excessive reliance on technology for daily tasks can lead to decreased interpersonal interactions and diminished social skills, as face-to-face interactions are sometimes replaced by digital communication.
- **Privacy and Security**: Increased use of connected devices raises concerns about data security, as these devices may be vulnerable to hacking or data breaches. Privacy settings and cybersecurity practices are essential for protecting personal information and ensuring safe internet use.

9.5 COMPUTERS IN SMALL BUSINESSES, SHOPS, AND CHURCHES

Computers have brought significant advancements to small businesses, shops, and even religious organisations, enhancing efficiency, customer service, and engagement within these communities. By leveraging digital tools, these entities can streamline operations, gain insights, and better serve their customers or members.

Applications in Various Sectors:

- **Retail**: Point of Sale (POS) systems have transformed the retail sector, enabling streamlined transactions, effective inventory management, and real-time sales data analysis. These systems can provide valuable insights on stock levels, popular products, and peak shopping times, helping business owners make informed decisions.
- **Service Industries**: Real estate agencies, beauty salons, and other service-oriented businesses use databases and scheduling software to manage listings, appointments, and customer interactions. This technology improves service delivery, enhances client satisfaction, and fosters stronger client relationships.
- **Religious Organisations**: Many churches and religious groups are adopting technology to manage finances, plan events, and communicate with congregants. Software solutions can help with donation tracking, membership directories, and automated notifications, allowing leaders to focus more on spiritual guidance and community building.

Benefits for Small Businesses:
- **Cost Efficiency**: By automating routine tasks, small businesses can reduce labour costs, streamline accounting, and minimise human error. For example, digital bookkeeping solutions can reduce the time spent on manual data entry while maintaining accurate financial records.
- **Improved Customer Experience**: Digital systems enable faster transaction processing, personalised service, and efficient customer data management. Small businesses can use customer data to tailor services, build loyalty programs, and enhance overall customer satisfaction.

Challenges:
- **Technological Barriers**: The initial cost of implementing technology solutions can be prohibitive for small businesses with limited budgets. Ongoing expenses, such as software updates, licensing fees, and hardware maintenance, can also strain resources.
- **Adaptation to Change**: Employees may need training to use new technologies effectively. This training period may impact short-term productivity, and some staff may be resistant to learning new systems, which can hinder full adoption.

9.6 COMPUTERS IN EDUCATION

The integration of computers in education has profoundly transformed learning environments, making education more interactive, accessible, and tailored to individual needs. This digital shift has also presented challenges that need to be addressed to ensure equitable and effective use of technology in education.

Historical Context:

- **Early Access**: During the 1970s, computers were expensive and uncommon in most schools, limiting access to only well-funded institutions. They were primarily used for administrative purposes or specialised technical training.

- **Current Landscape**: Today, computers are integral to educational institutions worldwide, with most schools equipped with computer labs, digital networks, and often one-to-one devices for students. This accessibility has encouraged widespread use of digital tools and resources in the classroom.

Applications in Education:

1. **Instructional Tools**: Computers enhance classroom instruction by providing interactive learning experiences, simulations, educational games, and virtual labs. Programs like digital whiteboards and subject-specific software make complex subjects more understandable and engaging.

2. **Research and Resources**: Computers open up vast online resources, allowing students to conduct research, access digital libraries, and use interactive databases. This immediate access supports self-guided learning and complements classroom materials.

3. **Skill Development**: Through various programs, students acquire essential digital skills, such as coding, typing, data analysis, and design. Specialised software for subjects like graphic design, computer programming, and video editing prepares students for the demands of the digital workplace.

Benefits of Technology in Education:

- **Personalised Learning**: Adaptive educational software responds to each student's learning pace and style, providing tailored resources and support. For example, math and reading applications can adjust difficulty levels based on student progress, offering a customised experience that enhances understanding.

- **Collaborative Learning**: Digital tools enable students and teachers to collaborate on projects, share resources, and engage in group discussions. Platforms like Google Classroom, Microsoft Teams, and educational forums support communication and project-based learning.

- **Expanded Learning Opportunities**: Virtual classrooms and online courses allow students to access subjects and programs that might not be available locally. For instance, rural students can learn advanced subjects online, and global classrooms connect students from different countries for cultural exchange and learning.

Challenges:

- **Equity in Access**: Not all students have equal access to technology at home, creating a digital divide that can impact academic performance and opportunities. Schools often need to address this gap by providing devices or offering extended computer lab hours.

- **Teacher Training**: Effective technology integration requires that educators are well-trained in digital tools and platforms. Without sufficient training, teachers may struggle to incorporate technology in ways that enhance learning, making professional development essential for effective implementation.

- **Data Privacy and Security**: With the rise of online learning, protecting students' personal information and ensuring secure online environments have become critical. Schools must adopt data protection policies and educate students on responsible digital behaviour to prevent cyber risks.

9.7 SOCIAL TRENDS STEMMING FROM THE USE OF COMPUTERS AND ICT

The adoption of computers and information and communication technology (ICT) has brought about transformative shifts in both personal and organisational interactions, with effects spanning various aspects of modern society.

Increased Reliance on Communications:

1. **Remote Work**: Telecommuting has surged in popularity, offering flexibility and enabling a balance between work and personal life. Employees can perform their duties from home or other remote locations, which has led to a shift in how workplaces operate.

2. **Distributed Operations**: Companies can now manage and coordinate activities across multiple locations, including global offices. This allows for greater collaboration and access to a diverse talent pool regardless of physical location.

3. **Automation of Services**: ICT has enabled automation in various industries, from utility management to transportation. Automated monitoring systems and IoT technology provide more efficient ways to track and manage resources remotely.

4. **Centralised Inventory Management**: Retailers benefit from real-time tracking of stock levels, demand, and sales through centralised systems. This helps optimise supply chains and reduce excess inventory, ultimately enhancing profitability.

5. **Digital Banking**: Online and mobile banking allow customers to manage finances, transfer funds, and pay bills conveniently. Digital banking solutions have significantly reduced the reliance on physical bank branches and facilitated financial transactions for many.

Decreased Use of Cash

The global shift toward digital transactions has significantly impacted financial habits and the infrastructure that supports them. As societies embrace technology-driven payment systems, the reliance on cash is steadily declining.

- **Electronic Funds Transfer (EFT):**
  EFT systems enable the movement of money without requiring physical cash or cheques. Transactions such as online banking and direct deposits are processed electronically, offering speed, convenience, and security.

- **Electronic Funds Transfer at Point of Sale (EFTPOS):**
  This technology allows consumers to make cashless payments directly at retail locations, using credit/debit cards or mobile payment solutions. It enhances the efficiency and security of transactions, reducing the need for carrying cash.

Challenges to a Cashless Society

While the transition to a cashless economy offers numerous advantages, it also poses challenges that must be addressed to ensure inclusivity and security.

- **Slow Adoption:**
  Certain populations, including the elderly and those in rural areas, continue

to rely on cash due to traditional habits, limited digital literacy, or concerns over cybersecurity.

- **Exclusion of Non-Banked Individuals:**
  People without access to banking services or digital platforms face significant barriers in a cashless economy. This highlights the need for financial inclusion initiatives, such as mobile banking and simplified account creation processes.

9.8 ARGUMENTS FOR AND AGAINST COMPUTERS

The role of computers and ICT in society sparks debates, with advocates and critics presenting contrasting perspectives on their impact.

First View: Limited Impact

- **Criticism:**
  Some argue that technological advancements predominantly benefit niche markets, such as gaming, without substantially improving everyday life.

- **Minimal Quality of Life Improvements:**
  Detractors question whether technology has significantly enhanced overall well-being or merely introduced temporary conveniences.

Second View: Transformative Power

- **Advocacy:**
  Proponents liken the digital revolution to the Industrial Revolution, citing widespread benefits across multiple sectors.

  - **Increased Leisure Time:**
    Automation and digital tools free individuals from repetitive tasks, allowing more time for leisure and self-improvement.

  - **Enhanced Quality of Life:**
    Technology has improved access to healthcare, education, and entertainment, contributing to overall societal well-being.

  - **New Opportunities:**
    The emergence of digital technologies creates new industries, job opportunities, and avenues for economic growth.

Third View: Risks and Inequities

- **Centralisation Risks:**
  The increasing centralisation of data raises concerns about privacy and potential misuse by governments or corporations.

- **Societal Inequities:**
  Access to technology remains unequal, with wealthier individuals enjoying greater benefits, thereby widening social and economic disparities.

Classroom Discussion

Students are encouraged to explore and critically examine the role of technology in society. Discussions should address ethical considerations, the societal impact of ICT, and personal experiences with technology. These conversations aim to foster a nuanced understanding of both the advantages and challenges of an increasingly digital world.

9.9 PERSONAL PRIVACY

The digital age has brought unprecedented challenges to personal privacy, with organisations collecting, storing, and sharing vast amounts of individual data. This has sparked ongoing debates about ethical data management and the protection of personal information.

Key Concerns

- **Data Collection Practices:**
  Organisations routinely gather user data for service optimisation and targeted marketing. However, the lack of transparency around these practices raises ethical concerns about consent and usage.

- **Comprehensive Dossiers on Individuals:**
  Aggregating diverse data sources creates detailed profiles, which can be used for marketing or surveillance. These practices often blur the lines between convenience and intrusion.

- **Access to Sensitive Information:**
  The unauthorised sharing or misuse of sensitive data, such as medical and financial records, poses significant risks, including identity theft and discrimination.

Advocating for Privacy Rights

To address privacy challenges, advocacy groups promote the following rights:

- **Right to Withhold Information:**
  Individuals should have the freedom to decide what data they share and understand the potential consequences of sharing.

- **Prevention of Unauthorised Data Sharing:**
  Strict regulations should mandate explicit consent for sharing personal data with third parties.

- **Access and Correction of Personal Records:**
  Individuals must have the right to review, verify, and correct personal data held by organisations to ensure accuracy and fairness.

Examples of Centrally Held Data Files

Centrally managed data systems maintain records across various sectors:

- **Healthcare:** Patient records with detailed medical histories are stored by hospitals and insurance companies.

- **Employment:** Employers and tax authorities track work history, roles, and salaries.
- **Finance:** Banks hold data on credit history, loan payments, and account balances.
- **Retail:** Retailers compile purchase histories and behavioural patterns for marketing purposes.
- **Law Enforcement:** Criminal records and personal identification details are maintained by government agencies.

Classroom Discussion

Students should analyse privacy challenges in a familiar context, considering:

- The types of records maintained in their country.
- Rights individuals have regarding data access, correction, and protection.
- Roles of governments and corporations in safeguarding privacy.

The discussion should include evaluating existing privacy protections and proposing improvements to address emerging challenges in the digital age.

9.10 THE EFFECT OF ICT ON EMPLOYMENT AND SKILL DEVELOPMENT

The integration of Information and Communication Technology (ICT) into workplaces is reshaping employment landscapes, creating both challenges and opportunities for the workforce. This section explores how job roles, skill demands, and organisational training needs evolve in response to ICT advancements.

Job Displacement

- **Automation of Routine Tasks**: As machines and software increasingly take on repetitive tasks, traditional roles in sectors like manufacturing, retail, and administration may face a decline, resulting in job displacement. This automation can particularly impact roles involving repetitive manual labour or standardised data processing, often requiring affected employees to reskill or find new employment paths.

- **Industry Transformation**: ICT-driven advancements have transformed entire industries, particularly in manufacturing, where mechanisation and robotics are reducing reliance on human labour. For example, assembly-line jobs are now more likely to be performed by automated systems, which demands that workers either adapt to new technical roles or consider transitioning into other fields.

New Job Creation

- **High Demand for Technology Skills**: ICT expansion has created numerous opportunities for skilled professionals in areas such as software development, data analysis, cybersecurity, network administration, and tech support. Roles requiring expertise in AI, cloud computing, and data science are increasingly in demand as digital transformation impacts more sectors.

- **Software Industry Growth**: With businesses relying on complex software solutions, there is a growing need for specialists who can design, develop, and maintain these systems. This demand for software engineers, UX designers, and application developers means new opportunities for employees who possess the necessary skills or are willing to upskill.

Managing Workforce Change

Businesses must anticipate and manage changes in workforce requirements by addressing both the impact of job displacement and the demand for new skill sets.

- **Importance of ICT Training**:
    - **Skill Development:** To remain competitive, employees need training in emerging technologies, software applications, and system operations. This training enables them to transition into new roles created by ICT advancements.
    - **Investment in Human Capital:** By investing in employee development, organisations can maintain productivity, meet evolving market needs, and retain valuable personnel. Reskilling can be a strategic asset for adapting to technology shifts and reducing turnover.
- **Challenges of ICT Integration**:
    - **Training Costs:** Funding comprehensive ICT training programs can strain an organisation's budget, particularly for smaller businesses.
    - **Reskilling Older Workers:** As technology evolves, older employees may find adapting to new systems more challenging. This can impact their job security unless adequate support, training, and resources are provided.

9.11 ESSENTIAL ICT SKILLS IN THE MODERN WORKPLACE

- **Hardware Operations**: Proficiency in operating hardware, such as monitors, keyboards, printers, and network devices, enables employees to troubleshoot basic issues and enhance efficiency.
- **System Management and Maintenance**: Regular updates, software patches, and security monitoring are essential to keep systems running efficiently. Understanding these processes helps staff prevent potential disruptions and maintain performance.
- **Software Setup and Initialisation**: Employees should know how to install applications, configure system settings, and manage user accounts, including knowledge of licensing and compatibility requirements.

- **Data Entry and Validation**: Accurate data entry is fundamental, with a need to understand data formats, validation techniques, and best practices to minimise errors.
- **Information Retrieval and Formatting**: Staff should be proficient in using software to generate reports, visualise data, and export information in various formats for analysis.
- **System Performance Evaluation**: Monitoring system effectiveness involves analysing output and identifying areas for improvement or adjustment, which is essential for ongoing productivity and alignment with goals.
- **Continuous Improvement**: Employees need the ability to propose and implement changes, such as system upgrades or process improvements, to enhance overall productivity.

9.12 SOURCES OF ICT TRAINING

Training programs can range from short workshops to extensive multi-week courses, with ongoing support through user assistance lines or on-site help to build staff confidence as they apply new skills. This continued support is crucial for ensuring that employees can effectively integrate ICT skills into their daily tasks, promoting long-term organisational adaptability and resilience.

Effective training ensures staff are skilled and comfortable using technology within their roles. Various training sources include:

- **Vendor Training**: Many computers or software vendors provide initial training sessions tailored to their products. These sessions help users understand specific features and functions.
- **Specialised Training Firms**: Professional agencies offer structured programs with hands-on experience and certifications, often covering diverse ICT skills from fundamental to advanced levels.
- **Community Colleges**: Local educational institutions provide IT courses for skill development, often supporting different levels of expertise and career-focused programs.
- **Peer Training**: Internal training, where skilled employees mentor colleagues, fosters a collaborative learning environment, allowing employees to learn practical skills within the specific context of their roles.

9.13 ROLE AND APPLICATIONS OF COMPUTERS AND ICT

ICT in Business

Within business organisations, ICT has transformed how operations are conducted, enabling efficiency and competitive advantage. Below are ways ICT is utilised in modern businesses:

- **Data Processing**: Organisations leverage ICT to collect, analyse, and manipulate vast amounts of data, which then inform decisions based on up-to-date insights and real-time information. For example, a retail chain might use customer data analytics to identify shopping patterns and stock products that better meet customer needs. Companies like Amazon utilise advanced data processing to optimise logistics, ensuring items are shipped from the nearest warehouse to reduce delivery times.

- **Information Management**: Effective data management systems generate real-time dashboards and analytical reports, supporting strategic planning and agile decision-making. For instance, a sales team could monitor weekly sales performance through a CRM (Customer Relationship Management) system, allowing for immediate adjustments to sales strategies.

- **Record Keeping**: ICT allows businesses to store records securely and access them easily, improving accuracy and regulatory compliance. Medical facilities, for instance, use electronic health record (EHR) systems to store patient records, making it easier to retrieve patient histories quickly, which enhances treatment decisions.

- **Enhanced Customer Service**: ICT enables businesses to provide personalised customer experiences. Banks, for example, offer digital services such as online banking, mobile apps, and AI-driven chatbots that provide 24/7 customer support. This accessibility improves customer satisfaction and loyalty.

- **Increased Efficiency**: Automated processes streamline repetitive tasks, allowing employees to focus on strategic initiatives. For instance, robotic process automation (RPA) can automate tasks like data entry in insurance claims processing, speeding up the workflow and reducing errors.

- **Cost Reduction**: ICT helps businesses cut costs by optimising resource usage and streamlining processes. For example, cloud storage reduces the need for physical servers and IT maintenance, lowering operational expenses while enhancing data accessibility and disaster recovery.

- **Speed up the production of information**: Automation of routine tasks allows employees to focus on more strategic initiatives, resulting in quicker information production and dissemination.

9.14 COMPUTERS & ICT IN FINANCIAL INSTITUTIONS

The finance sector was an early adopter of ICT, using technology to revolutionise how transactions are processed, and customer services are delivered:

- **Customer Records and Real-Time Processing**: Banks initially stored customer data on central mainframes, processing transactions in batch jobs daily. Modern banks now use real-time systems; for example, ATMs and mobile banking apps allow instant transactions, creating a more seamless customer experience.

- **Electronic Funds Transfer at Point of Sale (EFTPOS)**: Retailers and service providers enable customers to make immediate electronic payments, reducing cash dependency. Countries like Sweden have seen a significant shift towards cashless transactions, where even small purchases are made digitally.

- **Security Concerns and Paperwork Reduction**: While ICT allows quicker transactions, customers may worry about security, especially if deductions occur before services are received. Many banks employ multi-factor authentication and biometric systems to enhance security and mitigate such concerns.

- While this technology saves time and reduces paperwork for banks, it raises customer concerns about immediate fund withdrawal, particularly when transactions do not align with service delivery.

9.15 COMPUTERS IN HOSPITALS AND MEDICINE

The healthcare industry leverages ICT for efficient patient care and administration:

- **Digital Patient Records**: EHRs allow for quick data retrieval and patient information sharing among medical professionals, facilitating coordinated care. For instance, in emergency rooms, access to patient histories can be critical for immediate treatment.

- **Diagnostic Support via Expert Systems**: ICT supports clinical decision-making. For example, IBM's Watson for Oncology assists oncologists in treatment planning by analysing data on patient conditions and providing potential treatment options.

- **Medical Applications**:
    - **Therapeutic Radiology**: Computers plan radiation doses for cancer treatment, ensuring precision to minimise damage to healthy tissue.
    - **Vital Sign Monitoring**: In intensive care units (ICUs), computerised systems constantly monitor patient vitals, alerting healthcare staff to any concerning changes immediately.
    - **Automated Laboratories**: Medical labs utilise ICT to automate tests, allowing faster and more accurate results, such as blood analysis in diagnostic laboratories.

9.16 COMPUTERS IN THE HOME

The prevalence of computers in the home has skyrocketed, reflecting a significant cultural shift over the past four decades:

- **Personal Devices**: Smartphones, tablets, and PCs are now integral to daily life, enabling tasks ranging from communication to entertainment, online shopping and information access. Devices like Amazon's Alexa enable voice-activated controls over various household functions.

- **Smart appliances**: Various household items, such as microwaves, smart TVs, smart refrigerators, and home entertainment systems, utilise computer technology to enhance functionality and user experience. Refrigerators can track inventory, recommend recipes, and remind owners to restock items. For example, Samsung's Family Hub fridge lets users view contents remotely, facilitating better grocery management.
- **Automation and connectivity**: Smart home technologies, such as automated lighting and climate control, improve convenience and energy efficiency, allowing homeowners to manage their environments seamlessly. Smart thermostats, like Nest, learn user preferences and adjust heating/cooling to save energy, while apps allow remote control over lights and security systems, enhancing convenience and security.

19.17 COMPUTERS IN RETAIL

ICT has modernised retail operations by enhancing inventory control, sales processes, and customer insights:

- **Point of Sale (POS) Systems**: Integrated systems at checkout counters reduce transaction times and manage loyalty points, receipts, and stock updates. Major retailers like Tesco use this to streamline customer experiences and keep track of product turnover.
- **Inventory Management**: Automated systems track and reorder stock to avoid shortages, ensuring that shelves are always stocked with necessary items, enhancing customer satisfaction and particularly beneficial in high-demand areas like supermarkets.
- **Data Analytics for Customer Insights**: Retailers analyse transaction data to understand buying habits, allowing for tailored marketing and personalised promotions, as seen in loyalty programs like those used by Starbucks and Tesco.

9.18 ROLE OF ICT IN EDUCATION

The role of ICT in education has evolved significantly from historical development, transforming teaching and learning methods. While the benefits of technology in education are clear, challenges remain, particularly concerning access and equity. As we move forward, it will be crucial to address these issues while embracing the potential of ICT to enhance educational experiences for all learners.

Historical Development of ICT in Education

The evolution of ICT in education has seen significant milestones:

1. **1970s: Early Adoption**
    - **Mainframes:** Higher education institutions began using mainframes for computational tasks. Projects like ILEA in the UK aimed to teach programming to children, recognising their capacity to learn technology at a young age.

- **Programming Languages:** Seymour Papert's LOGO language and research into graphical user interfaces (GUIs) emphasized child-friendly programming, setting a foundation for future educational software.

2. **1980s: Microcomputers Enter Schools**

    - **Introduction of Microcomputers:** Affordable microcomputers like the Commodore PET, Amstrad, RM and BBC computers became common in schools. Governments invested in computer education, purchasing educational software to assist in teaching.
    - **Administrative Uses:** Schools began utilising ICT for administration tasks such as maintaining pupil records and handling exam entries.

3. **1990s: Rise of the Internet and CD-ROMs**

    - **Enhanced Computing Power:** The advent of large-scale integration (LSI) made computers cheaper and more powerful. Educational software transitioned to CD-ROMs, offering interactive learning experiences.
    - **Internet Integration:** By 1995, schools started incorporating the internet into administrative functions, marking a significant shift in how educational resources were accessed.

4. **2000s: Widespread Online Education**

    - **Computer-Based Training (CBT):** The 2000s saw a rise in CBT and online learning platforms, which became instrumental in delivering education across various contexts.
    - **Cloud Computing:** The development of wireless technology further enabled the use of ICT in education, allowing for greater accessibility and flexibility.

Impact of ICT in Education

The incorporation of ICT into education has led to several transformative changes:

1. **Enhanced Learning Experiences:**

    - **Interactive Learning Tools:** Tools like interactive whiteboards, digital projectors, and educational software foster engaging learning environments. Students can access multimedia content that caters to different learning styles.

2. **Improved Communication:**

    - **Emails and Messaging Apps:** ICT facilitates communication among students, teachers, and parents, enhancing collaboration and engagement through instant messaging and emails.

- **Reporting Systems:** Schools generate electronic report cards and notifications, allowing for quick and efficient updates on student progress.

3. **Data Management:**
    - **Efficient Record Keeping:** ICT systems streamline the management of student records, exam registrations, and performance tracking, enabling quick data retrieval and analysis.
    - **Data Protection Concerns:** While ICT enhances efficiency, it also raises issues of data security and privacy, necessitating robust measures to protect sensitive information.

4. **Access to Information:**
    - **Online Resources:** The shift from CD-ROMs to internet-based resources has democratised access to information. Students can utilise search engines and educational websites (like Wikipedia and educational platforms) for research and learning.

5. **Flexible Learning Environments:**
    - **Virtual Learning Environments (VLEs):** Platforms like Moodle, Blackboard and Padlet Wall allow for remote learning, enabling students to attend classes and submit assignments from anywhere - Turnitin software comes to mind here! This flexibility accommodates diverse learning needs and schedules.

ICT in Higher Education

Higher education institutions have long utilised computers and ICT for research and learning. The integration of technology in educational settings has accelerated, leading to transformative changes:

- **Administrative efficiency:** Institutions use IT to manage enrolment processes, student records, and course registrations, significantly reducing administrative burdens.
- **Enhanced learning experiences:** Interactive learning platforms and digital resources provide students with immediate access to information and facilitate collaborative learning.
- **Data-driven decisions:** Analytics derived from student performance data assist educators in identifying trends, tailoring instruction, and enhancing student outcomes.

Future Considerations in ICT for Education

As ICT continues to evolve, several trends and challenges emerge:

1. **Technological Advancements:**

- **E-books and Multimedia Learning:** The future of education may see a shift toward e-books and multimedia resources, reducing reliance on physical textbooks and materials.
- **Wearable Technology:** Devices like smartwatches and augmented reality glasses may enhance interactive learning experiences and provide real-time feedback.

2. **Changing Roles of Educators:**
   - **Facilitators of Learning:** With students increasingly proficient in ICT, teachers may transition to facilitators who guide learning rather than traditional teachers. This shift could lead to more personalised learning experiences.

3. **The Digital Divide:**
   - **Access Disparities:** While ICT advances are prevalent in developed countries, many developing nations face barriers to technology access. High costs of computers and internet connectivity can hinder educational progress.
   - **Affordability of Technology:** The cost of acquiring computers often exceeds that of textbooks, raising questions about the practicality of implementing ICT in resource-limited settings.

4. **Home Education Trends:**
   - **Rise of Homeschooling:** Increased interest in home education raises questions about the future of traditional schooling. Parents may seek alternative methods to educate their children, leading to shifts in educational norms and expectations.

5. **Need for Digital Literacy:**
   - **Preparing Students for the Future:** Educators must focus on enhancing digital literacy among students to equip them for a technology-driven world. This includes understanding how to use ICT tools effectively and responsibly.

9.19 ICT IN MANUFACTURING FIRMS

ICT in manufacturing increases productivity, quality, and safety:

- **Automation**: The use of computer-controlled devices, such as robots, has increased efficiency and precision in production processes, reducing reliance on manual labour for repetitive tasks.
- **Supply Chain Integration**: Manufacturers use ERP (Enterprise Resource Planning) software to monitor supply chains, coordinating resources and inventory for timely production. For example, Toyota's supply chain management optimises part delivery to assembly plants.

- **Quality control**: ICT facilitates real-time monitoring of production quality, allowing manufacturers to identify defects and adjust processes promptly.

9.20 ICT IN HEALTH AND SAFETY

The integration of ICT into hazardous work environments enhances safety and efficiency:

- **Robotic automation**: In sectors like nuclear and chemical industries, robots perform dangerous tasks, reducing the risk to human workers.
- **Data management**: ICT enables better tracking and management of safety protocols and compliance measures, contributing to a safer work environment.

Computers and the Disabled

Advancements in computer technology have significantly improved the quality of life for individuals with disabilities:

- **Assistive technologies**: Specialised software and hardware, such as voice recognition software and adaptive input devices, enable people with disabilities to engage with technology effectively.
- **Mobility solutions**: Innovations like robotic limbs and mobility aids allow greater independence for individuals with physical disabilities.
- **Communication tools**: Technologies that facilitate communication, such as text-to-speech devices and communication boards, enhance social interaction and participation in society.

9.21 COMPUTER-BASED TRAINING (CBT)

Computer-based training has become a popular method for skill development in various industries:

- **Flexible learning**: CBT offers employees the ability to learn at their own pace, accommodating various schedules and learning styles.
- **Cost-effectiveness**: Organisations benefit from reduced training costs as CBT eliminates travel and accommodation expenses associated with traditional training methods.
- **Self-paced learning**: Employees can revisit training materials as needed, reinforcing learning and enhancing retention of information.

9.22 ARTIFICIAL INTELLIGENCE (AI)

AI represents a significant frontier in computer technology, encompassing various applications that enhance ICT capabilities:

- **Adaptive learning**: AI can tailor educational experiences based on individual learning patterns, improving the effectiveness of training programs.

- **Decision support systems**: AI-driven tools assist in analysing data and providing recommendations, enhancing decision-making processes across industries.
- **Natural language processing**: Technologies like chatbots and virtual assistants enhance customer service and support, improving user interactions with businesses.

9.23 ROLE AND APPLICATIONS OF ICT IN FILMS & MOVIES

Production and Filmmaking:

- **Digital Filmmaking:** ICT has transformed traditional filmmaking processes. Digital cameras and editing software allow filmmakers to shoot, edit, and produce films more efficiently and with higher quality. Technologies like 4K and 8K resolution cameras provide stunning visuals, while software like Adobe Premiere Pro, Cap Cut and Final Cut Pro enables precise editing.
- **Visual Effects (VFX):** Advanced software and computing power have revolutionised the use of visual effects in films. Technologies like CGI (computer-generated imagery) create realistic environments, characters, and effects that enhance storytelling. Movies like *Avatar* and *Jurassic Park* showcase the power of VFX in creating immersive experiences.
- **Animation:** ICT has paved the way for the animation industry with tools like Maya, Blender, and After Effects. These programs allow animators to create intricate characters and worlds, leading to critically acclaimed animated films such as *Frozen* and *Toy Story*.

Distribution and Marketing:

- **Streaming Services:** Platforms like Netflix, Hulu, and Amazon Prime have transformed how films are distributed and consumed. This has made it easier for filmmakers to reach global audiences without the constraints of traditional theatrical releases.
- **Social Media Marketing:** Social media platforms (e.g., Instagram, Facebook, (Twitter) X) play a crucial role in promoting films. Trailers, behind-the-scenes content, and interactive campaigns engage audiences and create buzz before release.

Audience Engagement:

- **Interactive and Immersive Experiences:** With advancements in virtual reality (VR) and augmented reality (AR), filmmakers can create immersive experiences that allow viewers to engage with the story on a deeper level. VR films, like *The Invisible Man*, enable audiences to experience the narrative from unique perspectives.
- **Data Analytics:** Streaming services leverage data analytics to understand viewer preferences and behaviours, allowing for personalised recommendations and targeted marketing strategies.

9.24 ROLE AND APPLICATIONS OF ICT IN TRANSPORTATION

Smart Transportation Systems:

- **Traffic Management:** ICT facilitates real-time traffic monitoring and management through sensors, cameras, and GPS technology. Systems like Intelligent Transportation Systems (ITS) optimise traffic flow, reduce congestion, and improve road safety by providing real-time information to drivers and city planners.

- **Navigation and Routing:** Applications like Google Maps and Waze use ICT to provide accurate navigation, traffic updates, and alternative routes. These technologies enhance the efficiency of personal and public transportation.

Public Transportation:

- **Automated Ticketing:** ICT has streamlined ticketing systems in public transport. Smart cards and mobile ticketing apps (e.g., Oyster card in London, Ventra app in Chicago) simplify fare collection and reduce wait times for passengers.

- **Real-time Tracking:** Many public transportation systems employ GPS technology to provide real-time tracking of buses and trains. Passengers can receive updates on arrival times, enhancing convenience and reliability.

Logistics and Supply Chain:

- **Fleet Management:** Companies use ICT for fleet management, utilising software to monitor vehicle locations, optimise routes, and manage maintenance schedules. This leads to cost savings and improved service delivery.

- **E-commerce and Delivery Services:** The rise of e-commerce like Amazon has necessitated advancements in logistics. ICT enables efficient inventory management, order processing, and last-mile delivery tracking, transforming how goods are transported.

9.25 ROLE AND APPLICATIONS OF ICT IN GOVERNMENT

E-Government Services:

- **Digital Government Initiatives:** Many governments have adopted e-governance strategies to enhance service delivery and citizen engagement. Online portals allow citizens to access government services, submit forms, and pay taxes efficiently.

- **Transparency and Accountability:** ICT tools enable governments to provide real-time access to information, fostering transparency and accountability. Initiatives like open data platforms allow citizens to access government data and reports.

Public Safety and Security:

- **Surveillance Systems:** Governments utilise ICT for public safety through CCTV surveillance and data analytics. These technologies help monitor public spaces, prevent crime, and enhance emergency response efforts.

- **Disaster Management:** ICT plays a critical role in disaster management by facilitating communication, information sharing, and coordination during emergencies. Early warning systems, powered by ICT, enable governments to respond quickly to natural disasters.

Policy Development and Planning:

- **Data-Driven Decision Making:** Governments increasingly rely on data analytics to inform policy decisions and urban planning. By analysing data from various sources, such as census information and public feedback, policymakers can develop targeted initiatives that address citizens' needs.

- **Citizen Participation:** ICT enhances citizen participation in governance through online consultations and feedback platforms. This encourages active engagement in the decision-making process and fosters a sense of community involvement.

9.26 THE GLOBAL CONNECTIVITY

The Internet has redefined how people communicate, conduct business, and access information, fuelling an interconnected digital landscape:

- **Global Connectivity**: The Internet allows instant communication worldwide, facilitating remote work, e-commerce, and access to global information networks. With IoT (Internet of Things), connected devices can share data, such as wearable fitness trackers that monitor health and provide insights.

- **Advancements in AI and Machine Learning**: These technologies power applications like Google's AI-driven search engine, which tailors search results based on user intent, or smart assistants like Siri, which respond to user queries and control smart home devices.

Tutorial Activity 9 - Social Impact of Computers & ICT

Quizzes and Questions

Multiple Choice Questions (MCQs)

1. Which of the following is a positive social impact of ICT on the workplace?

   a) Increased isolation among employees

   b) Improved flexibility through remote work

   c) Greater reliance on manual labour

   d) Reduction in skill development opportunities

2. What is a major challenge associated with the use of ICT in personal communication?

   a) Faster message delivery

   b) Reduced face-to-face interactions

   c) Wider reach of communication

   d) Real-time feedback

3. ICT has significantly improved access to information. Which example best illustrates this?

   a) The growth of digital streaming services

   b) The availability of online educational resources

   c) The rise of social media influencers

   d) The development of wearable technology

4. What is one potential downside of computers replacing manual jobs?

   a) Increased productivity

   b) Job displacement

   c) Higher efficiency in production

   d) Reduction in operational costs

5. Which sector has seen major skill development opportunities due to ICT advancements?

a) Agriculture

b) Retail

c) IT and software development

d) Construction

True or False

1. ICT has eliminated all barriers to global communication.
2. Social media platforms are a direct result of advancements in ICT.
3. Over-reliance on ICT in the workplace always leads to better productivity.
4. ICT has helped bridge educational gaps in developing countries.
5. Automation through computers has only positive effects on employment.

Short Answer Questions

1. How has ICT influenced the way people interact socially?
2. List two arguments in favour of computers and two arguments against them.
3. What role does ICT play in skill development?
4. What are some ways ICT has transformed access to information?
5. Why is critical thinking important when evaluating the impacts of computers on society?

Essay/Discussion Questions

1. Discuss the ways ICT has reshaped employment opportunities and skill requirements in the 21st century.
2. Examine the dual nature of ICT in personal communication. What are its benefits and potential drawbacks?
3. Evaluate the role of ICT in bridging the gap between developed and developing nations.

Chapter 10: Network Systems Concepts

Learning Outcome

By the end of this chapter, learners will gain awareness of and develop an understanding of the following key concepts related to network systems:

1. Network Systems Concepts
    - Definition of a network system
    - Components of a network
    - The rationale for networking
    - Types of networks: LAN, WAN, WLAN, PAN
    - Network topology
2. Scenario: Designing a Network System
    - Practical aspects of planning and implementing network systems
3. Trends in Network System Design
    - Emerging trends and advancements in network architecture

10.1 NETWORK SYSTEMS CONCEPTS

In today's digital age, network systems form the backbone of communication, data transfer, and collaboration within organisations and across the globe. A network system enables the interconnection of multiple devices, allowing them to share resources, access information, and communicate efficiently. This chapter delves into the foundational concepts of network systems, exploring the various components, architectures, and technologies that drive modern networks. By understanding the principles of network design, including topology, protocols, and security considerations, readers will gain insight into how network systems are structured and managed to support seamless connectivity and optimise performance.

10.1.1 What is a Network System?

At its core, a network system refers to the interconnection of two or more computers or devices to facilitate communication and resource sharing in a cost-effective and efficient way. This may include sharing hardware like printers and storage devices or accessing software across multiple machines. A significant advantage of network systems is the ability to reduce costs through multi-user software licenses, which are generally cheaper than purchasing single-user licenses for each machine. Furthermore, network systems are designed to enhance collaboration, streamline processes, and improve access to information.

10.1.2 Components of a Network

Building a functional network involves integrating several hardware and software components that ensure efficient communication and resource sharing. Below are the essential components required to create a basic network, along with their roles:

1. File Server

A file server is the backbone of a network, acting as a central hub to manage network resources, store files, and control access.

- **Functions:**
    - Stores and organises shared data.
    - Runs network services such as databases or application hosting.
    - Manages security policies, user permissions, and access control.
    - Regulates and monitors network traffic to ensure smooth operations.
- **Note:** While "server" often refers to the hardware, it is the dedicated server software that performs these tasks.

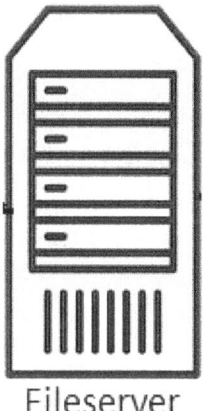
Fileserver

2. Workstation

A workstation is any computer or device used by end-users to interact with the network.

- **Uses:**
    - Accessing shared resources such as files, printers, and applications.
    - Running local or network-based tasks depending on the network configuration.
- **Evolution:** Historically, workstations were specialised, high-performance computers for tasks like CAD (Computer-Aided Design) and engineering. Modern desktops and laptops now serve as multi-purpose workstations.

Workstation/Client

3. RJ45 Connector

The RJ45 is the standard connector used for Ethernet networking.

- **Design:** It resembles a telephone connector but is larger, featuring 8 pins for connecting twisted-pair cables.
- **Role:** Establishes a physical link between computers, switches, routers, and other network devices.
- **Usage:** Primarily used in Local Area Networks (LANs).

4. Cables

Cables provide the physical medium for transmitting data between network devices.

- **Types:**

  - **Twisted-Pair Cables:** Commonly used for Ethernet, balancing cost and performance.
  - **Coaxial Cables:** Known for reliability and resistance to interference, often used in older networks or specific applications like cable TV.
  - **Fiber Optic Cables:** Used for high-speed data transmission over long distances with minimal signal loss.
- **Importance:** The choice of cable affects network performance, speed, and scalability.

5. Network Interface Card (NIC)

The NIC is a critical hardware component that connects a computer to a network.

- **Key Features:**
  - Converts data into electrical signals suitable for transmission over the network.
  - Each NIC has a unique MAC (Media Access Control) address for device identification.
- **Modern Variants:** Many devices now come with integrated NICs for wired or wireless connections.

6. Hubs and Switches

These are network devices that facilitate the transfer of data between connected devices.

- **Hub:**
  - A basic device that replicates and broadcasts incoming data packets to all connected devices.
  - Limited efficiency as it cannot distinguish between devices.

- **Switch:**
  - A more advanced device that forwards data only to the specific device intended to receive it.

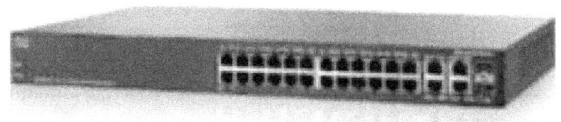

  - Reduces network congestion and improves overall performance.

7. Network Operating System (NOS)

A NOS is specialised software that manages network resources and communication between devices.

Example: Windows Server 2025 - latest Windows Server Version

The latest long-term servicing channel (LTSC) release of Microsoft's server operating system is Windows Server 2025, which was officially launched on November 1, 2024. It marks the 14th major LTSC release in the Windows NT family.

Features and Enhancements

Windows Server 2025 builds upon its predecessors by offering:

- Enhanced virtual machine (VM) support, including streamlined container management and better integration with Docker.
- Improved security, particularly for Hyper-V environments, with support for encryption.
- Updates to scalability and system management capabilities, catering to modern enterprise needs.

Most Widely Used Windows Server Version

Despite the availability of newer versions, Windows Server 2019 remains the most widely used Windows Server version.

- **Reasons for Popularity:**
  - Broad enterprise adoption due to its balance of stability, features, and support for hybrid cloud integration.

- o Trusted by organisations for running critical workloads and infrastructure.

Notable Previous Releases

- **Windows Server 2016:**
    - o Introduced significant features like native container support and improved virtualisation.
    - o Offered two main editions: Standard and Datacentre, catering to varying business needs.

Windows Server continues to evolve, with each release addressing modern technological demands while maintaining compatibility with existing enterprise systems.

10.1.3 Why Have Network Systems?

Networking offers a variety of benefits that enhance the efficiency and scalability of organisations, ranging from small businesses to large enterprises. Some key advantages include:

- **Centralised Data Storage**: In a network, all files and resources can be stored in a central location, enabling easier access and efficient backup. This centralisation ensures that all employees or users can retrieve the necessary data from any connected device, enhancing collaboration and data security.

- **Cost Savings**: Networks reduce the need for duplicate hardware and software. Shared printers, scanners, and servers can reduce an organisation's IT expenses, and multi-user software licenses further decrease costs.

- **Enhanced Communication**: Networks enable communication through emails, instant messaging, and video conferencing, making it easy for teams to collaborate in real-time, regardless of their physical locations.

- **Remote Access**: Users can access files and applications from remote locations through Virtual Private Networks (VPNs), enabling flexibility and remote working capabilities. Remote access also allows for secure communication and file sharing with encryption, ensuring data privacy.

10.1.4 Types of Networks

Networks are categorised based on their size, purpose, and geographical scope. Each type of network serves specific needs, from personal device connectivity to large-scale global communication. Understanding their characteristics helps in designing effective solutions for various environments.

Below are the most common types, along with explanations of their characteristics and applications:

Local Area Network (LAN)

A Local Area Network (LAN) is a network confined to a small geographic area, such as a single building, office, school, or campus. It enables devices within this localised space to communicate and share resources such as printers, file storage, and internet connections quickly and efficiently. LANs are typically characterised by high-speed connections and are cost-effective to set up and maintain. Technologies like Ethernet cables and switches are commonly used in LANs. LANs can also be secured with firewalls and passwords to ensure data protection.

Examples:

- Office networks where employees share files and printers.
- School computer labs with interconnected devices.

Wide Area Network (WAN)

A Wide Area Network (WAN) spans large geographic areas, such as cities, countries, or even continents. WANs often connect multiple LANs to facilitate communication between distant locations. The internet is the largest example of a WAN, interlinking millions of devices worldwide. WANs rely on technologies like fibre optics, satellite links, and telecommunication services for data transmission. They are typically more expensive to establish and maintain compared to LANs but are essential for global connectivity.

Examples:

- Corporate networks linking offices in different cities or countries.
- Banking systems enabling transactions across regions.

Wireless Local Area Network (WLAN)

A Wireless Local Area Network (WLAN) provides the functionality of a LAN but without physical cables, using wireless communication technologies such as Wi-Fi. WLANs allow devices like laptops, smartphones, and tablets to connect to the network within a specific range, offering greater mobility and convenience. Access points and wireless routers are used to extend the network's reach and ensure stable connections. WLANs are ideal for environments where flexibility and mobility are prioritised.

Examples:

- Home Wi-Fi networks enabling internet access for multiple devices.
- Public Wi-Fi hotspots in cafes, airports, and libraries.

Personal Area Network (PAN)

A Personal Area Network (PAN) is a short-range network designed for individual use, connecting personal devices such as smartphones, tablets, laptops, and printers. PANs use wireless technologies like Bluetooth, infrared, and near-field communication (NFC) to enable quick data transfer and resource sharing. Modern smartphones and devices often feature proprietary solutions, such as Apple's AirDrop and AirPlay, which allow seamless file sharing and media streaming.

Examples:

- Using Bluetooth to connect a smartphone to wireless earbuds.
- Sharing files between a laptop and a smartphone using AirDrop on Apple devices.
- Mirroring an iPhone screen to a smart TV or an Apple TV set via AirPlay.

10.1.5 Classifications of Network Systems

Network systems can be categorised by various criteria, including **range**, **topology**, **switching methods**, and the type of interconnectivity (server-based vs. peer-to-peer). These classifications help define the architecture, performance, and security of a network.

By Range:

1. **Local Area Network (LAN):**
   - A network confined to a small geographical area, such as a single building or campus.
   - **Typical Use Case:** Office environments, schools, and small businesses.
2. **Wide Area Network (WAN):**
   - **Definition:** A network that spans large geographical areas, connecting multiple LANs.
   - **Typical Use Case:** Connecting branch offices across different cities or countries.

By Topology:

1. **Bus Topology:**
   - All devices share a single communication line.
   - **Advantages:** Simple and cost-effective for small networks.
   - **Disadvantages:** Limited scalability and prone to data collisions.
2. **Star Topology:**
   - All devices are connected to a central hub or switch.
   - **Advantages:** Easy to manage and troubleshoot.
   - **Disadvantages:** Central hub failure can disrupt the entire network.
3. **Ring Topology:**
   - Each device is connected to two other devices, forming a ring.
   - **Advantages:** Data travels in one direction, reducing collisions.
   - **Disadvantages:** A single failure can disrupt the entire network.
4. **Mesh Topology:**
   - Every device is connected to every other device.
   - **Advantages:** High redundancy and reliability.

- **Disadvantages:** Expensive and complex to implement for large networks.
5. **Hybrid Topology:**
   - Combines elements of different topologies.
   - **Advantages:** Flexible and scalable.
   - **Disadvantages:** Complexity in design and implementation.

By Internetworking:

1. **Switched Networks:**
   - Use switches to manage data traffic.
   - **Advantages:** Efficient data handling and reduced collisions.
2. **Server-Based Networks:**
   - Utilise dedicated servers to manage resources.
   - **Advantages:** Enhanced security and centralised management.
   - **Disadvantages:** Higher cost and complexity, unsuitable for very small networks.
3. **Peer-to-Peer Networks:**
   - Each device can act as both a client and a server.
   - **Advantages:** Simple and cost-effective for small networks.
   - **Disadvantages:** Limited scalability and security.

By Switching Method:

1. **Circuit Switching:**
   - Establishes a dedicated communication path between two points for the duration of the connection.
   - **Advantages:** Guaranteed bandwidth and consistent performance.
   - **Disadvantages:** Inefficient for bursty traffic; resources are reserved even when not in use.
2. **Packet Switching:**
   - Divides data into packets that are transmitted independently over a shared network.
   - **Advantages:** Efficient use of bandwidth and flexibility.
   - **Disadvantages:** Variable latency and potential for packet loss.
3. **Cell Switching:**
   - Similar to packet switching but uses fixed-size cells for data transmission.
   - **Advantages:** Combines the benefits of circuit and packet switching; low latency and high throughput.
   - **Disadvantages:** More complex to implement.

Table: Network Classifications

Classification	Description	Advantages	Disadvantages
Range	LAN vs. WAN	LAN: High speed, low cost; WAN: Wide coverage	LAN: Limited range; WAN: Higher costs
Topology	Bus, Star, Ring, Mesh, Hybrid	Depends on topology: e.g., Star is easy to manage	Complexity varies by topology
Internetworking	Switched, Server-Based, Peer-to-Peer	Switched: Efficient; Server-Based: Secure	Server-Based: Costly; Peer-to-Peer: Limited
Switching Method	Circuit, Packet, Cell	Circuit: Reliable; Packet: Flexible; Cell: Efficient	Circuit: Inefficient for bursts; Packet: Variable

Server-based networks:

These systems utilise dedicated servers to manage and provide resources, such as a files or printers and applications. They offer robust security and reliability but may be inefficient for very small networks (less than 3 computers).

- **Advantages:**
    - **Enhanced Security:** Centralised control over access and data.
    - **Centralised Management:** Easier administration and resource management.
    - **Scalability:** Suitable for large networks with many users and devices.
- **Disadvantages:**
    - **Higher Cost:** Requires investment in server hardware and software.
    - **Complexity:** More complex to set up and maintain compared to peer-to-peer networks.
    - **Inefficiency for Small Networks:** Not cost-effective for networks with fewer than 3 computers.

Peer-to-peer networks:

In this configuration, computers share resources without a central server. Each computer (peer) can act as both a client and a server, sharing resources directly with other peers.

This system is easier and cheaper to set up, making it ideal for smaller networks but can suffer from performance and security issues, especially as the network grows.

- **Advantages:**
    - **Simplicity:** Easy to set up and manage without dedicated servers.
    - **Cost-Effective:** No need for expensive server hardware.
    - **Flexibility:** Suitable for small networks with up to 3 computers.
- **Disadvantages:**
    - **Limited Security:** Less control over data access and security.
    - **Poor Performance:** Performance degrades as the number of peers increases.
    - **Vulnerability:** If one peer fails, it can disrupt access to shared resources.

10.2 NETWORK TOPOLOGY

Network topology refers to the arrangement and configuration of various network elements, such as nodes, cables, hubs, and other devices, to establish connectivity between them. The choice of topology influences network performance, reliability, and scalability, and each topology has its own advantages and disadvantages. The basic topologies include Bus, Star, and Ring, and these can be combined in various configurations to create hybrid topologies.

10.2.1 Bus Topology

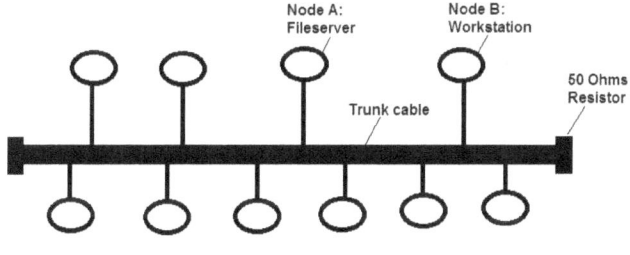

Diagram of Bus Topology

Bus topology, also known as a linear bus network, uses a single central cable (trunk) to which all nodes are connected sequentially. It is one of the simplest and most cost-effective topologies, commonly used in small Local Area Networks (LANs).

- **Configuration**: Nodes (like file servers and workstations) are connected in series to a single trunk cable. The topology typically uses twisted pair cables (10Base-2 Ethernet) with a transmission speed of 10 Mbps. The trunk ends are terminated with a 50-ohm resistor to prevent signal reflection.

- **Data Transmission**: Data travels in both directions along the bus, and a CSMA/CD (Carrier Sense Multiple Access with Collision Detection) protocol manages network access. Nodes listen for a clear channel before transmitting, and collisions are detected and managed by pausing and retrying transmission after a random delay.

Advantages of Bus Topology:

- Cost-effective and easy to set up.
- Decent data transmission rate of 10 Mbps.
- Uses CSMA/CD access method, effectively managing data collisions.

Disadvantages of Bus Topology:

- Single point of failure: if the trunk or one node fails, the entire network can go down.
- Difficult to troubleshoot faults.
- Performance degrades as the number of nodes increases due to collision likelihood.

10.2.2 Star Topology

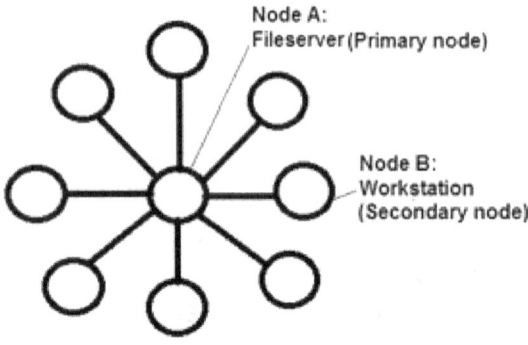

Diagram of Star Topology

Star topology is one of the most widely used network layouts. It consists of a central hub or switch (often a file server) that connects directly to each node in the network, creating a star-like structure.

- **Configuration**: Each node has an independent connection to the central hub or switch. Faults in individual nodes or cables do not affect the overall network unless the hub itself fails.
- **Data Transmission**: Uses Ethernet networks and employs CSMA/CD or polling access methods. Polling involves a designated controller node that manages data flow, acting as a master that coordinates communication among the connected nodes.

Advantages of Star Topology:

- Easy setup and maintenance with organised cable management.
- Fault isolation: individual node failures do not affect others.
- Centralised resource management and easy to trace faults.

Disadvantages of Star Topology:

- Higher costs due to increased cabling.
- Failure of the central hub results in network downtime.
- Polling can consume significant bandwidth, especially during heavy data exchange.

10.2.3 Ring Topology

Ring topology features a closed-loop configuration where each node is connected to two other nodes, forming a circular data path. This design can be physical or logical, and each node functions as a repeater.

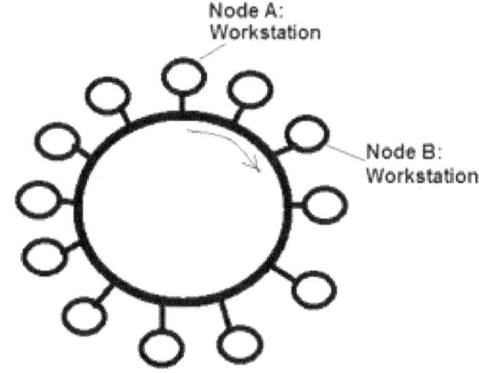

Diagram of Ring Topology

- **Configuration**: Data travels unidirectionally around the ring. Nodes receive data, check the address, and either pass it on or process it if it matches their address. No controlling node exists, and each node plays an active role in the network.
- **Data Transmission**: Uses a token-passing method, where a special data packet (token) circulates around the ring. Only the node holding the token can send data, ensuring orderly access and preventing collisions.

Advantages of Ring Topology:

- Efficient and deterministic network access due to token passing.
- Handles high traffic loads with minimal congestion.
- Predictable communication timing, beneficial for time-sensitive data.

Disadvantages of Ring Topology:

- Expensive and complex compared to Ethernet, especially due to token management.
- Difficult to scale and connect to Wide Area Networks (WANs).
- Entire network failure if a single node or connection is disrupted.

10.2.4 Mesh Topology

Mesh topology is a type of network that connects each node directly to every other node in the network, creating multiple pathways for data transmission. This design ensures high fault tolerance and redundancy but requires extensive cabling and configuration, making it costly and complex to implement.

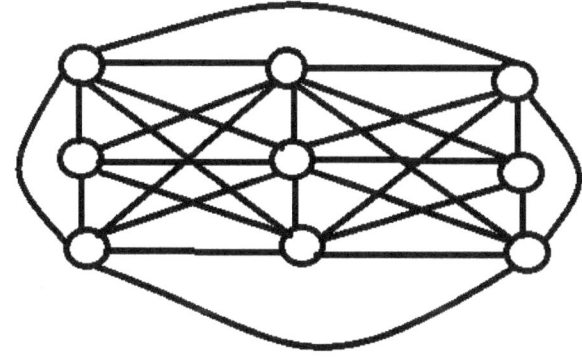

Diagram of Mesh Topology

Configuration: In a mesh topology, every node is connected to every other node, either fully or partially. In a full mesh, all nodes have direct links to one another, while in a partial mesh, only some nodes are directly interconnected. This creates multiple paths for data to travel, ensuring high redundancy and reliability.

Data Transmission: Data in a mesh topology travels via multiple routes, with each node acting as both a transmitter and a router. If one link fails, the data is rerouted through alternative paths, maintaining communication without disruption. This dynamic routing capability makes mesh topology robust and fault tolerant.

Advantages of Mesh Topology:

- **Redundancy and Reliability:** High resilience due to multiple pathways, ensuring network continuity even if some connections fail.
- **Scalability:** Can accommodate growth without significant reconfiguration, especially in partial mesh setups.
- **Efficient Traffic Management:** Direct links between nodes reduce congestion and enable faster data delivery.

Disadvantages of Mesh Topology:

- **High Cost:** Requires extensive cabling and hardware, especially in full mesh configurations.
- **Complex Setup and Maintenance:** The intricate connections can be challenging to configure, manage, and troubleshoot.
- **Resource-Intensive:** Consumes significant power and bandwidth for maintaining continuous connections and dynamic routing.

10.2.5 Hybrid Topology

Hybrid topology is a type of network that combines two or more basic network topologies, such as star, bus, or ring, to leverage the strengths of each while mitigating their weaknesses. It is highly scalable and flexible, but its complexity and cost depend on the specific configurations and the integration of different topologies.

Configuration: Hybrid topology combines two or more different types of network topologies (e.g., star, ring, bus, or mesh) to form a single cohesive network. Each segment of the hybrid network operates according to its native topology, but the segments are interconnected to enable seamless communication across the system.

Data Transmission: Data in a hybrid topology flows according to the characteristics of the integrated topologies. For example, a star segment may handle internal communication within a department, while a ring or bus segment connects multiple departments. Routers, hubs, or switches manage the flow of data between these segments, ensuring compatibility and efficiency.

Advantages of Hybrid Topology:

- **Flexibility:** Combines the strengths of multiple topologies, allowing customisation to meet specific network needs.
- **Scalability:** Easily accommodates expansion by integrating additional topologies without disrupting the existing network.
- **Fault Isolation:** Problems in one segment are less likely to impact the entire network, ensuring stability.

Disadvantages of Hybrid Topology:

- **Complexity:** The integration of diverse topologies increases design and management challenges.
- **High Cost:** Requires more resources, including specialised hardware and expertise, to implement and maintain.
- **Dependency on Central Devices:** If routers or switches fail, communication between different segments may be disrupted.

Summary

Each network topology offers distinct advantages and challenges, influencing overall network performance, cost, and scalability. Choosing the right topology depends on the specific requirements of the network, including cost, scale, fault tolerance, and ease of maintenance:

- Bus Topology is simple and cost-effective but suffers from poor fault tolerance and scalability.

- Star Topology is the most common due to its ease of maintenance and fault isolation, although it depends heavily on the central hub.

- Ring Topology provides deterministic access and efficient data management but is complex and costly, with significant impact from node failures.

- Mesh topology connects each node directly to every other node in the network, creating multiple pathways for data transmission. It ensures high fault tolerance and redundancy but costly and complex to implement.

10.2.6 Overview of Internetworking Devices

Network designers have a range of devices at their disposal to create and manage internetworks. Each device has specific functions that contribute to the overall performance, scalability, and security of the network.

1. Hubs (Concentrators)

- **Description**: Hubs are basic networking devices used to connect multiple computers or devices to a single network. They function primarily as repeaters, regenerating and retransmitting data signals across the network.

- **Use Case**: Suitable for small networks but limited in performance due to their inability to manage traffic efficiently.

2. Bridges

- **Description**: Bridges operate at the Data Link layer (Layer 2) of the OSI model and are used to logically divide a large network into smaller, manageable segments, improving network performance and reducing traffic congestion.
- **Use Case**: Helpful in segmenting networks but are largely being replaced by more advanced devices like switches.

3. Switches

- **Description**: Switches are advanced forms of bridges with multiple ports, each providing a separate collision domain. They manage data traffic more effectively by forwarding data only to the intended recipient device, thus improving network efficiency.
- **Use Case**: Commonly used in modern networks to replace hubs due to their superior traffic management, increased bandwidth, and the ability to create virtual LANs (VLANs).

4. Routers

- **Description**: Routers operate at the Network layer (Layer 3) and are responsible for directing data packets between different networks. They make forwarding decisions based on IP addresses, making them crucial for connecting and managing traffic between LANs, WANs, and external networks.
- **Use Case**: Essential for creating complex internetworks that connect multiple subnets and different network protocols.

5. Repeaters

- **Description**: Repeaters are simple devices with two ports that regenerate and retransmit signals between two network segments. They help extend the range of a network but do not filter or direct traffic.
- **Use Case**: Used in limited situations to extend the reach of a network without significant impact on traffic management.

Focus on Switches and Routers

With evolving networking demands, there is a clear shift towards using switches and routers as the primary devices for internetworking:

- **Switches** enhance network performance by reducing collisions and increasing bandwidth. Their ability to manage multiple ports efficiently allows for significant improvements in data flow and network speed.

- **Routers** are essential for connecting disparate networks, managing traffic effectively, and ensuring secure data transmission between internal and external networks. They also support dynamic routing protocols, which enable automatic route adjustments in response to network changes.

10.3 FROM NETWORK CONCEPTS TO STANDARDS

Having explored the fundamental building blocks of network systems, such as their classifications, components, types, and topologies, it is evident that networks are incredibly diverse in their design and purpose. While this diversity allows for tailored solutions to meet specific needs, it also presents a challenge: ensuring seamless communication and compatibility between different networks and devices.

This is where **standards in network systems** come into play. Standards provide a universal framework that governs how networks are structured, how data is transmitted, and how devices interact within and across networks. By adhering to these standards, network systems achieve:

- **Interoperability:** Ensuring devices from different manufacturers can work together.
- **Scalability:** Allowing networks to grow and adapt to future demands without losing functionality.
- **Efficiency:** Optimising resource use and minimising conflicts in data transmission.

In the next section, we will delve into key standards, including the **OSI model** and **TCP/IP model**, to understand how these frameworks provide structure and guidance to network operations. These models serve as blueprints, breaking down the complexities of communication into manageable layers, making it easier to analyse, design, and troubleshoot networks effectively.

By understanding these standards, we can bridge the gap between the physical and logical aspects of networking, enabling a comprehensive grasp of how modern networks function and evolve.

10.3.1 Standards in Network Systems

Standards in network systems is a customary agreement reached by international network consortium and laid down for the interconnection of network devices (hardware and/or software) on the network. Like protocols, standards are recommended and put in place in network systems for the fact that there are many different manufacturers from different countries of different components and connection media such as cables, fibre optics, telephone lines, switches, routers, computer systems, operating systems and network applications that are used in computer networks communication.

10.3.2 The OSI Model: An Overview

The OSI Model, or Open Systems Interconnection Model, is a conceptual framework developed by the International Standards Organisation (ISO) to standardise and facilitate communication between different network devices and systems. This model serves as a theoretical guide, helping designers and engineers understand how different protocols and technologies interact to enable network communication.

Key Features of the OSI Model

1. **Abstract and Theoretical Framework**:

   - The OSI Model is not an actual implementation but rather a reference model that outlines the functions required for communication between network systems. It provides a common language and guidelines for various technologies to interoperate.

   - **Purpose**: It helps in designing and troubleshooting network systems by breaking down the complex process of networking into more manageable and understandable layers.

2. **Layered Approach**:

   - The OSI Model divides network communication into seven distinct layers, each with a specific function and set of responsibilities. This layered approach simplifies the network architecture, making it easier to develop, maintain, and understand network protocols and services.

3. **Support for Connection-Oriented and Connectionless Protocols**:

   The OSI Model supports two main types of communication protocols:

   - Connection-oriented communication involves setting up a dedicated path, transmitting data reliably, and then closing the connection, similar to a telephone call. Connectionless communication, on the other hand, involves sending discrete messages independently without prior setup, much like sending individual letters or postcards through the mail.

10.3.3 Connection-Oriented Communication

1. Establishing a Connection:

- Before any data can be exchanged, the sender and receiver must first create a connection. This often involves a handshake process where both parties agree on the communication protocols and settings.

- Imagine two people setting up a phone call. Before they start talking, they need to dial each other's numbers, ensure their phones are working, and agree on when to start the conversation.

- This process might involve multiple steps, such as negotiating transmission rates or error-checking protocols, which could take seconds to minutes.

2. Data Transmission:

- Once the connection is established, data is transmitted in a continuous stream. The connection ensures that data arrives in the correct order and without errors.

- Think of this as a conversation over a secure telephone line where each person speaks in turn, and there is a clear, uninterrupted flow of dialogue.

- Data can be sent at a specified rate, such as 1 Mbps (Megabits per second), depending on the bandwidth of the connection.

3. Releasing the Connection:

- After the data exchange is complete, the connection is terminated. This involves a process to gracefully close the communication link.

- This is like hanging up a phone call after the conversation is over, ensuring that both parties have finished, and the line is properly disconnected.

- The release process could take milliseconds to seconds, depending on the complexity of the connection setup.

4. Example - Circuit Switching:

- Circuit switching establishes a dedicated path between the sender and receiver for the duration of the communication session.

- Traditional telephone systems use circuit switching, where a dedicated line is set up between two callers for the duration of their conversation.

- Each call uses a specific amount of network resources until the call is ended, which might be measured in terms of bandwidth used per minute.

10.3.4 Connectionless Communication

1. No Advance Setup:

- In connectionless communication, there is no need to establish a connection before sending data. The sender can transmit messages at any time without prior negotiation.

- Imagine sending a postcard through the mail. You don't need to arrange anything with the recipient before sending it; you simply drop it in the mailbox.

- The time to send a message is immediate, as there is no setup time involved.

2. Data Transmission:

- Data is sent in discrete units called datagrams. Each datagram is sent independently, and there is no guarantee of order, reliability or arrival.
- Sending a series of postcards, where each card might arrive at different times and in no particular order.
- Data packets might vary in size, and the transmission speed can be affected by network congestion or other factors. The size of each datagram can be limited, for example, to 1500 bytes.

3. Example - Surface Mail:

- Just as with surface mail, each message or datagram is sent individually without ensuring a continuous connection between the sender and receiver.
- Sending a letter through the postal service where each letter is treated as a separate entity, without the need for ongoing communication or setup.
- Delivery time can vary, and there is no guarantee that all messages will arrive in the order they were sent. The time for delivery can range from a few days to several weeks.

10.3.5 The Seven Layers of the OSI Model

The OSI model is a seven (7) layer configuration illustrated in the diagram below by Application Layer, Presentation Layer, Session Layer, Transport Layer, Network Layer, Data-Link Layer and Physical Layer. The model academically explains the communication process by which messages are transmitted and received over a typical network.

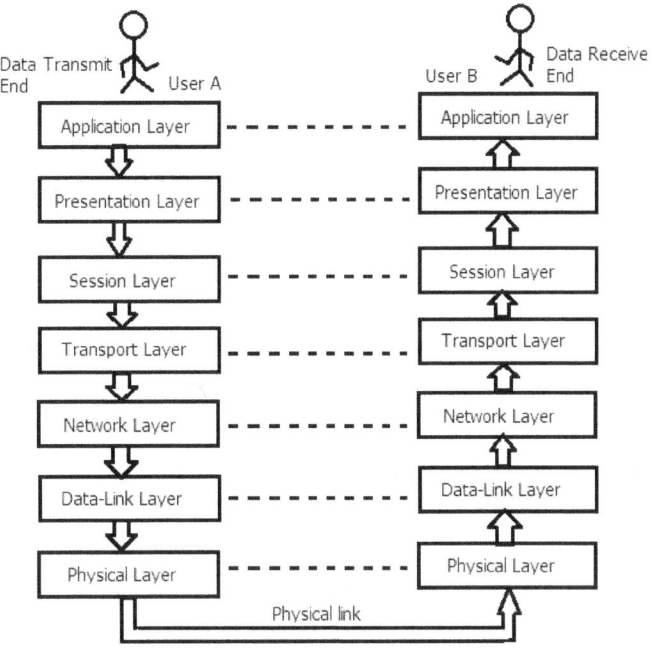

Diagram: The 7 Layers of the OSI Model

10.3.6 Basic Functions of the Layers of the OSI Model

The OSI Model consists of seven layers, each responsible for specific functions that enable communication between devices on a network. These layers work together to facilitate the transmission of data from a sending device to a receiving device, with each layer interacting with the layer directly above and below it. The process involves data encapsulation at the sender's end and decapsulation at the receiver's end, ensuring that the transmitted information is properly processed and delivered.

Layer-by-Layer Functions

1. **Application Layer (Layer 7)**

    - **Function**: The topmost layer that interacts directly with the user's application. It provides network services directly to end-users, such as web browsing, email, and file transfers.

    - **Key Responsibilities**:
        - Facilitates communication between software applications and lower network layers.
        - Provides network services such as HTTP (web browsing), FTP (file transfer), SMTP (email), and DNS (domain name resolution).

2. **Presentation Layer (Layer 6)**

    - **Function**: Translates data between the application layer and the lower layers, ensuring that the data is in a readable format for the application. It handles data encryption, decryption, compression, and translation.

- **Key Responsibilities**:
  - Converts data formats, such as translating character encoding schemes (e.g., ASCII to EBCDIC).
  - Encrypts and decrypts data to ensure secure communication.
  - Compresses data to reduce the size of transmitted files.

3. **Session Layer (Layer 5)**
   - **Function**: Manages and controls the dialog between two communicating devices, establishing, maintaining, and terminating sessions. It synchronises data exchange and manages communication checkpoints.
   - **Key Responsibilities**:
     - Establishes, manages, and terminates communication sessions.
     - Controls session flow to ensure that data is sent and received in the correct sequence.
     - Provides synchronisation points to recover from errors without restarting the entire process.

4. **Transport Layer (Layer 4)**
   - **Function**: Provides end-to-end communication control, ensuring reliable or unreliable data delivery based on the protocol used. It handles error recovery, flow control, and segmentation of data.
   - **Key Responsibilities**:
     - Manages data segmentation and reassembly, dividing large messages into smaller packets.
     - Implements flow control to prevent data overflow.
     - Provides error correction mechanisms and data acknowledgment for reliable transmission (e.g., TCP) or faster, unreliable delivery (e.g., UDP).

5. **Network Layer (Layer 3)**
   - **Function**: Determines the best path for data to travel across a network, handling packet forwarding, routing, and addressing. It is responsible for logical addressing and routing packets between devices.

- **Key Responsibilities**:
    - Routes data packets from the source to the destination using logical IP addresses.
    - Manages traffic congestion and packet forwarding decisions.
    - Handles fragmentation and reassembly of packets if they are too large for the data link layer.

6. **Data Link Layer (Layer 2)**
    - **Function**: Provides node-to-node data transfer and handles error detection and correction from the physical layer. It ensures that data is correctly formatted and prepared for transmission over the physical medium.
    - **Key Responsibilities**:
        - Establishes a reliable link between directly connected nodes.
        - Frames data packets and adds headers and trailers for error checking and flow control.
        - Uses MAC (Media Access Control) addresses to identify devices on the same network.

7. **Physical Layer (Layer 1)**
    - **Function**: The lowest layer that deals with the actual physical connection between devices, transmitting raw binary data over network media like cables, fibre optics, or wireless signals.
    - **Key Responsibilities**:
        - Defines the hardware components, electrical signals, and physical media used for communication.
        - Converts data into signals suitable for transmission (e.g., electrical pulses, light signals).
        - Manages the interface between the physical device and the transmission medium, including cable specifications and connector types.

10.3.7 Significance of the OSI Model

- **Standardisation**: The OSI Model standardises the process of network communication, allowing diverse systems to communicate effectively.
- **Troubleshooting and Design**: It aids network administrators and engineers in diagnosing network issues by isolating problems to specific layers.

- **Protocol Development**: Provides a structured approach to designing network protocols, ensuring compatibility and interoperability among different technologies.

10.3.8 Communication Process: Data Encapsulation and Decapsulation

1. **Encapsulation (Sender's Side)**:
    - Data starts at the application layer and moves down through each layer.
    - Each layer adds its own header (and sometimes a trailer) to the data, encapsulating it with necessary protocol information.
    - By the time data reaches the physical layer, it is fully encapsulated and ready for transmission.

2. **Transmission and Reception**:
    - The physical layer sends the encapsulated data across the network to the receiving device.

3. **Decapsulation (Receiver's Side)**:
    - The receiving device starts at the physical layer and moves the data up through each layer.
    - Each layer removes its corresponding header (and trailer if present), processes the data according to its protocol, and passes the remaining data to the next layer.
    - Finally, the application layer receives the original message, completing the communication process.

10.4 TCP/IP REFERENCE MODEL (INTERNET SUITE)

The **TCP/IP Reference Model**, also known as the **Internet Suite** or **Internet Model**, is the practical framework widely used for network communication today. While the OSI Model provides a detailed theoretical guide with seven distinct layers, the TCP/IP Model simplifies this into four key layers that handle all aspects of message transmission and reception over the network. This model serves as the backbone of the internet, guiding how data is packaged, transmitted, and received across interconnected devices globally.

10.4.1 Layers of the TCP/IP Reference Model

1. Application Layer
2. Transport Layer
3. Internet Layer
4. Host-to-Network Layer

10.4.2 Comparison with the OSI Model

The TCP/IP Model compresses the OSI Model's seven layers into four layers by merging certain functions. Here's a diagram and detailed breakdown of the TCP/IP layers and how they correspond to the OSI layers:

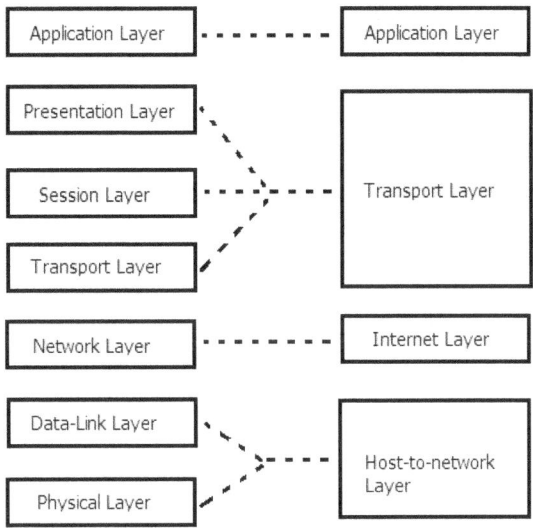

Diagram: OSI Model Vs. Internet Suite

1. **Application Layer (TCP/IP)**

   o **Correspondence to OSI**:

   - Equivalent to the **Application Layer, Presentation Layer, and Session Layer** of the OSI Model.

   o **Function**: Provides network services directly to user applications, handling data formatting, encryption, session management, and other tasks necessary for communication between networked applications.

   o **Key Protocols**:

   - **HTTP** (for web browsing),
   - **FTP** (for file transfers),
   - **SMTP** (for email),
   - **DNS** (for domain name resolution).

   o **Role**: Acts as the interface between user applications and the lower network layers, facilitating tasks such as sending emails, browsing websites, or accessing remote servers.

2. **Transport Layer (TCP/IP)**

   o **Correspondence to OSI**:

- Equivalent to the **Transport Layer** of the OSI Model.
   - **Function**: Manages end-to-end communication between devices, ensuring data is delivered reliably (or unreliably, if required) across the network.
   - **Key Protocols**:
     - **TCP (Transmission Control Protocol)**: Provides reliable, connection-oriented communication with error checking and flow control.
     - **UDP (User Datagram Protocol)**: Provides connectionless, faster communication without guaranteed delivery, suitable for applications like streaming.
   - **Role**: Handles data segmentation, error recovery, flow control, and ensures that data is sent and received in the correct order when using reliable protocols like TCP.

3. **Internet Layer (TCP/IP)**
   - **Correspondence to OSI**:
     - Equivalent to the **Network Layer** of the OSI Model.
   - **Function**: Responsible for packet routing, logical addressing, and forwarding data across networks, ensuring data packets find their way from the source to the destination.
   - **Key Protocols**:
     - **IP (Internet Protocol)**: Manages packet addressing and routing, ensuring that data reaches the correct destination across multiple networks.
     - **ICMP (Internet Control Message Protocol)**: Handles error reporting and diagnostic functions, such as ping tests.
     - **ARP (Address Resolution Protocol)**: Resolves IP addresses to physical MAC addresses within a local network.
   - **Role**: Routes data packets from one network to another, using IP addresses to identify devices and determine the optimal path.

4. **Host-to-Network Layer (TCP/IP)**
   - **Correspondence to OSI**:
     - Equivalent to the **Data Link Layer and Physical Layer** of the OSI Model.
   - **Function**: Handles the physical transmission of data over network media, including converting binary data into signals and managing device-to-device data frames.

- **Key Responsibilities**:
  - Manages the hardware and media used for communication, such as network adapters, switches, and cables.
  - Converts data packets into frames and bits suitable for transmission over the physical medium.
- **Role**: Establishes the physical connection between network devices and ensures that data is successfully sent and received at the hardware level.

10.4.3 Significance of the TCP/IP Model

1. **Simplicity and Practicality**:
   - Unlike the OSI Model, which is largely theoretical, the TCP/IP Model is practically implemented in real-world networks, including the internet. Its simplified four-layer structure makes it easier to understand and apply.

2. **Foundation of the Internet**:
   - The TCP/IP Model underpins all internet communication, defining how data is formatted, addressed, transmitted, routed, and received.

3. **Interoperability**:
   - The model ensures compatibility and interoperability between diverse hardware and software systems, allowing different network technologies to communicate seamlessly.

10.5 CASE STUDY 1

Scenario: Designing a Network System

Let's explore a hypothetical scenario where you are tasked with designing a network system for a small business. The company has two floors, with 20 employees distributed across several departments, and they require a robust network that will allow for file sharing, secure communication, and resource sharing, such as printers and servers.

Step 1: Assessing Requirements

Understanding the business's current and future needs is the first step. How many users need to be supported? What kind of data traffic is expected? Are there any security or privacy concerns, such as sensitive data that needs encryption?

Step 2: Choosing the Right Network Type

For a small business, a LAN might be appropriate. For remote employees, integrating a VPN would provide secure remote access.

Step 3: Selecting Hardware

Choosing suitable servers, NICs, hubs, switches, and routers based on user load is essential. Consider using wireless access points to support mobility and flexibility, as well as using security hardware, such as firewalls.

Step 4: Implementing Security

The network must be secured with strong firewalls, encryption methods, and secure password protocols. Additionally, installing network monitoring tools will allow the administrator to track traffic and detect security threats.

10.6 TRENDS IN NETWORK SYSTEM DESIGN

As technology evolves, so do network systems. The following are some emerging trends shaping the future of network architecture:

- **Software-Defined Networking (SDN)**: This technology allows network administrators to manage network services through abstraction of lower-level functionality. SDN is revolutionising how networks are designed and managed, allowing for more flexibility and central control.

- **Cloud Networking**: Businesses are increasingly shifting towards cloud-based services, where servers, storage, and applications are hosted remotely and accessed via the internet. Cloud networking reduces the need for on-site hardware and offers scalability and cost efficiency.

- **Network Function Virtualisation (NFV)**: Instead of using dedicated hardware, NFV enables the virtualisation of network services, allowing them to be run on standard hardware. This provides cost savings and greater flexibility.

- **5G and IoT**: The rise of 5G networks and the Internet of Things (IoT) is expanding the scope of networking, with billions of devices communicating over vast distances, enabling innovations such as smart cities and autonomous vehicles.

- **Edge Computing**: With edge computing, data processing happens closer to the source of data generation (the "edge" of the network), reducing latency and improving response times for applications like AI, autonomous driving, and real-time analytics.

10.6.1 Modern Network System Design

Network design has evolved to address the increasing complexity and demands of modern environments. Key trends include:

a. Shift to Layer 2 and Layer 3 Switching

A campus network where workgroups are connected via Layer 2 switches, and traffic between different VLANs is managed by a multilayer switch, ensuring efficient data flow and security.

- **Layer 2 (Data Link Layer) Switching:** Enhances performance by managing data traffic within the same network segment using MAC addresses.
- **Layer 3 (Network Layer) Switching:** Integrates routing functionalities, enabling inter-VLAN communication and advanced traffic management.
- **Multilayer Switches:** Combine Layer 2 and Layer 3 capabilities, providing a unified device for both switching and routing.

b. Increased Use of Virtual LANs (VLANs)

Implementing VLANs can reduce broadcast traffic by up to 70%, improving overall network performance.

- **Definition:** Logical segmentation of a network into smaller, isolated broadcast domains.
- **Benefits:** Enhances security, reduces broadcast traffic, and simplifies network management.
- **Example:** Separating the finance and HR departments into different VLANs to control access and enhance security.

c. Enhanced Security and Quality of Service (QoS)

- **Security Enhancements:** Use of ACLs, firewalls, and intrusion detection systems to protect network data.
- **QoS Implementations:** Prioritising critical applications (e.g., VoIP, video conferencing) to ensure low latency and high reliability.

Example: A network configured with QoS policies that prioritise video conferencing traffic over regular web browsing to maintain call quality.

d. Scalability and Control

Scalable network designs can support up to 10,000 devices without performance degradation, ensuring long-term usability.

- **Scalability:** Designing networks that can easily expand to accommodate more users and devices without significant reconfiguration.
- **Control:** Advanced routing protocols and traffic management tools provide better control over data flow and network resources.

e. Integration of Advanced Technologies

Implementing SDN allows network administrators to dynamically allocate bandwidth during peak usage times, ensuring optimal performance for all users.

- **Layer 3 Switching:** Facilitates efficient routing within the network.
- **Virtual Private Networks (VPNs):** Provide secure remote access for telecommuters and branch offices.
- **Software-Defined Networking (SDN):** Centralises network control, enabling dynamic adjustments to network configurations based on real-time needs.

Summary

Understanding network systems is critical in today's digitally connected world. Whether you're designing a network for a small business or a large enterprise, the concepts covered in this chapter - from network components and types to security and emerging trends - are essential in developing efficient, secure, and scalable networks. As technology continues to advance, network design and architecture will play an increasingly important role in connecting people, devices, and information.

10.6.2 Designing Local Area Networks (LANs)

Designing Local Area Networks (LANs) is crucial for ensuring efficient communication within a company's site, which could be a single building, or multiple buildings grouped together. Here's an overview of key concepts related to LAN design, including common technologies and considerations for optimising and future-proofing networks.

Key Characteristics of LANs:

1. **Ownership**: The company owns both the network infrastructure and the physical cabling within the site, allowing full control over network performance and maintenance.

2. **LAN Technologies**:

    - **Ethernet**: The most common LAN technology, using twisted-pair cabling or fibre optics to connect devices.
    - **Token Ring**: An older LAN technology that uses a token-passing protocol to prevent collisions; now largely obsolete.
    - **Fibre Distributed Data Interface (FDDI)**: Uses fibre optics and is used primarily for high-speed backbone networks.
    - **Fast Ethernet (100 Mbps)**: A faster version of Ethernet, offering increased data rates for demanding applications.
    - **Gigabit Ethernet (1 Gbps)**: Widely used in modern LANs, providing high-speed connections for servers, desktops, and network devices.
    - **Asynchronous Transfer Mode (ATM)**: A high-speed networking standard that uses fixed-size cells for data transmission, suitable for integrating voice, video, and data.

3. **Scaling with WAN Technologies**: For larger sites with multiple buildings, Wide Area Network (WAN) technologies can be used to connect buildings. Unlike traditional WANs, these site networks avoid high bandwidth costs because the company owns the cabling.

4. **Cost Considerations**:
   - **Initial Setup**: Installing the physical cabling and network hardware can be costly.
   - **Bandwidth Costs**: Once installed, there are no recurring costs from service providers, making high bandwidth relatively inexpensive.
   - **Upgrades**: Upgrading network infrastructure, such as replacing existing cables to support higher speeds, can be expensive.

5. **Optimising and Future-Proofing LAN Design**:
   - **Fast Functional Architecture**: Network designers aim to maximise performance on existing wiring. This often means using advanced LAN technologies (e.g., Gigabit Ethernet) compatible with current cabling.
   - **Layer 2 Switching**: Commonly used to provide dedicated bandwidth to each device (desktop, server) on the network, improving overall performance.
   - **Backbone Upgrades**: Technologies like Gigabit Ethernet and ATM can be used in the backbone, ensuring the network can handle high traffic loads.
   - **Futureproofing**: Planning network designs that accommodate future applications and technologies, minimising the need for frequent, costly upgrades.

10.6.3 Overview of Available Internetworking Technologies

Designing effective internetworks involves selecting and integrating a range of technologies tailored to specific needs. These technologies can be categorised into five critical areas:

1. Designing Local Area Networks (LANs)

LANs facilitate communication between devices within a building or a closely connected area, providing the foundation for most internetworking solutions.

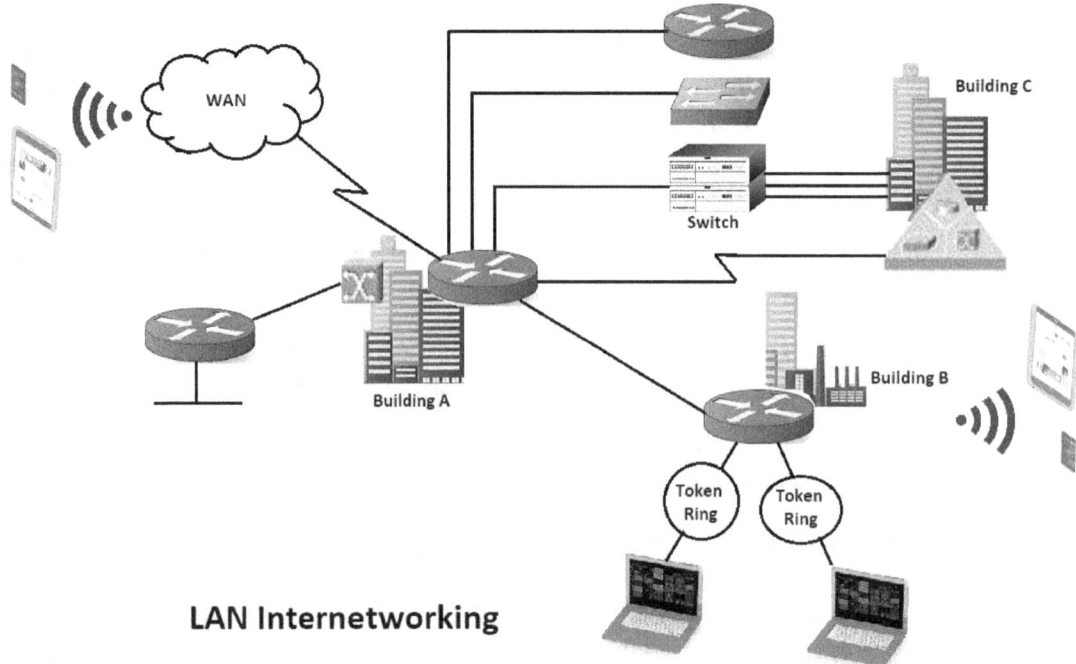

LAN Internetworking

Key LAN Technologies:

- **Ethernet:** The most widely used LAN technology, offering scalable and cost-effective solutions.

- **Token Ring:** A legacy technology with predictable performance, though largely replaced by Ethernet.

- **Fibre Distributed Data Interface (FDDI):** Offers high-speed connectivity over fibre-optic cables, suitable for backbone networks.

- **Fast Ethernet and Gigabit Ethernet:** Support high-speed data transfers essential for modern applications.

- **Asynchronous Transfer Mode (ATM):** Ideal for real-time voice, video, and data operations.

Trends in LAN Design:

- **Layer 2 Switching:** Enhances performance by dedicating bandwidth to specific devices.

- **Integrated Layer 3 Routing:** Adds intelligence to switching, improving security, traffic management, and scalability.

- **Gigabit Ethernet:** Provides a tenfold increase in speed compared to Fast Ethernet, becoming the backbone for high-performance networks.

2. Designing Wide Area Networks (WANs)

WANs connect geographically dispersed locations, enabling communication between remote sites and central offices.

Switching Technologies for WANs:

- **Circuit Switching:** Provides dedicated connections (e.g., ISDN, leased lines).
- **Packet Switching:** Efficiently shares bandwidth for bursty data traffic (e.g., Frame Relay, X.25).
- **Cell Switching (ATM):** Combines the advantages of circuit and packet switching for low latency and high throughput.

Emerging Trends in WANs:
Modern WAN designs emphasise:

- **Bandwidth optimisation** for cost-efficiency.
- **Scalable solutions** such as Frame Relay and ADSL.
- **Quality of Service (QoS):** Ensures reliable performance for applications like video conferencing and VoIP.

WAN Technology Examples:

- **Leased Lines:** Dedicated, secure point-to-point connections.
- **ADSL:** Cost-effective high-speed connections over existing telephone lines.
- **Frame Relay:** A popular choice for connecting multiple sites cost-efficiently.

3. Remote Connection Design

Remote connections are essential for enabling access to the internetwork from small branch offices or individual users.

Key Technologies for Remote Access:

- **Analogue Modems:** Legacy dial-up connections for low-speed access.
- **ISDN:** Provides digital connectivity for small-scale use.
- **ADSL and Leased Lines:** Offer faster and more reliable alternatives for remote sites.

Remote access solutions balance affordability with the need for stable, reliable connections, catering to both occasional and continuous usage scenarios.

4. Providing Integrated Solutions

As networks evolve, the integration of LAN and WAN functionalities becomes increasingly critical. Modern solutions merge voice, video, and data traffic into unified networks.

Technologies for Integration:

- **ATM:** Supports multiple Quality of Service (QoS) levels, making it ideal for diverse traffic types.
- **Unified Communication Platforms:** Facilitate seamless collaboration across different locations and devices.

5. Determining Internetworking Requirements

A successful internetwork design begins with a comprehensive assessment of specific requirements:

- **Environmental Factors:** Physical and logical topologies, geographical constraints.
- **Performance Constraints:** Bandwidth, latency, and reliability requirements.
- **Cost Considerations:** Balancing functionality with budgetary limits.

Best Practices in Design:

- **Hierarchical Models:** Segregate networks into core, distribution, and access layers to enhance scalability and fault isolation.
- **Traffic Analysis:** Ensures efficient routing and minimises bottlenecks.

LAN Technology Summary:

- **Routing Technologies**: Connect LANs within a local site network using Layer 3 switching or traditional routing.
- **Gigabit Ethernet**: Increases speed ten-fold over Fast Ethernet, providing high bandwidth for backbone designs.
- **LAN Switching Technologies**: Ethernet and Token Ring switching for dedicated network segments.
- **ATM Switching**: High-speed technology for voice, video, and data operations.

2. Designing WANs

Wide Area Networks (WANs) connect geographically separated areas, linking local and remote sites. Key switching technologies include:

- **Circuit Switching**: Provides dedicated bandwidth.
- **Packet Switching**: Offers flexible, efficient bandwidth usage.
- **Cell Switching (e.g., ATM)**: Combines circuit and packet switching benefits for low latency and high throughput.

Trends in WAN Design:

Modern WAN designs focus on optimising bandwidth, minimising costs, and maximising service quality. Technologies like Frame Relay, ISDN, and ATM provide scalable solutions for growing remote access and intranet needs.

WAN Technology Summary:

- **ADSL**: High-speed data over twisted-pair lines.

- **Analogue Modem (Dial-up)**: For occasional remote access or backup.
- **Leased Line**: Dedicated point-to-point connections.
- **Frame Relay**: Cost-effective, low-latency mesh topology.
- **X.25**: Legacy support and reliable circuits.
- **WAN ATM**: High bandwidth with quality-of-service options.

3. Utilising Remote Connection Design

Remote connections serve single users or small branch offices, offering dial-up or dedicated WAN options for cost efficiency. Technologies include:

- Analogue Modems
- ADSL
- Leased Lines
- ISDN

4. Providing Integrated Solutions

Internetworks increasingly integrate LAN and WAN functions, merging data, voice, and video traffic with technologies like ATM that support multiple Quality of Service (QoS) levels.

5. Determining Internetworking Requirements

Internetwork design involves assessing the environment, performance constraints, and topology variables to balance availability and cost. Hierarchical models (core, distribution, and access layers) facilitate scalable, reliable designs.

10.7 OUTPUT ANALYSIS

Despite advancements in equipment performance and media capabilities, designing a reliable internetwork is increasingly complex and requires a deep understanding of network technologies and emerging trends. Internetwork design involves connecting various networks into a cohesive, scalable, and secure system, often under different conditions and environments. Each major component of an internetwork - Local Area Networks (LANs), Wide Area Networks (WANs), and Remote Connections - has distinct design requirements.

Figure below is an example of a general network design process:

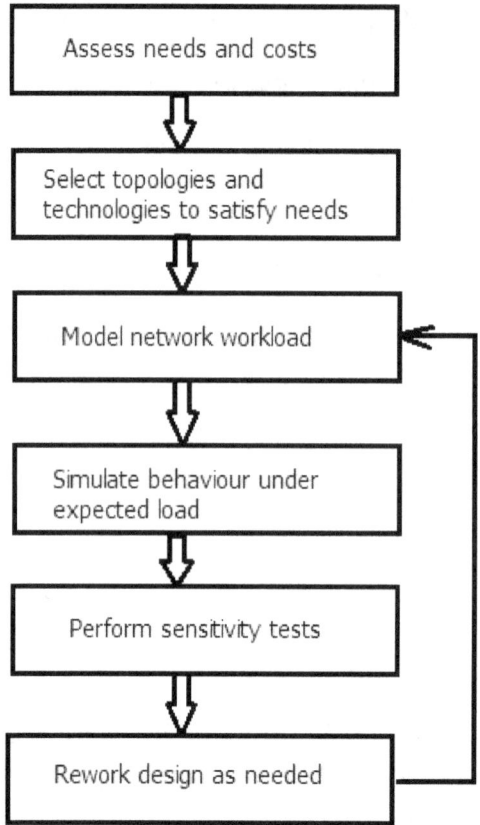

Diagram: Generic Network Design Process

10.7.1 Challenges in Internetwork Design:

1. **Complexity and Scalability:** Even a relatively small internetwork with about 50 interconnected routing nodes can present complex challenges, leading to unpredictable outcomes. Scaling up to thousands of nodes further complicates the design due to the need to manage extensive routing paths, data traffic, and network interactions.

2. **Diverse Environments:** Modern internetworks increasingly involve multiple media types (e.g., fibre optics, wireless, coaxial cables), various protocols (e.g., TCP/IP, MPLS, Ethernet), and connections to external networks beyond a single organisation's control, such as cloud services and third-party networks.

3. **Design Precision:** Careful design planning is essential to ensure that an internetwork can adapt to growth and evolving technologies without constant reconfiguration and performance degradation.

10.7.2 CASE STUDY 2

Scenario: Designing a Network System for EIA Training Centre

Terms of Reference / Statement of the Problem

EIA Training Centre requires a robust network system that connects two or more physical sites to ensure seamless communication, internet connectivity, and service availability across locations. The network design may involve creating a new network infrastructure from scratch or enhancing an existing one. The primary requirement is to facilitate effective "internetworking," a comprehensive approach to connecting computers and networks across various locations, encompassing both remote networking and internet services.

Solution: Desired Outcome

The goal is to design a network system that connects at least two remote sites, allowing computers and devices at each site to communicate and access internet services reliably. This configuration is crucial for operational efficiency, resource sharing, and maintaining constant communication between the sites.

Key Components of Internetworking

To build a large-scale internetwork, three essential components need to be considered:

1. **Local Area Networks (LANs)**

    - **Definition**: LANs are networks within a single physical location, such as a building or a campus, connecting users and devices locally. LANs enable the sharing of resources like files, printers, and applications among connected devices.

    - **Purpose**: Establish connectivity within a single site, supporting high-speed communication among local users.

    - **Typical Technologies**: Ethernet, Wi-Fi, switches, and routers.

2. **Wide Area Networks (WANs)**

    - **Definition**: WANs connect LANs across different geographical locations, such as multiple branch offices, cities, or even countries. They enable communication between sites and access to central resources over large distances.

    - **Purpose**: Ensure connectivity between different physical sites, supporting seamless communication and resource sharing.

    - **Typical Technologies**: Leased lines, MPLS (Multiprotocol Label Switching), VPN (Virtual Private Network), and SD-WAN (Software-Defined Wide Area Network).

3. **Remote Connections**
   - **Definition**: Remote connections facilitate the connection of individual users, such as telecommuters or mobile users, to the central network, enabling access to internal resources and internet services.
   - **Purpose**: Extend network access to offsite users, ensuring that they remain connected to the main office network.
   - **Typical Technologies**: VPNs, remote desktop access, secure tunnelling protocols, and cloud-based services.

10.7.3 Example of a Typical Enterprise Internetwork

In a typical enterprise internetwork setup, the interconnected LANs, WANs, and remote connections form a cohesive system that supports the organisation's communication and operational needs. Here's a diagram and an outline of how these components integrate:

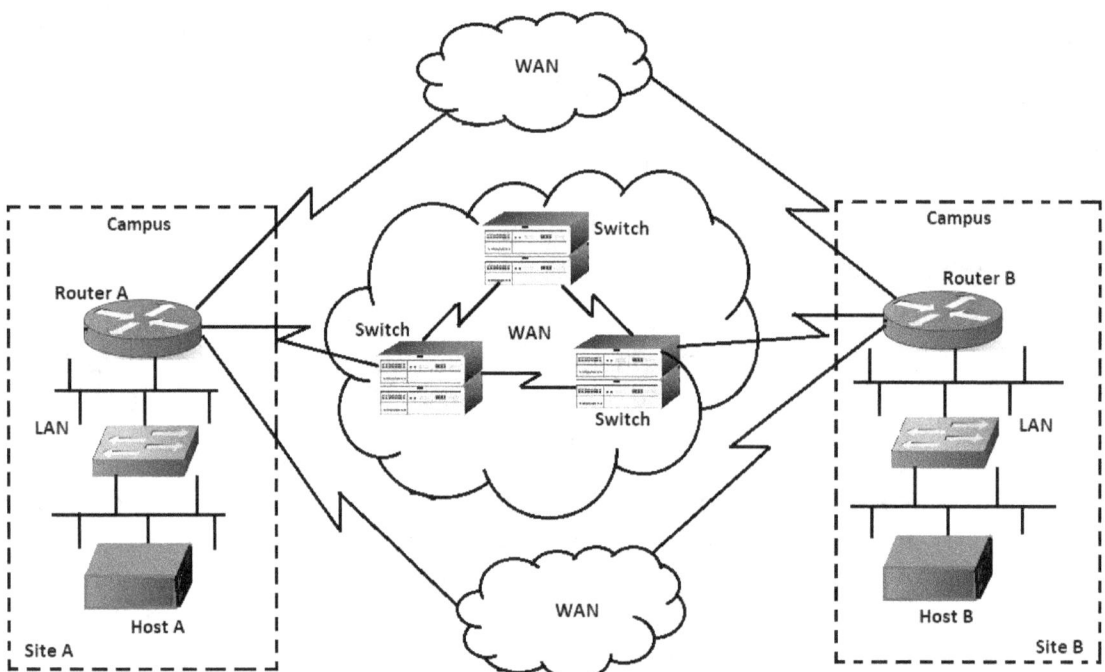

Typical LAN-WAN Enterprise Internetwork Systems

- **Site A (Head Office)**:
   - Hosts the primary LAN, which includes servers, desktop computers, printers, and other networked devices.
   - The LAN connects to the internet via a high-speed gateway router that manages traffic flow, security, and connectivity to other sites.

- **Site B (Branch Office)**:
    - Contains its own LAN setup, similar to the head office, with localised resources and devices.
    - Connected to Site A via a WAN link, such as an MPLS line or a dedicated VPN tunnel, ensuring continuous and secure data flow between the locations.
- **Remote Users**:
    - Access the network through secure VPN connections, allowing them to connect to either site from any location, enhancing flexibility and productivity.
- **Internet Access**:
    - Both sites and remote users have full internet connectivity, enabling access to external resources and cloud services.

10.7.4 Design Considerations for EIA Training Centre

1. **Network Redundancy and Reliability**:
    - Implement redundant connections, such as backup WAN links, to prevent downtime due to failures in the primary connections.
2. **Security**:
    - Use firewalls, VPNs, and secure access controls to protect the network from unauthorised access and cyber threats.
3. **Scalability**:
    - Design the network with the ability to expand, allowing additional sites and users to be easily integrated into the system.
4. **Performance Optimisation**:
    - Optimise traffic flow using Quality of Service (QoS) settings to prioritise critical data, ensuring high performance for essential applications.
5. **Network Management**:
    - Employ network management tools to monitor performance, manage configurations, and troubleshoot issues, minimising manual intervention.

With integration of these components and considerations, the EIA Training Centre can establish a reliable, secure, and efficient network that meets its current needs and scales for future growth.

10.7.5 Summary of LAN Technologies

LAN Technology	Typical Uses
Layer 2 Switching	High-speed data forwarding within the same network segment using MAC addresses.
Layer 3 Switching	Routing between different network segments, enabling inter-VLAN communication and traffic management.
Multilayer Switches	Combining Layer 2 and Layer 3 functionalities in a single device for efficient switching and routing.
Gigabit Ethernet	Providing high-speed (1 Gbps) connections for backbone networks and high-demand applications.
Fast Ethernet	Offering improved speeds (100 Mbps) over traditional Ethernet for demanding network segments.
VLANs	Logical network segmentation to enhance security and reduce broadcast traffic.
Quality of Service (QoS)	Prioritising critical network traffic to ensure reliable performance for essential applications.

10.8 NETWORK PERFORMANCE MEASUREMENT

Network performance refers to the effectiveness and efficiency of data transfer within a network. It is measured using several key parameters that collectively determine how well a network handles data transmission between devices. Understanding these metrics helps in diagnosing issues, optimising performance, and designing robust network systems.

10.8.1 Key Parameters for Measuring Network Performance

1. **Network Latency**

    - **Definition**: The time required to transfer an empty message between two known computers. It is the sum of various delays within the network, including processing, transmission, propagation, and queuing delays.

    - **Factors Influencing Latency**:

        - **Propagation Delay**: Time taken for the signal to travel through the medium.
        - **Transmission Delay**: Time taken to push all the packet's bits into the wire.

- **Processing Delay**: Time taken by devices (e.g., routers, switches) to process the packet header.
- **Queuing Delay**: Time packets spend waiting in queues due to network congestion.

2. **Network Data Transfer Rate**
   - **Definition**: Measured in bits per second (bit/s or bps), it represents the speed at which data is transferred between sender and receiver nodes once the transmission begins.
   - **Importance**: A higher data transfer rate implies faster data delivery, improving the overall user experience in applications such as streaming, online gaming, or large file transfers.

3. **Message Transfer Time**
   - **Definition**: The total time required to send a complete message from the sender to the receiver. It combines latency and the time it takes to transmit the actual data.
   - **Formula**: Message Transfer Time = Latency + (Length of Message/Data Transfer Rate)
   - **Example**: If the latency is 10 milliseconds, the message length is 1 megabit, and the data transfer rate is 10 Mbps, then:
   Message Transfer Time = 10 ms + 1 Mb/10 Mbps = 10 ms + 100 ms = 110 ms.

4. **Bandwidth (BW)**
   - **Definition**: The maximum volume of data that can be transferred across the network in a given time, typically measured in bits per second (bps). It represents the network's capacity and is crucial for determining how much data can flow through the network simultaneously.
   - **Role**: Bandwidth directly impacts how many users or data-intensive applications can run on the network without causing congestion.

5. **Maximum Data Rate (Shannon's Limit)**
   - **Definition**: The theoretical upper limit on the data transfer rate of a communication channel, determined by the channel's bandwidth and the signal-to-noise ratio (S/N). It provides a benchmark but is not achievable in practice due to real-world factors such as interference and imperfect hardware.
   - **Formula**: Maximum Data Rate = BW × $\log_2(1 + \text{Signal/Noise})$

- **Explanation**: This formula, derived from Shannon's theorem, shows that increasing the bandwidth or improving the signal-to-noise ratio will enhance the potential data rate of the channel.

10.8.2 Example Calculation of Maximum Data Rate

- **Scenario**: A telephone line with a bandwidth of 6 kHz and a signal-to-noise ratio (S/N) of 60 dB (decibels), where 60 dB corresponds to a ratio of 1000:1.

- **Calculations**:
  - **Signal-to-Noise Ratio (S/N)** in linear form: $S/N = 10^{(60/10)} = 1000$
  - **Maximum Data Rate**: Maximum Data Rate = 6,000 Hz × $\log_2(1+1000)$ ≈ 6,000 Hz × 9.97 ≈ 59,820 bps ≈ 60 kbit/s

10.8.3 Practical Considerations

- **Shannon's Limit** is theoretical and assumes perfect conditions, such as no interference, no signal distortion, and ideal hardware. In practice, environmental factors, imperfect equipment, and protocol overhead reduce the achievable data rates below this maximum.

- **Optimising Network Performance**: Network engineers often adjust bandwidth allocations, minimise latency through improved routing, and enhance the signal-to-noise ratio by using better cables or signal boosters to come closer to the theoretical limits.

Tutorial Activity 10 - Network Systems Concepts

Quizzes and Questions

Multiple Choice Questions (MCQs)

1. **What is the primary purpose of a network system?**
    a) To replace standalone computers
    b) To facilitate resource sharing and communication
    c) To increase the cost of technology implementation
    d) To restrict data access
2. **Which of the following is an example of a Personal Area Network (PAN)?**
    a) A home Wi-Fi router connecting multiple devices
    b) A Bluetooth connection between a phone and a smartwatch
    c) A corporate intranet
    d) A global internet connection
3. **In a star topology, all devices are connected to:**
    a) Each other in a loop
    b) A central hub or switch
    c) Multiple backbone cables
    d) A wireless access point
4. **Which component is responsible for directing data between different networks?**
    a) Switch
    b) Router
    c) Modem
    d) Access point
5. **Which type of network is typically used for connecting computers within a single building or campus?**
    a) WAN
    b) LAN
    c) WLAN
    d) PAN

True or False

1. A Wide Area Network (WAN) typically connects devices within a single office.
2. A network topology refers to the arrangement of devices in a network.
3. Bluetooth technology is commonly used in Local Area Networks (LAN).
4. The client-server model is a basic concept in network architecture.
5. Mesh topology provides high redundancy but is cost-effective to implement.

Short Answer Questions

1. Define a network system and explain its importance.
2. What are the key components of a network system?
3. List and briefly explain the four common types of networks.
4. What is the role of network topology in system design?
5. Why is network planning critical before implementation?

Scenario-Based Question

Scenario: A small business with 10 employees wants to set up a network for sharing files, printers, and internet access. The business requires minimal cost and ease of setup.

1. What type of network would you recommend and why?
2. Which hardware components are necessary for this network?

Essay/Discussion Questions

1. Discuss the advantages and disadvantages of different network topologies in terms of scalability, reliability, and cost.
2. How do emerging trends like Software-Defined Networking (SDN) and 5G impact modern network systems?
3. Explain the practical considerations a network administrator must address when designing a secure network for a medium-sized organisation.

Reference:

1. William Stallings, *Data and Computer Communications*, Pearson Prentice Hall, 7th Edition.
2. Bruce Hallberg, *Networking: A Beginner's Guide*, Osborne/McGraw Hill, 2nd Edition.
3. Peter Hodson, *Local Area Networks*, 2nd Edition.
4. Andrew S. Tanenbaum, *Computer Networks*, 3rd Edition, Prentice Hall.

Chapter 11: Basic Data Transmission Systems

Learning Outcome

By the end of this chapter, learners will be able to:

1. Understand key concepts related to data transmission and communication systems.

2. Differentiate between various data transmission media, including cables, radio signals, microwaves, and satellite communication.

3. Identify different transmission methods (baseband vs. broadband) and transmission modes (asynchronous vs. synchronous).

4. Recognise the differences between transmission directions (simplex, half-duplex, full-duplex, and asymmetric duplex).

5. Quantify data transmission speeds and comprehend the units of measurement like bits per second (bps) and baud rate.

11.1 Data Transmission & Communication Systems Concepts

In the interconnected world of today, data transmission systems form the foundation of all communication networks. Whether facilitating simple file transfers within an office or enabling complex global communications via satellites, understanding the principles and technologies behind data transmission is essential for designing efficient, reliable, and high-performance networks. This chapter explores the fundamental concepts of data transmission, various transmission media, methods, modes, directions, and rates. By delving into these topics, readers will gain a comprehensive understanding of how data moves from one point to another, the technologies that make this possible, and the considerations involved in selecting the appropriate transmission systems for different applications.

Data Transmission

Data transmission is the process of transferring data from one device or location to another through various communication channels. This transfer can occur between two computers, across a network, or between different components within a single system. The primary goal of data transmission is to enable communication and the sharing of resources, ensuring that information flows smoothly and efficiently.

Consider a corporate environment where multiple employees access shared resources such as printers, files, and databases. Data transmission systems facilitate the transfer of print jobs from individual computers to a shared printer, enable file sharing between workstations and servers, and support communication between different departments.

Quantification:

- **Cost Efficiency:** Utilising networked resources can reduce costs by up to 50% compared to individual setups.
- **Productivity Gains:** Centralised data access can increase employee productivity by approximately 20%.

11.2 Transmission Media

Transmission media are the physical pathways or channel through which data is transmitted from one device to another. They play a critical role in determining the speed, distance, and reliability of data transmission. This section explores the various types of transmission media, including cables, radio signals, microwaves, and satellite communications.

11.2.1 Cables

Cables are the most common transmission media used in wired networks. They come in various types, each with its own characteristics, advantages, and limitations.

i. Twisted Pair Cable

Twisted pair cable consists of two insulated copper wires twisted together to reduce electromagnetic interference (EMI). It is widely used in telecommunications and local area networks (LANs).

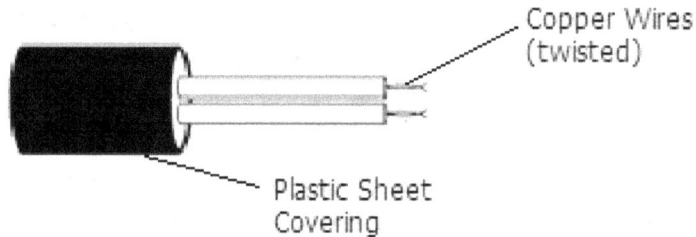

Twisted Pair Cable

- **Types:**
    - **Unshielded Twisted Pair (UTP):**
        - Lacks additional shielding around the wires.
        - **Advantages:** Cost-effective and flexible.
        - **Disadvantages:** More susceptible to EMI and crosstalk.
        - **Typical Use:** Ethernet networks (e.g., Cat5e, Cat6).
    - **Shielded Twisted Pair (STP):**
        - Includes a shielding layer to protect against EMI.
        - **Advantages:** Better protection against interference.

- **Disadvantages:** More expensive and less flexible.
            - **Typical Use:** Environments with high EMI, such as industrial settings.
    - **Quantification:**
        - **Bandwidth:** UTP can support speeds up to 10 Gbps (Cat6a).
        - **Distance:** Effective up to 100 meters without signal boosters.

ii. Coaxial Cable

Coaxial cable consists of a central conductor made of copper, surrounded by an insulating layer, a metallic shield, and an outer protective jacket. This design minimises signal loss and interference, making it suitable for high-frequency applications.

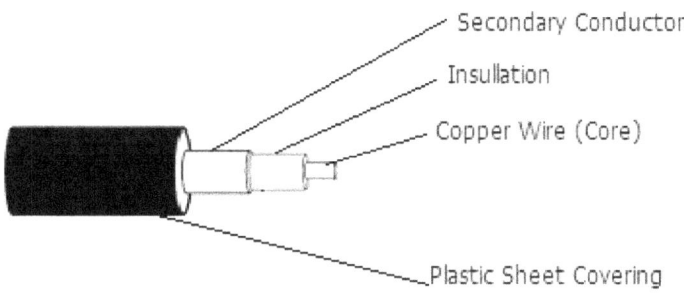

Coaxial Cable

- **Characteristics:**
    - **Central Conductor:** Carries the data signal.
    - **Insulation:** Prevents signal leakage.
    - **Shielding:** Protects against EMI and signal interference.
    - **Outer Jacket:** Provides physical protection.
- **Advantages:**
    - **High Bandwidth:** Supports higher frequencies and greater data rates than twisted pair.
    - **Durability:** More resistant to interference and physical damage.
- **Disadvantages:**
    - **Cost:** More expensive than twisted pair cables.
    - **Bulkiness:** Thicker and less flexible, making installation more challenging.
- **Quantification:**

- **Data Rate:** Can support up to 10 Mbps (traditional) to 1 Gbps (modern applications).
- **Distance Capability:** Effective up to 500 meters without significant signal loss.

iii. Fibre Optic Cable

Fibre optic cables use light to transmit data, offering unparalleled speed and bandwidth capabilities. They consist of thin strands of glass or plastic fibres that carry light signals modulated with data.

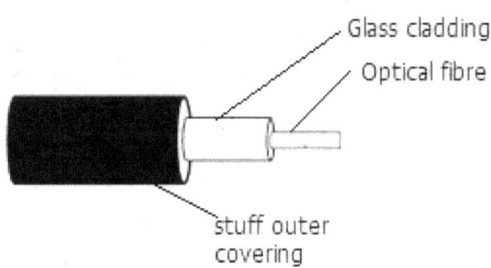

Fibre Optic Cable

- **Types:**
  - **Single-Mode Fiber (SMF):**
    - Has a small core (8-10 microns) that allows only one light mode to propagate.
    - **Advantages:** Supports long-distance transmission with minimal signal loss.
    - **Typical Use:** Long-haul telecommunications and high-speed data networks.
  - **Multi-Mode Fiber (MMF):**
    - Has a larger core (50-62.5 microns) that allows multiple light modes to propagate.
    - **Advantages:** Easier to splice and connect.
    - **Typical Use:** Shorter distance applications within buildings or campuses.
- **Advantages:**
  - **High Bandwidth:** Capable of supporting data rates from 100 Mbps to 100 Gbps and beyond.
  - **Long Distance:** Can transmit data over distances up to 100 kilometres without significant loss.

- o **Immunity to EMI:** No susceptibility to electromagnetic interference, ensuring signal integrity.
- **Disadvantages:**
    - o **Cost:** Higher initial cost compared to copper cables.
    - o **Fragility:** More delicate and prone to damage if not handled properly.
    - o **Installation Complexity:** Requires specialised tools and expertise for installation and maintenance.
- **Quantification:**
    - o **Bandwidth:** Up to 100 Gbps and beyond.
    - o **Distance Capability:** Up to 100 kilometres for SMF; up to 2 kilometres for MMF without amplification.

11.2.2 Radio Signal Transmission

Radio signal transmission uses radio waves to send information wirelessly between devices. This method is widely used in various applications, including broadcasting, mobile communications, and wireless networking.

- Radio waves are a type of electromagnetic radiation with frequencies ranging from 3 kHz to 300 GHz. They can carry information by modulating properties such as amplitude, frequency, or phase.
- **Components:**
    - o **Transmitter:** Converts data into radio signals.
    - o **Antenna:** Radiates the radio waves into the environment.
    - o **Receiver:** Captures and decodes the radio signals back into usable data.
- **Advantages:**
    - o **Mobility:** Allows devices to communicate without physical connections.
    - o **Flexibility:** Suitable for a wide range of applications, from short-range Wi-Fi to long-range broadcasting.

- o **Ease of Installation:** No need for extensive cabling infrastructure.
- **Disadvantages:**
  - o **Interference:** Susceptible to interference from other electronic devices and environmental factors.
  - o **Security Risks:** Wireless signals can be intercepted more easily than wired transmissions.
  - o **Limited Bandwidth:** Lower data rates compared to wired transmission methods.
- **Quantification:**
  - o **Frequency Range:** 3 kHz to 300 GHz.
  - o **Data Rates:** Varies from kilobits per second (e.g., AM/FM radio) to gigabits per second (e.g., Wi-Fi 6).
  - o **Applications:** AM/FM radio (sound), television broadcasting (audio and video), mobile phones, and Wi-Fi networks.

11.2.3 Microwave Transmission

Microwave transmission employs high-frequency radio waves (typically between 300 MHz and 300 GHz) for point-to-point communication. Unlike general radio signals, microwaves require line-of-sight between the transmitting and receiving antennas.

- **Characteristics:**
  - o **Wavelength:** Shorter than radio waves, ranging from one meter to one millimetre.
  - o **Frequency Bands:** UHF (Ultra High Frequency), SHF (Super High Frequency), and EHF (Extremely High Frequency).
- **Advantages:**
  - o **High Data Rates:** Supports large volumes of data transmission with low latency.
  - o **Long Distance:** Capable of spanning up to 30 miles with the right infrastructure.
- **Disadvantages:**
  - o **Line-of-Sight Requirement:** Requires unobstructed paths between antennas, making it vulnerable to physical barriers and the Earth's curvature.
  - o **Weather Sensitivity:** Susceptible to signal degradation due to rain, fog, and other atmospheric conditions.

- o **Installation Costs:** Requires precise alignment and more expensive equipment compared to lower-frequency radio transmissions.
- **Quantification:**
  - o **Frequency Range:** 300 MHz to 300 GHz.
  - o **Data Rates:** Up to several Gbps, depending on the technology and infrastructure.
  - o **Distance Capability:** Effective up to 30 miles (48 kilometres) with direct line-of-sight.
- **Applications:**
  - o **Telecommunication Networks:** Linking distant network nodes.
  - o **Broadcasting:** Transmitting television and radio signals over long distances.
  - o **Military Communications:** Secure and rapid data transmission.

11.2.4 Communication Satellite

Communication satellites are artificial satellites deployed in Earth's orbit to relay and amplify telecommunication signals. They serve as intermediary points for transmitting data between distant locations, overcoming the limitations of terrestrial transmission methods.

- Satellites in geostationary orbit (approximately 22,236 miles or 35,786 kilometres above Earth) remain fixed relative to a point on the ground, enabling continuous communication with specific regions.
- **Components:**
  - o **Transponders:** Receive, amplify, and retransmit signals between the ground stations.
  - o **Antennas:** Facilitate signal transmission and reception.
  - o **Power Systems:** Typically, solar panels provide energy for satellite operations.
- **Advantages:**
  - o **Global Coverage:** Enables communication across vast distances, including remote and inaccessible areas.

- o **Line-of-Sight Independence:** Signals can traverse the Earth's curvature, unlike microwave transmissions.
  - o **Versatility:** Supports a wide range of applications, including television broadcasting, internet services, and global positioning systems (GPS).
- **Disadvantages:**
  - o **Latency:** Significant delay (approximately 240 milliseconds round-trip) due to the long-distance signals must travel.
  - o **Cost:** High initial investment for satellite launch and maintenance.
  - o **Vulnerability:** Susceptible to space weather, debris impacts, and potential signal interception.
- **Quantification:**
  - o **Orbit Altitude:** Geostationary satellites at 22,236 miles above Earth.
  - o **Data Rates:** Can support data rates from several Mbps to Gbps, depending on the transponder and technology used.
  - o **Coverage Area:** Each geostationary satellite covers approximately one-third of the Earth's surface.
- **Applications:**
  - o **Telecommunications:** Facilitating international phone calls and internet services.
  - o **Broadcasting:** Delivering television and radio signals globally.
  - o **Navigation:** Providing accurate positioning data through systems like GPS.
  - o **Disaster Management:** Enabling communication in areas affected by natural disasters.

11.3 TRANSMISSION METHODS

Transmission methods define how data is encoded and sent over a communication medium. The two primary transmission methods are **baseband** and **broadband**.

11.3.1 Baseband Transmission

Baseband transmission sends a single signal over the communication channel at a time. It is typically used for short-distance communication and is the standard method for Ethernet networks.

- **Characteristics:**
  - o **Single Signal:** Only one data stream is transmitted at a time.

- o **Modulation:** Minimal modulation techniques are used, often transmitting digital data directly.
- **Advantages:**
  - o **Simplicity:** Easier to implement with straightforward encoding schemes.
  - o **Cost-Effective:** Requires less complex equipment, reducing costs.
  - o **Low Latency:** Minimal processing delays since data is transmitted directly.
- **Disadvantages:**
  - o **Limited Distance:** Effective only over short distances (up to 1,000 feet or 3,048 meters).
  - o **Single Channel:** Cannot carry multiple signals simultaneously without additional equipment like boosters.
- **Quantification:**
  - o **Distance:** Effective up to 1,000 feet (3,048 meters).
  - o **Data Rate:** Can support high-speed data rates, such as 10 Gbps with appropriate cabling.
- **Example:**
  - o **Ethernet Networks:** Most local area networks (LANs) use baseband transmission for connecting computers and devices within a building.

11.3.2 Broadband Transmission

Broadband transmission allows multiple signals to be transmitted simultaneously over the same medium by using different frequency bands for each signal. This method is ideal for longer-distance communication and high-capacity applications.

- **Characteristics:**
  - o **Multiple Channels:** Divides the available bandwidth into multiple channels, each carrying a separate signal.
  - o **Modulation:** Uses sophisticated modulation techniques to encode multiple data streams onto a single carrier wave.
- **Advantages:**
  - o **High Capacity:** Can carry multiple types of data (data, audio, video) simultaneously.
  - o **Long Distance:** Suitable for transmitting data over longer distances without significant degradation.

- o **Efficient Bandwidth Use:** Maximises the utilisation of the communication medium by allowing multiple transmissions concurrently.
- **Disadvantages:**
    - o **Complexity:** Requires more advanced equipment and modulation techniques.
    - o **Cost:** Higher initial investment due to the need for specialised hardware.
- **Quantification:**
    - o **Distance:** Can support data transmission over several kilometres with minimal loss.
    - o **Data Rate:** Capable of supporting multiple gigabits per second by aggregating multiple channels.
- **Example:**
    - o **Cable Television:** Uses broadband transmission to deliver multiple TV channels and internet services over a single coaxial cable.

11.4 TRANSMISSION MODES

11.4.1 Asynchronous Transmission

Asynchronous transmission is a method of sending data where individual characters or bytes are transmitted at irregular intervals. Each character is framed by specific control bits known as start and stop bits, which mark the beginning and end of the data packet.

- **Mechanism**
  This mode allows devices to send data when it is available, without needing to synchronise the transmission with the receiving device. The start bit indicates that a new character is being sent, and the stop bit signifies the end of that character. This flexibility makes asynchronous transmission particularly useful for devices that may not constantly generate data, such as keyboards or sensors. Each byte is sent independently, which means that the devices can operate at different speeds, accommodating variations in processing times.

- **Applications**
  Asynchronous transmission is commonly used in serial communication protocols like RS-232, which is often utilised for computer-to-peripheral communications. Additionally, this mode plays a significant role in various data communication technologies, including asynchronous transfer mode (ATM) networks, where data packets can be sent without the need for a dedicated circuit.

- **Advantages**
  One of the primary benefits of asynchronous transmission is its simplicity. The protocol is easy to implement, requiring minimal additional hardware for synchronisation. Because it does not require a constant connection between devices, it is well-suited for applications where communication does not need to be continuous, such as in remote monitoring systems or data logging.

11.4.2 Synchronous Transmission

Synchronous transmission is a more advanced method of data transmission that sends data in a continuous stream, synchronised by a clock signal shared between the sending and receiving devices.

- **Mechanism**
  Unlike asynchronous systems, synchronous transmission does not utilise start and stop bits. Instead, the timing of data transmission is governed by a clock signal, allowing for higher data throughput. This means that the sender and receiver are coordinated to send and receive data simultaneously in fixed time intervals. This synchronisation enables multiple bits to be sent at once, leading to more efficient communication.

- **Applications**
  Synchronous transmission is widely used in high-speed data transfer scenarios, such as fibre optic communication systems and digital subscriber lines (DSL). It is particularly advantageous in applications that require a high bandwidth and low latency, including video conferencing and online gaming.

- **Advantages**
  One of the key advantages of synchronous transmission is its efficiency. By eliminating the overhead associated with start and stop bits, this method allows for larger amounts of data to be transmitted in a shorter period. Additionally, it minimises delays and reduces the risk of data collisions, making it ideal for continuous data flow applications.

11.5 TRANSMISSION DIRECTIONS

11.5.1 Simplex

Simplex transmission is a unidirectional form of communication where data flows in only one direction. The sender transmits information without any expectation of a response from the receiver.

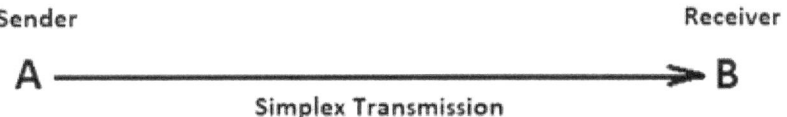

- **Example**
  Television broadcasting is a classic example of simplex transmission. In this scenario, the signal flows from the broadcaster to the viewers, and there is no feedback mechanism for the viewers to send information back to the broadcaster.

- **Characteristics**
  This method is simple and cost-effective, as it requires less complex hardware and fewer resources. However, it is limited in its application due to its one-way nature, making it unsuitable for interactions that require feedback.

11.5.2 Half-Duplex

Half-duplex transmission allows data to flow in both directions, but not simultaneously. Each device can send or receive data, but only one operation can occur at a time.

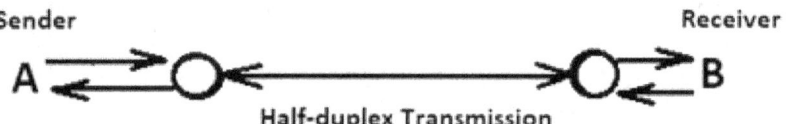
Half-duplex Transmission

- **Example**
  Walkie-talkies exemplify half-duplex communication. In this case, one party speaks while the other listens, and users must press a button to switch between speaking and listening modes.

- **Advantages**
  This method is more efficient than simplex communication, as it allows for bi-directional communication. However, it requires a simple control mechanism to manage when each device can transmit, which can add a slight delay to the conversation.

11.5.3 Full-Duplex

Full-duplex transmission enables simultaneous data flow in both directions. This means that two devices can communicate with each other at the same time without any interference.

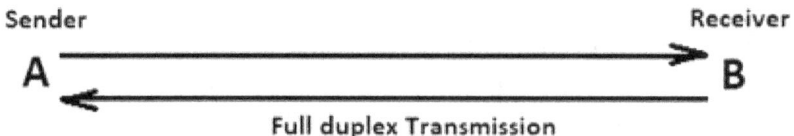
Full duplex Transmission

- **Example**
  Telephone conversations are a prime example of full-duplex communication. Both parties can talk and listen simultaneously, allowing for natural, real-time dialogue.

- **Advantages**
  Full-duplex transmission maximises data transfer efficiency, facilitating real-time communication without delays. This is especially important in applications that require immediate feedback, such as video conferencing or online customer support.

11.5.4 Asymmetric Duplex

Asymmetric duplex systems function similarly to half-duplex and full-duplex systems, but they feature different data rates (time lag) for sending and receiving information.

- **Example**
  Asymmetric Digital Subscriber Line (ADSL) is a common asymmetric duplex technology. It offers higher download speeds compared to upload speeds, catering to users who typically consume more data than they send.

- **Challenges**
  While asymmetric duplex systems can be efficient for typical internet usage, users may experience delays when uploading data due to the lower upload speeds. This disparity can affect performance in applications like cloud storage, video conferencing, or online gaming, where upload speeds are critical.

11.6 TRANSMISSION RATE

The transmission rate quantifies the speed at which data can be transferred between devices, typically measured in bits per second (bps). Understanding these rates is crucial for assessing the performance and suitability of communication systems for various applications.

- **Baseband Coaxial Cable:**
  Baseband coaxial cables can transmit data at rates of up to 10 million bps over short distances, making them well-suited for local area networks (LANs). This high transmission rate allows for fast communication between devices within a confined area, such as an office or building.

- **Fibre Optic Cables:**
  Fibre optic cables can achieve data rates ranging from 100 Mbps to over 100 Gbps, depending on the specific technology and application. The ability to transmit large volumes of data at such high speeds has made fibre optics the backbone of modern telecommunication infrastructure.

- **Baud Rate:**
  Baud rate represents the number of signal changes per second. In many cases, one baud corresponds to one bit transmitted per second; however, under certain conditions (such as modulation schemes that encode multiple bits per signal change), the baud rate can exceed the number of bits per second. For example, a signal that changes state multiple times per second

can convey more data than its baud rate might suggest, enabling more efficient data transmission.

Summary

The choice of transmission mode and direction plays a crucial role in determining the efficiency, speed, and reliability of data communication systems. By understanding the various methods of transmission, including asynchronous and synchronous modes, as well as the implications of simplex, half-duplex, full-duplex, and asymmetric duplex systems, users can make informed decisions about the most appropriate communication technologies for their needs. Furthermore, comprehension of transmission rates helps evaluate the performance of different communication media, ensuring that organisations and individuals can optimise their data transfer strategies effectively.

Tutorial Activity 11 - Basic Data Transmission Systems

Quizzes and Questions

Multiple Choice Questions

1. a. Which of the following is an example of a guided transmission medium?

    a. A) Radio Waves
    b. B) Fiber Optic Cable
    c. C) Satellite Signals
    d. D) Microwaves

    b. In which transmission mode does data travel in both directions simultaneously?

    e. A) Simplex
    f. B) Half-Duplex
    g. C) Full-Duplex
    h. D) Asynchronous

    c. What does the term "baud rate" measure?

    i. A) Data transfer rate in bytes per second
    j. B) Signal changes per second
    k. C) Total data capacity of a medium
    l. D) Number of data packets sent per second

2. **True or False Questions**
    a. Baseband transmission uses the entire bandwidth of a communication channel for a single signal.
    b. Asynchronous transmission requires data to be sent at a fixed rate without the use of a clock signal.
    c. In simplex transmission, data can flow in both directions but only one direction at a time.

Short-Answer Questions

1. **Question:** What are the differences between baseband and broadband transmission?
2. **Question:** List two advantages and two disadvantages of fiber optic cables as a transmission medium.
3. **Question:** Explain the concept of asymmetric duplex transmission and provide an example of its use.

Fill-in-the-Blank Questions

1. Transmission modes are categorised into _____, _____, and _____.
2. The unit "bps" stands for _____.
3. _____ transmission uses start and stop bits to indicate the beginning and end of data packets.

Scenario-Based Question

Question: A company wants to set up a secure communication link between its headquarters and a remote branch. They need high-speed data transmission with minimal interference. Which transmission medium and mode would you recommend, and why?

Chapter 12: The Internet and Security Challenges in ICT

Learning Outcomes

By the end of this chapter, learners will be able to:

- Understand the Internet: Explain its history, structure, core terminologies, and differences from the World Wide Web.
- Explore Internet Evolution: Describe technological advancements and predict future trends like AR and wearable devices.
- Identify Cybersecurity Threats: Recognise types of computer viruses, their sources, and impacts.
- Apply Security Practices: Use antivirus software, backups, and policies to protect against cyber threats.
- Evaluate ICT Security Issues: Analyse challenges and propose measures to enhance internet and ICT security.

12. THE INTERNET

The internet has become the backbone of modern communication, commerce, education, and entertainment, enabling unprecedented global connectivity. From its origins as a military research project to its evolution as the foundation of the digital age, the internet has transformed how individuals, organisations, and governments interact. Its versatility and scale have opened new opportunities while introducing complex challenges, particularly in the realm of cybersecurity.

This chapter delves into the core concepts, services, and evolution of the internet, providing a thorough understanding of its architecture and applications. It also examines the persistent and evolving threats posed by computer viruses, emphasizing the need for proactive protection measures in various environments. By understanding the mechanics of the internet and recognising the risks associated with its misuse, learners will gain a solid foundation for navigating and leveraging this critical technology securely and responsibly.

Key focus areas include:

- An exploration of the internet's history, core terminologies, and services.
- A detailed comparison of the internet versus the World Wide Web.
- An analysis of the evolution and future trends in internet technologies.
- A comprehensive guide to computer viruses, their types, impacts, and protective strategies.

Through this chapter, learners will develop the knowledge and skills needed to harness the internet's potential while mitigating its risks, preparing them to navigate an increasingly connected and digital world.

12.1 WHAT IS THE INTERNET?

The internet is a vast global network, linking millions of smaller, interconnected networks to facilitate worldwide data sharing and communication. Emerging from the Advanced Research Projects Agency (ARPA) in the United States in 1969, the internet initially served as a specialised network for military and academic research. Its foundational design, known as ARPANET, allowed for robust data exchange across computers, making it resilient and decentralised. Today, it operates on the Transmission Control Protocol/Internet Protocol (TCP/IP), a fundamental protocol suite that standardises data transmission and allows diverse systems to communicate through a network of interconnected routers. TCP/IP breaks data into packets, ensuring accurate delivery and reassembly at the destination, making it possible for devices around the globe to reliably share information.

12.1.1 Core Terminology of the Internet

To understand how the internet functions, it's essential to grasp key terms that underpin its architecture:

- **Internet Protocol (IP)**: This is responsible for defining addresses for devices and routing data packets, enabling accurate data transmission across networks.

- **IP Address**: A unique numerical identifier assigned to each device connected to the internet, facilitating location tracking and packet delivery (e.g., 192.168.1.1 for a local network).

- **Domain Name**: A human-readable address that represents an IP address, simplifying the process of accessing websites (e.g., example.com).

- **Domain Name Server (DNS)**: Often described as the "phonebook" of the internet, the DNS converts domain names into IP addresses, enabling users to access websites using familiar names rather than complex numeric strings.

12.1.2 Internet vs. World Wide Web

While "internet" and "World Wide Web" (WWW) are often used interchangeably, they denote different components. The internet refers to the global network of interconnected devices and systems, serving as the physical backbone that enables data transmission. In contrast, the World Wide Web is an information-sharing system that utilises the internet to retrieve and display content stored on web pages. Web pages are coded in HTML (HyperText Markup Language) and linked by URLs (Uniform Resource Locators), enabling users to navigate between sites and within pages through hyperlinks:

- **Intrapage links** connect within the same page,
- **Internal links** link to different pages within the same website, and
- **External links** lead to entirely different websites.

12.1.3 Internet Services

The internet supports a wide array of services, each catering to different communication, information-sharing, and collaboration needs:

- **Newsgroups/Usenet**: Early online forums that allowed users to discuss and share information on specific topics, often organised by subject or community.

- **Email**: A system for sending digital messages and multimedia attachments across the internet, serving as a cornerstone of both personal and professional communication.

- **Gopher**: An early protocol for searching and retrieving text-based information across networks, preceding the graphical capabilities of the web.

- **File Transfer Protocol (FTP)**: Facilitates the secure upload and download of files between a client and server, commonly used for website management and data sharing.

- **World Wide Web**: A graphical interface that allows users to access text, multimedia, and applications on the internet, becoming one of the most popular internet services globally.

12.1.4 Evolution of the Internet

Since its inception, the internet has undergone multiple generations of technological evolution:

- **Generation 1 - Static HTML**: The early internet featured static web pages, often with basic text and images. Access was primarily through dial-up connections with limited speeds.

- **Generation 2 - Web Applications**: This era introduced interactivity, allowing users to interact with dynamic content through early web applications and databases.

- **Generation 3 - Web Services**: The development of Software as a Service (SaaS) enabled online applications, including cloud-based tools that provided businesses and individuals with powerful, remote resources.

- **Generation 4 - Cloud Computing**: Characterised by scalable, internet-based infrastructure, cloud computing supports the storage, and processing needs of modern applications and services, allowing for high flexibility and remote accessibility.

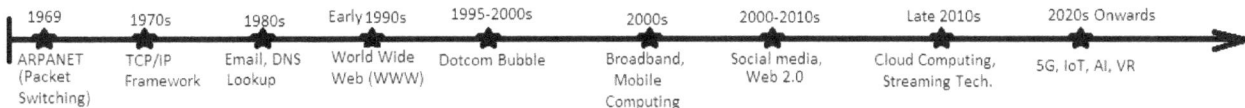

Diagram: Evolution of the Internet

12.1.5 The Future of the Internet: First World vs. Third World Perspectives

The future of the internet is marked by diverse advancements across both developed and developing regions. In many developed countries, households utilise digital TV and wireless technology, like WAP (Wireless Application Protocol), to access the internet on mobile devices, providing high-speed, convenient connectivity. Conversely, infrastructure challenges in developing regions can restrict internet availability and speed. Yet, technological solutions, such as mobile data hotspots and community internet programs, are helping to bridge these gaps.

Emerging internet technologies promise to reshape connectivity further:

- **Wearable Technology**: Devices like smart glasses could enable hands-free, on-the-go internet access, facilitating connectivity in professional, social, and personal contexts.

- **Augmented Reality (AR) and Virtual Reality (VR)**: These immersive technologies may transform education, training, entertainment, and communication, creating deeper, interactive experiences.

- **Public Access Points**: Hotspots and Wi-Fi access points are expanding, enabling users to connect to the internet in public spaces like parks, malls, and cafes, increasing internet accessibility.

12.2 IDENTIFYING CYBERSECURITY THREATS

12.2.1 Computer Viruses

In the digital age, where the internet and ICT play a central role in our lives, the threat of cybersecurity breaches has become a critical concern. Among these threats, computer viruses stand out as one of the most prevalent and disruptive forms of malicious software. They infiltrate systems, spread across networks, and cause harm ranging from minor inconveniences to devastating data losses and operational failures.

Understanding the types, sources, and impacts of computer viruses is essential for both individuals and organisations to safeguard their digital environments. This section explores the nature of computer viruses, their various forms, and how they exploit vulnerabilities to propagate. By recognising the warning signs of infection and the typical sources of viruses, learners will gain the foundational knowledge needed to anticipate and mitigate these threats effectively.

12.2.2 What is a Computer Virus?

A computer virus is a malicious program designed to replicate itself by attaching to other files or programs on a computer. Viruses activate when specific conditions are met, such as opening an infected file, launching a program, or reaching a certain date. These malicious programs often cause harm, ranging from displaying unexpected messages to slowing down system performance, corrupting files, or even deleting essential data.

Illustrative Example: Imagine a virus as a weed in a garden. If left unattended, it spreads and eventually overtakes other plants, damaging the ecosystem. Similarly, a virus hides in files and spreads each time an infected file or program is accessed, often causing harm to other parts of the computer system.

12.2.3 Why are Viruses Created?

People create computer viruses for a variety of reasons:

- **Financial Gain**: Some antivirus companies are rumoured to produce viruses to increase demand for their products, although these claims are often unsubstantiated.

- **Notoriety**: Some hackers seek recognition by creating viruses that cause significant disruption, gaining fame within certain communities.

- **Programming Challenges**: Certain developers create viruses as a personal challenge, treating it as a complex exercise in programming without fully considering the potential harm.

- **Targeted Attacks**: Viruses can also be designed for specific, malicious purposes, such as sabotaging organisations, individuals, or critical systems.

12.2.4 Warning Signs of a Virus Infection

Signs that a computer may be infected with a virus include:

1. **Slow Performance**: The computer's processing speed becomes unusually sluggish.

2. **Random Messages or Images**: Unwanted pop-ups or strange images suddenly appear.

3. **Erratic Mouse Movement**: The mouse pointer moves on its own or becomes difficult to control.

4. **Incomplete File Saves**: Files may not save properly or become corrupted.

5. **Missing System Files**: Important files disappear or are no longer accessible.

6. **Appearance of Unusual Characters**: Unexpected symbols or characters may show up on the screen.

12.2.5 Types of Computer Viruses

Computer viruses come in various types, each with unique behaviours and infection methods:

1. **Boot Sector Virus**
    - Targets the boot sector of a internal hard disk or external disk, making it difficult to remove.
    - **Example**: The "Brain" virus was among the first boot sector viruses.

- **Impact**: Since it activates each time, the computer starts up, it becomes deeply embedded and challenging to eliminate.

2. **Partition Sector Virus**
   - Infects the partition sector, responsible for dividing a hard disk into storage areas.
   - **Example**: The "Stoned" virus is a well-known example.
   - **Impact**: It resides deep within the system, making it harder to detect and remove using standard antivirus software.

3. **File Infector Virus**
   - Attaches itself to executable files (like .EXE and .SYS) and activates when these files are run.
   - **Example**: The "Jerusalem" virus, which activates every Friday the 13th.
   - **Impact**: Causes files to increase in size and can corrupt data in the infected files.

4. **Macro Virus**
   - Written using macros (automated tasks) within applications like Microsoft Word or Excel.
   - **Example**: The "Melissa" virus, which spread through Word documents in the late 1990s.
   - **Impact**: Automatically activates when opening infected documents, spreading rapidly through shared files or email.

5. **Worms**
   - Self-replicating programs that spread over networks independently, without attaching to files.
   - **Example**: The "ILOVEYOU" worm spread through email in 2000.
   - **Impact**: Consumes significant network bandwidth, slowing down or crashing systems.

6. **Trojan Horses**
   - Programs that appear harmless but perform malicious activities when opened.
   - **Example**: A game that, when launched, corrupts system files.
   - **Impact**: Trojans don't replicate but can steal data or allow attackers access to a system.

7. **Ransomware**

- A form of malware that encrypts files on a victim's computer, demanding payment (ransom) for decryption.
- **Example**: The "WannaCry" ransomware attack that affected thousands of computers globally in 2017.
- **Impact**: Can lead to significant financial losses and data breaches, as critical files may become inaccessible without paying the ransom.

12.2.6 Examples of Notorious Computer Viruses

- **Cascade Virus:** Known for its ability to make letters on the screen fall like a cascading waterfall.
- **Jerusalem Virus:** Activates on Fridays the 13th, leading to file deletion and system disruptions.
- **ILOVEYOU Worm:** An infamous worm that spread through email and caused billions in damages worldwide.

12.2.7 How to Protect Against Viruses

To safeguard computers from viruses, a multi-layered defence strategy is essential:

1. **Antivirus Software**: Install and maintain reputable antivirus software, ensuring regular updates to protect against emerging threats. Popular options include Norton, McAfee, Kaspersky, Microsoft Defender, and Bitdefender.

2. **Regular Scans**: Schedule routine virus scans to detect and remove infections early. Most antivirus software offers automated scheduling features.

3. **System Backups**: Regularly back up critical files using secure methods, such as external hard drives or cloud storage solutions, to prevent data loss.

4. **Employee Education**: Conduct training sessions to teach employees about recognising phishing emails, suspicious downloads, and safe browsing practices.

5. **Restrict File Transfers**: Implement policies that limit the sharing of executable files and enforce scanning of external devices before use.

Illustrative Example: A company may implement strict security policies, requiring all USB drives to be scanned before use on any company computer, minimising the risk of infection from external devices. Some organisations have configured their systems to completely block the use of USB devices.

12.2.8 Sources of Virus Infection

Viruses can infiltrate systems through various channels:

- **Email Attachments**: Malicious files disguised as legitimate attachments can spread viruses when opened.
- **Infected Software**: Downloading pirated or compromised software often carries hidden malware.
- **USB Drives**: Viruses can easily spread through shared USB drives or external storage devices.
- **Internet Downloads**: Free software or dubious pop-up ads may contain hidden viruses. Always download software from reputable sources.

12.2.9 Actions a Company Should Take Against Viruses

To ensure robust protection against viruses, companies should adopt proactive measures:

1. **Limit Software Installations**: Only permit installation of approved software on company devices to minimise exposure to threats.
2. **Use a Designated Directory for Files**: Store all executable files in a secure directory with restricted access to prevent unauthorised execution.
3. **Maintain Clean Boot Disks**: Keep a clean boot disk readily available to start systems without loading infected software.
4. **Conduct Regular Training**: Offer ongoing training to employees about emerging virus threats, safe computing practices, and incident reporting.
5. **Ensure Updated Antivirus**: Regularly update antivirus solutions to protect against newly discovered viruses and vulnerabilities.

12.2.10 List of Popular Antivirus Software

Below is a list of widely recognised antivirus programs that individuals and organisations can use to protect their systems:

1. Norton Antivirus
2. McAfee Antivirus
3. Kaspersky Antivirus
4. Microsoft Defender
5. AVG Antivirus
6. Bitdefender
7. Avast Antivirus
8. ESET NOD32
9. Sophos Antivirus

12.2.11 Issues with Viruses in Academic Environments

Academic settings face particular challenges regarding virus management due to its limited IT resources and high volumes of public-access computers. To mitigate these issues, educational institutions can adopt the following strategies:

1. **Designate a "Sheep-Dip" Computer**: Establish a dedicated computer used solely for scanning and disinfecting USB drives before they are connected to networked systems.

2. **Implement Cryptographic Checksums**: Use checksums to verify that files remain unchanged and uninfected by viruses.

3. **Run Regular Scans**: Conduct routine virus scans in shared computer labs to prevent infections from proliferating.

4. **Educate Students**: Regularly hold workshops and informational sessions including broadcast emails to raise awareness about virus threats and promote best practices for safe computing.

5. **Develop IT Policies**: Create clear guidelines for using personal devices on campus networks, ensuring that devices meet security standards before connecting.

6. Configure all systems to completely block the use of USB devices.

Tutorial Activity 12 - The Internet and Security Challenges in ICT

Quizzes and Questions

These questions will test learners' understanding of the chapter and help reinforce key concepts while encouraging analytical thinking about cybersecurity and internet evolution.

Quiz 1: Understanding the Internet

1. **What year did the internet originate, and under which project?**

    a) 1979, under CERN
    b) 1969, under ARPANET
    c) 1991, under the World Wide Web
    d) 1983, under TCP/IP

2. **Which protocol suite is fundamental to the operation of the internet?**

    a) HTTP/HTML
    b) DNS/IP
    c) TCP/IP
    d) FTP/SMTP

3. **What is the primary function of the Domain Name System (DNS)?**

    a) To route data packets across the internet
    b) To convert IP addresses into human-readable domain names
    c) To host websites and applications
    d) To secure data transmissions with encryption

Quiz 2: Exploring Internet Evolution

4. **Which generation of the internet introduced cloud computing and scalable infrastructure?**

    a) Generation 1: Static HTML
    b) Generation 2: Web Applications
    c) Generation 3: Web Services
    d) Generation 4: Cloud Computing

5. **Name one emerging technology that may transform connectivity in the future.**

6. **True or False:** The World Wide Web and the internet are interchangeable terms.

Quiz 3: Identifying Cybersecurity Threats

7. **What is a computer virus?**

    o (a) A self-replicating program that spreads across systems

    o (b) A protective software used to prevent hacking

- (c) A harmless coding error in software
- (d) A physical device that disrupts internet signals

8. **Which of these is NOT a source of computer virus infection?**
    - (a) Email attachments
    - (b) USB drives
    - (c) Encrypted backups
    - (d) Downloaded software from unknown sources

9. **List three types of computer viruses and their impacts.**

Quiz 4: Applying Security Practices

10. **What is the primary purpose of antivirus software?**
    - (a) To backup files
    - (b) To prevent system overheating
    - (c) To detect and remove malicious software
    - (d) To create complex passwords

11. **Which of these is NOT a recommended security practice?**
    - (a) Regularly updating antivirus software
    - (b) Downloading pirated software
    - (c) Backing up data frequently
    - (d) Educating employees about cybersecurity

12. **Match the following terms with their descriptions:**
    - **Firewall**: Controls incoming and outgoing network traffic.
    - **Encryption**: Protects data by converting it into unreadable code.
    - **Phishing**: A fraudulent attempt to obtain sensitive information.

Quiz 5: Evaluating ICT Security Issues

13. **What are two major security challenges in academic environments?**
14. **Propose one strategy to enhance internet security in an organisation.**
15. **True or False:** Cryptographic checksums help ensure data integrity by verifying that files remain unchanged.

Chapter 13: Web Technology and Emerging Web Trends

Learning Outcomes

By the end of this chapter, learners will be able to identify and explain:

Section 1: Fundamentals of Web Architecture and Networking

1. Web Architecture and Components: Describe the key components of web architecture and illustrate the three-tier system.

2. Networking Concepts and Devices: Differentiate between the internet, intranet, and extranet, and explain the roles of networking devices like routers and switches.

3. Client/Server Communication: Explain the client/server model, including request-response cycles and DNS resolution.

Section 2: Web Standards, Tools, and Security

4. Web Standards and Tools: Discuss the importance of web standards and evaluate popular browsers and servers.

5. Security Mechanisms: Explain the role of proxy servers, firewalls, and OpenRSM in web security and system management.

6. Performance Metrics: Quantify metrics like latency, response time, and bandwidth to evaluate network performance.

Section 3: Web Protocols and Communication

7. TCP/IP and Related Protocols: Explain the TCP/IP model and its four layers, highlighting data encapsulation.

8. Web Communication Protocols: Describe HTTP/HTTPS protocols, their functionality, and security features.

9. Email Communication Protocols: Differentiate between SMTP, POP3, and IMAP in email handling and storage.

Section 4: Web Applications and Their Impact

10. Applications of Web Technology: Identify and evaluate web technologies supporting e-commerce, e-learning, and communication.

11. Key Applications in the Web Ecosystem: Highlight the significance of cloud computing, e-commerce, and online collaboration tools.

Section 5: Evolution and Future of the Web

12. Evolution of the Web: Differentiate Web 1.0, Web 2.0, and Web 3.0, focusing on their features and user interactions.

13. Characteristics of Web 2.0: Identify the participatory and interactive elements of Web 2.0 with real-world examples.

14. Characteristics of Web 2.5: Explain the transitional phase of Web 2.5, merging Web 2.0 interactivity with decentralisation.

15. Features of Web 3.0 and Emerging Technologies: Define Web 3.0, its decentralisation focus, and its transformative applications.

16. Emerging Web Technologies: Explore Web 4.0 and Web 5.0, highlighting intelligent, emotional, and immersive web advancements.

17. Future Trends: Predict the global impact of technologies like AI, AR/VR, blockchain, and quantum computing on industries and human interactions.

13 INTRODUCTION TO WEB TECHNOLOGY

This chapter provides an in-depth exploration of web technologies, focusing on their evolution, current applications, and future potential. By the end of the chapter, learners will understand the fundamental components of web architecture, networking, and client-server communication, which form the backbone of modern internet operations.

Through a detailed analysis of web standards, tools, and security mechanisms, learners will appreciate the importance of interoperability, accessibility, and safeguarding data in a connected world. They will also examine key web protocols, including TCP/IP, HTTP, HTTPS, and email communication systems, to understand how these frameworks facilitate seamless data transmission and secure communication.

The chapter also highlights the transformative impact of web technologies on global industries such as e-commerce, education, and entertainment, illustrating their role in fostering collaboration, productivity, and innovation. Learners will explore the characteristics of Web 2.0, Web 2.5, and Web 3.0, as well as the groundbreaking capabilities of Web 4.0 and Web 5.0, gaining insight into the semantic, intelligent, and emotional dimensions of emerging technologies.

Finally, learners will delve into future trends, including blockchain, AI, AR/VR, and quantum computing, to understand their potential to redefine the web landscape and revolutionise industries, shaping a more interconnected and adaptive digital future.

13.1 FUNDAMENTALS OF WEB ARCHITECTURE AND NETWORKING

In the digital age, Web Technology serves as the cornerstone of global communication, information dissemination, and business operations. Understanding the intricacies of web architecture, functionalities, design tools, and web applications is essential for anyone aspiring to excel in the field of information technology. This chapter delves into the fundamental components of web technology, explores the functionalities and performance metrics that define effective web systems, and introduces the tools and techniques necessary for designing robust websites and web applications.

This comprehensive exploration of web technology equips students with the knowledge and skills necessary to navigate and innovate within the digital landscape. By understanding the architecture, functionalities, design tools, and applications of the web, students are prepared to contribute effectively to the ongoing evolution of information and communication technologies.

13.1.1 Web Architecture and Components

Understanding web architecture is pivotal to grasp how web systems operate seamlessly across the globe. Web architecture refers to the design and structure of a website or web application, outlining how different components interact to deliver content and services to users.

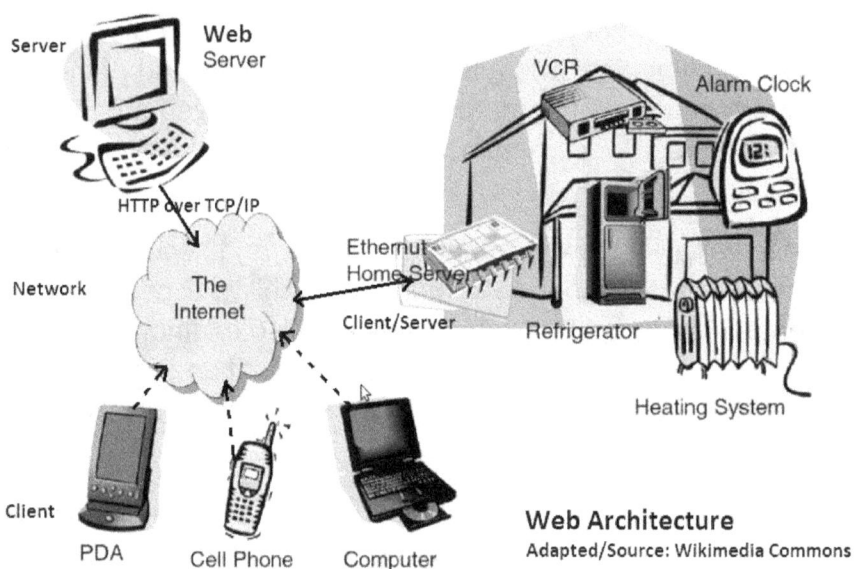

Web Architecture
Adapted/Source: Wikimedia Commons

13.1.2 N-Tier System Architecture

An **N-tier system** is a client/server architecture in which the presentation, application processing, and data management functions are physically separated. This separation enhances scalability, maintainability, and flexibility.

- **Three-Tier Architecture**:
    - **Presentation Tier (Client Side)**: The user interface running on the user's device, typically a web browser.
    - **Business Logic Tier (Middle Tier)**: The server-side application handling data processing, business rules, and decision-making.
    - **Data Tier (Database Server)**: Manages data storage, retrieval, and management through databases.

Three-Tier Architecture Diagram

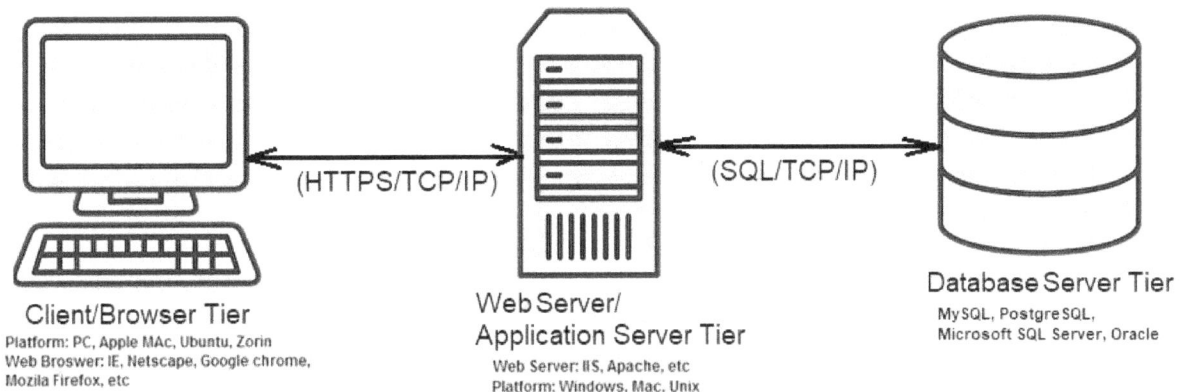

Diagram of 3-Tier Architecture

Quantification:

- **Common Technologies**:
    - **Client Side**: Browsers like Google Chrome, Mozilla Firefox (over 80% market share collectively).
    - **Web Servers**: Apache (over 40% market share), Nginx (over 30%), Microsoft IIS (over 20%).
    - **Databases**: MySQL, PostgreSQL, Microsoft SQL Server, Oracle.

13.1.3 Client/Server (Request/Response) Model

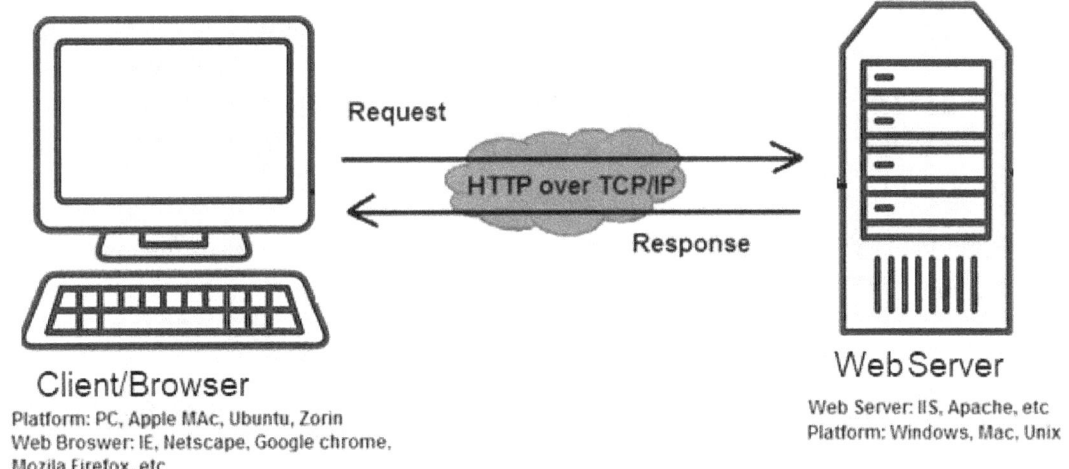

Diagram of Client/Server Architecture

The **Client/Server Model** is a foundational concept in web technology, describing how interactions between two entities - **clients** and **servers** - occur over a network. In this model, the **client** initiates a request, while the **server** processes that request and returns an appropriate response. This interaction is essential for the functioning of web applications and websites.

- **Client**: A client is typically a user's device, such as a computer, smartphone, or tablet, running a web browser or another application that requests resources from a server. For example, when a user enters a URL into their browser, the browser becomes the client, initiating the communication with the web server.
- **Server**: The server is a remote computer or system that hosts the requested resources (like web pages, images, or files) and is responsible for processing client requests. Web servers, database servers, and application servers are all examples of servers that can fulfil client requests by sending back data or content.

Process Flow:

- **Client Request**: The process begins when the client sends a request for a resource, such as a web page, through a browser. This request is typically sent using the **HTTP/HTTPS** protocol.
- **DNS Resolution**: The client browser contacts a **DNS (Domain Name System)** to resolve the domain name (e.g., www.example.com) to its corresponding **IP address**.
- **HTTP Request**: Once the IP address is obtained, the browser initiates an **HTTP request** to the web server, specifying the desired resource (e.g., index.html).
- **Server Processing**: The web server receives the request, processes it, and checks its **data storage** (such as a database) or filesystem for the requested resource. It may also execute server-side scripts or applications to generate dynamic content (like results from a search).
- **Server Response**: After processing, the server sends an **HTTP response** back to the client, which includes the requested resource (e.g., an HTML file, image, or JSON data).
- **Rendering**: The client (browser) then interprets and renders the response, allowing the user to interact with the web page or application.

Examples:

- **Simple Scenario**: A user types "www.example.com" into their browser. The browser (client) sends an HTTP request to the server hosting "example.com", which then returns the requested HTML page. The browser displays the page to the user.
- **Dynamic Scenario**: A user submits a form on a website, triggering a request to a server to process the data. The server interacts with a database, processes the data, and sends back an updated web page or confirmation message.

Quantification:

- **Latency**: Typical round-trip time for a client-server request should be under **200 milliseconds** for an optimal user experience.
- **Data Size**: The size of a single HTTP request varies, but modern web pages can require transferring 1 MB to 5 MB of data, including multimedia content.
- **Concurrent Users**: High-performing servers may handle thousands of concurrent requests per second, depending on hardware and server architecture.
- **Response Time**: Average web server response time should be under 200 milliseconds for optimal user experience.
- **Bandwidth Usage**: Modern web pages can range from 1 MB to 5 MB per page load.

13.1.4 Internet Service Provider (ISP)

An Internet Service Provider (ISP) is an organisation that provides users with the ability to access the internet, typically through broadband connections like DSL, fibre optics, or satellite. In addition to offering internet access, ISPs may provide other essential services such as domain registration, which allows individuals or businesses to register unique domain names for their websites. ISPs often offer web hosting services, allowing users to store their website data on servers, making it accessible to the public. Some ISPs also offer email services, virtual private networks (VPNs), and cloud storage solutions. ISPs are essential in connecting homes, businesses, and institutions to the internet, and they are typically subject to national regulations regarding data security and net neutrality.

Types of ISPs:

- **Commercial ISPs**: Offer services for a fee (e.g., Comcast, AT&T).
- **Community ISPs**: Operate in specific regions, often non-profit.
- **Government ISPs**: Provide internet services as part of public services.

Quantification:

- **Market Leaders**: Companies like Comcast and AT&T dominate the U.S. market, each holding approximately 20% market share.
- **Global Reach**: ISPs serve over 4.9 billion internet users worldwide as of 2023.

13.2 WEB STANDARDS, TOOLS, AND SECURITY

13.2.1 Web Standards

Web Standards ensure consistency, accessibility, and interoperability across the web. They are established by organisations like the Internet Engineering Task Force (IETF) and the World Wide Web Consortium (W3C).

- **IETF**: Focuses on developing and promoting voluntary internet standards, such as TCP/IP and DNS.
- **W3C**: Oversees the development of web standards, ensuring that technologies like HTML, CSS, and JavaScript work seamlessly across different browsers and devices.

Quantification:

- **W3C Members**: Over 450 member organisations from various industries, academia, and governments.
- **Standards Adoption**: 95% of modern browsers comply with W3C standards, ensuring uniform web experiences.

13.2.2 Web Browsers

A **Web Browser** is a client-side application that retrieves, interprets, and displays web content to users. Browsers handle HTML, CSS, JavaScript, and multimedia content.

Popular Browsers:

- **Google Chrome**: Leading with over 65% global market share.
- **Mozilla Firefox**: Approximately 4% market share.
- **Safari**: Around 18% market share, dominant on Apple devices.
- **Microsoft Edge**: Gaining traction with about 8% market share.
- **Opera**: Smaller niche with around 2% market share.

Special Browsers:

- **Lynx**: Text-based browser for users with visual impairments.
- **Jaws**: Assistive technology browser with screen reading capabilities.

Browser Market Share Pie Chart

Browser Market Share Pie Chart	
Google Chrome:	65%
Safari:	18%
Microsoft Edge:	8%
Mozilla Firefox:	4%
Others:	5%

Browser Market Share Pie Chart

- Google Chrome: ■ Safari: ■ Microsoft Edge: ■ Mozilla Firefox: ■ Others:

13.2.3 Web Servers

A **Web Server** is both a physical machine (hardware) and a program (software) that delivers web content to users who request it via their web browsers. The server handles HTTP requests, which are generated when a user enters a website's URL into a browser. Once the server receives the request, it processes it by retrieving the necessary resources (such as HTML files, images, or scripts) and sending them back to the client (browser) in an HTTP response. Web servers often incorporate functionalities for load balancing (distributing traffic evenly) and security protocols (like SSL/TLS for encrypting data). They can be configured to handle both static content (like images and text) and dynamic content (generated by server-side scripts). Popular web servers include Apache, Nginx, and Microsoft's IIS (Internet Information Services).

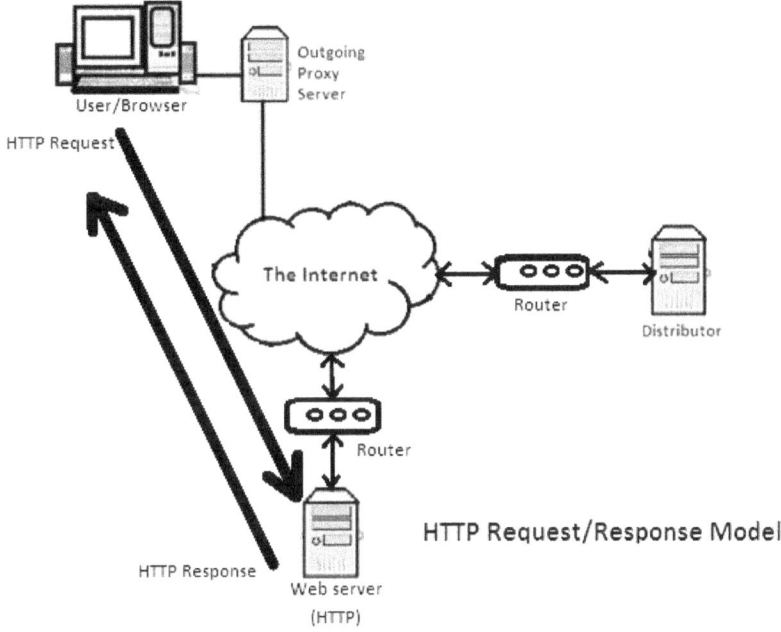

Popular Web Servers:

- **Apache HTTP Server**: Dominates with over 40% of the market.
- **Nginx**: Fast-growing with around 35% market share, known for handling high concurrency.
- **Microsoft IIS**: Approximately 15% market share, integrated with Windows Server.
- **LiteSpeed**: Emerging with about 5% market share, known for performance and security.

Quantification:

- **Apache**: Handles approximately 32% of all active websites.
- **Nginx**: Manages about 28% of active websites, increasing rapidly due to its performance benefits.

13.2.4 Proxy Server & Firewall

Proxy Server: A Proxy Server acts as an intermediary between the client (user) and the destination server (internet). When a user requests access to a website, the proxy server intercepts the request, forwards it to the appropriate web server, and then returns the requested data to the client. This setup can be used to cache frequently requested content, speeding up response times for users by delivering pre-stored data instead of making new requests to the web server. Proxy servers also filter web traffic for security, blocking malicious websites or unwanted content. Additionally, they can anonymise user activity by hiding the user's IP address, thus protecting their privacy and location from external tracking.

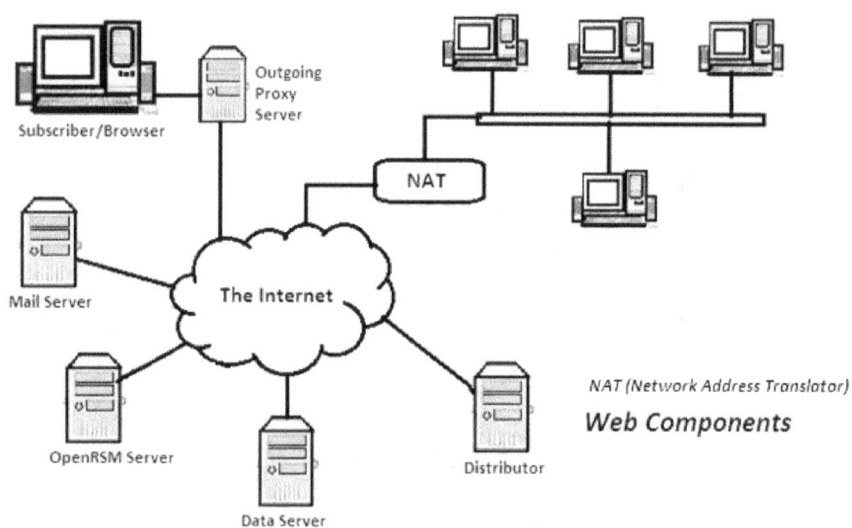

Functions of Proxy Server:

- **Caching**: Reduces bandwidth usage by storing frequently accessed resources.
- **Filtering**: Blocks access to unauthorised or harmful websites.
- **Anonymisation**: Hides client IP addresses for privacy.

Firewall: A Firewall is a security device, either hardware or software, designed to monitor and control incoming and outgoing network traffic. Firewalls establish a barrier between trusted internal networks (like private corporate networks) and untrusted external networks (like the internet), using predefined security rules. Firewalls can block suspicious or unauthorised traffic, protect systems from cyberattacks, and prevent sensitive data from leaving a network. They are a critical part of any network's security infrastructure, ensuring that only permitted traffic flows through while denying or flagging harmful requests. Firewalls work alongside proxy servers to enhance network security by controlling access and protecting sensitive information.

Functions of Firewall:

- **Access Control**: Permits or denies traffic based on security policies.
- **Threat Prevention**: Blocks malicious traffic and potential attacks.
- **Network Segmentation**: Divides networks into segments to contain breaches.

Quantification:

- **Proxy Servers**: Approximately 30% of enterprises use proxy servers for enhanced security and performance.
- **Firewalls**: Over 90% of organisations deploy firewalls as part of their security infrastructure.

13.2.5 OpenRSM Server

OpenRSM Server is an open-source solution designed for remote systems and network management, allowing administrators to monitor, control, and manage a network of computers or systems from a central location. It is built to enhance the efficiency of system administration tasks by providing a comprehensive platform for managing multiple devices remotely.

Key Components of OpenRSM Server:

- **Server**: The core component that organises and dispatches tasks to different subsystems. It coordinates communication between agents and user consoles, ensuring that administrative commands are executed properly.
- **Agent**: Installed on each managed system, the agent remains inactive until it receives a command from the server. Once activated, it performs the necessary tasks such as updating software, applying configurations, or collecting system data.
- **User Console**: The interface used by administrators to interact with the OpenRSM system. From this console, administrators can send commands to agents, monitor system health, view logs, and track network performance.

Features and Benefits:

- **Centralised Management**: OpenRSM Server allows system administrators to manage and monitor multiple remote machines from a single interface, reducing the complexity of handling large-scale networks.
- **Task Automation**: Routine tasks such as software updates, security patches, and performance monitoring can be automated, freeing up time and reducing the chance of human error.
- **Scalability**: OpenRSM can handle networks of varying sizes, from small networks with a few computers to large enterprise environments with thousands of systems.

- **Open-Source Flexibility**: Being open-source, OpenRSM can be customised to fit specific needs, and its source code can be modified or extended by users or developers.

Typical Use Cases:

OpenRSM Server provides a robust solution for organisations seeking efficient, scalable, and cost-effective remote systems management, with flexibility for both small businesses and large enterprises.

- **IT Infrastructure Management**: Used in data centres and enterprise IT departments to maintain and troubleshoot servers and workstations remotely.
- **Educational Institutions**: Deployed in schools or universities to manage computer labs and student devices.
- **Government Agencies**: For managing secure networks and ensuring compliance with operational protocols across distributed systems.

Quantification:

- **Adoption Rate**: OpenRSM Server is used by over 5,000 organisations worldwide for remote system management, including businesses, educational institutions, and government agencies.
- **Scalability**: The system supports management of up to 10,000 agents simultaneously, making it suitable for large-scale network management tasks.

13.2.6 Internetworking Technology

Internetworking Technology refers to the practice of connecting multiple independent computer networks to create a larger, cohesive network, allowing for seamless communication and resource sharing between the interconnected systems. This interconnected network is commonly known as an internet, of which the global Internet is the most prominent example.

Through internetworking technology, modern businesses and individuals can access global communication, services, and information, fostering innovation and collaboration on a global scale.

By using internetworking devices such as routers, switches, and gateways, data packets can be transmitted across different networks, even when they use different protocols, ensuring efficient and reliable communication between various systems.

Key Devices in Internetworking:

- **Routers**: These devices direct data packets between networks, choosing the most efficient path for data transmission based on the network topology. Routers connect different networks, ensuring that data reaches its intended destination.

- **Gateways**: Gateways act as bridges between networks that use different protocols or architectures. They perform protocol conversions, enabling smooth communication between otherwise incompatible systems.
- **Switches**: Switches connect devices within the same network (local area network or LAN) and manage data traffic by ensuring that data is sent only to the intended device within the network.

Benefits of Internetworking:

- **Resource Sharing**: Internetworking allows multiple networks to share resources such as files, applications, and devices like printers, across large distances, boosting productivity and collaboration.
- **Scalability**: Networks can be easily expanded as business needs grow, allowing for the addition of new devices or networks without overhauling the entire system.
- **Cost Efficiency**: By sharing resources and centralising services (like cloud-based storage), internetworking reduces the need for redundant infrastructure, lowering overall operational costs.
- **Reliability**: By interconnecting different networks, organisations can implement redundancy and failover mechanisms, ensuring continuous operation even if parts of the network experience issue.

Applications of Internetworking Technology:

- **Web Applications**: Allowing users to access software over the web without the need for installation on their local machines.
- **E-Commerce**: Powering online marketplaces and payment systems that span multiple networks and geographical regions.
- **E-Learning**: Supporting online education platforms that connect students and educators from across the globe.
- **E-Government**: Facilitating online public services and enhancing citizen-government interactions.
- **Streaming and social media**: Enabling media streaming services (such as Netflix) and social platforms (like Facebook, X (Twitter)) to deliver content seamlessly across networks.

13.2.7 Scope of Networks

Internetworking connects various types of networks, creating a cohesive communication infrastructure. Networks can be classified based on their scope:

- **Internet**:
    - **Definition**: A global network of interconnected computers using the TCP/IP protocol.

- - **Origin**: Developed from the ARPANET in 1969 by the U.S. Defence Advanced Research Projects Agency (DARPA).
  - **Usage**: Facilitates global communication, information sharing, and access to resources.
- **Intranet**:
  - **Definition**: A private network accessible only to an organisation's members.
  - **Purpose**: Enhances internal communication, collaboration, and information sharing within the organisation.
  - **Security**: Protected by firewalls to restrict access to authorised users only.
- **Extranet**:
  - **Definition**: An extension of an intranet that allows limited access to external users.
  - **Purpose**: Facilitates collaboration with partners, suppliers, and customers while maintaining security.
  - **Accessibility**: Controlled through authentication mechanisms like usernames and passwords.

Quantification:

- **Internet Users**: Over 5 billion active users globally as of 2023.
- **Intranet Usage**: Approximately 95% of large organisations use intranets for internal communication.
- **Extranet Adoption**: Around 60% of businesses utilise extranets to collaborate with external partners.

13.2.8 How Does a Computer Send a Request to a Web Server on the Other Side of the World?

Understanding the journey of a web request enhances comprehension of web functionalities and performance.

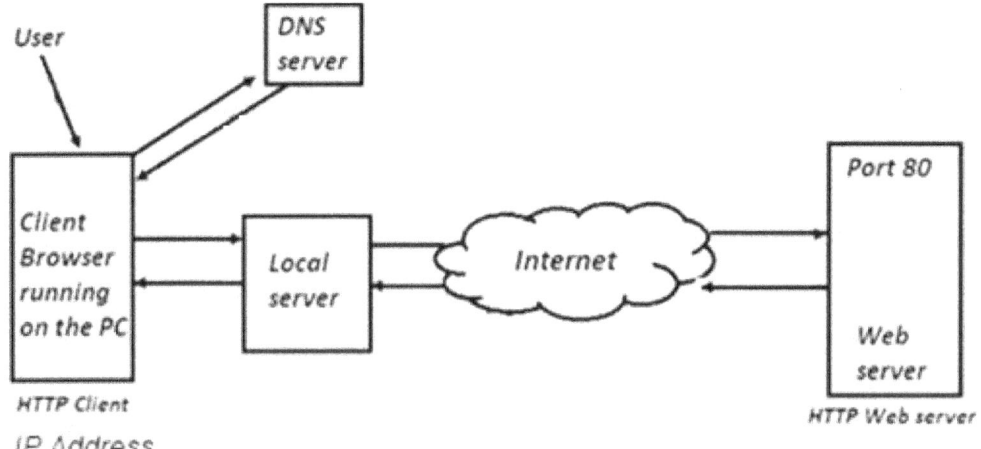

Client/Server (Request/Response) dialogue

Here's a step-by-step illustration of how a browser retrieves a web page from a distant server:

- **URL Verification**:
  - **Action**: The browser checks if the entered URL is syntactically correct.
  - **Example**: Ensuring "https://www.example.com" follows proper URL structure.

- **DNS Resolution**:
  - **Action**: The browser requests the **Domain Name System (DNS)** to resolve the domain name to an IP address.
  - **Example**: Resolving "www.example.com" to "93.184.216.34".

- **DNS Response**:
  - **Action**: DNS returns the corresponding IP address or an error message if the domain is not found.
  - **Example**: Receiving "93.184.216.34" as the IP address.

- **TCP Connection**:
  - **Action**: The browser (HTTP client) establishes a **TCP connection** to the web server on port 80 (HTTP) or port 443 (HTTPS).
  - **Example**: Connecting to the server at IP "93.184.216.34" on port 443.

- **HTTP Request**:
  - **Action**: The HTTP client sends an HTTP request (e.g., GET /index.html HTTP/1.1) to the server through the established TCP connection.
  - **Example**: Requesting the homepage of "www.example.com".

- **Server Processing**:
  - **Action**: The web server processes the request, retrieves the requested resource, and prepares an HTTP response.
  - **Example**: Fetching "index.html" from the server's file system.
- **HTTP Response**:
  - **Action**: The server sends the HTTP response containing the requested resource back to the client via the TCP connection.
  - **Example**: Delivering the HTML content of the homepage.
- **Connection Termination**:
  - **Action**: The server instructs TCP to close the connection after ensuring the client has received the response correctly.
  - **Example**: Closing the TCP connection after successful data transfer.
- **Resource Rendering**:
  - **Action**: The browser parses the HTML, fetches additional resources like images, CSS, and JavaScript files by establishing new TCP connections for each resource.
  - **Example**: Loading images and stylesheets to display the complete web page.

Web Request Flow Diagram

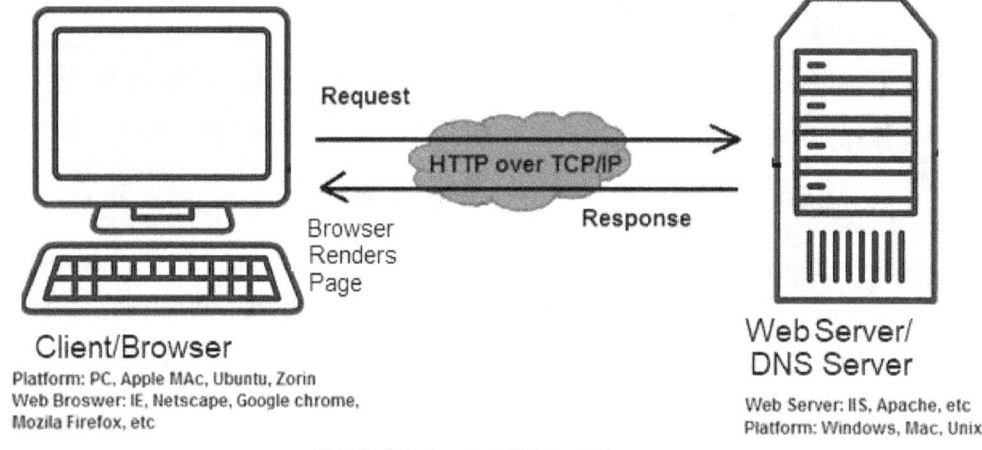

Web Request Flow Diagram

Quantification:

- **Average DNS Lookup Time**: Approximately 20-120 milliseconds.
- **Average HTTP Request Size**: Varies, but typically around 500 KB per webpage.
- **Average Page Load Time**: Under 3 seconds for optimal user experience.

13.3 WEB PROTOCOLS AND COMMUNICATION

Overview

Transmission Control Protocol/Internet Protocol (TCP/IP) is the foundational suite of communication protocols that govern how data is transmitted over the internet. It is the standard for network communication, ensuring that data can be sent between devices across networks, regardless of their hardware, software, or location. TCP/IP divides data into packets, which are transmitted across the network and reassembled upon arrival.

13.3.1 Importance of TCP/IP:

TCP/IP is the most widely adopted networking protocol and is used in both local and global networks. It enables seamless communication between different computer systems (including those from various vendors) by standardising how data is exchanged. TCP/IP ensures that devices running different operating systems can communicate as long as they both use this protocol suite.

13.3.2 Key Components of TCP/IP:

- **Transmission Control Protocol (TCP)**: TCP ensures reliable transmission of data. It breaks down large data into smaller packets, sends them, and ensures that they are reassembled correctly at the destination. If any packet is lost or corrupted during transmission, TCP can detect this and request the missing data to be resent.

- **Internet Protocol (IP)**: IP specifies how data packets are addressed and routed. It defines the structure of the packets and manages the addressing system, ensuring that packets reach the correct destination by determining the best path through the network.

Together, TCP and IP create a robust, efficient, and secure communication framework capable of handling errors, resending missing packets, and ensuring reliable delivery.

13.3.3 TCP/IP Protocol Architecture

The TCP/IP suite operates on a layered model, commonly referred to as the **TCP/IP Stack**, consisting of four distinct layers:

- **Application Layer**: This layer provides the protocols for various software applications, such as web browsers and email clients, to communicate with the network. It handles user data.
    - Example protocols: HTTP, HTTPS, SMTP, IMAP, FTP.
    - Data format: (user data)

- **Transport Layer**: The transport layer manages the delivery of data between devices. TCP is the key protocol here, ensuring that data is sent and received correctly.

- Data format: {TCP header + (user data)}
- **Internet Layer**: This layer deals with packet routing across the network. It uses the Internet Protocol (IP) to route data to the appropriate destination.
  - Data format: [IP header + {TCP header + (user data)}]
- **Network Access (Physical) Layer**: This is the layer responsible for data transmission over physical networks (e.g., Ethernet). It ensures that packets reach the correct physical destination.
  - Data format: N/W header [IP header + {TCP header + (user data)}]

Application Layer	consists of applications and processes that use the network	(user data)
Transport Layer	provides end-to-end data delivery services	{TCP header + (user data)}
Internet Layer	defines the datagram and handles the routing of data	[IP header + {TCP header + (user data)}]
Network Access (physical) Layer	consists of routines for accessing physical networks	N/W header [IP header + {TCP header + (user data)}]

As data moves from one layer to another, it is encapsulated with headers containing control information. Encapsulation ensures that each layer operates independently while working together to complete the communication.

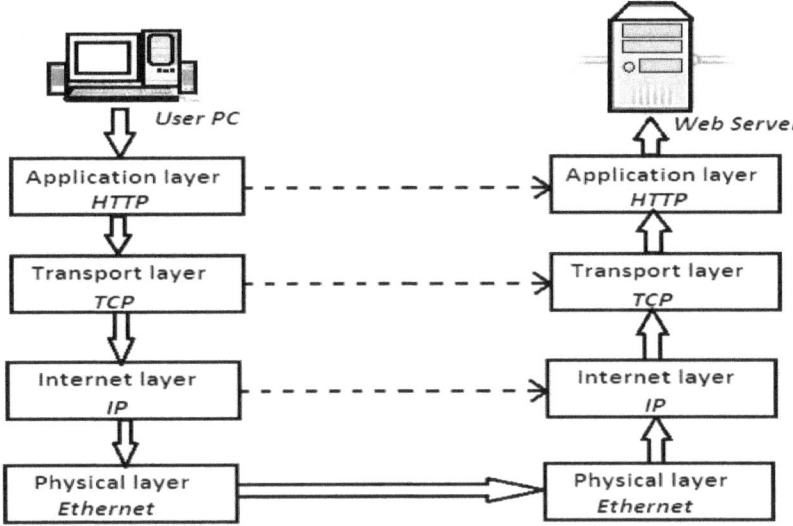

Internet Model & Protocol Stack

Data Transmission: From Source to Destination

When a user sends a request, for instance, to load a webpage, the request travels through the protocol stack, moving down from the Application Layer to the Physical Layer on the sender's side. The data packets then travel across the network (usually via Ethernet), pass through routers, and arrive at the destination, where they move back up the stack, eventually reaching the Application Layer on the server.

Routers: The Network Navigators

A **router** is a device that directs data packets along the most efficient path through the network. Routers use routing tables to identify potential pathways and can detect and avoid damaged or unavailable network connections, rerouting packets as necessary. Routers and TCP/IP work together to ensure accurate and reliable delivery of packets.

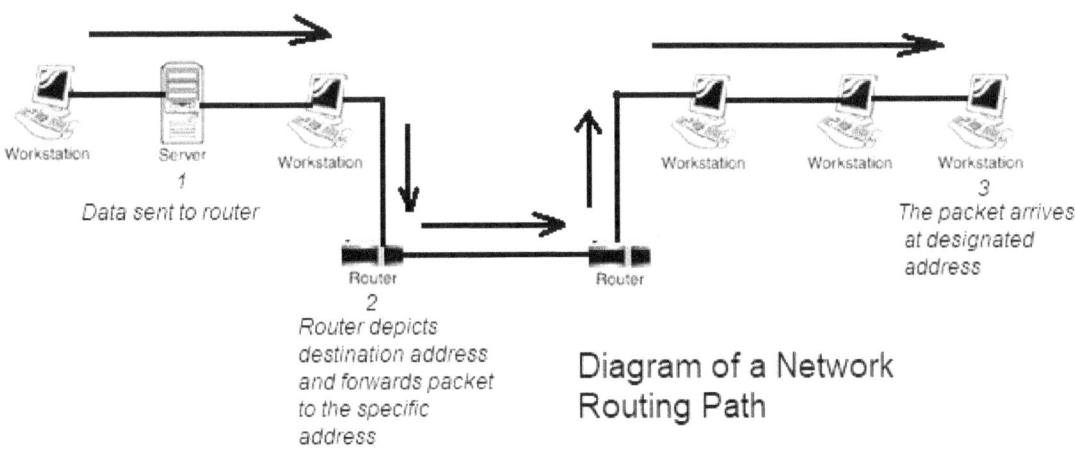

Diagram of a Network Routing Path

13.3.4 HTTP and HTTPS: Web Communication Protocols

Hypertext Transfer Protocol (HTTP) is the foundational protocol that enables the loading of web pages through a web browser. It governs how information is transmitted from a web server to a client (typically a browser). Each HTTP request made by the browser is sent to the server, which then processes the request and sends back the corresponding data (webpages, images, multimedia content, etc.).

- **How HTTP Works**: When you type a URL into your browser, an HTTP request is sent to the web server. The server processes the request and sends an HTTP response back to the browser, which renders the webpage for the user. This request-response cycle happens quickly, and multiple requests are made to display a full webpage (HTML files, images, CSS, and JavaScript are all separate requests).
- **Limitations of HTTP**: HTTP is a stateless protocol, meaning that each request is independent of the previous one, with no memory of past interactions. This can be a limitation for certain applications, requiring developers to implement session management systems.

Hypertext Transfer Protocol Secure (HTTPS) is the secure version of HTTP. It encrypts the data transferred between the client and server, ensuring privacy and protection against eavesdropping, tampering, and forgery. HTTPS uses SSL (Secure Socket Layer) or TLS (Transport Layer Security) encryption protocols to provide a secure communication channel.

- **How HTTPS Works**: When a browser makes an HTTPS request, a secure connection is established between the browser and the server. This includes verifying the website's SSL/TLS certificate, encrypting the session, and exchanging data securely. This encryption ensures that even if someone intercepts the data being transmitted, they cannot read or modify it without the decryption key.
- **Benefits of HTTPS**: HTTPS is especially critical for sensitive transactions such as online banking, e-commerce, and login authentication. Websites that use HTTPS are more trustworthy, and browsers like Chrome now mark HTTP sites as "Not Secure."

13.3.5 Email Protocols

Email protocols define how email is sent, received, and stored across mail servers. These protocols enable communication between email clients (such as Outlook or Gmail) and mail servers.

1. **SMTP (Simple Mail Transfer Protocol)**: SMTP is used specifically for sending outgoing mail. It ensures that emails are properly addressed and delivered to the recipient's mail server.
    - **How SMTP Works**: When you send an email, your email client connects to the SMTP server. The server processes the message, including the email

address of the recipient, and forwards the email to the recipient's mail server. If the recipient's server is unavailable, the SMTP server may retry sending the email or queue it for later delivery.

- **Advantages**: SMTP is widely supported and essential for sending emails. It is reliable and ensures the delivery of messages.

- **Limitations**: SMTP is not used for receiving or storing emails. It also doesn't support the retrieval of email from the server.

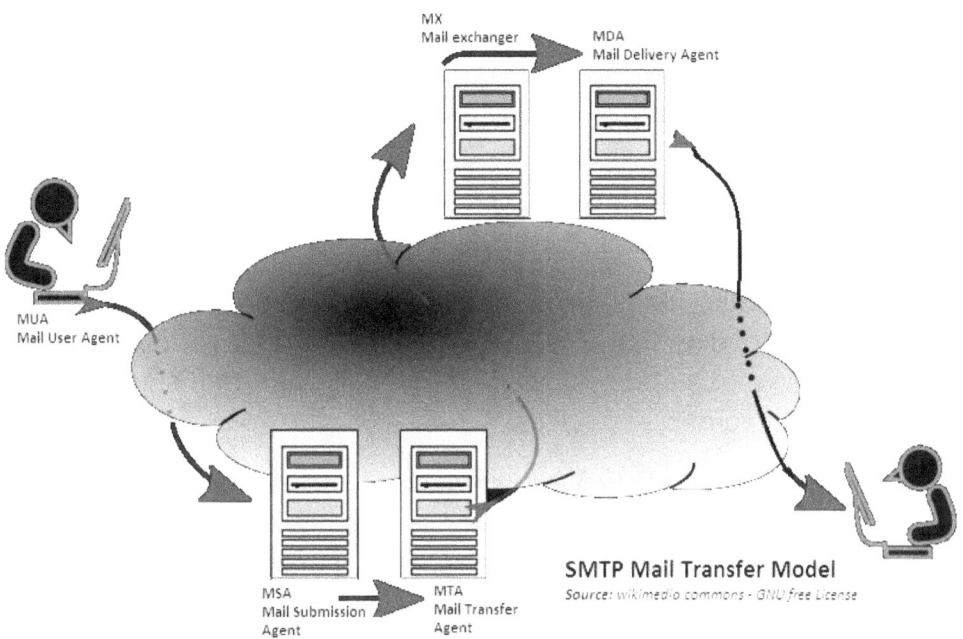

SMTP Mail Transfer Model
Source: wikimedia commons - GNU free License

2. **POP3 (Post Office Protocol version 3)**: POP3 is an incoming mail protocol that allows users to download emails from the mail server to their device.

   - **How POP3 Works**: After authentication (via username and password), the POP3 server retrieves all the emails stored on the server for the user. Once the emails are downloaded, they are usually deleted from the server, meaning they can only be accessed locally from the user's device.

   - **Advantages**: Emails can be read offline since they are downloaded to the device. This can be particularly useful when a stable internet connection is not available.

   - **Limitations**: Once the email is downloaded and deleted from the server, it cannot be accessed from another device. This makes POP3 less suitable for users who need to access their email from multiple devices.

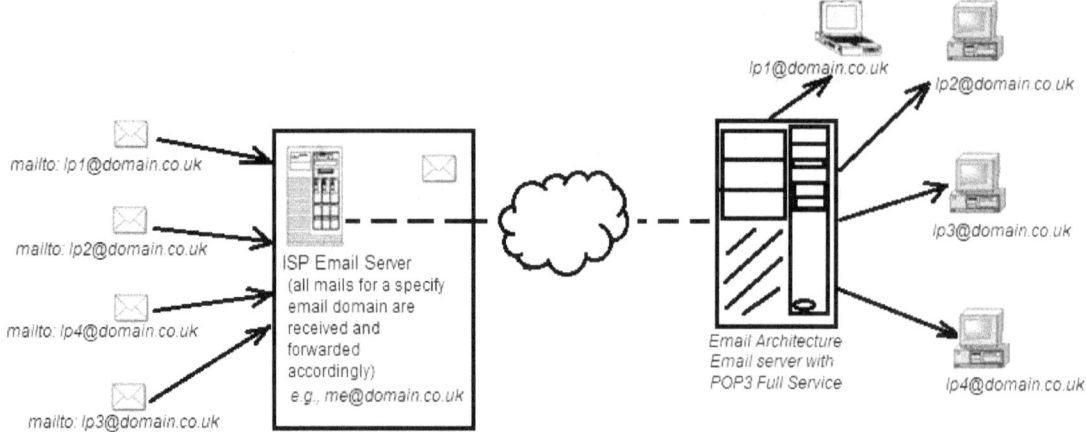

Diagram of Email Architecture with POP3 Full Service

3. **IMAP (Internet Message Access Protocol)**: IMAP is a more advanced email retrieval protocol that allows users to manage their emails directly on the server, providing flexibility in accessing emails from multiple devices.

    - **How IMAP Works**: IMAP allows users to browse emails stored on the server without downloading them first. Emails remain on the server until deleted, and changes made (such as reading, deleting, or organising emails) are synchronised across all devices.

    - **Advantages**: IMAP is ideal for users who need to access their email from multiple devices (e.g., phone, laptop, and desktop). It also supports advanced email management features, like message flags and folder management.

    - **Limitations**: Accessing email using IMAP requires an internet connection since the emails remain on the server. Offline access is possible only if emails are downloaded or cached.

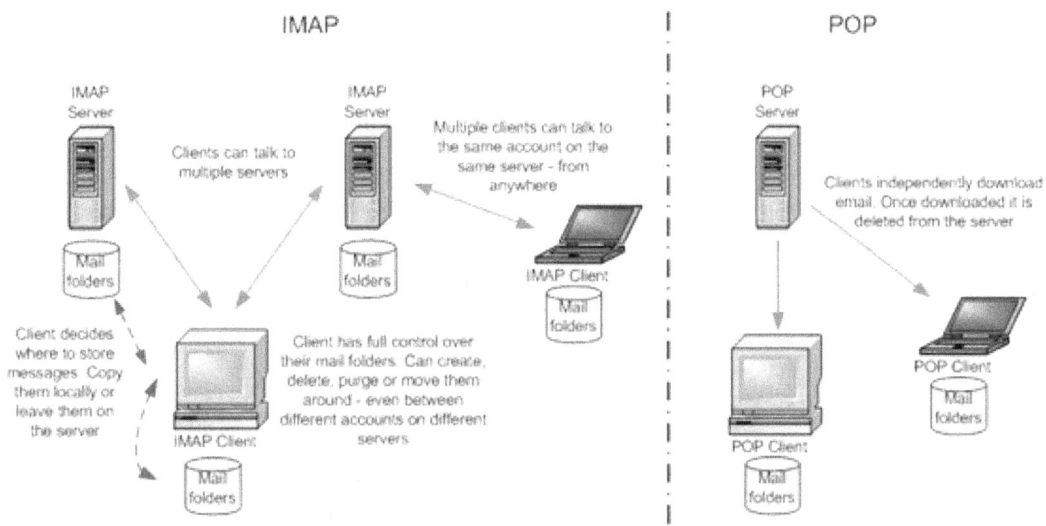

Diagram of IMAP Vs. POP Services

13.4 WEB APPLICATIONS AND THEIR IMPACT

13.4.1 Other Applications in the Web Ecosystem

1. **Cloud Computing**:
   Cloud computing services such as Amazon Web Services (AWS), Google Cloud, and Microsoft Azure have revolutionised how data is stored, managed, and processed. These platforms offer businesses and individuals the ability to access vast computing power without relying on local infrastructure. With cloud services, users can store large volumes of data, host websites and applications, and run complex algorithms, all on remote servers.

   Key benefits of cloud computing include:

   o **Scalability**: Cloud services allow businesses to easily scale their resources up or down based on demand. This flexibility makes it easier for companies to handle fluctuations in traffic or processing needs.

   o **Cost-Effectiveness**: By eliminating the need for expensive local infrastructure, cloud computing offers a pay-as-you-go model that helps businesses reduce costs.

   o **Accessibility**: Cloud platforms provide users with access to their data and applications from anywhere in the world, as long as there is internet connectivity. This is particularly valuable for global teams and remote workers.

- **Collaboration**: Cloud-based applications like **Google Drive** and **Dropbox** facilitate easy collaboration by allowing multiple users to access and edit documents in real-time.

2. **E-commerce**:
E-commerce platforms such as **Amazon**, **eBay**, and **Alibaba** have transformed the global retail industry by creating virtual marketplaces that connect buyers and sellers across the world. These platforms enable businesses to reach customers beyond their local geographic location and offer a wide variety of products and services.

Key elements that power e-commerce include:

- **Secure Payment Gateways**: Services like **PayPal**, **Stripe**, and **Square** enable online transactions by securely processing payments through credit cards, digital wallets, or bank transfers.

- **Inventory Management**: E-commerce platforms integrate inventory systems that automatically update stock levels as items are sold. This helps businesses manage their stock and avoid over-selling or under-selling.

- **Real-time Shipping Logistics**: Companies like **FedEx**, **UPS**, and **DHL** use advanced tracking systems to offer customers real-time updates on their purchases, allowing for faster and more reliable shipping.

- **Customer Experience**: Personalised recommendations, reviews, and customer service channels have helped improve the shopping experience, making it more tailored and convenient for consumers.

3. **Online Collaboration Tools**:
The rise of remote work and digital collaboration has driven the development of tools like Zoom, Slack, Google Workspace, and Microsoft Teams. These platforms enable virtual meetings, document sharing, and real-time communication, making them essential for modern work environments.

Benefits of online collaboration tools include:

- **Remote Work Enablement**: Tools like Zoom have made it possible for businesses to conduct meetings without being physically present, providing flexibility for teams working from different locations.

- **Team Collaboration**: Platforms like Slack allow teams to communicate in real-time, organise conversations into channels, and share files, improving overall productivity.

- **Document Sharing and Real-time Editing**: Google Workspace allows users to collaborate on documents, spreadsheets, and presentations simultaneously, making teamwork more efficient.

- **Post-Pandemic Workplace**: The COVID-19 pandemic accelerated the adoption of these tools, and they have become integral to hybrid work models, where employees split their time between the office and remote locations.

4. **Streaming Services**:
Streaming platforms such as Netflix, Spotify, and YouTube have changed the way users consume media. These services allow users to access movies, TV shows, music, and videos over the internet in real-time, without the need to download files.

Key aspects of streaming services include:

- **Data Compression**: To optimise streaming, these platforms use advanced data compression algorithms that reduce file sizes without sacrificing quality. This allows content to load faster and minimises buffering.

- **Content Delivery Networks (CDNs)**: CDNs are distributed networks of servers that deliver content to users based on their geographical location. By caching content at multiple points, CDNs reduce latency and enhance the user experience by delivering data faster.

- **Personalisation**: Streaming platforms use algorithms to recommend content based on users' viewing habits, ensuring that users are consistently engaged with content that matches their interests.

- **Global Reach**: Services like Netflix and YouTube are available in multiple languages and countries, providing content to a global audience and democratising access to entertainment.

5. **Virtual and Augmented Reality (VR/AR)**:
Virtual Reality (VR) and Augmented Reality (AR) are emerging technologies that are gradually being integrated into web applications. These immersive technologies offer innovative ways for users to interact with digital content and have a growing presence in industries like gaming, education, real estate, and e-commerce.

Applications of VR and AR include:

- **Gaming**: VR technologies like **Oculus Rift** and **HTC Vive** provide fully immersive gaming experiences, allowing players to interact with virtual worlds in ways that were previously impossible.

- **Education**: AR can overlay educational content onto the real world, enabling students to engage in interactive learning experiences. For instance, AR applications allow students to visualise complex concepts like the human anatomy or astronomical phenomena in 3D.

- **Real Estate**: Virtual tours powered by VR and AR allow potential buyers to explore properties remotely, saving time and providing more comprehensive views of homes and buildings.
- **Online Shopping**: E-commerce platforms are beginning to incorporate AR features, allowing users to virtually try on clothes or preview furniture in their homes before making a purchase. For example, IKEA's AR app lets customers see how a piece of furniture would look in their living space.

These technologies have the potential to revolutionise how we interact with the internet, creating more dynamic, immersive, and personalised web experiences.

13.5 EVOLUTION AND FUTURE OF THE WEB

13.5.1 Web 1.0: Static Web

Web 1.0, often referred to as the "Static Web," was the first version of the internet that emerged in the early 1990s. It was characterised by simple, static websites that were primarily used for delivering information. Key features, functionalities, and uses of Web 1.0 include:

- **Static Content**: Websites were made up of static HTML pages, meaning that the content did not change dynamically. Users could only read information but could not interact with the content.
- **Limited User Interaction**: There were minimal options for user engagement. Users could browse websites, but there were no interactive features such as commenting or social media integration.
- **Basic Design and Navigation**: Web 1.0 websites often had simple, text-heavy designs with limited images and basic navigation menus. Web pages were primarily informational, with few multimedia elements.
- **Read-Only Web**: Content was mainly read-only, meaning users could not contribute or alter the information on websites. The internet was largely a one-way communication channel.
- **Limited Multimedia**: Websites in Web 1.0 typically contained only text and basic images, with limited support for audio, video, or interactive features.
- **Use Case**: Web 1.0 was primarily used for informational purposes - businesses, educational institutions, and individuals used it to share content and showcase products or services. It was essentially a digital brochure or catalogue for most users.

13.5.2 Web 2.0: The Dynamic and Interactive Web

Web 2.0, often called the "Social Web," marks the transition from static websites to dynamic, interactive platforms. Introduced in the early 2000s, Web 2.0 emphasizes user-generated content, greater collaboration, sharing, and social interaction. Key features and characteristics of Web 2.0 include:

- **User Interaction**: Platforms such as social media, Facebook, YouTube, and Wikipedia wikis, and blogs allow users to contribute and interact, create, share, and collaborate on content rather than merely consuming it.

- **Interactivity**: Websites became more dynamic, allowing for real-time content updates and user interaction (e.g., comment sections, likes, and shares).

- **Rich User Experiences**: The web's visual and functional aspects were enhanced through technologies like **AJAX**, enabling smooth and responsive interfaces without full page reloads.

- **Cloud Computing**: Cloud-based services enable data storage, processing, and sharing across devices.

- **Social media & Networking**: Web 2.0 introduced widespread social networking, allowing users to connect, communicate, and share experiences.

Examples of Web 2.0 Applications:

- **Social Networking**: Facebook, X (Twitter), Instagram.
- **Video Sharing**: YouTube, TikTok.
- **Collaborative Platforms**: Wikipedia, Google Docs.

The rise of **Web 2.0** has paved the way for modern digital ecosystems, transforming how individuals, businesses, and communities engage with the internet.

13.5.3 Web 3.0: The Semantic and Intelligent Web

Web 3.0, often referred to as the "Semantic Web," represents the next stage of the internet, focusing on decentralisation, AI, and greater data privacy. It envisions a web that is more intelligent, context-aware, and data-driven. While Web 2.0 focused on user-generated content and interactivity, Web 3.0 is about structuring and linking data in a way that machines can understand and process. It leverages emerging technologies such as blockchain and artificial intelligence.

Key features and characteristics of Web 3.0 include:

- **Decentralisation**: Decentralisation is a key aspect of Web 3.0, where Blockchain technology empowers decentralised applications (dApps) ensure data privacy, security, and trust, and removes the need for centralised control by large corporations.

- **Semantic Understanding**: Web 3.0 aims to make the web smarter by allowing machines to understand and process data contextually, improving search results and personalisation. Thus, websites and applications will be able to interpret the context and meaning of data. This allows for more accurate and personalised search results, intelligent recommendations, and better data interoperability.

- **Enhanced Privacy and Security**: Web 3.0 incorporates advanced encryption and user control over personal data.

- **AI and Virtual Assistants**: Artificial intelligence enhances user interaction with smarter search engines, recommendation systems, and voice-controlled assistants. AI and machine learning will play a critical role in Web 3.0, enabling systems to understand user preferences and provide more intuitive and automated experiences.

- **Real-World Applications**:
    - **Smart Assistants**: AI-driven platforms like Siri and Alexa use semantic web principles to understand and respond to user queries.
    - **Decentralised Applications (dApps)**: Applications built on blockchain technology allow for greater transparency and security.

Web 3.0 aims to create a more intelligent, secure, and decentralised internet, empowering users with greater control over their data and interactions, including non-fungible token (NFT).

A **non-fungible token (NFT)** is a distinctive digital identifier stored on a blockchain, serving to verify ownership and authenticity. It cannot be duplicated, exchanged, or divided. Ownership of an NFT is documented on the blockchain and can be transferred by the owner, enabling the buying and selling of NFTs.

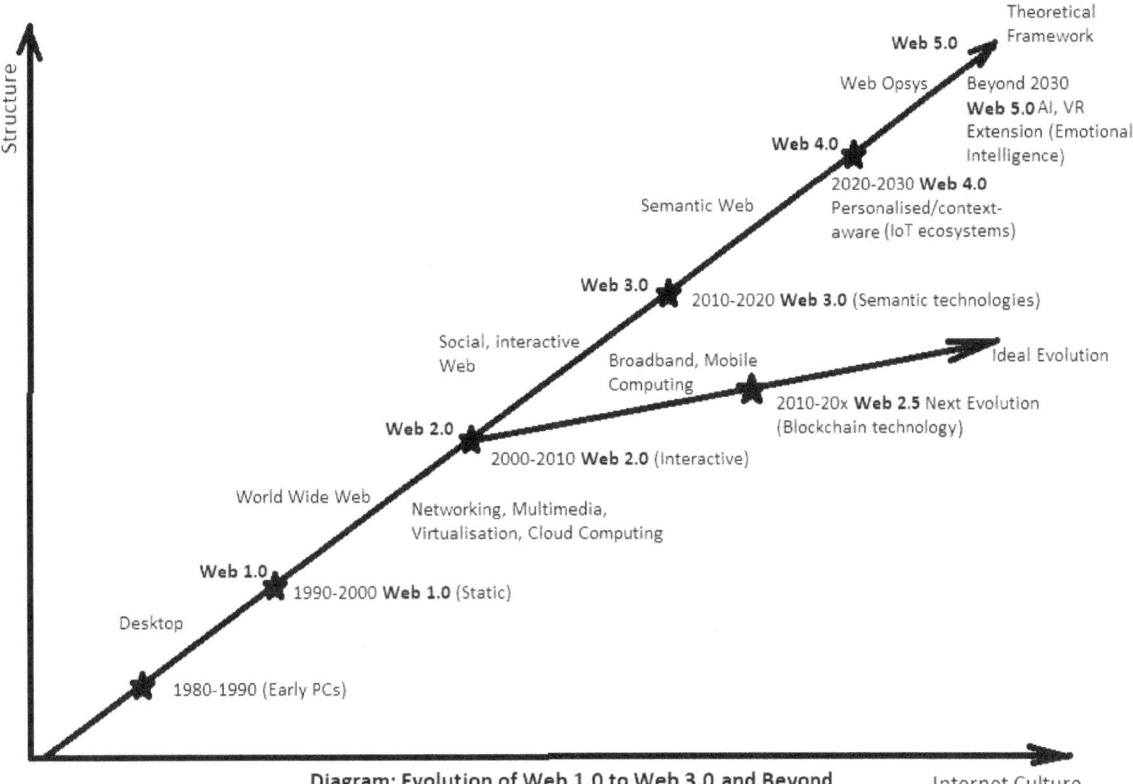

Diagram: Evolution of Web 1.0 to Web 3.0 and Beyond

13.6 CHARACTERISTICS OF WEB 4.0: THE INTELLIGENT WEB

13.6.1 Key Features of Web 4.0

- **Ubiquitous Connectivity:** Web 4.0 integrates advanced AI with Internet of Things (IoT) devices, enabling seamless connectivity across all smart systems and environments.

- **Personalised Experiences:** Offers hyper-personalisation through advanced data analytics and adaptive AI systems that predict user needs.

- **Real-Time Interaction:** Focuses on immediate, context-aware interactions between users, devices, and services.

13.6.2 Applications of Web 4.0

- **Smart Cities:** Integration of IoT and AI for efficient city management, such as traffic control, energy optimisation, and public safety systems.

- **Healthcare:** AI-driven diagnostics and real-time patient monitoring through connected medical devices.

- **Retail:** Personalised shopping experiences using AR/VR and predictive AI for recommendations.

13.7 CHARACTERISTICS OF WEB 5.0: THE EMOTIONAL WEB

13.7.1 Key Features of Web 5.0

- **Emotional Interaction:** Focuses on creating emotionally intelligent systems that can detect, interpret, and respond to human emotions.

- **Deep Integration:** Combines AI, brain-computer interfaces (BCI), and advanced biometrics for immersive and intuitive user experiences.

- **Enhanced Ethical Considerations:** Prioritises transparency, security, and privacy as technology becomes deeply integrated with personal and emotional aspects of life.

13.7.2 Applications of Web 5.0

- **Mental Health Support:** AI-driven tools that provide emotional support and real-time stress management.

- **Education:** Learning platforms that adapt to a student's emotional state to enhance engagement and retention.

- **Entertainment:** Fully immersive, emotionally responsive gaming and media experiences using advanced VR and haptic feedback.

13.8 FUTURE OF WEB TECHNOLOGIES

Emerging web technologies continue to evolve, shaping how we interact with the internet. Web 3.0 introduces a decentralised and semantic web, where blockchain, smart contracts, and AI-driven personalisation enable more secure, efficient, and user-focused online experiences. This paradigm shift empowers users with greater control over their data while enhancing machine-readable content for seamless integration across platforms.

Building on this foundation, Web 4.0 integrates advanced AI and IoT technologies to create intelligent systems that offer ubiquitous connectivity and context-aware interactions. This phase envisions smart environments where users can engage with connected devices in real-time, enhancing productivity and convenience in everyday tasks.

Looking further ahead, Web 5.0 aims to forge emotional and intuitive interactions between humans and technology. Leveraging AI, brain-computer interfaces, and biometric feedback, it creates emotionally intelligent systems capable of responding to users' feelings and intentions. These advancements promise transformative applications in fields like mental health, education, and immersive entertainment.

One example of these future trends includes 3D web browsers, which could revolutionise online experiences. These browsers will enable users to navigate immersive virtual environments, shop in realistic virtual stores, or participate in interactive virtual meetings, blending the digital and physical worlds more seamlessly than ever before.

Tutorial Activity 13 - Web Technology and Emerging Web Trends

Quizzes and Questions

Section 1: Fundamentals of Web Architecture and Networking

Question 1:

What is the primary role of a router in a network?
A. To connect devices within the same network
B. To manage email communications
C. To forward data packets between different networks
D. To store files and documents

Question 2:

Which of the following best describes a three-tier system architecture in web technology?
A. A model that involves a single database, application, and client interface
B. A structure consisting of a presentation layer, business logic layer, and data layer
C. A model that integrates client-side and server-side communication
D. A two-level system consisting only of client and server

Question 3:

In a client/server communication model, what happens when a user types a URL into their browser?
A. The server sends a request to the DNS to resolve the IP address.
B. The server directly processes the request without needing DNS.
C. The client receives an immediate response without contacting the server.
D. The request is routed directly through a proxy server.

Section 2: Web Standards, Tools, and Security

Question 4:

Which organisation is responsible for setting global web standards, including HTML and CSS?
A. IETF
B. W3C
C. ICANN
D. IEEE

Question 5:

What is the main purpose of a proxy server?
A. To route data packets through the internet
B. To filter and monitor internet traffic for security purposes
C. To host websites and manage servers
D. To store emails and other data

Question 6:

Which performance metric measures the delay between sending a request and receiving a response from a server?
A. Bandwidth usage
B. Latency
C. Response time
D. Server concurrency

Section 3: Web Protocols and Communication

Question 7:

Which of the following is NOT a layer of the TCP/IP model?
A. Application
B. Transport
C. Internet
D. Physical

Question 8:

What is the main difference between HTTP and HTTPS?
A. HTTP is used for secure communication, while HTTPS is not.
B. HTTPS includes encryption, while HTTP does not.
C. HTTP is faster than HTTPS.
D. HTTP uses IP addresses, while HTTPS uses domain names.

Question 9:

What is the primary function of SMTP in email communication?
A. To retrieve emails from the server
B. To manage email folders
C. To send emails from the client to the server
D. To encrypt email content

Section 4: Web Applications and Their Impact

Question 10:

What is a key benefit of cloud computing in modern web technologies?
A. It ensures local storage of all user data.
B. It increases the complexity of web applications.
C. It offers scalability and flexibility in accessing resources.
D. It eliminates the need for web browsers.

Question 11:

How has e-commerce impacted global trade?
A. By allowing customers to shop without internet access
B. By enabling secure online transactions and efficient logistics systems
C. By limiting the number of goods sold online
D. By reducing online customer interactions

Section 5: Evolution and Future of the Web

Question 12:

Which of the following is a defining feature of Web 3.0?
A. Static web pages with limited user interaction
B. Semantic understanding, AI, and decentralisation
C. Focus on social media platforms
D. Enhanced search engine optimisation

Question 13:

What is the role of blockchain in Web 3.0?
A. To improve website design
B. To enhance data privacy, security, and trust
C. To optimise video streaming
D. To support cloud storage solutions

Question 14:

What technology is often used in immersive web experiences such as gaming and education?
A. Virtual Reality (VR)
B. Email Protocols
C. TCP/IP
D. Proxy Servers

Chapter 14: Cloud Computing

Learning Outcome

By the end of this chapter, learners will be able to:

- Compare and contrast public, private, and hybrid cloud models, outlining their benefits and appropriate use cases.

- Identify and describe the different cloud service models (IaaS, PaaS, SaaS) and their applications in modern computing environments.

- Examine the security challenges in cloud computing, focusing on data protection and compliance issues.

14. CLOUD COMPUTING

Cloud computing is a transformative technology that delivers computing services - including servers, storage, databases, networking, and software - via the internet. This model provides users with on-demand access to a shared pool of configurable resources, enabling businesses and individuals to utilise virtualised hardware hosted on physical machines in remote data centres, often referred to as "the cloud."

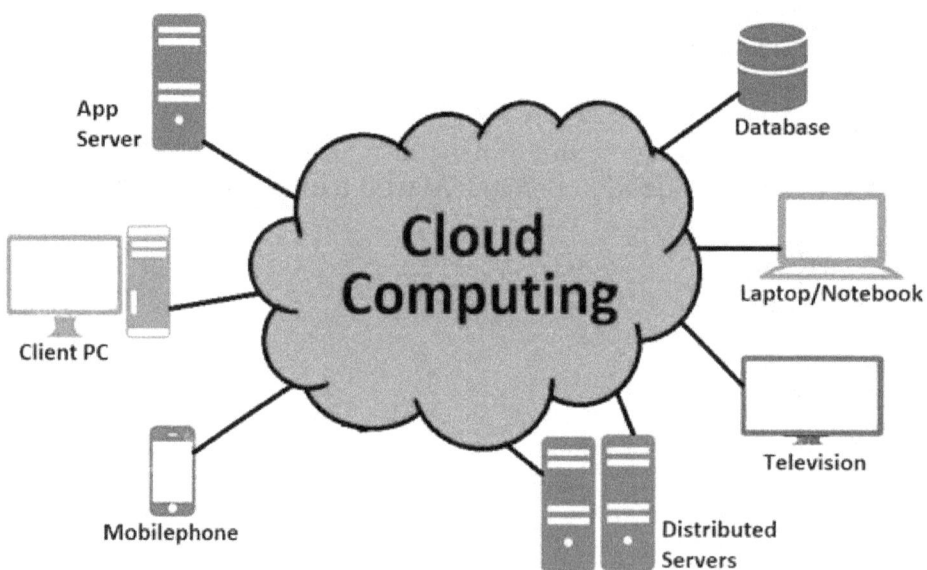

Diagram of Cloud Computing

At its core, cloud computing is a network of interconnected servers, each performing specific functions such as delivering applications or services. These resources are accessed as needed, allowing users to experience them as though dedicated solely to their use, even though they are shared among multiple users. This abstraction eliminates the need for users to understand the underlying architecture or configurations, allowing them to focus entirely on their tasks rather than the technical details of cloud infrastructure.

The scalability of cloud computing is one of its most significant benefits. Resources can be adjusted dynamically to meet real-time demands, ensuring that users only pay for what they use. This flexibility enables businesses to accommodate fluctuations in workload without incurring unnecessary costs or compromising performance. Whether experiencing a surge in demand or scaling down during slower periods, cloud computing ensures operational efficiency and cost-effectiveness. Moreover, the cloud fosters innovation by providing access to advanced tools and services that may be too expensive or impractical to implement on-premises.

Leading cloud providers, such as Amazon (Simple Storage Service, or S3), Google (offering tools like Gmail, Google Maps, and Translate), Salesforce (platforms for customised cloud solutions), and Microsoft, have shaped the landscape of cloud computing. Microsoft's Office 365 suite exemplifies the integration of cloud capabilities, offering a unified experience with cloud-based data storage (OneDrive), global team collaboration, and online availability of all its applications. Unlike its predecessors that required local installation, Office 365 eliminates the need for on-site hardware while enhancing accessibility and productivity.

Cloud computing represents a paradigm shift in how computing resources are accessed and managed. By housing virtualised environments in distributed data centres, it provides users with efficient, scalable, and cost-effective solutions. This innovative approach not only reduces capital and operational costs but also enables businesses of all sizes to optimise resource allocation, enhance efficiency, and focus on driving growth.

14.1 TYPES OF CLOUD COMPUTING

Cloud computing offers versatile models designed to meet diverse business and operational needs. The three primary types of cloud computing and deployment models are Public Cloud, Private Cloud, and Hybrid Cloud, each catering to specific use cases and offering unique benefits:

14.1.1 Public Cloud

The public cloud model involves resources that are owned and managed by third-party cloud service providers. These resources, such as servers and storage, are shared among multiple users (also known as tenants) over the Internet. This model is widely adopted due to its cost-effectiveness and scalability.

- **Key Features:**
    - Operated and maintained by external providers, such as Amazon Web Services (AWS), Google Cloud, and Microsoft Azure.
    - Accessible to any individual or business willing to subscribe to the service.
    - Users are billed based on usage, such as storage capacity or computing power consumed.

- **Advantages:**
  - **Cost-Effective:** Eliminates the need for businesses to invest in expensive hardware and maintenance.
  - **Scalable:** Resources can be scaled up or down based on demand.
  - **Ease of Access:** Services can be accessed from anywhere with an internet connection.
  - **Minimal Maintenance:** Providers handle updates, security, and maintenance.
- **Common Use Cases:**
  - **Hosting Websites:** Public clouds are ideal for hosting websites due to their ability to handle fluctuating traffic.
  - **Application Development and Testing:** Developers leverage the cloud for creating, testing, and deploying applications quickly without requiring physical infrastructure.

14.1.2 Private Cloud

The private cloud model is tailored to meet the needs of a single organisation. It offers a dedicated environment, ensuring that resources are not shared with other users, which enhances security and control. The private cloud can be hosted on-premises or managed by a third-party provider.

- **Key Features:**
  - Exclusive to a single organisation.
  - Provides full control over resources, infrastructure, and security protocols.
  - Customisable to meet specific organisational needs and compliance requirements.
- **Advantages:**
  - **Enhanced Security:** Ideal for managing sensitive data with robust access controls and encryption.
  - **Greater Customisation:** Offers flexibility to configure the environment according to business requirements.
  - **Regulatory Compliance:** Simplifies adherence to industry-specific regulations, such as GDPR, HIPAA, or PCI-DSS.
- **Common Use Cases:**
  - **Sensitive Data Management:** Widely used in industries like finance and healthcare, where data privacy is a top priority.

- - **Enterprise Applications:** Suited for large organisations running mission-critical workloads requiring stringent security measures.

14.1.3 Hybrid Cloud

The hybrid cloud model combines the benefits of both public and private clouds, allowing businesses to seamlessly share data and applications between the two environments. This model is designed to optimise flexibility, performance, and cost-efficiency.

- **Key Features:**
  - Enables businesses to keep sensitive data in a private cloud while utilising the public cloud for less-critical operations.
  - Provides a unified infrastructure that integrates on-premises and cloud-based systems.
  - Facilitates workload migration between environments as needed.
- **Advantages:**
  - **Flexibility:** Adapts to changing workloads and business requirements.
  - **Optimised Resource Allocation:** Businesses can allocate workloads to the most cost-effective or performance-appropriate environment.
  - **Improved Security:** Sensitive operations can be confined to private environments while leveraging the scalability of public clouds.
- **Common Use Cases:**
  - **Fluctuating Workloads:** Ideal for businesses with seasonal spikes in demand, such as e-commerce platforms during sales events.
  - **Data Segmentation:** Useful for organisations handling both sensitive and non-sensitive data, ensuring that confidential information remains secure while other operations benefit from public cloud efficiency.

Summary

Each type of cloud computing offers distinct features and benefits that cater to varying business needs:

- **Public Cloud:** Cost-effective and scalable, suited for general-purpose tasks like hosting and development.
- **Private Cloud:** Secure and customisable, ideal for organisations managing sensitive data or adhering to strict regulations.
- **Hybrid Cloud:** Combines the best of both worlds, providing flexibility for businesses with diverse and fluctuating requirements.

By understanding the unique attributes of each model, organisations can select the cloud computing approach that aligns with their operational goals, ensuring optimal performance, security, and cost-efficiency.

Types of Cloud Computing

CC-BY-SA 3.0by Sam Johnston

Diagram showing the relationship between Public, Private, and Hybrid Clouds

14.2 CLOUD SERVICES AND SECURITY: IaaS, PaaS, SaaS, and Compliance

Cloud computing has revolutionised the way businesses and individuals utilise technology by providing scalable resources over the internet. Three primary service models in cloud computing – Infrastructure as a Service (IaaS), Platform as a Service (PaaS), and Software as a Service (SaaS) – cater to different organisational needs. This section explores each model's applications, the technology driving them, the advantages and disadvantages, and the security considerations organisations must address.

14.2.1. Cloud Services Technology Model

Cloud computing services are typically divided into three main categories based on the level of user control and capacity management:

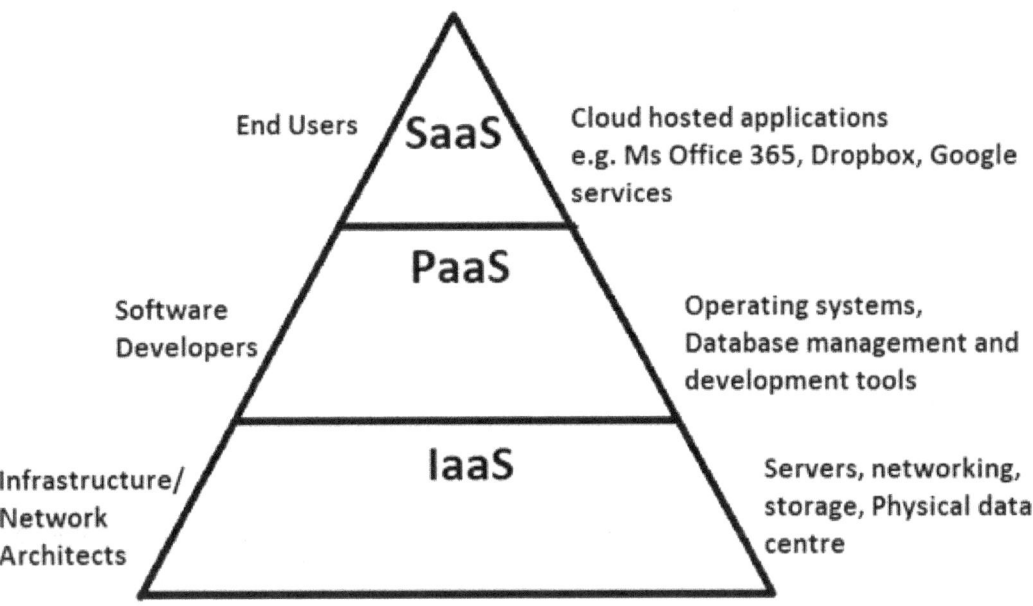

Diagram of Cloud Services Technology Model and Actors

14.2.2 Infrastructure as a Service (IaaS)

- **Definition**: IaaS offers virtualised computing resources over the internet. Users rent virtual servers, storage, and networking capabilities, enabling flexible scaling of infrastructure on a pay-as-you-go basis.

- **Applications**:

    - **Data Storage**: Examples include Amazon S3, Google Cloud Storage, and Microsoft OneDrive, where organisations can store large amounts of data without physical hardware.

    - **Web Hosting**: Providers like Microsoft Azure and DigitalOcean allow companies to host websites on virtual servers, ensuring high availability and scalability.

    - **Development and Testing**: Developers can test applications on virtual machines without investing in physical hardware.

    - **Disaster Recovery**: IaaS enables robust disaster recovery plans, offering quick data recovery and business continuity after outages.

- **Advantages**:

    - **Scalability:** Resources can be adjusted based on demand.
    - **Cost-Effective:** Pay-per-use pricing model reduces upfront costs.
    - **Flexibility:** Users can choose specific infrastructure components.

- **Disadvantages**:

    - **Complexity:** Managing virtual machines and resources can require technical expertise.

- o **Security Risks:** Users are responsible for securing their data and applications, increasing vulnerability to breaches.
- o **Dependency on Providers:** Downtime or outages from the provider can disrupt business operations.

14.2.3 Platform as a Service (PaaS)

- **Definition**: PaaS provides a platform allowing developers to build, deploy, and manage applications without the complexity of managing the underlying infrastructure.

- **Applications**:
  - o **Application Development**: Platforms like Google App Engine and Heroku streamline coding while managing infrastructure, scaling, and deployment.
  - o **Integration Services**: PaaS helps integrate various organisational applications and services, facilitating smoother workflows.
  - o **API Management**: PaaS tools allow easy creation and management of APIs, enabling better communication between software systems.
  - o **Collaboration Tools**: These platforms often include version control, testing, and collaboration features, enhancing team productivity.

- **Advantages**:
  - o **Simplified Development:** Developers can focus on writing code without worrying about infrastructure management.
  - o **Faster Time to Market:** Ready-to-use platforms speed up application deployment.
  - o **Integrated Tools:** Many PaaS platforms provide tools for version control, testing, and monitoring.

- **Disadvantages**:
  - o **Limited Customisation:** Platforms may not allow full control over underlying infrastructure.
  - o **Vendor Lock-In:** PaaS solutions often tie users to a specific provider's ecosystem.
  - o **Performance Issues:** Depending on the provider, performance may vary based on the resource-sharing model.

14.2.4 Software as a Service (SaaS)

- **Definition**: SaaS delivers software applications over the internet on a subscription basis, enabling users to access software without installation or maintenance.

- **Applications**:
    - **Business Applications**: Examples include Salesforce (CRM), Microsoft 365 (productivity tools), and Google Workspace (collaboration).
    - **Email and Communication**: Services such as Gmail and Slack offer communication tools hosted in the cloud.
    - **Financial Management**: SaaS platforms like QuickBooks Online and FreshBooks offer accessible financial solutions.
    - **Human Resources**: Tools such as Workday and BambooHR streamline HR management, from recruitment to employee services.

- **Advantages**:
    - **Ease of Use:** SaaS applications are ready to use, requiring minimal setup.
    - **Accessibility:** Users can access applications from anywhere with an internet connection.
    - **Cost-Efficiency:** SaaS typically eliminates the need for installation and maintenance.

- **Disadvantages**:
    - **Limited Customisation:** SaaS products may not cater to specific organisational needs or workflows.
    - **Data Security:** Since data is hosted by a third party, there may be concerns regarding its security and privacy.
    - **Vendor Dependence:** Reliance on a single provider can cause problems if the service is discontinued or experiences downtime.

14.2.5 Everything as a Service (XaaS)

As organisations grow and globalise, the integration of various software tools and services via cloud infrastructure is increasing, leading to the concept of Everything as a Service (XaaS). This model provides an extensive range of services and products over the internet instead of on-premises installations.

14.3 CLOUD SERVICES COMPLIANCE AND DATA PRIVACY

Organisations using cloud services must trust their cloud providers to ensure data privacy, security, and availability. This trust is essential because cloud data must remain protected from unauthorised access, misuse, and theft. Data stored in the cloud should be accessible only by authorised individuals and secure from breaches.

14.3.1 Cloud Services Compliance and Policy

Cloud services operations must comply with industry regulations and policies, along with internal organisational policies. For example, the General Data Protection Regulation (GDPR) governs the storage and processing of personal data in the European Union. The complexity of compliance increases when cloud services span multiple jurisdictions, requiring legal oversight and clear data management protocols. Some industries, like healthcare (e.g., NHS), must comply with stringent data protection rules that add further complexity to the cloud services framework.

14.3.2 Security Considerations and Challenges in Cloud Computing

While cloud computing offers various benefits, such as cost savings, scalability, and improved accessibility, it also brings significant security challenges. Organisations need to address these concerns proactively to ensure data security and compliance with legal and regulatory standards.

14.3.3 Data Protection and Privacy

- **Data Breaches**: Unauthorised access to sensitive data in the cloud remains a major concern. Implementing strong access controls and robust encryption is essential to safeguard data both in transit and at rest.

- **Data Loss**: While cloud providers are generally reliable, data loss can still occur due to accidental deletions, service outages, or corruption. Regular backups and comprehensive data recovery plans are necessary for mitigating such risks.

- **Shared Responsibility Model**: Cloud security follows a shared responsibility model where the cloud provider ensures the security of the infrastructure, and the customer is responsible for securing their data and applications.

14.3.4 Compliance Issues

- **Regulatory Compliance**: Organisations must ensure compliance with various data protection and privacy regulations, such as GDPR, HIPAA, and CCPA. This can be more challenging when data is distributed across multiple jurisdictions.

- **Vendor Compliance**: Organisations must also ensure that their cloud service providers comply with relevant regulations. Regular vendor assessments and audits are crucial to ensuring compliance.

- **Audit Trails**: Maintaining audit trails for data access and changes is essential for compliance. Organisations should implement monitoring tools to track user activities and ensure transparency.

14.3.5 Security Challenges

- **Identity and Access Management**: Controlling user identities and permissions is crucial for preventing unauthorised access. Multi-factor authentication (MFA) and identity management tools can enhance cloud security.

- **Insecure APIs**: APIs are central to cloud services, but poorly secured APIs can expose vulnerabilities. Organisations should implement secure coding practices and regularly test APIs for security weaknesses.

- **Vendor Lock-In**: Relying on a single cloud provider can lead to challenges in migrating data or applications to other platforms. Adopting a multi-cloud strategy can reduce this risk and offer greater flexibility in managing cloud services.

14.3.6 Gartner's 7 Advisory Considerations for Cloud Adoption

Gartner provides seven advisory considerations that organisations should evaluate when considering cloud adoption:

1. **Governance and Compliance**: Ensure that cloud services meet industry-specific regulatory and legal requirements and establish clear governance policies for data and resource management.

2. **Security and Privacy**: Assess the security measures implemented by cloud providers. Ensure robust encryption, identity management, and access control mechanisms are in place.

3. **Cloud Integration**: Evaluate how well the cloud service integrates with existing on-premises infrastructure and applications, ensuring minimal disruption to business operations.

4. **Cost Management**: Understand the cost structure of the cloud services and establish strategies to manage and optimise cloud expenditure to avoid overspending.

5. **Performance and Availability**: Assess the service-level agreements (SLAs) for uptime and response times, ensuring that the provider can meet performance requirements.

6. **Scalability and Flexibility**: Ensure that the cloud service can scale according to the organisation's growth needs and that it offers enough flexibility to adapt to changing business requirements.

7. **Vendor Lock-In**: Evaluate the risk of being tied to a specific vendor. Consider multi-cloud strategies or exit strategies to mitigate the risks of relying on a single cloud provider.

Tutorial Activity 14 - Cloud Computing

Quizzes and questions

Quiz 1: Cloud Deployment Models

1. Which of the following is a characteristic of a public cloud model?
(a) Exclusively used by a single organisation
(b) Highly scalable and accessible over the internet
(c) Built for specific, proprietary use
(d) Operates within an organisation's private network

2. What is a key advantage of a private cloud?
(a) Reduced cost for small-scale operations
(b) Enhanced control and customisation for an organisation
(c) Easy integration with third-party providers
(d) Requires no in-house IT expertise

3. True or False: A hybrid cloud combines elements of public and private clouds to enable flexible operations.

4. Match the following deployment models to their characteristics:

- Public Cloud: Accessible to anyone over the internet.
- Private Cloud: Exclusively managed for one organisation.
- Hybrid Cloud: Combines benefits of public and private models.

Quiz 2: Cloud Service Models

1. Which cloud service model provides a platform for developers to build, test, and deploy applications without managing infrastructure?
(a) IaaS
(b) PaaS
(c) SaaS
(d) FaaS

2. What is an example of Software as a Service (SaaS)?
(a) Microsoft Azure
(b) Google Workspace (formerly G Suite)
(c) AWS Elastic Compute Cloud (EC2)
(d) Docker

3. True or False: Infrastructure as a Service (IaaS) allows users to access virtualised computing resources like servers, storage, and networks.

4. Name a benefit of SaaS over traditional software delivery models.

Quiz 3: Security Challenges in Cloud Computing

1. What is the primary concern with data stored in a public cloud?
(a) Cost of storage
(b) Lack of scalability
(c) Data security and compliance risks
(d) Limited accessibility

2. Which of the following is a key security measure for cloud computing?
(a) Using shared access keys for all users
(b) Encrypting sensitive data before uploading to the cloud
(c) Relying solely on the cloud provider for security measures
(d) Disabling multi-factor authentication

3. List two compliance standards relevant to cloud computing security.
4. True or False: Cloud providers are solely responsible for the security of data stored in the cloud.

Extended Questions

1. Explain the differences between public, private, and hybrid cloud models, providing an example use case for each.

2. Discuss the role of encryption in mitigating security risks in cloud computing.

3. Compare IaaS, PaaS, and SaaS in terms of user responsibility and control.

Reference

Buyya, R., **Yeo, C. S.**, & **Venugopal, S.** (2008). *Market-Oriented Cloud Computing: Vision, Hype, and Reality for Delivering IT Services as Computing Utilities*. IEEE.

- This paper provides a foundational understanding of cloud computing, its models, and applications.

Mell, P., & Grance, T. (2011). *The NIST Definition of Cloud Computing*. National Institute of Standards and Technology (NIST).

- The NIST definition is critical for understanding cloud computing models and their standards.

Armbrust, M., **Fox, A.**, **Griffith, R.** (2010). *A View of Cloud Computing*. Communications of the ACM.

- Discusses the key elements of cloud computing and its impact on businesses.

Chapter 15: The Role of Communication Systems and Telematics

Learning Outcomes

By the end of this chapter, readers should be able to:

- Understand the Importance of Communication Systems: Explain their role in enhancing business efficiency, reducing costs, and improving customer service.

- Define and Trace the Development of Telematics: Describe telematics and its evolution from GPS technology to its applications across industries.

- Analyse Telematics Applications: Explore its use in sectors like logistics, healthcare, traffic management, and insurance, focusing on operational efficiency and safety.

- Evaluate Business Impacts: Assess how telematics enhances productivity, safety, and decision-making through real-time data exchange.

- Identify Emerging Trends: Recognise advancements like IoT, machine learning, and data analytics in telematics and communication systems.

- Appreciate Real-Time Data Exchange: Highlight its benefits for agility, safety, and proactive management in industries.

- Recognise Business Benefits: Understand how communication systems streamline processes, improve collaboration, and elevate customer experiences.

15.1 INTRODUCTION TO COMMUNICATION SYSTEMS AND TELEMATICS

Modern communication systems are integral to business, industry, and commerce, allowing organisations to operate seamlessly and foster innovation. Communication systems in both digital and telecommunications formats connect departments, automate processes, and improve workflows across various sectors. These systems enable organisations to reduce operational costs, enhance productivity, improve security, and optimise customer service delivery.

A significant advancement in communication technology is telematics, which merges telecommunications with informatics (information science) to facilitate real-time data exchange and monitoring. Telematics is crucial in industries such as transportation, logistics, and healthcare, where remote monitoring and data transfer enable better asset management, operational efficiency, and safety.

15.2 THE DEVELOPMENT OF TELEMATICS

Telematics, often referred to as "telecommunication informatics," integrates telecommunications, data transfer, and informatics to capture, process, and transmit information about remote objects or systems. The field originated in the 1960s with the advent of GPS (Global Positioning System) technology for military navigation. Over time, the technology expanded to commercial logistics and fleet management, evolving into a sophisticated system for real-time monitoring, data storage, and remote diagnostics.

The term informatics emphasizes data processing and technology-assisted information management, similar to Information Technology in the UK. While the UK and US primarily use terms like IT or Computer Science, many European countries, such as the Netherlands, use "informatics" to emphasize the data-centric aspect of technology applications. In a business setting, informatics focuses on using data and communication technology to improve decision-making, efficiency, and information access.

A significant push for telematics came from collaborative research projects in the European Union, notably the Telematics Application Programme. This initiative, conducted under the EU Directorate General XIII, explored the use of telematics in areas like transport, healthcare, education, and public administration. The programme encouraged research and development of communication tools that improved these sectors' efficiency, safety, and reliability.

15.3 APPLICATIONS AND IMPACT OF TELEMATICS

Telematics has become indispensable across various industries, transforming operations, improving resource management, and enhancing safety. Key applications include:

- **Fleet Management**: Telematics systems are widely used in transportation and logistics, allowing companies to track fleet performance, vehicle location, fuel consumption, and driver behaviour in real time. GPS-based tracking and data analytics improve route planning, reduce fuel costs, and enhance fleet security. For example, companies like UPS and FedEx rely on telematics for route optimisation, helping them meet delivery timelines and minimise environmental impact.

- **Healthcare**: In healthcare, telematics enables remote patient monitoring through wearable devices that transmit patient data (e.g., heart rate, blood pressure) to healthcare providers. This real-time information allows providers to monitor patients outside traditional settings, improving response times in emergencies. For example, telematics supports managing chronic diseases, as continuous monitoring can prevent complications and reduce hospital visits.

- **Traffic Management and Road Safety**: Telematics improves road safety by enabling technologies like speed cameras, real-time traffic monitoring, and incident response systems. These tools support law enforcement, help manage traffic flow and reduce accident rates. Cities worldwide use telematics-based smart traffic systems to improve urban mobility by adjusting traffic signals based on real-time congestion data.

- **Insurance Industry**: Telematics has revolutionised vehicle insurance through usage-based insurance (UBI) models, where insurers offer premiums based on real-time driving data (e.g., speed, braking). This enables personalised insurance plans, rewarding safe driving behaviours and reducing accident-related costs.

- **Construction and Heavy Equipment**: Construction companies leverage telematics to monitor heavy equipment, track fuel usage, and manage maintenance schedules. This data-driven approach ensures equipment availability, reduces downtime, and extends the lifespan of expensive machinery.

As telematics expands, software and hardware solutions that combine telecommunications and informatics are growing rapidly. Advances in wireless networks, sensors, and data analytics have enabled the integration of telematics with other technologies, such as IoT (Internet of Things) and machine learning. Publications like Informatics Digest and industry resources from organisations such as VNU Business Publications provide updates on telematics advancements and its growing applications across sectors.

15.4 THE ROLE OF COMMUNICATION SYSTEMS IN BUSINESS

With the rapid advancement of telematics and digital communication technologies, businesses are leveraging these systems to revolutionise their operations, improve customer engagement, and drive efficiency. These innovations are reshaping how companies manage data, automate processes, and deliver value, setting new benchmarks for operational excellence and customer satisfaction.

Effective communication systems are vital for businesses to remain competitive and achieve sustainable growth. They play a significant role by:

Reducing Operating and Labour Costs

Automation enabled by telematics and advanced communication systems significantly lowers reliance on manual processes, resulting in reduced labour expenses and streamlined operations. For instance, fleet management systems automate route optimisation, driver monitoring, and fuel usage analysis, minimising the need for manual dispatch personnel and reducing operational overhead. Similarly, automated customer service chatbots reduce the need for extensive call centre staff while maintaining efficiency.

Enhancing Productivity

Real-time data sharing and seamless communication across departments improve collaboration, reduce delays, and optimise workflows. Businesses equipped with IoT-enabled devices can access critical operational insights instantaneously. For example, a manufacturing facility using smart sensors and connected devices can predict equipment failures, schedule maintenance proactively, and minimize production interruptions, boosting overall productivity.

Improving Safety and Security

Modern communication systems enhance safety protocols and risk management through real-time monitoring, reporting, and alerting. Businesses can respond swiftly to potential threats or emergencies, reducing risk and ensuring a secure environment. For example:

- Logistics companies use telematics to track vehicle health and driver behaviour, preventing accidents and ensuring compliance with safety standards.
- Security systems with live video feeds and AI-based threat detection enable swift responses to breaches, safeguarding personnel and assets.

Elevating Customer Service

Communication systems empower businesses to deliver responsive and personalised customer service. Leveraging data insights, companies can anticipate customer needs, address inquiries efficiently, and build stronger relationships. Examples include:

- Retailers using inventory management systems integrated with telematics to ensure stock availability, avoiding out-of-stock situations.
- Delivery services offering real-time package tracking and predictive delivery updates, enhancing customer trust and satisfaction.

Driving Strategic Decision-Making

Communication systems provide businesses with actionable insights through data analytics and visualisation tools. Leaders can monitor performance metrics, evaluate market trends, and adjust strategies quickly. For example, telematics systems in supply chains enable businesses to analyse delivery efficiency, identify bottlenecks, and implement data-driven solutions to improve overall performance.

In conclusion, telematics and communication systems are indispensable for modern businesses, enabling cost efficiency, operational excellence, safety, and superior customer experiences. As technology evolves, their role will continue to expand, driving innovation and creating new opportunities across industries.

Tutorial Activity 15 - The Role of Communication Systems and Telematics

Quizzes and Questions

Quiz 1: Understanding Communication Systems

1. What is the primary purpose of communication systems in business?
   (a) Automating manual tasks
   (b) Enhancing operational efficiency and customer satisfaction
   (c) Monitoring employee productivity
   (d) Expanding physical office spaces

2. Which of the following is NOT a benefit of communication systems in businesses?
   (a) Real-time collaboration
   (b) Cost reduction through automation
   (c) Increased hardware dependency
   (d) Enhanced customer service

3. Match the following examples to their corresponding benefits:
   - Real-time tracking of deliveries:
     - Improves customer service
   - Automated inventory updates:
     - Reduces operational costs
   - IoT-enabled sensors in manufacturing:
     - Enhances productivity

Quiz 2: Tracing the Development of Telematics

1. What is telematics?
   (a) A method of telecommunication used exclusively in healthcare
   (b) A field combining telecommunications and information technology to enable real-time data transfer
   (c) A software tool for designing communication networks
   (d) A system solely for tracking vehicles

2. What technology marked the beginning of telematics?
   (a) IoT networks
   (b) Blockchain systems
   (c) GPS tracking
   (d) 5G connectivity

3. True or False: Telematics only applies to logistics and fleet management.

Quiz 3: Analysing Telematics Applications

1. Which industry uses telematics to monitor patient health remotely and schedule emergency responses?
   (a) Logistics
   (b) Healthcare
   (c) Insurance
   (d) Retail

2. How does telematics improve traffic management?
   (a) By eliminating traffic signals
   (b) By providing real-time traffic updates to reduce congestion
   (c) By automating vehicle production
   (d) By tracking employee attendance

3. List two ways telematics benefits the insurance industry.

Quiz 4: Evaluating Business Impacts

1. What aspect of telematics helps businesses make faster and better decisions?
   (a) High-speed internet
   (b) Real-time data exchange
   (c) Manual reporting systems
   (d) Employee performance reviews

2. True or False: Telematics reduces downtime by enabling predictive maintenance in industries.

3. Which of these is a direct benefit of telematics in enhancing safety?
   (a) Improved office layouts
   (b) Real-time monitoring of vehicle conditions
   (c) Reducing employee training costs
   (d) Automating payroll systems

Quiz 5: Emerging Trends in Telematics

1. What role does IoT play in advancing telematics?
   (a) Establishing manual processes
   (b) Enabling connected devices to share data seamlessly
   (c) Replacing cloud computing services
   (d) Reducing network infrastructure

2. Name two emerging technologies influencing telematics and communication systems.

3. Which of the following is NOT an emerging trend in telematics?
   (a) Autonomous vehicle data exchange
   (b) Integration of neural interfaces for vehicle control
   (c) Reduction of global internet accessibility
   (d) Predictive analytics for operational efficiency

1. **Research and Reports from Technology Firms**: Companies like Cisco, Microsoft, and IBM frequently publish white papers and reports detailing ICT trends, cybersecurity, the Internet of Things (IoT), and other emerging technologies and their impacts on business and society.

2. **Academic Journals on ICT and Society**: Journals like *Computers in Human Behaviour*, *Information Systems Research*, and *Journal of Information Technology* provide peer-reviewed articles that explore the social and economic impacts of ICT, with studies on e-commerce, digital privacy, cybersecurity, and social media influence.

Chapter 16: E-Commerce

Learning Outcomes

By the end of this chapter, learners will be able to:

- Define e-commerce and its key components, including its various models and applications.
- Assess the performance of different e-commerce applications and explore their impact on businesses and consumers.

16. UNDERSTANDING E-COMMERCE

E-commerce, short for electronic commerce, refers to the buying, selling, and exchanging of goods, services, and information over a network, primarily the internet. E-commerce has become a cornerstone of modern business, leveraging technologies that allow organisations to carry out transactions globally, efficiently, and cost-effectively.

Historically, e-commerce's roots date back to the 1970s with the introduction of Electronic Funds Transfer (EFT) in the banking sector, which allowed for the digital transfer of money between accounts. The advent of Electronic Data Interchange (EDI) followed, allowing companies to electronically exchange standardised business documents such as purchase orders and invoices with partners, vendors, and customers.

16.1.1 E-Commerce Today

The global commercialisation of the internet in the 1990s ignited a massive surge in e-commerce applications. Small businesses, which previously couldn't compete with large corporations, now found themselves operating on a level playing field through online commerce. With the widespread adoption of internet technologies, e-commerce became a vital tool for businesses, government agencies, and individuals to trade, communicate, and share information. The rise of cloud computing, mobile technologies, and nanotechnology has further accelerated the growth of e-commerce, with more interconnected devices and systems in use than ever before.

16.1.2 E-Commerce Models and Applications

1. **Buying and Selling Goods and Services (Electronic Markets or e-Markets):**
    - E-markets are virtual environments where buyers and sellers conduct transactions without the need for physical interaction. E-markets handle everything from the transfer of money to logistics, providing an efficient marketplace for goods and services.

2. **Facilitating Organisational Communication and Collaboration:**

- E-commerce technologies streamline communication within and between organisations. This may include the use of extranets, intranets, and collaborative software that allows seamless information sharing and cooperation among business partners.

3. **Customer Service and Support:**
    - E-commerce platforms also facilitate customer service functions, such as e-CRM (Customer Relationship Management) and e-Government solutions that enhance the interaction between the public and government institutions.

16.1.3 E-Commerce Transaction Models

E-commerce transaction models define the interactions between various parties involved in online commercial transactions. Each model has its unique characteristics, catering to different needs within the business ecosystem. Below is an expanded discussion on the various e-commerce transaction models:

- **Business-to-Business (B2B):**
  In the B2B model, transactions occur between businesses, typically involving manufacturers, wholesalers, and suppliers. This model is foundational in supply chain management, where large volumes of goods or services are exchanged. B2B e-commerce usually involves Inter-organisational Information Systems (IOS), which automate and streamline the ordering process, payment systems, and inventory management. These transactions are generally characterised by bulk orders, long-term relationships, and negotiated contracts. Platforms like Alibaba and Grainger provide B2B services where businesses can buy and sell products in bulk, often with complex pricing structures and contractual terms.

- **Business-to-Consumer (B2C):**
  B2C is the most widely recognised e-commerce model, where businesses sell products or services directly to individual consumers. This model encompasses a vast range of online retailing, such as physical goods, digital products, and services. The B2C model has revolutionised how consumers shop, allowing them to purchase items from anywhere, at any time, via platforms like Amazon, eBay, and Walmart's online store. Key features of B2C transactions include product catalogues, secure online payment gateways, and consumer-driven shopping experiences. These platforms often offer personalisation and recommendation algorithms to enhance the consumer shopping experience and drive sales.

- **Consumer-to-Consumer (C2C):**
  The C2C model facilitates direct transactions between consumers, typically mediated through third-party platforms that provide the infrastructure for these interactions. The most common examples of C2C platforms include eBay, Craigslist, and Facebook Marketplace. Consumers can sell new or used goods to other consumers, either through fixed-price listings or auctions. This model empowers individuals to act as both buyers and sellers

in an online marketplace, creating a peer-to-peer economy. C2C platforms often rely on reputation systems (e.g., user ratings and reviews) to build trust and ensure the quality of transactions.

- **Consumer-to-Business (C2B)**:
  In the C2B model, individuals sell goods or services to businesses. This model is increasingly common in the freelance and gig economy, where individuals offer specialised services, such as web development, graphic design, or writing, to businesses. Popular platforms like Upwork, Fiverr, and 99designs operate on a C2B model, allowing freelancers to connect with companies in need of specific expertise. Unlike traditional business-to-consumer transactions, the C2B model places the consumer in the position of offering value to the business, making it a flexible and evolving e-commerce model.

- **Non-Business E-Commerce**:
  non-business e-commerce includes transactions conducted by non-profit organisations, such as charities, educational institutions, and government agencies, to improve their services and reduce operational costs. For example, academic institutions may sell course materials, while charities may use online platforms for donation processing or to raise funds through crowdfunding. These organisations leverage e-commerce technologies to increase accessibility, streamline operations, and reach a broader audience. They often operate on a smaller scale compared to traditional businesses but have significant social impact through their use of online platforms.

- **Intra-Business E-Commerce**:
  Intra-business e-commerce focuses on internal transactions within a business organisation. It involves the use of e-commerce technologies, such as intranets, to manage internal processes like resource planning, supply chain management, and inventory control. For instance, companies may use e-commerce solutions to automate procurement, track shipments, or manage employee purchasing programs. By utilising secure internal platforms, businesses can streamline operations, improve efficiency, and reduce costs associated with traditional manual processes. This model often enhances collaboration between departments and facilitates better management of organisational resources.

Each of these e-commerce models plays a vital role in the global digital economy, with various applications that cater to specific business needs, consumer preferences, and technological advancements. The continuous evolution of e-commerce technologies is enabling these models to be more interconnected, efficient, and accessible to users across different industries.

16.1.4 Inter-Organisational Information Systems (IOS)

An IOS integrates various organisations - typically suppliers and customers - onto a unified system platform. This system streamlines transactions and communications by enabling partners to exchange data without relying on physical documents or time-consuming phone calls. Common IOS applications include:

Electronic Data Interchange (EDI):
EDI is a standardised method that enables businesses to exchange electronic documents, such as purchase orders and invoices, between partners. It ensures secure, automated, and efficient B2B (business-to-business) communication, reducing the need for paper documents and manual processing, thereby speeding up transactions and reducing errors.

Extranets:
Extranets provide secure access to a company's internal network for external business partners, clients, and suppliers over the internet. It allows organisations to share relevant information, such as inventory levels or project updates, while maintaining security and privacy, enhancing collaboration and communication between the business and its partners.

Electronic Funds Transfer (EFT):
EFT is a system used to transfer money electronically between banks or financial institutions. It facilitates payments for goods and services without the need for paper-based transactions like cheques. EFT is commonly used in payroll processing, supplier payments, and online purchases, offering a faster, more secure way to handle financial exchanges.

Supply Chain Management (SCM):
SCM systems streamline the flow of goods, services, and information between a business and its suppliers. By optimising logistics, inventory management, and production scheduling, SCM systems improve efficiency, reduce costs, and help ensure that products are delivered to customers in a timely manner. Integration with IOS allows real-time data sharing across the entire supply chain.

16.1.5 Benefits of IOS

Inter-Organisational Information Systems (IOS) provide a framework that allows businesses to seamlessly share data, processes, and systems across organisational boundaries. This collaboration enhances operational efficiency, cost management, and trust among partners. Below are the key benefits of IOS:

1. Efficient Transaction Processing

- **Streamlined Workflows:** IOS automates routine processes, such as purchase orders, inventory updates, and payment confirmations, eliminating manual intervention and reducing human error.

- **Faster Operations:** Transactions are processed in real time, significantly reducing the time required to complete business exchanges compared to traditional methods.

- **Error Reduction:** By eliminating the need for physical documentation and manual entry, IOS reduces errors in data handling, ensuring greater accuracy in transactions.

2. Cost Savings

- **Lower Operational Costs:** Automating processes reduces dependency on manual labour, cutting costs associated with wages and employee management.

- **Reduced Administrative Overheads:** The shift from physical to digital documentation eliminates expenses on paper, printing, and storage.

- **Savings on Physical Infrastructure:** Businesses that operate through IOS reduce reliance on traditional brick-and-mortar setups, saving on costs like office space, utilities, and maintenance.

- **Advertising and Marketing Efficiency:** Digital platforms within IOS offer cost-effective methods for advertising and reaching targeted audiences without relying on costly traditional media.

3. Trust and Collaboration

- **Enhanced Transparency:** Shared data systems within an IOS ensure all partners have access to the same accurate and up-to-date information, fostering trust and mutual accountability.

- **Improved Communication:** Partners in an IOS can interact through integrated software and networks, reducing communication gaps and ensuring clarity in joint operations.

- **Collaborative Decision-Making:** Access to shared analytics and reporting tools allows partners to make informed decisions collaboratively, benefiting all stakeholders involved.

- **Resource Sharing:** Organisations can share technological resources like software and databases, reducing duplication of efforts and promoting operational efficiency.

- **Strengthened Partnerships:** Long-term collaboration through IOS builds stronger business relationships by aligning goals and fostering mutual benefits.

16.1.6 Globalisation and E-Commerce

The integration of global markets through globalisation has significantly transformed e-commerce, enabling businesses to operate across borders and reach international audiences. This evolution provides immense economic opportunities while also introducing unique challenges and competition in a highly interconnected world.

Globalisation's Role in Expanding E-Commerce

- **Access to International Markets:** Businesses can sell products and services to customers worldwide, breaking down traditional geographic barriers.

- **Diverse Consumer Base:** E-commerce platforms cater to a global audience with varied preferences, increasing the potential for revenue growth.
- **Competition Across Borders:** International companies, particularly from Asia, have emerged as significant players in e-commerce, offering competitive pricing and innovative solutions.
- **Economic Opportunities:** Globalisation fosters job creation in developing countries by opening new markets and encouraging trade.
- **Shifting Consumer-Business Dynamics:** E-markets have redefined how consumers interact with businesses, with online reviews, social media, and instant communication influencing buying decisions.

Challenges of Global E-Commerce

- **Intense Competition:** Businesses face increased competition from international brands with lower production costs.
- **Job Displacement:** While globalisation creates jobs in developing regions, it can lead to job losses in developed economies as companies offshore operations to reduce costs.
- **Customs and Regulations:** Managing international logistics, tracking orders, and navigating customs regulations remain significant hurdles.
- **Cultural Barriers:** Differences in language, preferences, and payment systems require businesses to localise their operations for different markets.

Key Statistics

In 2006, data relating to globalisation and e-commerce provided in context:

- **Limited Global Reach:** 70% of U.S. e-businesses did not deliver internationally due to logistical challenges such as order tracking and customs management.
- **Domestic Revenue Dominance:** 90% of online revenue in the U.S. came from domestic sales, indicating limited international penetration.
- **European Export Constraints:** Only 5% of businesses in EU countries exported goods outside Europe, highlighting the localised nature of e-commerce operations.

Key Statistics for the UK

Recent data relating to UK globalisation and e-commerce might vary, but these provide a useful context:

E-Commerce in the UK

- **Market Size:** The UK e-commerce market is among the largest in Europe, with a total market value of £121 billion in 2023, reflecting strong growth compared to previous years.

- **Online Shopping:** Over 80% of UK consumers shop online, making it one of the highest e-commerce adoption rates globally.
- **International Reach:**
  - Approximately 55% of UK e-commerce businesses export to international markets, highlighting their global focus.
  - The EU and the U.S. remain the top destinations for UK exports via online platforms.

16.1.7 Globalisation and Trade

- **Cross-Border E-Commerce:**
  - Around 40% of UK online shoppers buy from international websites, particularly from the EU, China, and the U.S.
  - Fashion, electronics, and cosmetics are the most purchased categories internationally.
- **Impact of Brexit:**
  - Brexit introduced challenges for UK e-commerce businesses due to new customs regulations, tariffs, and shipping delays, with over 30% of SMEs reporting disruptions in their cross-border trade.

Digital Infrastructure

- **Broadband Access:** With 97% of households having internet access, the UK boasts a highly connected population.
- **Mobile E-Commerce (M-Commerce):** Mobile devices account for 60% of e-commerce sales, driven by the UK's high smartphone penetration rate.

Economic Impact

- **Employment:** The e-commerce sector directly employs over 1.5 million people in the UK, with additional jobs created indirectly in logistics, IT, and marketing.
- **Contribution to GDP:** E-commerce contributes approximately 10% to the UK's GDP, highlighting its importance in the overall economy.

These statistics reflect the UK's strong position as a leader in e-commerce while underscoring challenges like international competition, regulatory compliance, and maintaining consumer trust in a globalised digital economy.

16.1.8 The Impact of E-Commerce

E-commerce has revolutionised the way businesses operate and interact with customers, providing numerous benefits while also posing risks and challenges.

Positive Impacts of E-Commerce

1. **Cost Savings:**

- Eliminates the need for physical stores, reducing overhead costs like rent, utilities, and maintenance.
- Streamlines operations by minimising administrative expenses such as paper-based processes and manual labour.

2. **24/7 Access:**
   - Customers can shop at any time, offering unmatched convenience and increasing potential sales.
   - Businesses can operate around the clock without additional costs for extended hours.

3. **Global Reach:**
   - E-commerce platforms allow businesses to scale globally, reaching new markets with minimal additional investment.
   - Digital advertising enables precise targeting of international audiences, boosting visibility.

4. **Efficient Communication:**
   - Real-time updates on inventory, pricing, and promotions improve transparency and customer satisfaction.
   - Instant communication between businesses and consumers fosters trust and flexibility.

Risks and Concerns in E-Commerce

1. **Security Risks:**
   - Vulnerability to cyberattacks, including hacking and phishing, jeopardises sensitive customer and business data.
   - Fraudulent activities, such as fake transactions, can erode trust and incur financial losses.

2. **Data Protection and Privacy:**
   - Businesses must comply with strict regulations like GDPR to ensure customer data security.
   - Mishandling or breaches of sensitive data can lead to reputational damage and legal consequences.

3. **Virus and Malware Attacks:**
   - Malicious software can disrupt operations, resulting in downtime and data loss.
   - Companies must invest in robust antivirus and firewall solutions to mitigate risks.

4. **Intellectual Property Theft:**
   - Proprietary information may be stolen or misused by internal employees, contractors, or competitors.
   - Securing intellectual assets with legal protections and IT safeguards is essential.

5. **Technical Failures:**
   - Server downtimes and system errors can lead to lost revenue and frustrated customers.
   - Regular maintenance, backups, and scalable infrastructure are critical to ensuring uninterrupted operations.

Summary

Globalisation and e-commerce have fundamentally reshaped the business landscape, creating unparalleled opportunities for growth, innovation, and global connectivity. E-commerce empowers businesses of all sizes to compete in international markets, offering tools to improve efficiency, expand market reach, and enhance customer experiences. However, these advancements also bring challenges such as heightened competition, security vulnerabilities, and the need for reliable technological infrastructure.

By understanding the core components of e-commerce, its operational models, and the technological systems that support it, businesses can harness its transformative potential to drive growth and success. To thrive in this increasingly digital and globalised economy, organisations must not only leverage the benefits of globalisation but also implement strategies to mitigate risks, ensuring sustainability and competitiveness in a dynamic marketplace.

Tutorial Activity 16 - E-Commerce

Quizzes and Questions

Quiz 1: Defining E-Commerce and Its Key Components

1. **What is the definition of e-commerce?**
   (a) The sale of physical goods through a brick-and-mortar store
   (b) The exchange of goods, services, or information over the internet
   (c) The manufacturing of electronic goods
   (d) The delivery of physical products by postal service

2. **Which of the following is NOT a key component of e-commerce?**
   (a) Online transactions
   (b) Digital marketing
   (c) Customer service
   (d) Brick-and-mortar retail

3. **Briefly define the following e-commerce models:**
   - B2B (Business-to-Business):
   - B2C (Business-to-Consumer):
   - C2C (Consumer-to-Consumer):

Quiz 2: E-Commerce Models and Applications

1. **Which of the following is an example of a B2C (Business-to-Consumer) e-commerce application?**
   (a) Amazon
   (b) Alibaba
   (c) eBay
   (d) Uber

2. **What is a key feature of C2C (Consumer-to-Consumer) e-commerce?**
   (a) Companies selling products to other companies
   (b) Individual consumers selling goods or services to other consumers
   (c) Businesses providing digital services to consumers
   (d) Businesses using the internet for marketing

3. **Which of the following is a primary characteristic of B2B e-commerce?**
   (a) Direct sale of products to individual customers
   (b) Large-scale transactions between businesses
   (c) Peer-to-peer transactions between consumers
   (d) Small purchases made by individuals for personal use

Quiz 3: Assessing the Performance of E-Commerce Applications

1. **Which of the following metrics is used to assess the performance of an e-commerce website?**
   (a) Customer acquisition cost
   (b) Click-through rate (CTR)
   (c) Bounce rate
   (d) All of the above

2. **True or False:** One of the benefits of e-commerce applications for businesses is the ability to reach a global market.

3. **Which of the following is a major impact of e-commerce on consumers?**
   (a) Ability to shop from anywhere at any time
   (b) Limited access to customer service
   (c) Restrictions on product choices
   (d) Reduced speed of purchasing process

Quiz 4: Impact of E-Commerce on Businesses and Consumers

1. **How does e-commerce impact the operational costs of a business?**
   (a) Increases operational costs due to higher shipping expenses
   (b) Decreases operational costs by reducing the need for physical stores
   (c) Increases costs for customer support
   (d) Has no impact on operational costs

2. **Which of the following is a benefit of e-commerce for businesses?**
   (a) Ability to offer a personalized shopping experience
   (b) Increased reliance on physical retail space
   (c) Increased cost of inventory management
   (d) Limited consumer reach

3. **What is one major challenge for businesses in e-commerce?**
   (a) High physical retail space costs
   (b) Cybersecurity threats and online fraud
   (c) Limited product availability
   (d) Lack of customer data

Quiz 5: Exploring E-Commerce Applications in Business

1. **Which of the following is an example of a B2B e-commerce application?**
   (a) Alibaba
   (b) Etsy

(c) Netflix
(d) Pinterest

2. **How does e-commerce impact consumer purchasing behaviour?**
   (a) Consumers have to visit physical stores to make purchases
   (b) Consumers can easily compare products and prices online
   (c) Consumers are less likely to return purchased products
   (d) Consumers have limited product choices

3. **What is a potential disadvantage for consumers when using e-commerce platforms?**
   (a) Limited access to customer reviews
   (b) Inability to physically examine products before purchasing
   (c) Decreased availability of global shipping
   (d) Inconsistent product quality

Chapter 17: Web Design and Development

Learning Outcomes

By the end of this chapter, learners will be able to explain:

- Principles of Website Design: Understand the types and purposes of websites and key web elements, while applying principles of website development using HTML and CSS to create functional and appealing websites.
- Design Tools and Concepts: Use design tools and coding languages like HTML, CSS, and JavaScript to develop static and dynamic websites that meet client and user needs.
- Development Process: Analyse the website development process, including SDLC, to ensure the final product meets usability, performance, and security standards.
- Interactive Features in Websites: Design and test interactive features such as shopping carts, animations, and multimedia to enhance engagement in e-commerce and educational websites.
- Web Design Principles: Apply core web design principles to create visually appealing, accessible, and user-friendly websites for various audiences and devices.

17.1 WEBSITE DESIGN

A website is essentially a network of interconnected pages that share resources, providing users with information and services. The design of a website is a critical factor in ensuring its functionality, user experience, and the successful achievement of business objectives. It is not only about how the site looks but also about how well it works for the user, how it communicates its purpose, and how it supports the business goals.

17.1.1 Types of Websites

Websites can be classified based on their primary functions and target audiences. Below are common types:

- **Commercial Websites**: These sites are primarily designed to sell products or services. They focus on generating revenue through e-commerce and online transactions. Examples include online stores such as Amazon or eBay, where the main objective is to facilitate shopping and sales.
- **Portal Websites**: A portal is a website that acts as a gateway to other websites and online services. These sites provide a wide range of content and services, such as news, email, search engines, and other utilities. Popular examples include Yahoo, Google, and MSN, which aggregate diverse information in one place, making it a convenient access point for users.

- **Informational Websites**: These sites are dedicated to providing factual content on specific subjects. They serve as a resource for users seeking knowledge or understanding on a particular topic. Wikipedia, for example, is an informational website where users can find detailed entries on various topics contributed by a community of users.

- **Educational Websites**: Educational websites offer learning resources, tools, and materials, often in the form of online courses, tutorials, and instructional videos. Websites like Khan Academy or Coursera are great examples, offering a wide range of subjects and opportunities for learning in various fields, from arts to sciences.

- **Personal Websites**: These are often created by individuals to share their personal experiences, interests, or creative works. Personal websites include blogs, portfolios, and online journals, such as those found on platforms like WordPress or personal blog sites, where individuals can express their opinions, share stories, or showcase their talents.

17.1.2 Common Web Elements

Web elements are the building blocks of a website's design and functionality. These elements are essential for creating an interactive and engaging user experience.

- **Text**: Text provides the bulk of the content on a website, offering information, instructions, labels for images, and descriptions of navigation options. Clear, well-written text is crucial for user understanding and navigation.

- **Graphics**: Graphics are visual components of a website, including images, charts, icons, and buttons. They serve both aesthetic and functional purposes, helping to attract the user's attention, guide them through the site, and illustrate information in a more digestible format. Graphics can also enhance the branding of the site, making it more visually appealing.

- **Multimedia**: Multimedia includes audio, video, and animations that can help make a website more engaging and dynamic. These elements are used to enhance user interaction and can communicate complex ideas more effectively than static text alone. Videos, for example, are often used in e-commerce to showcase products, while animations can be used in educational websites to explain concepts in a visual format.

17.1.3 Purpose of Text & Graphics

- **Text**:
  - Text serves as the primary medium of communication on a website. It offers essential information about the site's content and context, including product descriptions, company details, and other important data.
  - Text is used to describe navigation options, explain the purpose of buttons, and provide links to other pages or resources, thus guiding the user through the site.

- **Graphics**:
    - Graphics serve multiple purposes: they can capture the user's attention, create an inviting atmosphere, and provide a visual break from text-heavy content. They also aid in simplifying complex ideas or making abstract concepts easier to understand.
    - For example, charts and infographics help explain data in a clear and visually appealing way, making the information more accessible to a wider audience.

17.1.4 Hyperlinks

Hyperlinks are one of the most important elements of a website, as they enable users to navigate from one page to another, access external resources, or jump to specific sections within a page. They can be categorised into three main types:

- **Internal Links**: These links allow users to navigate between different pages within the same website. They are commonly used for navigation menus, footer links, or any other section that requires users to access different content without leaving the site. For example, a blog may have links to other articles within the same site.

- **Intrapage Links**: These links take the user to a different section of the same page. Typically used for long-form content, such as FAQs or product listings, they help users quickly access relevant information without needing to scroll manually. For instance, a table of contents at the top of a page may have intrapage links that jump to specific sections further down.

- **External Links**: External links direct users to websites outside of the current site. These links are often used to provide additional information or resources related to the content on the website. For example, a news article may have external links to the source of a cited study or other relevant websites for further research.

The effective use of these web elements and features ensures that a website not only functions well but also meet the needs and expectations of its users, helping businesses achieve their goals and providing users with a seamless, informative, and engaging experience.

17.2 WEBSITE DEVELOPMENT PROCESS

The process of designing and developing a website follows many of the same fundamental principles used in software development, particularly in adhering to established software engineering guidelines. This ensures that the website is built efficiently, meets user requirements, and functions as expected. A key framework used in this process is the Systems Development Life Cycle (SDLC), which provides structured stages for the development, testing, and deployment of the website.

The SDLC is a systematic process that guides developers through each phase of the website development, ensuring quality control, scalability, and functionality. It helps ensure that the final product aligns with both client needs and user expectations.

17.2.1 Key Stages of the Website Development Process

1. **Planning and Requirement Analysis**:
   - In this initial phase, developers and stakeholders gather the requirements and goals for the website. This includes understanding the target audience, determining the website's purpose, and setting clear objectives.
   - The analysis will also involve evaluating technical requirements, such as the hosting environment, content management systems, and other essential tools for development.

2. **Design**:
   - During the design phase, the website's structure, layout, and user interface (UI) are created. This stage may include the development of wireframes, mockups, and prototypes to illustrate how the website will look and function.
   - Key design decisions will focus on the website's aesthetics, navigation, and overall user experience (UX), ensuring that the site is both visually appealing and easy to use.

3. **Development**:
   - The development phase is where the actual coding takes place. Developers write the necessary code to build the website's functionality using coding languages such as HTML, CSS, JavaScript, and server-side languages like PHP or Python.
   - Content is also integrated into the site, and any interactive features (e.g., forms, shopping carts) are developed to enhance user engagement.

4. **Testing**:
   - After development, the website undergoes thorough testing to identify any bugs or issues. This testing phase ensures that the site functions correctly across different devices, browsers, and operating systems.
   - The website's performance, security, and usability are also evaluated, with tests for loading speed, mobile compatibility, and user-friendliness.

5. **Deployment**:
    - Once the site is fully tested and approved, it is deployed to a live server. This phase involves uploading the website to the hosting environment and ensuring it is accessible to the public.
    - The deployment process may include configuring databases, ensuring SEO optimisation, and conducting final checks to ensure the site is working as intended.

6. **Maintenance and Updates**:
    - After deployment, the website enters the maintenance phase, which involves ongoing monitoring and updates. This may include addressing issues that arise, improving functionality, adding new features, and ensuring security patches are applied regularly.
    - Regular updates and content changes ensure the website remains relevant and continues to meet the needs of its users.

17.2.2 Importance of the SDLC in Website Development

The SDLC provides a structured framework that ensures the website development process is methodical and efficient. By following these stages, developers can minimise errors, reduce costs, and deliver a high-quality product that meets both technical specifications and user expectations. Additionally, the SDLC helps manage time and resources, making it easier to track progress and ensure deadlines are met. This systematic approach also makes it easier to make adjustments and improvements throughout the development process, which is crucial for maintaining a successful website in the long term.

By adhering to the SDLC, developers ensure that the website not only meets the initial requirements but is also scalable, secure, and adaptable to future needs and technologies.

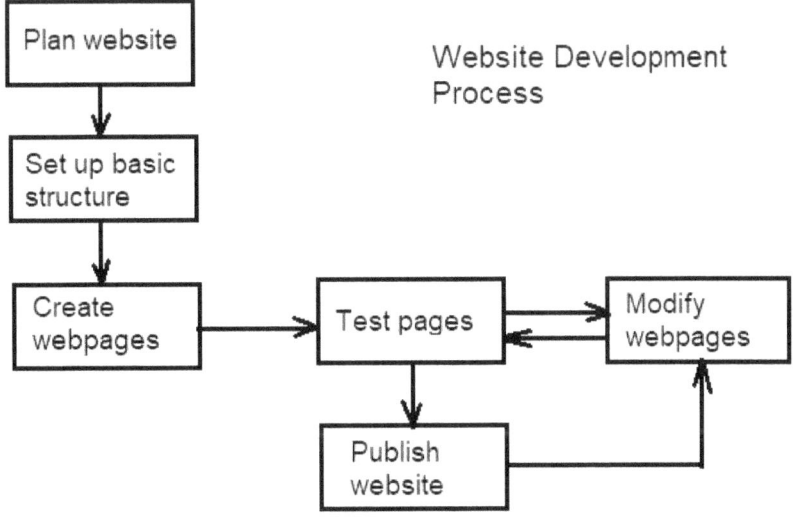

17.2.3 Considerations for Designing Website

When designing a website, several critical criteria must be considered:

1. **Identification of Need**

   - Purpose and Goals: Define the website's purpose and target audience. Determine whether the website will be static (informational) or dynamic (interactive with user inputs, such as online transactions).

   - Client and User Needs: Understand the client's requirements regarding content, security, development timelines, support, overall experience and maintenance.

   - End-User Experience: Consider how the website will appear to visitors. Ensure that the design and layout are user-friendly, visually appealing, and suitable for the target audience.

   - Consider development costs and timeframes.

2. **Design Tools and Concepts**

   - Concept Designs: Use tools like mood boards and storyboards to plan the website's overall look and feel, focusing on colours, layout, and the structure of pages.

   - Software Tools: Languages like HTML and CSS are the foundation of web design. For dynamic websites, additional tools like JavaScript, PHP, and databases like MySQL are essential for interactive features.

3. **Development and Implementation**

   - Coding the Site: Actual development requires knowledge of HTML and CSS for basic websites. For dynamic, interactive websites, server-side scripting (e.g., PHP) and client-side scripting (e.g., JavaScript) are necessary to communicate with databases and create user engagement.

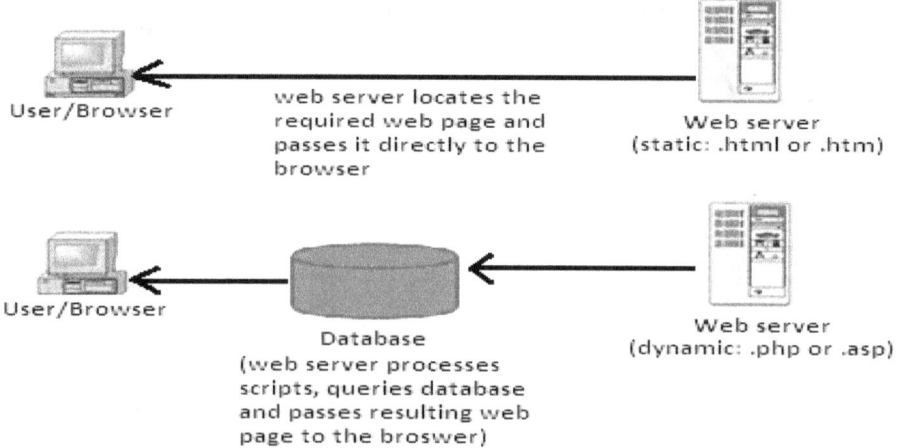

17.2.4 Implementation

Also referred to as 'development phase' or 'coding phase'. When implementing a website, its structure and organisation are crucial to ensuring functionality, user experience, and design consistency. Below are the key elements involved in implementing a website:

Website Structure

The structure of a website is fundamental to how its content is organised and presented. It typically includes the following components:

- **Page Layout**: This defines how information is arranged on each page. Designers can use frames, templates, or no frames at all depending on the needs of the website.

- **Navigation Types**:
  - **Local navigation**: Focuses on navigating within sections of the site (e.g., global area, navigation area, content area).
  - **Internal navigation**: Includes tools like sitemaps, functional navigation, breadcrumb trails, and dynamic or step navigation that help users find content within the site.
  - **External navigation**: Links to external sites or resources outside of the website itself.

Formatting Content

Content on a website is formatted using tags that structure the webpage. These tags define different parts of the content, ensuring that they display correctly.

- **HTML Tags**: HTML uses tags to structure a website's content, which includes opening and closing tags (e.g., <p> for paragraphs, <strong> for bold text). Some tags, such as <hr> for a horizontal rule or <br> for a line break, do not require closing tags.
  - Main HTML structure tags include:
    - <html>: Defines the document as an HTML document.
    - <head>: Contains metadata like the title and links to CSS files.
    - <title>: Sets the title of the webpage.
    - <body>: Contains the main content that is displayed to users.

- Common HTML content tags include:
  - **Header tags** (<h1> to <h6>) to define headings.
  - **Paragraph tag** (<p>) for text.
  - **Bold tag** (<strong>) for emphasis.
  - **Italic tag** (<em>) for italics.
  - **Unordered/Ordered list tags** (<ul>, <ol>, <li>) for bullet points or numbered lists.
  - **Table tags** (<table>, <tr>, <th>, <td>) for displaying tabular data.
  - **Image tag** (<img>) for inserting images.
  - **Anchor tag** (<a>) for creating hyperlinks.
  - **Division tag** (<div>) and **span tag** (<span>) for structuring content into sections or grouping inline elements.
  - **Underline tag** <u> for underling texts
  - **Thematic/semantic break tag** <hr> for horizontal ruler
  - **Line break tag**
 for line break to mention a few.

17.2.5 Example HTML Structure

A simple HTML document is structured as follows:

```
<html>
  <head>
    <title>Website Title</title>
  </head>
  <body>
    <h1>Welcome to My Website</h1>
    <p>This is a paragraph of text. </p>
  </body>
</html>
```

In this basic structure:

- The <html> tag encloses the entire webpage.
- The <head> section contains metadata, including the page title.

- The <body> section includes all the content, such as headings, paragraphs, images, and links that users interact with.

By understanding these core principles, developers can successfully implement a website that is functional, visually appealing, and easy to navigate.

Cascading Style Sheets (CSS)

CSS, or Cascading Style Sheets, is a style sheet language used to describe the presentation of a document written in HTML or XML. It enhances the visual appearance of a webpage by defining styles such as fonts, colours, spacing, and layout, allowing for uniformity and consistency across multiple pages. By separating content (HTML) from design (CSS), developers can manage the look and feel of a site more efficiently.

CSS is an essential tool for web designers and developers, enabling the creation of visually appealing, responsive, and user-friendly websites.

Key Functions of CSS:

- **Colors**: Set background, text, and link colours.
- **Fonts**: Control font styles, sizes, and types.
- **Layout**: Manage the placement of elements (e.g., grids, columns).
- **Spacing**: Define padding, margins, and borders around elements.
- **Responsiveness**: Allow webpages to adjust their layout on different screen sizes.

Basic CSS Example:

```
<!DOCTYPE html>
<html>
<head>
 <title>My Webpage</title>

<style>
 body {
 background-color: #f0f0f0;
 font-family: Arial, sans-serif;
 color: #333;
 margin: 0;
 padding: 20px;
 }
 h1 {
  color: #0056b3;
 }
 p {
 font-size: 18px;
 line-height: 1.5;
 }
 .highlight {
```

```
    background-color: yellow;
    }

</style>
</head>
<body>
  <h1>Welcome to My Website</h1>
  <p>This is a simple webpage styled with CSS. </p>
  <p class="highlight">This text is highlighted with a yellow background using CSS. </p>
</body>
</html>
```

Explanation of the Example:

- **body**: Sets the background colour, font family, and text colour for the entire page.
- **h1**: Defines the colour for the main heading.
- **p**: Specifies the font size and line spacing for paragraph text.
- **.highlight**: This is a class selector that adds a yellow background to elements with the class "highlight."

Visual Breakdown:

- **Text Styling**: The h1 heading is styled with a blue colour (#0056b3), and paragraph text is 18px in size with line-height set to improve readability.
- **Background Styling**: The body background is a light grey (#f0f0f0), while specific paragraphs can have their own styles like the yellow background in .highlight.

Illustration using CSS Code:

```
/* Text Styling */
h1 { color: #0056b3; /* Blue colour for the h1 heading */
}

p { font-size: 18px; /* 18px font size for paragraphs */
 line-height: 1.6; /* Line height to improve readability */
}

/* Background Styling */
body { background-color: #f0f0f0; /* Light grey background for the entire body
*/ }

 .highlight { background-color: yellow; /* Yellow background for paragraphs
with the 'highlight' class */
}
```

Explanation of the CSS code:

- Styles the h1 heading with a blue colour (#0056b3).
- Sets the paragraph text (p) to 18px with a line height of 1.6 for better readability.
- Applies a light grey background (#f0f0f0) to the whole page.
- Highlights specific paragraphs with a yellow background using the .highlight class.

Benefits of Using CSS:

- **Consistency**: The same style can be applied across multiple pages, ensuring a unified design.
- **Flexibility**: Easy to update. Changing the CSS file will instantly affect all linked pages.
- **Separation of Concerns**: HTML handles content structure while CSS focuses on presentation.
- **Performance**: CSS reduces the size of HTML files and improves load times when applied effectively.

Interactive Features

In modern web design (Web 2.0), websites often include interactive features to engage users and provide a dynamic experience:

- **Catalogues of products**: Common in e-commerce sites for displaying items for sale.
- **Shopping carts**: Allow users to add items they want to purchase.
- **Images and animation**: Enhance the visual appeal and user engagement by displaying products, showcasing events, or explaining processes through moving visuals or animated graphics.

17.2.6 Evaluation and Testing

The evaluation and testing phase is critical to ensuring the website functions as expected and provides a seamless user experience. The following testing procedures should be conducted:

- **Browser Compatibility Testing:** It is essential to test the website across various web browsers (e.g., Google Chrome, Mozilla Firefox, Safari, Edge) to ensure that it renders correctly and provides the same experience to all users, regardless of the browser they use. This can include checking for issues such as layout distortions, missing elements, or broken JavaScript functions that might occur on certain browsers.

- **Device and Mobile Responsiveness Testing:** As websites must work across different devices, testing on various screen sizes is essential. Ensure the website adapts appropriately to desktops, tablets, and smartphones. Responsive web design techniques such as media queries should be tested to guarantee proper layout, font size, navigation functionality, and interaction.

- **User Acceptance Testing (UAT):** UAT involves real users or stakeholders testing the website in a controlled environment to validate whether it meets their needs and expectations. Feedback from this phase helps identify any usability issues, design flaws, or functionality gaps, ensuring the site meets the intended user requirements.

- **Link Functionality Testing:** It's vital to test all links on the website (internal and external) to ensure they point to the correct locations. Broken links can lead to poor user experience, so they must be identified and fixed. Tools like link checkers can automate this process.

- **Content Accuracy Testing:** Review all the content on the site, including text, images, and multimedia, for accuracy and consistency. Ensure all data is up-to-date, error-free, and that all multimedia content loads correctly. This also involves proofreading the content to eliminate spelling or grammar mistakes.

- **Load Speed Testing:** Test the website's load speed using tools like Google PageSpeed Insights or GTmetrix. Fast load times are crucial for user satisfaction and SEO. Optimising images, minifying CSS and JavaScript, and leveraging browser caching are common practices to improve site speed.

17.2.7 Publishing the Website

Publishing a website, also known as "going live," is the final step in the website development process. It involves transferring the website's files from your local development environment to a web server where it can be accessed by users. Here's how the publishing process works:

- **File Transfer Protocol (FTP):** The website's files (HTML, CSS, JavaScript, images, etc.) are transferred to the server using FTP. This protocol allows files to be moved from a local computer to the hosting provider's web server. FTP software like FileZilla or Cyberduck is commonly used for this purpose. Users need the FTP credentials provided by their hosting provider to connect to the server.

- **Web Hosting Configuration:** Before publishing, ensure the web hosting account is correctly configured with the necessary files and server settings. This includes setting up databases (if applicable), configuring DNS (Domain Name System) settings, and ensuring the correct file structure on the server.

- **Domain Name Association:** Once the files are uploaded, the website must be associated with a domain name. This involves pointing the domain to the correct server by updating DNS records. This allows users to access the website by typing in its domain name (e.g., www.example.com).

- **Final Testing Post-Publishing:** After publishing, conduct a final round of testing to ensure everything functions properly on the live server. Sometimes issues such as broken links, missing files, or incorrect server configurations may arise post-launch, which need to be addressed immediately.
- **Ongoing Maintenance:** Once live, the website requires ongoing maintenance to ensure it stays secure, functional, and up to date. Regular updates, backups, and monitoring for performance issues or security vulnerabilities are essential to keep the website running smoothly.

17.2.8 Web Server

A **web server** is a specialised computer system designed to host websites and manage the delivery of web content to users over the Internet. It has a unique IP address that identifies it on the network, allowing clients (such as browsers or mobile devices) to send requests to it and receive the requested web pages. The web server serves as the central hub for hosting the website's files, including HTML documents, CSS, JavaScript, images, and other media.

When a user accesses a website, their browser sends a request to the web server for the website's files. The server then processes the request and returns the appropriate content, such as the website's home page, images, or data from a database. The web server's functionality is critical because it handles multiple user requests concurrently, ensuring the smooth operation and accessibility of the website.

Before a website can be viewed by others online, it needs to be uploaded to the web server. This process involves transferring all the website's files (using protocols like FTP or SFTP) to the server's storage, where they can be accessed by users around the world. Once the website's files are on the server, and the appropriate domain name is associated with the IP address, the website becomes publicly accessible to anyone who enters the domain name in their browser's address bar.

In summary, the web server is a vital component in the functioning of a website, ensuring that the website's content is available on the Internet and accessible to users globally.

17.2.9 Maintenance

Website maintenance is an ongoing process that ensures the website stays secure, up-to-date, and functional over time. Regular maintenance activities are essential to keep the website running smoothly and ensure a good user experience. Below are key aspects of website maintenance:

- **Regular Updates and Security Audits**
  - **Regular Updates:** Websites often rely on third-party software, content management systems (CMS), plugins, and frameworks. These components are frequently updated by their developers to fix bugs, introduce new features, or enhance performance. It's critical to keep all these elements up to date to avoid compatibility issues and to take advantage of the latest advancements. This can include updating the website's software, libraries, themes, and plugins.
  - **Security Audits:** Conducting regular security audits is crucial to identify vulnerabilities in the website's infrastructure. Security audits involve reviewing server configurations, checking for outdated software, ensuring the use of secure protocols (like HTTPS), and scanning for potential threats such as malware or hacking attempts. A comprehensive security audit helps prevent unauthorised access and protects sensitive data, such as customer information or payment details.
  - **Backup and Disaster Recovery:** Regular backups should be scheduled to protect the website's data in case of unexpected failures or attacks. This includes database backups, media files, and website configurations. In the event of an issue, having a recent backup allows you to restore the website to its previous state quickly and minimise downtime.

- **Maintaining an Audit Trail for Database Changes**
  - **Audit Trail:** It is essential to track all changes made to the website's database, especially when it involves user activities such as adding, updating, or deleting content. An audit trail is a record of all modifications to the database, which helps administrators monitor user interactions and ensure that actions are legitimate and authorised. It can help identify any unusual or unauthorised activities that could indicate a security breach or misuse.
  - **Prevent Unauthorised Access:** The audit trail also helps in maintaining **accountability** by identifying the individual responsible for each action. This is critical for maintaining the integrity of the website, particularly when multiple users have access to sensitive parts of the website or database. An audit trail can also assist in identifying and addressing any issues related to **data manipulation**, fraud, or data loss.
  - **Database Security Measures:** Along with the audit trail, it's important to implement **access controls** that limit who can modify the database. Regularly reviewing permissions and enforcing strong password policies for

administrators and users can help prevent unauthorised access and ensure the overall security of the website's data.

In conclusion, **website maintenance** is a critical ongoing process to ensure a website remains functional, secure, and up to date. By conducting regular updates, security audits, and maintaining a robust audit trail for database changes, website owners can enhance performance, prevent security breaches, and ensure a smooth user experience.

17.3 CAREERS IN WEBSITE DEVELOPMENT

- **Web Author**: A web author is responsible for crafting the written content that appears on a website. This includes everything from blog posts, articles, product descriptions, and metadata to more technical content like FAQs and policy pages. They ensure that the content is clear, engaging, and optimised for both users and search engines (SEO). Web authors often work closely with designers and developers to ensure that the text aligns with the overall site structure and goals.

- **Web Designer**: A web designer focuses on the aesthetic and visual aspects of a website. They create the layout, choose the colour scheme, design the user interface (UI), and ensure the site is visually appealing and easy to navigate. Web designers use tools like Adobe Photoshop, Sketch, and Figma to develop wireframes and mock-ups, paying close attention to user experience (UX) principles. Their goal is to create an attractive, functional, and responsive design that works well across various devices.

- **Web Developer**: A web developer is responsible for turning the designs created by web designers into a functional website. They use programming languages like HTML, CSS, JavaScript, PHP, and Python to write code that ensures a site's functionality. There are two main types of developers:
    - **Front-End Developers** work on the parts of the website that users interact with directly (e.g., the layout, buttons, navigation).
    - **Back-End Developers** focus on server-side operations, databases, and application logic that make the website run smoothly. Full-stack developers handle both front-end and back-end tasks.

- **Webmaster**: The webmaster is responsible for the ongoing management and maintenance of a website after its development. They ensure that all components are working correctly, update content, monitor site performance, troubleshoot technical issues, and maintain security protocols. Webmasters also oversee software updates, backup processes, and monitor website traffic to optimise performance and security. Their role is critical to keeping the website functional, secure, and up to date.

Tutorial Activity 17 - Web Design & Development.

Quiz and Questions

Quiz 1: Principles of Website Design

Question 1: Which of the following is NOT a common type of website?

- a) Commercial
- b) Informational
- c) Multimedia
- d) Personal

Question 2: What are key web elements commonly used in websites?

- a) Text, graphics, multimedia, and hyperlinks
- b) Text, audio, and navigation
- c) Audio, forms, and video
- d) Images, links, and animations

Quiz 2: Design Tools and Concepts

Question 1: What is the purpose of a mood board in web design?

- a) To display a website's final look
- b) To collect and showcase design ideas
- c) To test user interactions
- d) To code the website's functionality

Question 2: Which coding languages are commonly used in web design for static and dynamic websites?

- a) HTML, CSS, JavaScript
- b) HTML, Python, Ruby
- c) JavaScript, SQL, CSS
- d) HTML, PHP, JavaScript

Quiz 3: Development Process

Question 1: What does the Systems Development Life Cycle (SDLC) ensure in the web development process?

- a) The website is optimised for search engines
- b) The final product meets usability, performance, and security standards

- c) The website has interactive features
- d) The website is visually appealing

Question 2: Which of the following is NOT a phase of the SDLC?

- a) Design
- b) Implementation
- c) Data entry
- d) Testing

Quiz 4: Interactive Features in Websites

Question 1: What is an example of an interactive feature used in e-commerce websites?

- a) Video backgrounds
- b) Shopping carts
- c) Static images
- d) Text-only navigation

Question 2: Why are animations important in website design?

- a) They increase website speed
- b) They enhance user engagement and interaction
- c) They reduce file size
- d) They make websites more static

Quiz 5: Web Design Principles

Question 1: Which of the following principles is key to making websites accessible?

- a) Using a single colour scheme
- b) Using text-to-speech features
- c) Clear navigation and legible fonts
- d) Using animations for all content

Question 2: When designing a website, it is important to ensure that it is visually appealing and functional across:

- a) Only desktop devices
- b) Only mobile devices
- c) Various audiences and devices
- d) Only smartphones and tablets

Quiz 6: Website Performance Evaluation

Question 1: Which of the following is NOT a common metric used to evaluate website performance?

- a) Loading time
- b) Bounce rate
- c) Customer satisfaction score
- d) Server response time

Question 2: What does the term "responsiveness" refer to in website performance?

- a) How quickly the website loads
- b) How well the website adjusts to different screen sizes
- c) How fast a user can log in
- d) How much data the website uses

Quiz 7: Optimisation Techniques

Question 1: Which technique is used to improve website functionality by reducing the amount of data transferred?

- a) Increasing server capacity
- b) Resource minimisation
- c) Caching static content
- d) Adding more graphics

Question 2: What is the purpose of caching in website optimisation?

- a) To speed up loading times by storing frequently accessed content
- b) To reduce the need for animations
- c) To secure the website from hacking attempts
- d) To change the website's appearance

Reference

- **W3C. (2021).** "Web Technologies: An Overview." W3C. Retrieved from https://www.w3.org/
- **Moore, A. (2018).** "Web Development and Design Foundations with HTML5" (8th ed.). Pearson.
- **Garrett, J. J. (2010).** "The Elements of User Experience: User-Cantered Design for the Web and Beyond." New Riders.
- **Krug, S. (2014).** "Don't Make Me Think: A Common-Sense Approach to Web Usability" (3rd ed.). New Riders.
- **Koller, D.**, **Harris, S.**, & **Mansfield, T.** (2019). *Web Development and Design Foundations with HTML5* (9th ed.). Pearson.
  - A foundational textbook for learning web design and development, focusing on HTML5, CSS, and modern practices.
  - **Duckett, J.** (2011). *HTML and CSS: Design and Build Websites*. Wiley.
    - A practical guide to building websites using HTML and CSS, focusing on design principles and techniques.
- **Keith, J.** (2010). *HTML5 for Web Designers*. A Book Apart.
  - A practical introduction to HTML5 for creating modern websites with attention to user experience and design
- **Zeldman, J.** (2016). *Designing with Web Standards* (4th ed.). New Riders.
  - This book explains the principles of web design with an emphasis on standards and best practices.

Chapter 18: Cybersecurity Strategies for ICT Systems

Learning Outcomes

Upon successful completion of this chapter, learners will be able to:

- Identify cybersecurity risks associated with ICT systems and their potential impacts.
- Analyse common vulnerabilities and threats in ICT infrastructure.
- Evaluate key cybersecurity principles and their application in protecting ICT systems.
- Develop strategies to mitigate cyber risks and ensure system integrity.
- Assess tools and techniques for monitoring and responding to cybersecurity incidents.

18. Modern Cybersecurity Practices and Risk Mitigation

In today's digital era, cybersecurity plays a pivotal role in safeguarding ICT systems from ever-evolving threats. As businesses and individuals increasingly rely on interconnected technologies and cloud computing, understanding and implementing robust cybersecurity strategies has become essential. This chapter explores the risks, mitigation techniques, and emerging technologies in cybersecurity, providing a comprehensive framework to protect information systems effectively.

18.1 CYBERSECURITY RISKS AND RISK MANAGEMENT

18.1.1 Cybersecurity Risk

Cybersecurity risk refers to the potential threats, damages, or losses that arise from the exploitation of weaknesses or vulnerabilities within an organisation's Information and Communication Technology (ICT) systems, networks, and data storage. With the increasing reliance on digital technologies, especially the internet and cloud computing services, the potential attack surface for cybercriminals has expanded significantly. This has heightened the exposure of organisations, making them more susceptible to a wide variety of cyberattacks that could compromise sensitive information, disrupt operations, or lead to significant financial losses.

In today's digital age, cybersecurity risk encompasses a wide range of possible threats, including but not limited to:

- **Data Breaches:** A data breach occurs when sensitive or confidential information, such as personal, financial, or proprietary data, is accessed, stolen, or exposed without authorisation. These breaches can occur through hacking, insider threats, or accidental leaks, and often lead to severe financial and reputational damage. Stolen data may include personal details, credit card numbers, social security numbers, trade secrets, or intellectual property, all of which can be sold on the dark web or used to commit identity theft.

- **Identity Theft:** This is the fraudulent use of an individual's personal information, often obtained through cyberattacks like phishing, data breaches, or social engineering. Cybercriminals can use stolen identities to commit financial fraud, access restricted services, or impersonate victims for illegal activities. The consequences for victims can include financial loss, damaged credit, and long-term personal or professional harm.

- **Denial-of-Service (DoS) Attacks:** A DoS attack disrupts the normal functioning of a server, service, or network by overwhelming it with a flood of traffic or requests. This causes the system to become slow, unreliable, or completely unavailable to users. DoS attacks are often used to disrupt business operations or as a form of protest, and they can cause significant harm, especially if critical online services or e-commerce platforms are targeted.

- **Ransomware Attacks:** Ransomware is malicious software that encrypts a victim's data, rendering it inaccessible until a ransom is paid to the attacker. These attacks can severely impact an organisation's operations, especially when important data is held hostage. While some organisations may pay the ransom, there is no guarantee that the attacker will provide the decryption key, and paying the ransom can encourage future attacks. Ransomware attacks have become more sophisticated, with some cybercriminals even threatening to release sensitive data if the ransom is not paid.

To manage cybersecurity risks effectively and reduce the likelihood and impact of such threats, organisations must implement a structured approach that involves several key steps:

- **Identify Vulnerabilities:** The first step in managing cybersecurity risk is identifying potential vulnerabilities in an organisation's ICT systems, networks, and processes. Vulnerabilities can exist in software, hardware, network configurations, or human processes, such as poor password practices or insufficient security training. Conducting regular security audits, penetration testing, and vulnerability assessments helps organisations detect weaknesses before they can be exploited by cybercriminals.

- **Assess Potential Impacts:** Once vulnerabilities are identified, organisations need to assess the potential impact of these risks. This involves understanding the severity of each risk, the value of the assets at risk, and the potential consequences of an exploit. For example, a breach of a database containing customer financial information could result in legal penalties, reputational damage, and financial losses, while a DoS attack on a company's website may only result in temporary disruption. Risk assessments help prioritise which vulnerabilities need immediate attention, and which can be addressed over time.

- **Implement Targeted Strategies to Mitigate Risks:** After identifying vulnerabilities and assessing their potential impacts, the next step is to implement targeted cybersecurity strategies to mitigate or reduce these risks. This may include deploying security technologies such as firewalls, encryption, antivirus software, and intrusion detection systems. Additionally, organisations should establish comprehensive cybersecurity policies and training programs to educate employees about best practices for data protection, secure communication, and recognising potential threats like phishing emails. Incident response plans should also be developed to guide the organisation's response in the event of a cyberattack, ensuring that recovery and containment measures are in place to minimise damage.

Cybersecurity risk is a dynamic and evolving challenge that organisations must continuously monitor, and address as new threats emerge. The growing complexity of the cyber threat landscape means that proactive, comprehensive risk management strategies are essential for minimising potential harm. Effective risk management helps ensure that sensitive data remains protected, operations remain uninterrupted, and the organisation's reputation remains intact in the face of increasing cyber threats.

18.1.2 Cybersecurity Risk Assessment

Cybersecurity risk assessment is a critical process in the development of a strong defence against cyber threats. It is a systematic approach to identifying, evaluating, and prioritising potential cybersecurity risks based on their impact and likelihood. The primary objective is to understand and anticipate the various threats that may compromise an organisation's critical assets and develop strategies to mitigate those risks effectively.

A thorough risk assessment includes:

- **Identifying Threats:** The first step in the risk assessment process is identifying potential threats to the organisation. These threats may include external factors, such as cybercriminals or state-sponsored hackers, as well as internal threats, such as employees or contractors with malicious intent. Common examples of threats include phishing attacks, malware infections, ransomware, and insider threats. Identifying these threats allows organisations to understand the scope of potential cyber risks they may face.

- **Analysing Vulnerabilities:** After identifying potential threats, organisations must assess vulnerabilities within their systems. Vulnerabilities refer to weaknesses or gaps that could be exploited by threats to gain unauthorised access to information or systems. These vulnerabilities may include weak passwords, outdated software or hardware, unpatched security flaws, or poorly configured network infrastructure. By identifying and addressing these vulnerabilities, organisations can significantly reduce the risk of exploitation.

- **Prioritising Risks:** Once threats and vulnerabilities are identified, the next step is to prioritise risks based on their likelihood and potential impact on the organisation. This involves assessing the severity of each risk, considering the value of the assets at risk, and evaluating how likely the risk is to occur. High-priority risks, such as attacks targeting sensitive financial data or critical infrastructure, should be addressed first. Risk prioritisation allows organisations to allocate resources effectively, focusing on the most critical risks that pose the greatest threat.

18.1.3 Cybersecurity Risk Management

Risk management is the process of applying strategies and measures to minimise the impact of cybersecurity risks. It involves proactive steps to reduce the likelihood of threats exploiting vulnerabilities, as well as preparing for recovery in the event of an attack. Risk management is an ongoing process that requires constant evaluation, adaptation, and improvement to stay ahead of emerging threats.

Key components of cybersecurity risk management include:

- **Administrative Controls:** Administrative controls encompass policies, procedures, and training designed to promote cybersecurity awareness and foster a security-conscious culture within the organisation. This includes establishing clear security protocols, such as access control policies, incident response procedures, and guidelines for the secure handling of sensitive data. Regular staff training and awareness programs help employees recognise and respond to cybersecurity threats, such as phishing attacks, reducing the risk of human error.

- **Technical Safeguards:** Technical safeguards are tools and technologies implemented to prevent unauthorised access and protect against cyber threats. These include firewalls, intrusion detection systems (IDS), encryption, antivirus software, and other security solutions. Firewalls act as the first line of defence by filtering network traffic and blocking unauthorised access attempts. Encryption secures data by converting it into unreadable code, ensuring that sensitive information remains confidential. Intrusion detection systems monitor network traffic for suspicious activity and alert security teams to potential threats.

- **Contingency Plans:** Contingency plans are disaster recovery protocols and procedures that ensure business continuity in the event of a cyberattack or other disruptive incidents. These plans outline how to respond to and recover from cybersecurity breaches, minimising downtime and ensuring that critical operations can continue. Regular testing of contingency plans through simulated cyberattack scenarios helps organisations identify gaps in their recovery processes and improve overall resilience.

Effective cybersecurity risk management is not a one-time task but an ongoing effort that evolves with the changing threat landscape. As new technologies and attack vectors emerge, organisations must continuously update their risk management strategies to mitigate evolving risks. Regular risk assessments, combined with strong risk management practices, enable organisations to stay ahead of cyber threats and maintain a secure environment for their assets and operations.

18.2 MITIGATION, CONTROL, AND PROTECTION MECHANISMS

Cybersecurity mitigation and protection mechanisms are essential tools in defending against cyber threats. These technologies and practices are designed to prevent attacks, detect malicious activity, and respond to incidents when they occur. By implementing a combination of protective measures, organisations can significantly reduce their exposure to cybersecurity risks and improve their overall security posture.

Encryption

Encryption is one of the most effective tools for ensuring data confidentiality and integrity. It works by transforming readable data into an unreadable format using encryption algorithms, making it inaccessible to unauthorised users. Encryption is applied to data both at rest (stored data) and in transit (data being transmitted).

Software Encryption: Software-based encryption tools, such as those provided by Microsoft Office or VeraCrypt, allow organisations to encrypt files, ensuring that only authorised users can access sensitive data. Strong passwords are essential for software encryption, requiring a mix of uppercase and lowercase letters, numbers, and special characters to strengthen security.

It is the process of securing data, either stored on a disk or transmitted via email, by converting it into a coded format that can only be accessed with a specific decryption key (usually a password). A common example of software encryption can be seen with Office documents. For instance, when saving a Word document, you can encrypt it to protect its contents.

Steps to Encrypt a Word Document:

1. Open the document in Microsoft Word.
2. Click on the **File** menu and select **Info**.
3. In the "Protect Document" section, click on the **Protect Document** icon.
4. A dropdown list of protection options will appear. Select **Encrypt with Password**.
5. The **Encrypt Document** dialogue box will appear. Enter a strong, case-sensitive password and click **OK**.

6. Once encrypted, the document can only be accessed by entering the correct password. If the password is forgotten or lost, it cannot be recovered, so it's essential to store it securely.

Password Requirements:

A strong password should be:

- At least 8 characters long
- A mix of upper- and lower-case letters
- Include numbers
- Contain special characters (e.g., #, @, *, &)

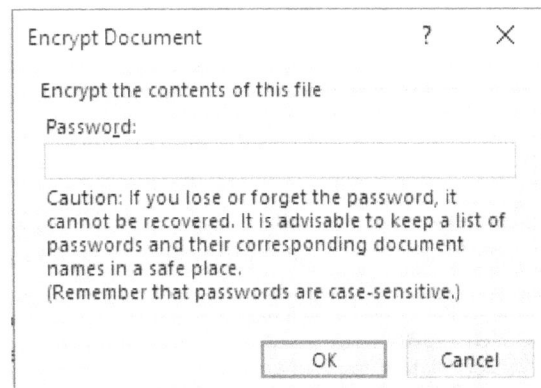

When sending the encrypted document, the recipient will need the exact password to decrypt it and access the contents. Without the correct password, the file remains inaccessible.

Hardware Encryption: Hardware encryption uses dedicated hardware devices or components to protect data. For example, USB drives with built-in encryption or BitLocker-protected drives provide an additional layer of security by securing data at the hardware level, reducing the risk of unauthorised access if the device is lost or stolen.

Biometric Security

Biometric security systems use unique physical traits for authentication, providing a highly secure and convenient alternative to traditional password-based systems. These biometric traits may include fingerprints, facial recognition, iris scans, or voice patterns. Modern smartphones and other devices frequently use biometric security to grant access to applications or data, reducing the reliance on passwords and enhancing user experience.

Biometric systems are particularly useful in environments where security is a top priority, as they are difficult to replicate or forge, providing stronger protection against unauthorised access.

Two-Factor Authentication (2FA)

Two-factor authentication (2FA) enhances user verification by requiring two forms of identification: something the user knows (e.g., a password) and something the user has (e.g., a code sent to a phone or generated by an authentication app). This added layer of security makes it more difficult for attackers to gain unauthorised access to accounts or systems, even if they have obtained a user's password.

However, while 2FA is highly effective, it is not immune to threats like social engineering attacks. As a result, it is important to implement 2FA alongside other security measures to create a multi-layered defence strategy.

Remote Find and Wipe Software

Remote find and wipe software provides the ability to locate, lock, or remotely erase sensitive data from a lost or stolen device. For instance, tools like Apple's "Find My iPhone" or Dropbox's remote wipe feature allow users to locate their device or delete personal information, reducing the risk of a data breach. These tools are especially important for protecting sensitive data on mobile devices, which are more likely to be lost or stolen.

Automatic Account Lockout

Automatic account lockout is a security feature that restricts access to an account after a predetermined number of failed login attempts. This mechanism helps prevent brute-force attacks, where attackers attempt to guess a user's password through repeated login attempts. By limiting the number of incorrect attempts, automatic lockouts mitigate the effectiveness of these attacks and enhance system security.

Firewall Protection

Firewalls are essential for network security, acting as a barrier between trusted internal networks and external, potentially dangerous networks. They monitor and filter incoming and outgoing network traffic based on predefined security rules, blocking unauthorised access while allowing legitimate communication. Firewalls can be either hardware-based, software-based, or a combination of both, depending on the organisation's needs.

Antivirus Software

Antivirus software plays a critical role in defending against a wide range of malware, including viruses, ransomware, spyware, and trojans. These programs continuously scan devices for malicious files and activities, blocking or removing threats before they can cause harm. To maintain effectiveness, antivirus software should be updated regularly to recognise the latest threats and perform routine scans.

Secure Wireless Connections

Secure wireless connections are essential for protecting data transmitted over Wi-Fi networks. Protocols like WPA2 and WPA3 provide encryption for Wi-Fi connections, making it more difficult for unauthorised users to intercept or gain access to sensitive information. It is crucial to avoid using outdated and insecure protocols like WEP, as they are highly vulnerable to attacks.

Virtual Private Networks (VPNs)

A Virtual Private Network (VPN) creates a secure, encrypted tunnel for internet traffic, masking a user's IP address and providing privacy when browsing online. VPNs are especially useful for individuals accessing public Wi-Fi networks, as they protect sensitive information from being intercepted by attackers. Organisations use VPNs to securely connect remote employees to corporate networks, ensuring that all data transmitted over the internet remains encrypted and protected.

18.3 DATA BACKUP AND CONTINGENCY PLANNING

In the digital age, safeguarding data is critical for organisations to ensure operational continuity and resilience against potential disruptions such as hardware failures, cyberattacks, or natural disasters. Effective backup strategies, combined with well-structured contingency plans, enable quick recovery and minimise the impact of such incidents.

Types of Backups

1. **Full Backup**
   A full backup creates an exact, comprehensive copy of all data within a system. This type of backup is the most complete and serves as a foundational snapshot of the entire dataset. However, it can be time-consuming and requires significant storage space, making it suitable for periodic rather than frequent use.

2. **Incremental Backup**
   Incremental backups save only the data that has changed since the last backup, whether full or incremental. This method is highly efficient in terms of storage and time but may require multiple backup files for restoration, increasing complexity during recovery.

3. **Differential Backup**
   Differential backups store all changes made since the last full backup. While

it consumes more storage than incremental backups, it simplifies recovery by reducing the number of files needed to restore the system.

4. **Offsite and Cloud Backup**
Offsite backups involve storing data copies in remote physical locations, while cloud backups use virtual storage platforms accessible via the internet. Both methods provide additional protection by ensuring data remains available even if local infrastructure is compromised. Cloud backups also offer real-time syncing, encryption, and accessibility, making them a popular choice for modern organisations.

Recommended Practices

1. **Scheduled Backups**
Regularly scheduled backups are vital to maintaining data integrity and availability. Organisations should tailor backup schedules to the sensitivity and importance of their data:
    - Daily backups for mission-critical systems and databases.
    - Weekly or monthly backups for less frequently accessed data.

2. **Secure Backup Storage**
Utilise encrypted storage solutions, such as Google Drive, OneDrive, or other secure cloud platforms, to ensure data privacy and protect against unauthorised access. Encryption safeguards sensitive information, adding an extra layer of security against cyber threats.

3. **Contingency Plans**
Contingency planning is essential for swift recovery from unexpected incidents. Effective plans include:
    - Clearly defined recovery processes to restore operations with minimal delay.
    - Designated personnel responsible for executing backup and recovery procedures.
    - Regular testing and updating of backup systems to ensure reliability during crises.

4. **Multiple Backup Locations**
Diversifying backup locations further mitigates risks. For example:
    - Maintain on-premises backups for quick access.
    - Store secondary backups in geographically dispersed offsite locations or cloud environments to protect against localised disasters.

5. **Backup Verification**
Periodically verify the integrity of backups to ensure that data can be successfully restored. Regular testing helps identify potential issues and reinforces confidence in the backup system's reliability.

Integrating robust backup strategies and contingency planning into their cybersecurity framework allows organisations to significantly enhance their resilience to data loss and ensure seamless recovery during unforeseen events. These practices not only protect valuable assets but also uphold business continuity, safeguarding the organisation's reputation and operations.

18.4 Emerging Technologies in Cybersecurity

As cybersecurity threats continue to evolve, new technologies emerge to combat these challenges and enhance protection across digital environments. Among these technologies are Near-Field Communication (NFC) and AI-based cybersecurity solutions, both of which bring innovative approaches to securing sensitive data and systems.

Near-Field Communication (NFC)

Near-Field Communication (NFC) is a wireless communication technology that enables the exchange of data over short distances, typically a few centimetres. NFC is primarily used in mobile payments, identity verification, and authentication systems. This technology is widely seen in applications like contactless payment cards, smartphones, and smartwatches, allowing users to perform secure transactions or access systems without physical contact.

One of NFC's most significant advantages is its ease of use. Consumers can tap their mobile devices or cards on compatible readers to complete transactions or authenticate themselves quickly, making it highly convenient for daily activities. Despite its simplicity, NFC also incorporates strong security measures, such as encryption and tokenisation, to protect sensitive data during transmission. By ensuring that data is only exchanged between close proximity devices, NFC reduces the risk of interception by malicious actors, providing a secure method for conducting transactions and verifying identities.

AI-Based Cybersecurity Solutions

Artificial Intelligence (AI) is revolutionising the field of cybersecurity by providing advanced systems capable of autonomously detecting and responding to threats in real-time. AI platforms, such as MixMode, leverage machine learning and deep learning algorithms to analyse vast volumes of data and identify potential security risks with minimal human intervention. These AI-driven systems can autonomously adapt to new threats and evolving attack vectors, making them highly effective in defending against zero-day vulnerabilities, sophisticated attacks, and emerging cybersecurity risks.

AI-based solutions continuously monitor networks, systems, and user behaviour to detect abnormal patterns that may indicate a cybersecurity breach. These platforms are capable of identifying both known and unknown threats by recognising anomalies in network traffic, user activity, and system performance. For instance, AI can detect malicious behaviour such as phishing attempts, malware infections, or insider threats by analysing deviations from normal operational patterns.

Furthermore, AI cybersecurity systems can respond to these threats automatically, mitigating risks before they escalate into full-blown attacks.

One of the major benefits of AI in cybersecurity is its ability to work at scale, processing large datasets and monitoring extensive systems without the need for continuous human oversight. This scalability allows AI-driven solutions to offer real-time protection across vast networks, identifying threats faster and more accurately than traditional security measures. Additionally, AI-based systems are capable of learning from past incidents and improving their detection capabilities over time, making them increasingly effective in anticipating and preventing future cyber threats.

The integration of AI into cybersecurity is not without its challenges, however. AI systems require significant amounts of data to train and operate effectively, and they need to be continuously updated to adapt to evolving threat landscapes. Additionally, while AI can assist in threat detection, it is not a replacement for human expertise in cybersecurity. A hybrid approach, combining AI's capabilities with human oversight, is often the most effective way to secure ICT systems.

Overall, the emergence of NFC and AI-based cybersecurity solutions is a game-changer in the fight against cyber threats. NFC offers a secure, convenient method for transactions and identity verification, while AI enhances threat detection and response, providing advanced, real-time protection for organisations and individuals alike. As these technologies continue to evolve, they will play an increasingly pivotal role in shaping the future of cybersecurity.

Summary

Modern cybersecurity practices require a proactive, multi-layered approach to safeguard ICT systems from persistent threats. By identifying risks, implementing robust mitigation strategies, and leveraging emerging technologies, organisations can ensure the integrity, confidentiality, and availability of their digital assets. This comprehensive framework empowers businesses and individuals to navigate the complexities of cybersecurity effectively.

18.5 Independent Tutorial Activity

Use the following prompts to assess and enhance understanding of cybersecurity practices:

1. Propose strategies for securing Wi-Fi networks.
2. Identify benefits and limitations of VPNs.
3. Suggest methods to ensure imported and exported data is safe.
4. Recommend techniques to block malicious websites.
5. Discuss the implementation of anti-malware policies.
6. Define cybersecurity risks and their implications.
7. Compare and contrast risk assessment and risk management.

Using these tools and strategies, organisations can effectively protect their assets and ensure operational resilience against cybersecurity threats.

Tutorial Activity 18 - Cybersecurity Strategies for ICT Systems.

Quizzes and Questions

Quiz 1: Cybersecurity Risks and Impacts

Question 1:
Which of the following is a common risk associated with ICT systems?
a) Data loss
b) Increased productivity
c) Reduced system availability
d) All of the above

Question 2:
What is the potential impact of a data breach in an ICT system?
a) Loss of financial data
b) Loss of customer trust
c) Legal consequences
d) All of the above

Quiz 2: Common Vulnerabilities and Threats

Question 1:
Which of the following is a common vulnerability in ICT systems?
a) Outdated software
b) Strong passwords
c) Regular updates
d) Firewalls

Question 2:
What is a Denial-of-Service (DoS) attack?
a) A method to gain unauthorised access to sensitive data
b) An attack that disrupts the availability of a service
c) A type of virus that damages computer files
d) An attack that exploits system vulnerabilities for financial gain

Quiz 3: Cybersecurity Principles and Protection

Question 1:
Which of the following is a key principle of cybersecurity?
a) Confidentiality
b) Accountability
c) Availability
d) All of the above

Question 2:
Which cybersecurity principle focuses on ensuring that authorised users have access to systems and data when required?
a) Confidentiality
b) Integrity

c) Availability
d) Non-repudiation

Quiz 4: Mitigating Cyber Risks

Question 1:
Which of the following is a strategy for mitigating cyber risks?
a) Regular system backups
b) Ignoring security updates
c) Using weak passwords
d) Disabling firewalls

Question 2:
What is a common method for ensuring system integrity in cybersecurity?
a) Encrypting sensitive data
b) Allowing unrestricted access to sensitive information
c) Disabling user authentication
d) Ignoring software patches

Quiz 5: Tools and Techniques for Monitoring Cybersecurity

Question 1:
Which tool is commonly used to monitor network traffic for potential cybersecurity threats?
a) Antivirus software
b) Intrusion Detection System (IDS)
c) Email filtering software
d) Backup software

Question 2:
What is the purpose of using security information and event management (SIEM) tools in cybersecurity?
a) To encrypt sensitive data
b) To track user behaviour
c) To collect and analyse security data from different sources
d) To perform regular system updates

Chapter 19: Foundations of Software Design and Development.

Learning Outcomes

Upon completing this chapter, students will be able to:

1. **Understand the Software Development Process:**
   - Explain the stages involved in the software development lifecycle, including design, documentation, testing, and maintenance.

2. **Identify Key Elements in Software Development:**
   - Differentiate between programming languages, their syntax, and applications.
   - Utilise modelling tools such as use-case diagrams and data flow diagrams in software planning.
   - Compare and apply development methodologies like Agile and Waterfall.

3. **Recognise Roles and Responsibilities:**
   - Describe the various roles in the software development industry and their duties, such as programming, systems analysis, and software engineering.

4. **Distinguish Programming Paradigms:**
   - Define and differentiate procedural, object-oriented, and event-driven programming paradigms.
   - Evaluate the advantages and limitations of each paradigm.

5. **Explore Programming Features and Data Types:**
   - Understand core programming constructs like sequence, selection, and iteration.
   - Compare methods of program translation, including interpreted and compiled languages.
   - Explain the importance of variables, data types, and syntax in programming.

6. **Examine Computer Programming Languages:**
   - Outline the evolution of programming languages from first-generation machine code to fourth-generation high-level languages.
   - Analyse the characteristics and real-world applications of low-level and high-level languages.

- Apply knowledge of programming languages to solve problems through hands-on coding tasks.

7. **Apply Knowledge through Practical Activities:**
    - Engage in hands-on programming projects, such as designing programs for expense tracking, invoice calculation, and tile cost estimation.
    - Collaborate on group presentations exploring programming paradigms and language features.

8. **Develop Problem-Solving Skills:**
    - Utilise programming principles to design and implement solutions for real-world problems, fostering analytical and creative thinking.

19.1 Introduction

In the digital age, software is at the heart of technological innovation and everyday operations. Whether it's the applications that run on our smartphones, the systems that manage critical infrastructure, or the platforms facilitating global communication, software development has become an indispensable field. This chapter serves as an in-depth introduction to software design and development, providing foundational knowledge for students and aspiring programmers.

Software development is not merely about writing code; it encompasses a comprehensive process that includes requirements gathering, design, implementation, testing, and maintenance. Each of these stages plays a crucial role in delivering reliable and effective software solutions. Throughout this chapter, we will explore the various elements that contribute to successful software development, including programming languages, development methodologies, and the key roles involved in the process.

We will also delve into the different programming paradigms that shape how software is structured and executed. Understanding these paradigms - such as procedural, object-oriented, and event-driven programming - equips developers with the versatility needed to tackle diverse programming challenges. Additionally, we will examine the features of programming languages, their syntax, and the importance of data types, laying the groundwork for effective problem-solving in programming.

Finally, this chapter will cover the evolution of computer programming languages, tracing their development from low-level machine code to high-level languages that enhance productivity and ease of use. By the end of this chapter, you will have a comprehensive understanding of the software design and development landscape, preparing you for further exploration into specialised topics within the field.

Let's embark on this journey to discover the intricacies of software design and development!

19.1.1 Overview of Software Design & Development

Definition of Software

Software, often referred to as applications or computer programs, consists of a series of instructions that a computer follows to perform specific tasks. Software enables users to accomplish various functions, ranging from simple calculations to complex data analysis and gaming.

Software Development Process

The software development process encompasses a series of stages that go beyond just writing code. It includes:

- **Designing**: Creating the architecture of the software, which outlines its structure and interaction.
- **Documenting**: Writing detailed descriptions of the software's functionality and user interfaces to assist in understanding and future development.
- **Testing**: Verifying that the software performs as intended and is free of bugs, ensuring accuracy and reliability.

19.1.2 Elements of Software Development

Programming Languages

Programming languages, such as C++, C#, Java, HTML, and Visual Basic, are essential tools for writing software. Each language has unique syntax, capabilities, and suitable applications. For instance:

- **C++**: Often used for system software and applications that require high performance.
- **Java**: Known for its portability across platforms, making it ideal for web applications and enterprise solutions.

Modelling Tools

Modelling tools help visualise and plan software architecture. Two key tools are:

- **Use-Case Diagrams**: Illustrate how users will interact with the software, outlining system functions from the user's perspective.
- **Data Flow Diagrams (DFDs)**: Represent the flow of data within the system, helping to clarify the processes and data management.

Methodology

Software development methodologies provide frameworks for guiding the development process. These methodologies dictate how the project will be planned and executed. Common methodologies include:

- **Agile**: Focuses on iterative development and flexibility in responding to change.

- **Waterfall**: A linear approach where each stage must be completed before moving on to the next.

19.1.3 Roles in Software Development

Titles in the Industry

The software development field encompasses various roles, each contributing to the overall process:

- **Computer Programmer**: Writes and maintains the code.
- **Systems Analyst**: Analyses system requirements and designs solutions.
- **Software Developer**: Engages in the overall development process, from conception to deployment.
- **Software Engineer**: Applies engineering principles to software design, ensuring quality and efficiency.
- **Web Developer**: Specialises in building applications for the web, focusing on user interface and experience.

Duties

Key responsibilities of professionals in software development include:

- **Client Communication**: Engaging with clients to understand their needs and gather requirements.
- **User Requirements Documents**: Creating detailed documents that specify user needs and system functionality.
- **Preliminary Design Reviews**: Discussing initial designs with clients to ensure alignment with expectations.
- **Software Analysis and Design**: Utilising methodologies to create effective software solutions.
- **Code Writing and Testing**: Developing the program and creating test plans to ensure functionality.
- **Documentation**: Producing system documentation and user manuals to facilitate understanding and usage.

19.2 Programming Paradigms

A programming paradigm is a fundamental style of programming that provides developers with a framework to structure and solve problems effectively. It dictates how programs are designed, implemented, and executed, influencing the way developers think about and write code. Paradigms often reflect different approaches to problem-solving, ranging from sequential task execution to modular and interactive designs.

Programming paradigms are essential because they shape the strategies used in creating software, ensuring that developers can choose the most suitable method for a given problem or project. By understanding these paradigms, programmers gain the versatility to tackle a wide range of challenges and adapt to evolving technological needs.

In this section, we explore the major programming paradigms, their characteristics, and their applications. Each paradigm has distinct principles, advantages, and limitations, providing developers with unique tools to approach their tasks. The primary paradigms include:

1. **Procedural Programming**: Focuses on structured steps and functions.
2. **Object-Oriented Programming (OOP)**: Centre's around objects that encapsulate data and behaviour.
3. **Event-Driven Programming**: Emphasizes responding to events, such as user interactions.

These paradigms are not mutually exclusive and can often be combined to achieve optimal results in software development. Understanding the strengths and appropriate use cases of each paradigm equips developers with the knowledge to make informed design decisions in programming projects.

19.2.1 Procedural Programming

Procedural programming focuses on a sequence of tasks or procedures. Programs are structured as a set of procedures or functions that operate on data.

Example: A simple program in Pascal, which is widely used for teaching due to its clear syntax:

```pascal
program HelloWorld;
begin
    WriteLn('Hello, World!');
end.
```

Advantages:

- Typically, faster than object-oriented languages due to direct execution of procedures.
- Facilitates straightforward and quick program development.

Disadvantages:

- Less flexible and more challenging to modify in response to changes in requirements.

19.2.2 Object-Oriented Programming

Object-oriented programming (OOP) centres around the concept of "objects," which bundle data fields and methods that operate on the data.

Example: A basic C++ program demonstrating OOP:

```cpp
#include <iostream>
using namespace std;
class Rectangle {
  private:
    int width, height;
  public:
    void set_values(int w, int h) {
      width = w;
      height = h;
    }
    int area() {
      return width * height;
    }
};
int main() {
  Rectangle rect;
  rect.set_values(5, 3);
  cout << "Area: " << rect.area() << endl;
  return 0;
}
```

Advantages:

- Encourages code reusability and modular design.
- Easier to maintain and modify code due to encapsulation.

19.2.3 Event-Driven Programming

Event-driven programming focuses on responding to events or user actions, such as mouse clicks or key presses.

Example: A simple Visual Basic program demonstrating event-driven programming:

```
Public Class Form1
    Private Sub Button1_Click(sender As Object, e As EventArgs) Handles Button1.Click
        MessageBox.Show("Hello, World!")
    End Sub
End Class
```

Advantages:

- User-friendly and easier for beginners to learn.
- Enables the creation of dynamic and interactive applications.

19.3 Programming Features and Data Types

Programming languages provide a range of features and data types that enable developers to create functional and efficient software solutions. These features encompass the fundamental building blocks of programming, such as control structures, modularity, abstraction, and data manipulation. Mastery of these elements allows programmers to design, write, and optimise code effectively.

Programming Features refer to the capabilities and constructs offered by a programming language to facilitate software development. Key features include:

- **Control Flow Constructs**: Loops, conditionals, and branching statements for managing program execution.
- **Functions and Modularity**: Tools for dividing code into reusable components.
- **Error Handling**: Mechanisms for detecting and managing errors gracefully.
- **Concurrency**: Support for multi-threading and parallel processing.
- **Memory Management**: Techniques to allocate and deallocate memory efficiently.

Data Types are fundamental to programming as they define the nature of data that can be manipulated within a program. Common data types include:

- **Primitive Data Types**: Such as integers, floating-point numbers, characters, and booleans.
- **Composite Data Types**: Including arrays, lists, and dictionaries that hold collections of values.
- **User-Defined Data Types**: Custom data structures like classes and enums.

Understanding the features and data types of a programming language is crucial for selecting the right tools for specific tasks and optimising performance. This section delves into these concepts, exploring their characteristics, examples, and real-world applications. By the end of this section, readers will have a comprehensive understanding of the features and data types necessary to write robust, maintainable, and efficient programs.

19.3.1 Features of Programming Languages

The features of programming languages describe three (3) main programming constructs, specifically, sequence, selection and iteration.

19.3.2 Programming Constructs

- **Sequence**: The order in which statements are executed.

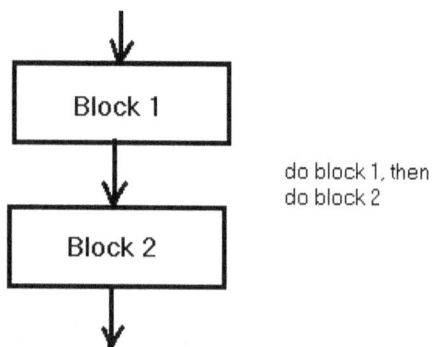

- **Selection**: Selection is a form of 'branching' in programming and used to control the execution sequence, it tests a condition or asks a question and depending on the answer to the question, follows a predetermined program path. It enables decision-making through conditional statements such as if...then...else. This type of construct can also take place within a switch statement to achieve a much neater program codes, e.g. Case... of...

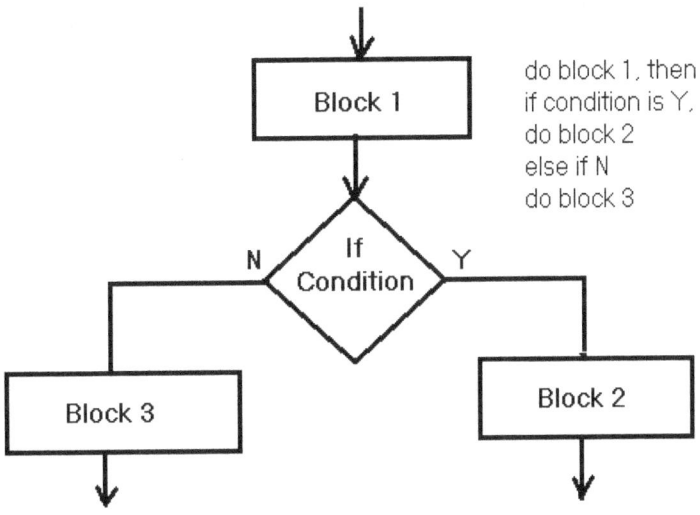

- **Iteration**: Iteration in computing is a process of repeating or looping a block of statements in a computer program in order to reach a desired outcome. This process may occur in an order or in an irregular order although each individual item is visited only once whilst counting from say, 1 to 10, this mean that you are iterating over the first 10 numbers. It allows repetition of code blocks through loops such as for, while, and repeat...until.

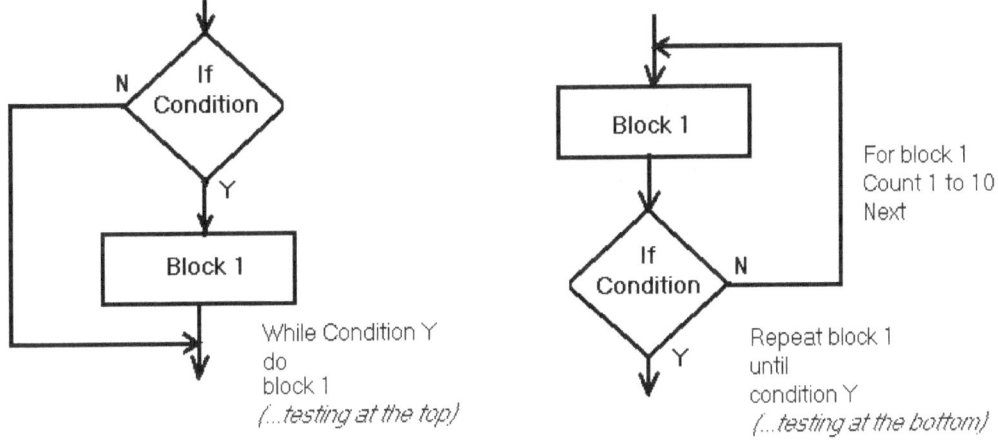

19.3.2 Methods of Translation

- **Interpreted Languages**: Execute code line-by-line during runtime, which can slow down performance (e.g., Python).
- **Compiled Languages**: Translate the entire program into machine code before execution, resulting in standalone executable files (e.g., C++).

19.3.3 Understanding Syntax and Keywords

- **Syntax**
  - **Comparison**:

- **English Language**: Flexible grammar that allows for various interpretations.
- **Programming Language**: Strict syntax; any errors can result in program failure or crashes.

Keywords

- **Definition**: Reserved words in programming languages that cannot be used as variable names (e.g., print, end, case).

19.3.4 Variables and Data Types

- **Variables**
  - **Definition**: Named locations in memory that hold data.

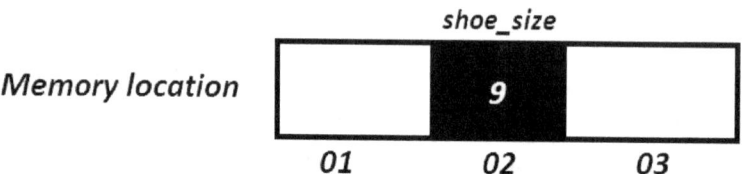

  Example: shoe_size = 9.
- **Data Types**
  - **Definition**: Specifies the type of data a variable can hold.
- **Basic Data Types**:
  - **Numbers**: Used for arithmetic operations.
  - **Strings**: Represents a sequence of characters.

19.3.5 Common Types of Data Types

Type	Used for	Range of values
Boolean	Values that can be true or false	True or false
Byte	Whole numbers	0 to 255
Integer	Whole numbers	−32,768 to +32,767
Long	Very large whole numbers	Approximately plus or minus 2 billion
Currency	Decimal numbers with 2 digits after the decimal	
Single	Floating point numbers	Up to 7 significant digits
Double	Large floating point numbers	Up to 14 significant digits
Date	Date and time	
Variant	Any type of data	
String	Any type of text	

19.3.6 Benefits of Data Types

- **Memory Efficiency**: Different data types of help optimise memory usage.
- **Performance Improvement**: Smaller data sizes can lead to faster execution.
- **Error Reduction**: Clear data types can help prevent mistakes in the program.

19.4 Computer Programming Languages

19.4.1 Definition of Computer Programming Languages

A computer programming language is a set of software codes that programmers use to design, write, and develop programs that solve business problems, either general or specialised. Each language has specific commands and syntax that programmers must follow.

19.4.2 Generations of Computer Programming Languages

Overview of Generations:

1. **1st Generation (Late 1940s)**
    - **Type:** Machine Code
    - **Example:** 0100100101001100
    - **Characteristics:** Very difficult to program; directly interacts with hardware.
    - **Application:** Used in early computing for basic tasks and operations.

2. **2nd Generation (Early 1950s)**
    - **Type:** Assembly Language
    - **Example:** LD RE, Price
    - **Characteristics:** More readable than machine code but still challenging.
    - **Application:** Used in system-level programming and performance-critical applications.

3. **3rd Generation (Late 1950s - 1970s)**
    - **Type:** High-Level Languages
    - **Example:** total = price * quantity
    - **Characteristics:** User-friendly, portable, and structured; includes languages like Pascal, C, C++, and Visual Basic.

- **Application:** Widely used in software development across various domains.

4. **4th Generation (Late 1970s Onwards)**
    - **Type:** Very High-Level Languages, Query Languages
    - **Characteristics:** Visual programming and object-oriented programming; includes languages like VB.Net, Visual C++, C#, and Java.
    - **Application:** Focused on application development with reduced programming effort.

19.4.3 Characteristics of Programming Languages

- **Low-Level Languages (e.g., Assembly Language)**
    - **Characteristics:**
        - Machine-oriented and processor-specific.
        - Each instruction corresponds to one machine code instruction.
        - Efficient for hardware manipulation and speed-critical applications.
    - **Real-World Application:** Device drivers for hardware.

- **High-Level Languages (e.g., C++, Java)**
    - **Characteristics:**
        - Not machine-oriented; generally portable.
        - Problem-oriented with structures tailored to user needs.
        - Resemble English sentences or mathematical expressions; one statement may translate into several machine instructions.
        - Additional features include selection structures, iteration structures, built-in functions, and data structures.
    - **Real-World Application:** Developing business applications, web development, and software for various platforms.

- **Additional Features of High-Level Languages:**
    1. Selection structures (e.g., if...then...else, case).
    2. Iteration structures (e.g., for...do, while...do).
    3. Built-in routines for input/output.
    4. Built-in functions (e.g., sqr, log).
    5. Data structures (e.g., strings, records).

19.4.4 Examples of Common Programming Languages

1. **Scientific Languages: FORTRAN**
   - First scientific programming language, popular for mathematical and engineering applications.

2. **Commercial Languages: COBOL**
   - Developed for data processing, featuring good screen painting facilities and data validation commands.

3. **General Purpose Languages:**
   - **PL/1:** Combines best features of COBOL and FORTRAN.
   - **BASIC:** Designed for ease of learning; criticised for leading to poor coding practices.
   - **Pascal:** Focuses on teaching good programming practices.
   - **C:** Block structured, efficient for systems programming.
   - **C++:** Extends C to include object-oriented features.

4. **High-Level Programming Languages:**
   - **Visual Basic:** Event-driven and close to English, designed for rapid application development.
   - **C#:** Designed for .NET development; simple and modern.
   - **Java:** Platform-independent and object-oriented; compiled and interpreted.
   - **Python:** Interpreted and known for readability; supports multiple programming paradigms.
   - **Ruby:** High-level and reflective, focusing on simplicity and productivity.

5. **Specialised Languages:**
   - **Ada:** Developed for embedded systems; emphasizes readability and maintainability.
   - **Concurrent Programming:** Allows tasks to be executed simultaneously, useful in real-time systems (e.g., Occam).

19.4.5 Fourth Generation Languages (4GLs)

4GLs provide tools for building applications with minimal traditional programming. They often include:

- Database management systems
- Query languages

- Report generators
- Screen painting facilities

19.4.6 Advantages of 4GLs:

1. Faster system development.
2. Enhanced communication between developers and users.
3. Increased programmer productivity.
4. Easier maintenance.

19.4.7 Activities for Reinforcement

1. **Comparative Analysis:**
    - Create a table comparing the characteristics and applications of different programming languages across generations.

2. **Hands-On Programming Tasks:**
    - Write simple programs in different languages (e.g., a calculator in Python, a sorting algorithm in C++) to understand syntax and application.

3. **Discussion Topics:**
    - Discuss the impact of programming languages on technology evolution.
    - Analyse how different programming paradigms (procedural, object-oriented, functional) influence software development.

4. **Real-World Project:**
    - Choose a problem to solve (e.g., developing a simple inventory management system) and use a suitable programming language to design, implement, and present the solution.

19.4.8 Tasks to do...

a. **Group Presentations:**
    - Research and present your findings on a specific programming paradigm, covering its history, characteristics, and notable applications.

b. **Explain the Key Features of an Event-Driven Programming Language**
    - *Explore how event-driven programming facilitates user interaction and application responsiveness.*

c. Design and Implement a Program to Show Monthly Expenses
- *Develop a simple application that tracks and displays monthly expenses, incorporating user inputs and data display.*

d. Design and Implement an Invoice Calculation Program
- *Create a program that calculates and displays an invoice, including subtotal, VAT, and total payable amounts for a training centre.*

e. Activity: Garden Area Calculation and Fence Cost Estimation

Objective: Write a program that calculates the area of a garden based on user inputs, estimates the length of fencing required, and calculates the total cost with discounts and VAT.

Analysis and Design: Write a program that:

1. **Inputs**:
   - Accepts the length (minimum 5 meters) and width of a garden (in meters).

2. **Calculations and Outputs**:
   - Calculates and displays the area of the garden (in square meters).
   - Calculates and displays the perimeter of the garden (in meters) to determine the fencing required.

3. **Cost Estimation**:
   - Calculates the cost of fencing at £15 per meter.
   - Applies a 10% discount for orders over £300.
   - Adds 20% VAT on the discounted amount.
   - Displays the final amount payable.

Tutorial Activity 19 - Foundations of Software Design and Development

Quiz Questions, Exercises

Quiz 1: Understanding Software Development

1. **Question**: Define software development and outline its primary stages.

2. **Question**: Why is maintenance considered a critical stage in the software development lifecycle?

Quiz 2: Identifying Elements of Software Development

1. **Question**: Match the following tools to their purpose:
   - a) UML Diagrams:
   - b) IDEs (Integrated Development Environments):
   - c) Version Control Systems:

2. **Question**: List three programming languages commonly used in software development and their primary use cases.

Quiz 3: Roles in Software Development

1. **Question**: Match the following roles to their responsibilities:
   - a) Software Developer:
   - b) Systems Analyst:
   - c) Software Engineer:

2. **Question**: What is the role of a quality assurance (QA) engineer in software development?

Quiz 4: Programming Paradigms

1. **Question**: Differentiate between procedural programming and object-oriented programming.

2. **Question**: Give an example of an event-driven programming use case.

Quiz 5: Features of Programming Languages

1. **Question**: Explain the difference between interpreted and compiled languages with examples.

2. **Question**: Define "syntax" in programming and explain its importance.

Quiz 6: Data Types and Variables

1. **Question**: Match the data type to its description:
    - a) Integer:
    - b) String:
    - c) Boolean:
2. **Question**: Why is choosing the correct data type important in programming?

Quiz 7: Evolution of Programming Languages

1. **Question**: Categorise the following languages into their respective generations:
    - a) Assembly Language
    - b) Python
    - c) FORTRAN
2. **Question**: Describe one advantage of high-level programming languages over low-level languages.

Practical Activities

1. Write a simple program in Python to calculate the area of a rectangle.
2. Compare the syntax of a "Hello, World!" program in Python and C++.

Conclusion

As we come to the end of our journey through the world of Information and Communication Technology (ICT), it is clear that we are living in a rapidly evolving digital age, one where technology is transforming every aspect of our lives. From the way we work and communicate to the way we learn and interact with the world around us; ICT is the backbone of modern society.

Throughout this book, we have explored the key concepts, skills, and challenges that shape the ICT landscape. We began by understanding the basic building blocks of computer systems and software, before delving into the logic that drives these technologies. We examined the laws and ethical considerations that govern the digital world and highlighted the societal impacts of ICT, both positive and negative. We also explored emerging trends such as cloud computing, web development, e-commerce, and cybersecurity, and how these innovations are shaping industries and education.

Importantly, we have also considered the critical role of digital skills in today's education systems. The digital divide remains a significant barrier, and bridging that gap is essential to ensuring that all students, regardless of their socio-economic background, have access to the tools and knowledge they need to thrive in an increasingly digital world. By fostering digital literacy, we are not only preparing students for the demands of the workforce but also empowering them to navigate the complexities of modern life.

This book has been designed to serve as a comprehensive guide for educators, students, and anyone interested in gaining a deeper understanding of ICT. It provides practical insights, case studies, and real-world applications to ensure that learners not only acquire theoretical knowledge but also develop the practical skills needed to succeed in the digital age.

As you conclude this chapter of learning, it is essential to remember that the world of ICT is always evolving. The technologies we have discussed in this book are continually advancing, and new innovations are emerging every day. To remain competitive and relevant, it is important to continue building on the knowledge and skills gained here. Embrace lifelong learning, stay curious, and keep adapting to the ever-changing digital landscape.

In closing, ICT is not just about the tools and technologies we use, but about the people who use them. It is about the ability to create, communicate, solve problems, and innovate. The opportunities that ICT provides are limitless, and as we move forward into the future, the possibilities are boundless for those who are equipped with the right knowledge and skills.

Thank you for taking this journey with us. We hope that this book has not only expanded your understanding of ICT but also inspired you to become an active participant in shaping the future of technology.

References

Some chapters in this book draw upon general knowledge and an understanding of the capabilities and limitations of computers and ICT in commerce, industry, and society at large without referencing specific sources. For instance, the chapters on data privacy, digital rights, and the structure of privacy legislation, regulations, and practices are largely based on established principles and common practices.

To provide readers with a deeper understanding of the subjects discussed and to offer reliable avenues for further exploration, the following references and resources are included. These sources offer factual, comprehensive, and insightful perspectives on how ICT reshapes various sectors, addressing both its potential and its challenges:

- World Bank Reports on Digital Development: Comprehensive studies and statistics on ICT's role in economic growth, digital transformation, and poverty reduction globally.

- International Telecommunication Union (ITU) Publications: Global standards, data, and research on telecommunications and ICT usage, addressing topics like internet access and digital skills.

- OECD Reports on Digital Economy and Innovation: Research on digital transformation and innovation in various sectors, alongside trends and policy recommendations.

- UNESCO Resources on ICT in Education: Frameworks and studies focusing on ICT's role in improving educational access and quality.

- Eurostat and U.S. Bureau of Labour Statistics Data: Detailed data on ICT's impact on industries, job creation, and productivity.

- McKinsey Global Institute (MGI) Reports: Insights on digital and technological transformations, including AI, automation, and workforce shifts.

- Research and Reports from Technology Firms: Companies like Cisco, Microsoft, and IBM offer white papers and reports on cybersecurity, IoT, and other emerging technologies.

- Academic Journals on ICT and Society: Journals such as *Computers in Human Behaviour*, *Information Systems Research*, and *Journal of Information Technology* provide peer-reviewed research on ICT's social and economic impacts.

Legal and Regulatory Frameworks

- **UK Legislation**:
  - Copyright, Designs, and Patents Act 1988
  - Computer Misuse Act 1990
  - Data Protection Acts of 1998 and 2018
  - Health and Safety at Work Act 1974
- **European Union**:
  - General Data Protection Regulation (GDPR)
- **Nigeria**:
  - Nigerian Data Protection Regulation (NDPR)

Notable Organisations and Initiatives

- Electronic Frontier Foundation (EFF): Advocates for digital privacy, free expression, and innovation.
- International Association of Privacy Professionals (IAPP): Offers resources and certifications on data privacy.
- Information Commissioner's Office (ICO): UK authority providing guidance on data protection and cybersecurity.
- Nigerian National Information Technology Development Agency (NITDA): Regulates ICT development and data protection in Nigeria.

Consolidated References Grouped by Theme:

1. Computer Architecture and Operating Systems

- Tanenbaum, A. S., & Austin, T. (2012). *Operating Systems: Design and Implementation.* Pearson.
- Stallings, W. (2018). *Operating Systems: Internals and Design Principles.* Pearson.
- Tanenbaum, A. S., & Austin, T. (2013). *Structured Computer Organisation* (6th ed.). Pearson.
  - This textbook provides a comprehensive look at computer architecture, covering topics such as logic gates, circuits, and processor design.
- Hennessy, J. L., & Patterson, D. A. (2019). *Computer Architecture: A Quantitative Approach* (6th ed.). Morgan Kaufmann.

- Focuses on the principles of computer architecture, with an emphasis on logic gates and data representation.
- Sharma, A. (2011). *Digital Logic and Computer Design.* McGraw-Hill Education.
  - A detailed introduction to digital circuits and logic gates, foundational to understanding computer architecture.

2. E-Commerce and Digital Business

- Laudon, K. C., & Traver, C. G. (2020). *E-commerce: Business, Technology, Society* (15th ed.). Pearson.
  - A comprehensive guide to e-commerce concepts, models, and applications.
- Turban, E., King, D., Lee, J. K., Li, X., & Turban, D. C. (2018). *Electronic Commerce: A Managerial and Social Networks Perspective* (9th ed.). Springer.
  - Focuses on e-commerce strategies, technologies, and the social network aspect.
- Chaffey, D. (2019). *Digital Marketing: Strategy, Implementation, and Practice* (7th ed.). Pearson.
  - Offers an overview of digital marketing and its integration with e-commerce strategies.
- Stair, R., & Reynolds, G. (2019). *Principles of Information Systems* (13th ed.). Cengage Learning.
- Chaffey, D. (2022). *Digital Business and E-Commerce Management* (7th ed.). Pearson.
- Kalakota, R., & Robinson, M. (2001). *E-Business: Roadmap for Success.* Addison-Wesley.
- Geyskens, I., Gielens, K., & Gijsbrechts, E. (2006). "The Market Valuation of E-Business Strategies: An Empirical Study." *Journal of Marketing Research, 43*(2), 119-130.
- Hof, R. D. (1999). "The E-Commerce Revolution: The Internet and the Future of Business." *Business Week, 15.*
- He, Y., & Wang, L. (2018). "Research on the Application of E-commerce in Supply Chain Management." *Journal of Logistics, 2*(3), 3-10.
- Laudon, J. P., & Laudon, E. (2017). *Management Information Systems: Managing the Digital Firm* (15th ed.). Pearson.

3. Web Development and Design

- W3C. (2021). "Web Technologies: An Overview." Retrieved from https://www.w3.org/

- Moore, A. (2018). *Web Development and Design Foundations with HTML5* (8th ed.). Pearson.

- Garrett, J. J. (2010). *The Elements of User Experience: User-Centred Design for the Web and Beyond.* New Riders.

- Krug, S. (2014). *Don't Make Me Think: A Common-Sense Approach to Web Usability* (3rd ed.). New Riders.

- Koller, D., Harris, S., & Mansfield, T. (2019). *Web Development and Design Foundations with HTML5* (9th ed.). Pearson.
  - A foundational textbook focusing on HTML5, CSS, and modern practices.

- Duckett, J. (2011). *HTML and CSS: Design and Build Websites.* Wiley.
  - A practical guide to building websites with HTML and CSS.

- Keith, J. (2010). *HTML5 for Web Designers.* A Book Apart.
  - A practical introduction to HTML5.

- Zeldman, J. (2016). *Designing with Web Standards* (4th ed.). New Riders.
  - Explains principles of web design with emphasis on standards and best practices.

4. Cybersecurity

Books and Textbooks:

- Stallings, W. (2017). *Network Security Essentials: Applications and Standards* (6th ed.). Pearson.

- Andress, J. (2014). *The Basics of Information Security: Understanding the Fundamentals of Infosec in Theory and Practice.* Syngress.

- Justus, P. (2024). *Mastering Cybersecurity Excellence: Securing the future beyond cyberthreats.*

Research Papers and Articles:

- "Understanding Cybersecurity Risks and Mitigation Strategies in ICT Infrastructure." *Journal of Cyber Security Technology.*

- "Cybersecurity Risks and Their Impact on Business Operations: A Case Study Approach." *International Journal of Information Technology and Security.*

Government and Industry Reports:

- National Institute of Standards and Technology (NIST). (2018). *Framework for Improving Critical Infrastructure Cybersecurity* (Version 1.1).
- European Union Agency for Cybersecurity (ENISA). (2020). *Cybersecurity Threat Landscape.*

Online Resources and Tools:

- OWASP (Open Web Application Security Project). *Top 10 Web Application Security Risks.*
- Cybersecurity & Infrastructure Security Agency (CISA). *Cybersecurity Best Practices.*
- Kaspersky Labs. (2023). *Cybersecurity Threats and Solutions: Best Practices for Protecting ICT Systems.*